THE
MIGHTY
MOO

THE MIGHTY MOO

The USS *Cowpens* and Her Epic World War II
Journey from Jinx Ship to the Navy's First
Carrier into Tokyo Bay

Nathan Canestaro

GRAND
CENTRAL

New York   Boston

Grand Central Publishing
Hachette Book Group
1290 Avenue of the Americas, New York, NY 10104
grandcentralpublishing.com
X.com/grandcentralpub

First Edition: June 2024

Grand Central Publishing is a division of Hachette Book Group, Inc. The Grand Central Publishing name and logo is a registered trademark of Hachette Book Group, Inc.

The publisher is not responsible for websites (or their content) that are not owned by the publisher.

The Hachette Speakers Bureau provides a wide range of authors for speaking events. To find out more, go to hachettespeakersbureau.com or email HachetteSpeakers@hbgusa.com.

Grand Central Publishing books may be purchased in bulk for business, educational, or promotional use. For information, please contact your local bookseller or the Hachette Book Group Special Markets Department at special.markets@hbgusa.com.

Library of Congress Cataloging-in-Publication Data

Names: Canestaro, Nathan, author.
Title: The Mighty Moo : the USS Cowpens and her epic World War II journey from jinx ship to the Navy's first carrier into Tokyo Bay / Nathan Canestaro.
Other titles: USS Cowpens and her epic World War II journey from jinx ship to the Navy's first carrier into Tokyo Bay
Description: First edition. | New York ; Boston : Grand Central Publishing, 2024. | Includes bibliographical references and index.
Identifiers: LCCN 2023036596 | ISBN 9781538742716 (hardcover) | ISBN 9781538742730 (ebook)
Subjects: LCSH: Cowpens (Aircraft carrier) | World War, 1939–1945—Naval operations, American. | World War, 1939–1945—Aerial operations, American. | Sailors—United States—Biography. | United States. Navy—Airmen—Biography. | Aircraft carriers—United States—History—20th century. | CYAC: World War, 1939–1945—Campaigns—Pacific Area.
Classification: LCC D774.C69 C37 2024 | DDC 940.54/5973—dc23/eng/20230810
LC record available at https://lccn.loc.gov/2023036596

ISBNs: 978-1-5387-4271-6 (hardcover), 978-1-5387-4273-0 (ebook)

Printed in Canada

MRQ

Printing 1, 2024

*To my grandfather, Aviation Ordnanceman First Class
Herbert Todd, who could not tell us the stories of his
time aboard the* Cowpens…

*…and to sixty of his shipmates who never got
the chance to tell theirs.*

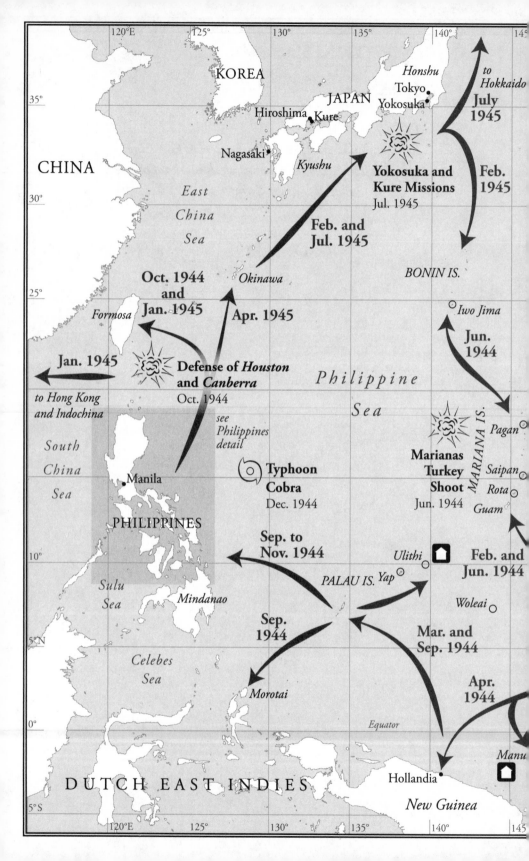

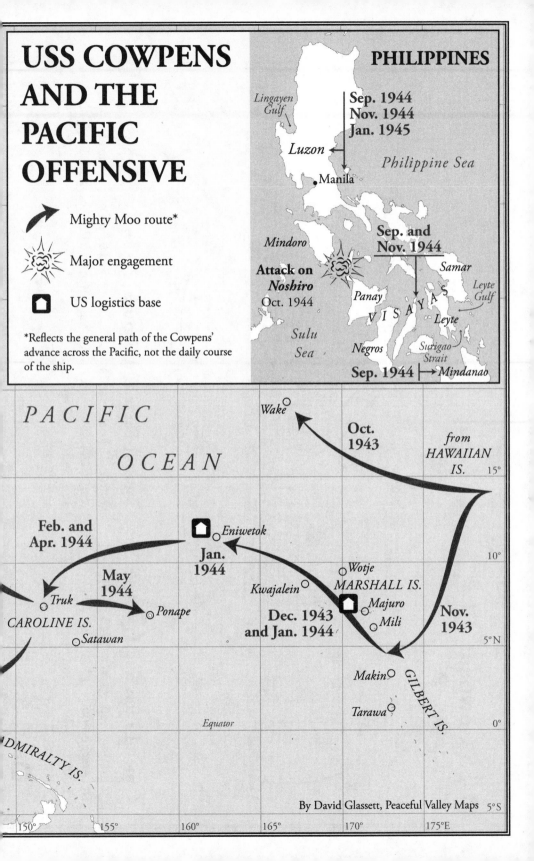

USS COWPENS AND THE PACIFIC OFFENSIVE

➤ Mighty Moo route*

✳ Major engagement

⬢ US logistics base

*Reflects the general path of the Cowpens' advance across the Pacific, not the daily course of the ship.

PHILIPPINES

Lingayen Gulf

Sep. 1944
Nov. 1944
Jan. 1945

Luzon

• Manila

Mindoro

Attack on Noshiro
Oct. 1944

Sep. and Nov. 1944

Philippine Sea

Samar

Leyte Gulf

Panay

V I S A Y A S

Leyte

Sulu Sea

Negros

Surigao Strait

Sep. 1944 → Mindanao

PACIFIC

OCEAN

Wake

Oct. 1943

from HAWAIIAN IS.   15°

Feb. and Apr. 1944

Eniwetok

Jan. 1944

May 1944

Wotje

MARSHALL IS.   10°

Kwajalein

Truk

Ponape

Dec. 1943 and Jan. 1944

Majuro

Mili

Nov. 1943   5°N

CAROLINE IS.

Satawan

Makin

GILBERT IS.

Equator

Tarawa   0°

ADMIRALTY IS.

By David Glassett, Peaceful Valley Maps   5°S

150°   155°   160°   165°   170°   175°E

USS Cowpens
"The Mighty Moo"

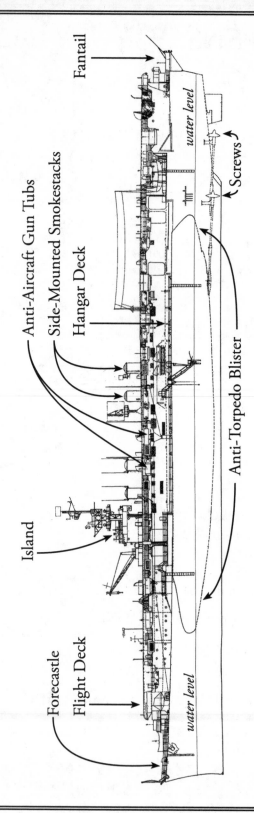

Forecastle
Flight Deck

Island

Anti-Aircraft Gun Tubs
Side-Mounted Smokestacks
Hangar Deck

Anti-Torpedo Blister

Fantail

water level

Screws

water level

General Facts and Figures

Commissioned: 28 May 1943
Decommissioned: 13 January 1947
11,000 tons displacement
Length: 622.5 feet
Speed: 32 knots (37 mph)

Combat Facts and Figures

Awarded 12 battle stars
Steamed 211,615 miles
Launched 11,275 aircraft
Sank 16 ships

Destroyed 93 planes in the air
Destroyed 512 planes on the ground

By David Glassett, Peaceful Valley Maps

Contents

Introduction

Like many of his generation, my grandfather Herbert Todd never talked much about the war. He joined the Navy in 1942 at the age of twenty-one, following the example of his father, a World War I veteran who earned the Navy Cross on convoy duty in the Atlantic. Our family understood the broad outlines of my grandfather's wartime service; he was a tail gunner on an Avenger torpedo bomber in the Pacific, flew missions in the Philippines, and survived a terrible typhoon. While he was proud to be a veteran and displayed his framed service ribbons in his home, it was clear my grandfather decided to put that part of his life behind him. He rarely told stories about the war, and when he did they were always humorous or upbeat. Once, while we were attending an air show in small-town Ohio, the sight of a type of aircraft that he trained in decades before jarred loose a memory. My grandfather described how he and his pilot buzzed a free-range chicken farm, recalling with a mischievous grin, "If you've never seen a few hundred thousand chickens take to the air all at once, it is a sight you will never forget."

My grandfather tolerated my interest in his service, but I don't think he understood it. He was particularly puzzled when, after I returned from my own wartime deployment to the Middle East, I went to the South Pacific on a scuba-diving trip. My itinerary included two islands that my grandfather's squadron bombed—Truk and Palau. To him, these were hostile islands on the edge of the world, and he didn't understand why I paid to go there. I explained to him that after seven months in the desert, all I wanted to do was surround myself with water. He got a wistful look on his face, and commented on the irony that "you went to war and missed the water—I went to war and missed the land."

Toward the end of his life, I made a determined effort to learn my grandfather's story, but it seemed like my questions only caused him pain. He told me more about his time in Hawaii and aboard the aircraft carrier USS *Cowpens*, but he was frequently vague and the discussion repeatedly brought him to tears. Afterward, I felt guilty for asking him to relive such a traumatic time in his life. To make matters worse, I did not know much more about his service than when I started. As someone who researches military conflict for a living, I grew determined to learn about his Navy years on my own, starting a decade-long odyssey that has culminated in this book. I hoped to answer the questions that my grandfather could not or would not: What was it like for a young man who had never been far away from home to live on and fly from a carrier in the Pacific? Where did you go and what missions did you fly? How did your carrier contribute to the overall course of the war?

Over several years, I searched archives, collected official records, and accumulated piles of books and other secondary sources. In the end, I came to the disappointing conclusion that there was simply not enough information to piece together my grandfather's story. With the exception of a few photos, a basic personnel record, and a mention in the Navy's muster rolls, he was like millions of other Americans whose service made little mark on the historical record. This was largely due to factors beyond his control; my grandfather was an enlisted man, while the Navy's record-keeping focused on its officers. Unless an enlisted man conducted some act of heroism or was wounded or killed, the records rarely mentioned him.

A few tantalizing details emerged suggesting my grandfather had some close calls. The TBF Avengers that he flew in were vulnerable to ground fire, and several of his squadronmates were shot down. The pilot that my grandfather flew with the most, Silas Johnson, went down over the Philippines, losing his radioman and spending several weeks on the run with Filipino guerrillas. But my grandfather's moment of greatest fear was not in combat—it was at the hands of Mother Nature. While he would not talk of his combat missions, he spoke freely of the terrifying experience of Typhoon Cobra, when seventy-foot waves and winds of 120 knots rocked his top-heavy ship so severely that its crew feared it would capsize. They had good reason to be scared; three destroyers foundered and sank in the storm, killing almost eight hundred men.

This book, then, is not my grandfather's story. He died in 2010 and kept his secrets until the end. But in my attempt to retrace his steps, I found another, larger story—that of his ship and the men who served aboard it. It's a tale that is representative of the experiences of countless Americans who served aboard aircraft carriers in the Pacific and helped me understand what my grandfather's wartime service was like.

It's a story of underdogs, with a ship and crew who were hardly the stuff of naval legends. It features a humble and forgotten light aircraft carrier, the USS *Cowpens*, affectionately known as "the Mighty Moo." She started her career as a jinx ship, beset by accidents and bad luck. But she found her stride in battle, earning a distinguished combat record in service with the Navy's task force of larger fast carriers. *Cowpens'* virtue was her endurance; she spent more time in combat and earned more battle stars—twelve total—than her sister ships. With the exception of the Okinawa campaign, she participated in every major carrier operation from the 1943 raid on Wake Island to the final surrender in Tokyo Bay in 1945. Moreover, she did so without taking any hits from enemy action, even though bombs and torpedoes fell all around her. And at the end of the war, only one US aircraft carrier sat triumphantly in Tokyo Bay to witness the Japanese surrender—the Mighty Moo.

This story is as much about the men who served aboard the *Cowpens* as the ship itself. They were no strangers to adversity, suffering through both the hard years of the Great Depression and the dark early days of the war, when the US military reeled from one defeat to another. From a twenty-first-century eye, these men came of age during a remarkable period of national cohesion and moral clarity, a time when our wars united rather than divided us. Characteristic of many of their generation, the men of the *Cowpens* denied they were anything special. "We're not heroes," said the ship's official narrative from early 1945. "We're just a bunch of guys serving our country aboard an aircraft carrier. We have enormous pride in a mass of steel labelled by the Navy as the *Cowpens*, and by us the Mighty

Moo."[1] "We were a close organization," recalled one of the ship's last combat squadrons. "We had no outstanding characters, nor did we have any non-entities. We were just average men who played only a small part in winning the Second World War."[2]

The men aboard the *Cowpens* were not the Navy's elite. Most of her officers and men were reservists who had been in uniform barely longer than the ship had been afloat. Even the handful of career officers aboard were often second-class citizens in the Navy before Pearl Harbor, lacking the pedigree or seniority to qualify for better commands. The Moo's personnel were from all backgrounds and walks of life, a slice of the America that had sent them to war. Her captains were in turn unlucky, toxic, and stalwart—her pilots brave, loyal, and sometimes vainglorious. They suffered and celebrated together, sometimes fighting each other almost as hard as they did the enemy. There was a tragic hero and an ace in a day, epic storms, feckless admirals and courageous ones. There were endless days at sea, hard-fought successes, Pyrrhic victories, and more close calls than anyone cared to count. There were men lost in life rafts, and others shot down and left on the run behind enemy lines. Sixty men did not come home. Some died bravely, in combat—in defense of their friends or pursuit of the enemy. Others lost their lives tragically, the result of accidents. And still others just disappeared, never to be seen again, swallowed up by the Pacific.

This is their story.

THE
MIGHTY
MOO

CHAPTER 1

Origins: The Stopgap Sisters

*C*owpens and her eight sisters of the *Independence* class were never intended to be aircraft carriers at all. They were designed as light cruisers, a sleek greyhound of a warship with a middle-weight punch of five- and six-inch guns. But the US Navy had a problem; it was losing its carriers at a rapid rate. Of the six US flattops that served in the Pacific in 1942, four—*Wasp, Hornet, Lexington,* and *Yorktown*—fell prey to the Japanese, and the remaining two took turns in the shipyard patching up their battle damage. So desperate was the situation in late 1942 and early 1943 that first *Enterprise* and then *Saratoga* were at times the only American carriers operating in the Pacific.

The Navy wanted the heavy *Essex*-class fleet carriers to be the backbone of the fleet. These 27,100-ton ships were everything it was looking for in a flattop: fast, resilient to battle damage, and with the striking power of almost one hundred planes. Their size and complexity made them slow to build, and the first few did not arrive in the Pacific until mid-1943—and not in sufficient numbers to replace battle losses until 1944. What was needed were additional carriers to fill the gap until more of the *Essex*es arrived. These stopgap ships would need to be quickly built from resources already on hand and had to be capable of keeping up with the full-size fleet carriers on their long forays across the Pacific.

The Navy had already contracted for three dozen *Cleveland*-class light cruisers, and on the orders of President Franklin D. Roosevelt—and over the objections of the Navy's hidebound bureaucracy—nine of these ships were rebuilt to host aircraft. And so the ships of the *Independence* class of light carriers, designated "CVL" (carrier, aircraft, light) were born. These nine ships filled out the ranks of the fleet at the precise moment they were needed most. Collectively, they earned eighty battle stars, carried future presidents Gerald Ford (USS *Monterey*) and George H. W. Bush (USS *San Jacinto*) into harm's way, and accounted for more than half of the American carrier decks during the Battle of the Philippine Sea—which broke the back of Japanese naval aviation. They were workhorses of the fleet and critical supporting players in winning the war. But afterward they were discarded and forgotten, and virtually no trace of them remains.[1]

They were not beautiful ships. The compromises necessary to fit a flight deck on the smaller hull of a light cruiser made them downright ungainly. They were short and stubby in comparison to a full-size carrier—622 feet from bow to stern, roughly two-thirds the length of an *Essex*. Their eleven-thousand-ton bulk was narrow and tall, with uncharitable handling characteristics in heavy weather, including a tendency to pitch and roll badly when wind and waves picked up. With their high center of gravity and the uncompensated weight of an island—a small, towerlike structure that was the ship's nerve center for flight operations—on the starboard side, the CVLs were always just a little off balance. They had a natural four- to six-degree list to starboard when fully fueled, although when there was some room in the tanks the crew could compensate by pumping more fuel to the port-side tanks. The smokestacks were side-vented, and they curled upward like sprouting mushrooms. The flight deck stopped fifty feet short of the bow, giving the ship the appearance of having a broken nose. The *Independence*-class carriers were, as one sailor observed, "as dumpy and dowdy a sea-going scow as ever outraged a shellback's critical eye."[1]

Their capabilities were also modest, primarily due to space constraints. They held only thirty-three aircraft, a third of the *Essex* class. The CVLs had the narrowest flight deck in the Navy, at only seventy-three feet, making landings aboard what one *Cowpens* pilot called "lively."[2] Another word for it was dangerous. They were difficult to fly from and had some of the highest accident rates in the fleet. They were not comfortable ships and were cramped even by Navy standards: 159 officers and 1,410 men packed into quarters that were initially designed for only 1,250. Another compromise in the CVLs' design was ventilation, and when the ship was buttoned up for battle in the warm South Pacific waters, temperatures in some compartments soared to over 130 degrees.

It was a sign of the Navy's desperation that they could accept ships of such modest capability and with such obvious limitations. But the CVLs had two major advantages. First, they were fast enough to keep up with the fleet carriers. They retained the power plants of their cruiser progenitors: four oil-fired boilers drove their turbines, producing more than 100,000 horsepower. When teamed with their four manganese bronze screws— each 6.3 tons and almost 12 feet in diameter—the CVLs could manage over 31 knots. At a more efficient speed of 15 knots, they could steam 13,000 miles without refueling, long enough to complete raids deep into Japanese territory. The second advantage of these light carriers was they were relatively quick to build. While it took fifteen to eighteen months to complete an *Essex*-class, all nine CVLs were in service within twenty-two months of the first conversion contract.

While US planners and strategists had long considered how they might fight Japan, the fleet needed to win that war was assembled at the last minute, resulting from the fear that the United States might have to face all three Axis powers by itself. In 1940, with the French having surrendered and the British fighting a desperate battle for survival, the United States set about to build a fleet capable of defeating the Axis at sea without Allied support.

Private shipbuilders were a major beneficiary of this unprecedented expansion in naval construction. One such firm was the misleadingly named New York Shipbuilding Company in Camden, New Jersey— where *Cowpens* and her sisters soon took form. Established in 1899, New York Ship, as it was called, was just up the Delaware River from the government-owned Philadelphia Naval Shipyard, then one of the biggest shipyards in the world. The firm had only barely survived the lean years of the interwar period, with the 1920s being especially difficult. Contracts were hard to find, and the yard constructed only a handful of warships for the Navy—as well as any other job that kept it operating, such as barges and ferries. The firm took drastic measures to stay afloat, cutting its workforce nearly 70 percent, and engaging in some illegal collusion on contract bidding with its two largest rivals in order to limit competition on the few government contracts available.

Once the United States began preparing for war, the company's growth was explosive. Buoyed by a $25 million federal grant, the shipyard devoted itself to building warships. And build ships it did—in one twelve-month period from March 1942 to 1943, New York Ship delivered more than $217 million in naval construction, mostly of heavy combatant ships from 12,000 to 35,000 tons, all of it months ahead of schedule. This increase in work demanded a massive increase in personnel; the company had only 3,000 employees in 1938, but by 1942 this number swelled to an army of more than 34,000.

Desperate Times and Desperate Measures: Cruisers to Carriers

Much of the credit for pushing the concept of light aircraft carriers onto a reluctant Navy goes to President Franklin D. Roosevelt. He was no stranger to the Navy, with years of experience in its administration. He had served as assistant secretary of the Navy for eight years in the Wilson administration, longer than he had occupied any other job besides the presidency. The future commander in chief, then a thirty-one-year old former New York state senator, ran the day-to-day operations of the Navy and helped it mobilize for the First World War. In this role, FDR became acquainted with most of the men who eventually led the US Navy in the 1940s while they were midlevel officers.

The Navy was unhappy with FDR's hands-on management style, regarding it as unhelpful meddling. As president, FDR quipped that he was his own secretary of the Navy and sought to take charge in a variety of matters normally well below the interest of any other commander in chief. He routinely monitored individual ships and personnel and sometimes even influenced assignment boards. FDR enjoyed intervening in the Navy's affairs, and he was not intimidated by the gold braid of its admirals. Not that the Navy blithely went along with the president's instructions, of course. Its leadership employed a variety of tactics to keep him at bay, from slow rolling to outright refusal—and overall the president lost more bureaucratic battles than he won. FDR once complained to a friend: "The admirals are really something to cope with—and I should know. To change anything in the Navy is like punching a feather bed. You punch it with your right and you punch it with your left until you are finally exhausted, and then you find the damn bed just as it was before you started punching."[3]

FDR was especially critical of the Navy's tendency for "gold plated" solutions to problems, a preference for expensive naval systems when something more austere could meet the need. One such dispute with the Navy bureaucracy produced *Cowpens* and her sisters. In August 1941, worried about the slow pace of delivery of the *Essex*-class carriers, FDR directed the Navy to convert several *Cleveland*-class light cruisers already under construction into flattops to bolster the fleet until the larger ships arrived. The Navy bureaucracy rejected the idea, arguing that the small size of these ships would limit their effectiveness, make them difficult to fly from, and that they would be available only about ninety days faster than the *Essex*es. FDR was not interested in excuses, he just wanted more carriers for the expected war with Japan—and it was only by conceding the Navy's arguments that he convinced them to comply with his order. On January 2, 1942, the Navy finally relented and directed New York Ship to convert the partially constructed light cruiser *Amsterdam* into an aircraft carrier, soon to be renamed as *Independence*.

Although the Navy had finally agreed to the project, the question of how to make a light cruiser into an aircraft carrier remained. New York Ship did most of the design work for the *Cleveland* class, and so the Navy's Bureau of Ships allowed the firm to also take the lead on its carrier conversions, an arrangement that likely reflected its overall disdain for the project. New York Ship threw itself into the work, tackling each of the major issues with remarkable speed.

The first question was how to put a flight deck on top of a hull never designed to carry that much weight so far off the water. In an attempt to compensate for their high center of gravity, New York Ship's naval architects steadied the CVLs by broadening them. They added long blisters down both sides of the hull, extending 3.5 feet beyond the normal hull amidships and tapering at the bow and the stern. While this slowed the ship's top speed by 1.5 knots, it offered storage of an additional 635 tons of bunker oil and aviation gasoline. But even with these additions, topside weight remained a problem throughout the design process, and New York Ship's designers looked to trim wherever they could. The flight deck stopped fifty feet short of the full length of the hull, to avoid overloading the sleek cruiser bow. The island structure on the flight deck was cramped—only a small bridge, plus the captain's and navigator's sea cabins, a chart room, and lookout platforms. But even as small as it was, the addition of so much weight on the starboard needed compensating ballast on the port, and so the shipyard added eighty-two tons of concrete to that side of the hull.

Other weight continued to add up, including an aircraft crane capable of hoisting fourteen thousand pounds, a hydraulic catapult, and an extension of the flight deck on the port side to allow aircraft to bypass the elevator well when they were jettisoned over the side in an emergency. New York Ship did its best to counter these necessary additions by reducing weight elsewhere. Every cut counted—even small changes like replacing all doors on the officers' quarters with cloth curtains. But the designers could only do so much, and they never could fully resolve the CVLs' list or their top-heavy nature.

There were other problems, too. The room that the designers found in the belly of the light carriers for a tank capable of holding one hundred thousand gallons of aviation gasoline came at the expense of additional room for the larger complement needed to operate an aircraft carrier. As a result, the CVLs were cramped for their crew. The conversion from cruiser to carrier also restricted space for the ships' defenses, including its antiaircraft batteries and armor. There was little room for the Navy's preferred antiaircraft weapon—five-inch guns—and so the light carriers made do with shorter-range 20mm and 40mm batteries in gun tubs along the perimeter of the flight deck. Moreover, while their design called for armor of the same thickness as the cruisers, it was of reduced quality to save weight. Despite these limitations, New York Ship was proud of its work. The light carriers were fast, more capable than the Navy's naysayers predicted, and built in record time—a fact that the company touted in wartime advertisements.

The *Cowpens* Is Born: The US Navy Down to Its Last Carrier

The wisdom of FDR's insistence on more carrier decks for the war soon proved itself, as one by one US carriers were damaged or sunk. The first was *Saratoga*, on her way to gaining a reputation as a magnet for enemy fire. On January 11, 1942, Japanese submarine *I-6* caught her southwest of Hawaii, tearing open one of her flanks with a torpedo and killing eleven men. She limped back to the United States for five months of repairs. The Navy looked to New York Ship to help make up for her absence, and on February 3, 1942, it directed that work begin on two more CVLs— *Princeton* and *Belleau Wood*.

Lexington was the next of the Navy's losses—a casualty of the Battle of the Coral Sea in May, the first naval battle in history fought primarily by carrier aircraft. Tipped off by US codebreaking, the Navy sortied *Lexington* and *Yorktown* to block a Japanese invasion fleet bound for Port Moresby, on the southern coast of New Guinea, that would put them in a position to threaten the sea routes between the United States and Australia. While a strategic victory for the US in that the battle turned back the Japanese invasion fleet, it was a tactical victory for the Japanese in terms of ships lost. In the exchange of carrier strikes, Lady Lex fell prey to multiple torpedo and bomb hits while *Yorktown* suffered bomb damage in exchange for the sinking of Japanese light carrier *Shoho*.

Back in Camden, *Lexington's* loss led the Navy to add three more carrier conversions to New York Ship's workload—the former cruisers *Huntington*, *Dayton*, and *Fargo*. With the addition of these three ships the work of building the CVLs constituted the bulk of New York Ship's construction program, and the yards were by then buzzing with activity to try and keep up with the Navy's need for additional carriers.

In the spring of 1942, President Roosevelt received a postcard from George Dean Martin, a drugstore owner in the small town of Cowpens, South Carolina. Martin inquired whether the Navy could name an aircraft carrier *Cowpens*, in honor of the nearby Revolutionary War battle after which the town was named. Cowpens was hardly the place where one would expect a connection to the Navy. It was a landlocked town with only 1,343 residents, nearly two hundred miles from the Atlantic. While other Revolutionary War battles such as Lexington, Yorktown, and Saratoga were firmly entrenched in the American historical memory, both the town and the Battle of Cowpens were more obscure. One Cowpens resident visiting Philadelphia dealt with a flummoxed telephone operator while trying to call home. In those days, operators connected long-distance calls, and this one had never heard of Cowpens and even struggled to spell it. "Don't worry," the resident assured her, "many people in Cowpens don't know where Philadelphia is either."[4]

Were it not for a postcard from a pharmacist more than 150 years later, the contributions of the town of Cowpens to American military history might have stopped with the Revolution. But the White House approved George Martin's suggestion and passed it along to the Navy Department, who in turn directed that the former cruiser *Huntington* should carry the name USS *Cowpens* (CVL-25).

As work on the *Cowpens* got underway, New York Ship was losing its battle to build carriers faster than the Japanese could sink them. Every ship launching was seemingly followed by a loss at sea, as if the enemy was taunting the shipyard to keep up. US codebreakers again provided the tipoff that the Japanese fleet was on the move, this time bound for Midway in June. Adm. Chester W. Nimitz, who had commanded the Pacific Fleet only since January, concentrated his three available carriers—*Enterprise*, *Hornet*, and *Yorktown*—to try and ambush them there. In the climactic battle that followed, American dive bombers sunk four Japanese fleet carriers—*Akagi*, *Kaga*, *Hiryu*, and *Soryu*—in return for *Yorktown*, which had been hurriedly repaired after Coral Sea. The victory was worth the sacrifice; Midway ended the unchecked Japanese expansion across the Pacific and brought the two opposing navies to near parity in terms of aircraft carriers. Despite the magnitude of the victory, the Navy's carrier situation remained difficult, and within a month the Navy queued up additional replacements at New York Ship. The final batch of CVLs were built from cruisers *Wilmington*, *Buffalo*, and *Newark*—becoming *Cabot*, *Bataan*, and *San Jacinto*, respectively.

Fighting throughout the rest of 1942 shifted to the Southwest Pacific as US forces for the first time went on the offensive. The US Marine Corps landed on Guadalcanal in August, and the battle for control of that island was hard-fought for months, with the advantage repeatedly shifting back and forth between the American invaders and Japanese defenders. Aircraft carriers are most effective when they remain mobile and on the offensive, but the need to support US troops ashore kept the Navy close to Guadalcanal—making its flattops an easier target. By the end of the year, an American victory ashore looked likely, but the US Navy paid the price: two carriers lost and a third damaged. The wounded carrier was again *Saratoga*, who found herself in a submarine's crosshairs while transiting a patch of ocean between Noumea, Espiritu Santo, and Guadalcanal that was notorious as "torpedo junction."

Wasp followed not long after. On September 15, 1942, she was in the company of *Hornet*, the battleship *North Carolina*, and ten other warships, escorting transports carrying the Seventh Marine Regiment to Guadalcanal. But that afternoon, Japanese submarine *I-19* managed to score three torpedo hits on *Wasp*'s side. The attack came at the worst possible time; she was launching aircraft and so her fuel lines were full. The fuel and ammunition of her ready-to-launch planes contributed to the blaze, creating an inferno aboard. The blaze soon grew unmanageable, and a gasoline vapor explosion ripped through the ship less than twenty minutes after the initial attack. *Wasp* went down by the bow, still ablaze and with some of her hull plating growing bright orange from the fires burning within. Nearby ships pulled all but 173 of her men from the water and finished off the burning wreck with three torpedoes.

US aircraft carrier production finally came to fruition in early 1943, and new flattops began arriving in the Pacific just a few weeks later. With the assistance of its greatly increased numbers, New York Ship delivered one CVL after another to the Navy anywhere from ten months to two years ahead of schedule. A ship's launching and her commissioning are the two most important dates in her early life. Blessing a new ship on her launching day is a tradition that stretches back to antiquity, and sometimes resembles a baptismal ceremony. But for the US Navy, a new ship formally receives her name on her launching day while a female sponsor breaks a bottle of christening wine or spirits over her bow as she slides from the shipyard ways into the water. The new ship does not year bear the USS in her title or fly any ensign, jack, or pennant, as she is not yet in the naval service. Months of work known as "fitting out" are required before the ship is commissioned—designated ready for sea. *Independence* was commissioned on January 14, 1943, and *Princeton* and *Belleau Wood* followed in February and March, only one month apart. *Cowpens* was not far behind. Her launching day was January 17, 1943, the 162nd anniversary of the battle for which she was named, and only three days after her sister *Independence* was commissioned.

Cowpens' sponsor was Mrs. Margaret Halsey Spruance, the daughter of Adm. William "Bull" Halsey. He was one of the Navy's best known admirals, famous not only for his battle record but for his fiery personality. He commanded several of the early raids against Japanese-held islands in 1942, led the carriers that brought Jimmy Doolittle's raiders within striking range of Tokyo, and then commanded the South Pacific forces in the Solomon Islands. The American public loved his bombastic statements, which boosted morale on the home front at times when the news coming from the Pacific was almost uniformly bad. Upon seeing the damage the Japanese inflicted at Pearl Harbor, Halsey swore that "before we're through with 'em, the Japanese language will be spoken only in Hell!" During the Guadalcanal campaign, Halsey had a sign posted that urged his men to "Kill Japs, Kill Japs, and Kill More Japs," and he promised to ride Japanese emperor Hirohito's famed white stallion through the streets of Tokyo.[5] *Cowpens* repeatedly served under Halsey's command in the months to come, and the bellicose admiral proved to have a soft spot for the little carrier that his daughter christened.

CHAPTER 2

The Moo's Veteran Officers:
McConnell and Price

The war's desperate first eighteen months not only remade the US Fleet, but it also shaped the generation of officers who suffered through it. Two such men played an important role in *Cowpens*' story, helping make the ship the success it eventually became. Like the ship itself, both were underdogs. They were second-class citizens in the Navy before the war, lacking the pedigree needed for prestigious assignments. Both men survived early Allied losses or bore the costs of one of its Pyrrhic victories, and once they returned to action they were motivated to take the fight to the enemy. Robert P. McConnell escaped the destruction of the US Asiatic Fleet only by the narrowest of margins, having two ships sunk out from underneath him in the Java Sea in the early days of the war. He went on to serve as *Cowpens*' first commanding officer, and under his steady leadership the crew evolved from a mob of raw recruits to a capable wartime team. Bob Price was an experienced fighter pilot and natural leader who escaped the fall of Singapore in early 1942. Price set the example of combat leadership for all the air groups that followed. He served aboard *Cowpens* in a series of increasingly important positions, first as commander of one of its fighter squadrons, then as air group commander, and finally as the ship's air officer.

Cowpens' First Captain: Robert P. McConnell

Robert P. McConnell was one of many US and Allied officers who narrowly escaped the initial Japanese offensive that followed Pearl Harbor. The handsome, silver-haired McConnell was forty-six years old and a rarity in the prewar Navy—a "mustang," an officer who started his career as an enlisted man. McConnell studied mining engineering at the University of California at Berkeley before dropping out to join the Navy in 1917. Although the 1918 armistice ended World War I before McConnell saw action in Europe, the practical and conscientious young man secured a commission, starting a Navy career in 1920 as a lieutenant.

McConnell's unconventional background and lack of a Naval Academy degree nearly hamstrung his career before it began. Amid the draconian personnel cuts that followed the war, the Navy became more parochial, with an officer's professional pedigree just as important in determining advancement as his performance. Through sheer determination and persistence, McConnell managed to survive and advance in rank in this unforgiving environment. But it wasn't easy. His daughter Doreen McConnell Johnson recalled how her father had to work harder than the Naval Academy graduates who surrounded him, and he was constantly nettled by reminders that he would always be an outsider in the service's old boys' network. Even among the families, Doreen recalled the first question asked in any social engagement was "Oh, what Academy class was your father in?"[1]

McConnell was assigned to the Asiatic Fleet in the Philippines, where he briefly served as the executive officer (second in command) of seaplane tender *Langley* before assuming command of that ship in early 1942. While every naval officer dreamed of commanding a ship, the *Langley* was no prize and neither was the Asiatic Fleet. In fact, the assignment was likely the Navy's way of telling Commander McConnell that his career advancement had come to an end. Despite its grandiose name, the Asiatic Fleet was a ragtag collection of obsolete ships primarily intended to "show the flag" in East Asia rather than do much fighting. It was a place of exile, where the Navy shipped its over-the-hill or incapable officers to wait out their retirement. Similarly, the *Langley* was exactly the sort of misfit that ended up in the Asiatic Fleet. She'd started life as a humble collier (coal ship), but in 1920 was rebuilt into the Navy's first aircraft carrier. *Langley* was more of a test bed for naval aviation than a warship, never really intended to go into harm's way. She was desperately vulnerable— slow, unmaneuverable, and with little in the way of antiaircraft defenses. Deemed no longer useful as an aircraft carrier, in 1936 she suffered through a conversion to a seaplane tender that cost her almost half her flight deck. *Langley* lost the ability to launch and land planes in return for the space to winch aboard one of her flock of long-range PBY Catalina seaplanes for maintenance.

Although the Asiatic Fleet had been bracing for the outbreak of hostilities, news of the attack on Pearl Harbor arrived like a bolt out of the blue in the predawn hours of December 8. It caught Commander McConnell and his crew entirely by surprise. *Langley* received her orders to raise steam and head south as fast as she could, only barely keeping ahead of Japanese air strikes on her home port of Cavite, Manila. They escaped to Australia, where *Langley* and McConnell had a two-month reprieve patrolling its northern coast before being called back to the war.

Singapore surrendered on February 15, and three days later the Japanese landed on Bali. The Japanese were now poised to attack the Dutch territory of Java from two directions and controlled all the approaches to the island. Although most Allied commanders were skeptical it could be defended, the Netherlands government-in-exile was determined to hold on. They were desperate for reinforcements and pressured the US Navy to send McConnell and *Langley* to deliver thirty-two P-40 Warhawk fighters to the port of Tjilatjap on the southern coast of Java. The mission was as futile as it was dangerous. *Langley* was a sitting duck at sea, such a small number of planes would never hold back the Japanese tide, and the P-40 was no match for the Japanese Zeke. To make matters worse, Tjilatjap did not have an airfield. The planes would have to be unloaded at the dock and towed to a nearby field that could serve as an airstrip. The streets were too narrow to fit the P-40s' wings, and so Dutch officials planned to bulldoze buildings to make way.

Commander McConnell was a practical man and knew the odds were against him, but he was also not in a position to refuse his orders. His only consolation was that the mission was choreographed so that *Langley* steamed the last and most dangerous leg of the trip under the cover of darkness. Unfortunately, McConnell's superior officers—Dutch admiral Conrad Helfrich and his American subordinate Vice Admiral William Glassford—sabotaged the plan by micromanaging it. A series of back-and-forth orders as to who would escort *Langley* into port—a Dutch minelayer or two US destroyers, *Whipple* and *Edsall*—cost McConnell eight hours. Now, instead of arriving in the early morning, *Langley* would have to steam the final leg of the trip in broad daylight.

The result was a foregone conclusion: Japanese bombers spotted *Langley* a full one hundred miles short of Tjilatjap on February 27. Flying above the range of her few antiaircraft guns, the enemy planes homed in on her as if on a training exercise. Despite McConnell's desperate attempts to evade, the Japanese smothered his ship in bombs. Afire above decks and taking on water below, *Langley* was in trouble. With propulsion lost and the weight of the P-40s topside contributing to a dangerous list, she seemed ready to capsize. McConnell ordered his men to abandon ship, and *Edsall* and *Whipple* picked up 308 survivors. Unfortunately, the crippled *Langley*—while still afire—did not sink. Worried that the Japanese might return at any moment, *Whipple* attempted to finish her off with gunfire and torpedoes, but the stubborn old collier refused to die. After a brief discussion—and with only two torpedoes remaining—McConnell and the two destroyer captains agreed to depart without waiting for her to go under, a decision that would soon bring McConnell no end of trouble.

Edsall and *Whipple* transferred their survivors at sea to the oiler *Pecos* on February 28; she headed south for Australia while the destroyers returned to Java. *Pecos* did not get far, however. At about 10 a.m. on March 1, Japanese reconnaissance planes spotted her. McConnell had a terrible sense of déjà vu, and he remarked to *Pecos'* captain, Cmdr. Elmer Abernethy, "We're in for it now."[2]

Japanese bombers appeared overhead within two hours. As with the *Langley*, the *Pecos'* meager battery of antiaircraft guns posed little threat to the attacking planes. They put two bombs on her upper decks, but it was a close miss near the bow on the port side that proved to be fatal, caving in the hull below the waterline. Tons of seawater poured in, and *Pecos* immediately started going down by the bow. McConnell and the other *Langley* survivors went into the ocean for the second time in four days as *Pecos* stood vertical in the water for a brief moment before taking her final plunge into the abyss.

Unbeknownst to the survivors in the water, *Whipple* had heard the *Pecos* distress call and rushed to the scene. Her crew manned the rails to help bring the exhausted, battered, and oil-coated survivors aboard. The rescue operation was painfully slow, as there were more survivors in the water than the destroyer had men aboard. After two hours, sonar reports of a Japanese submarine nearby forced a difficult decision. McConnell, Abernethy, and the commanding officer of the destroyer division, Cmdr. William Crouch, met to discuss whether it was better to remain in the area and pick up as many men as possible and risk being sunk, or depart the area with the survivors they had. *Whipple* was the sole survivor of the mission, low on fuel and overloaded with men. All three officers agreed it was better to depart and save some than remain and lose all. *Whipple* increased her speed to sixteen knots and sped away, leaving as many as five hundred men to the mercy of the sea.

Having narrowly survived two Japanese attacks at sea, upon returning to Australia McConnell soon discovered that his career was the next target. Because McConnell had not actually seen *Langley* sink, Admiral Glassford accused him of abandoning the ship prematurely.[3] McConnell responded with a seven-page handwritten report that justified his abandonment of the *Langley* on the basis of the danger that Japanese planes could have returned at any moment and that the overloaded and heavily listing ship was about to capsize. Both accounts worked their way up the chain of command to the desk of Adm. Ernest King, the most powerful man in the US Navy and the first to simultaneously hold the offices of commander in chief of the US Fleet and chief of naval operations.

McConnell spent several anxious weeks with his career hanging in the balance, waiting for King's decision. The admiral was not a merciful man.

He was a hard-charging, heavy-drinking, quick-tempered taskmaster who had made it his personal mission to rid the service of poor performers. Stories of his hard-nosed leadership style were legend. Gen. Douglas MacArthur described him as "perpetually mean," while Gen. Dwight Eisenhower once mused that shooting King would help the war effort.[4] Even one of King's six daughters described him as "the most even-tempered man in the Navy. He is always in a rage."[5]

On June 2, 1942, King ruled in favor of McConnell—concluding that his actions were reasonable under the difficult circumstances—and ordered the matter closed. McConnell had dodged the bullet, although it was only a partial delivery of justice. He remained stoic while his superior officers who had mismanaged the mission escaped accountability and others whose actions were similar to his own were commended for their bravery. *Pecos'* commanding officer, Elmer Abernethy, for example, received the Navy Cross—the service's second highest decoration—for his heroism in his defense of the doomed oiler and then for evacuating his men. But despite his outward calm, *Langley's* sinking and the loss of nearly a quarter of his crew affected McConnell greatly. His daughter Doreen said afterward that he was "never the same."[6]

The Squadron Commander: Robert H. Price

Another future *Cowpens* officer staring down the barrel of the Japanese offensive in Southeast Asia was Bob Price. Originally from Webster Grove, Missouri—a suburb of St. Louis—Price was twenty-seven years old, with a wide, friendly face and straight brown hair that he parted in the middle. He was much like McConnell in that he was not one of the "trade school boys," as Naval Academy graduates were known. Instead, Price graduated from the University of Illinois in 1937. Times were still hard in the civilian economy, and Price had a lifelong passion for flying that he shared with his father, an Army aviator in the First World War. He joined the Navy as an aviation cadet, earning his wings at Pensacola in June 1938.

After training, Price reported aboard the *Saratoga* to fly with Fighting

Squadron Three (VF-3)—one of the famed "First Team" of prewar naval aviators. VF-3 had a lineage as proud as any squadron in the Navy. Formed in 1923 as VF-2, the squadron was the first to fly from McConnell's future command, the *Langley*. In 1928, the squadron took as its insignia the mischievous cartoon character Felix the Cat, and its aircraft soon sported the iconic black-and-white feline clutching a bomb with a lit fuse.

For Price, his time in VF-3 was a master class in both flying and leadership. He served with two of the finest fighter pilots of his generation—Jimmy Thach and Edward "Butch" O'Hare—and under their tutelage, Price learned many of the skills he would need both to survive in combat and to run his own squadron. The earnest and humble Price threw himself into the job and loved every minute of it. Writing in his journal at sea during training maneuvers in January 1939, Price stated, "Nobody can tell me that a fighting squadron isn't the best duty. Whenever there is any action, we're the first ones in it."[7] But in VF-3, Price was at the bottom of the officer pecking order in the squadron. During the two years he was a cadet, he was inferior in rank to a brand-new ensign but something more than a senior enlisted man.

Price departed VF-3 in the spring of 1941 and headed for his next assignment as an assistant US naval observer in Singapore. The city anchored British colonial possessions in the Far East and served as the administrative hub of the Empire's lucrative Asian rubber and tin industries. A polyglot city of nearly two million people, Singapore caps the end of the Malay Peninsula, only eighty-five miles north of the equator. The British had spent nearly twenty years and the then-outrageous sum of £60 million to build a world-class fleet anchorage there, defended by a garrison of eighty-eight thousand men, judged sufficient to hold the island for the three months it might take for reinforcements to arrive from Europe. The press dubbed it "Fortress Singapore," or the "Gibraltar of the East." While war was raging at home in Britain, Singapore's defenders were convinced that nothing in Asia could threaten their security. In fact, many of the troops were disgruntled about the potential for action because they were convinced there wouldn't be any.

Bob Price arrived in Singapore on June 11, 1941, running headlong into the city's oppressive heat. He wrote to his wife soon after his arrival that he had never been "so hot and uncomfortable in my life. Humidity is about 99.9%!"[8] But he soon acclimatized and spent five largely uneventful months in Singapore before Pearl Harbor. The day before the attack started like any other. Price and his officemates gathered for a dinner party to honor a retiring officer returning to Washington. In Price's journal, the only sign of the impending crisis was the notation that his colleague had gone back to the office "to send ultra-secret message concerning Jap movements."[9] Another batch of cables arrived late that evening, and Price went into the office about 2 a.m. on December 8 to decode them and draft a response.

Unbeknownst to Price, as he finished up his cable in the wee hours of the morning, a Japanese air raid was underway. British radar detected the approaching enemy bombers more than an hour before they arrived over Singapore, but no one at the city's civil defense headquarters answered the phone, and RAF commanders refused to scramble their fighters to intercept for fear that friendly antiaircraft fire would endanger their pilots. As a result, the streets were brightly lit, allowing the Japanese planes to easily find their targets. One group of Japanese bombers struck near the British naval base, unimpeded by a spray of inaccurate antiaircraft fire. Others dropped their bombs on Raffles Square, the commercial heart of the city and only a few yards from Price's office. In his journal the next day, he wrote how "about 0310 I had started to type the dispatch up when I heard anti-aircraft fire, approaching planes, then 'whammo,' what seemed to be a 500-pound bomb landed in back of our office in the Union Building on Raffles Square."[10] Not yet realizing the city was under attack, Price exited the building to investigate, and as he did another bomb fell nearby, just close enough to give him a jolt. Price added news of the attack to his dispatch and rushed to the cable office to send it. There he ran into several newspapermen who informed him about the Japanese attack on Pearl Harbor. Price was dumbfounded by the news, later writing that it "seemed incredible but true beyond doubt."[11]

Over the following ten weeks, Price documented for his superiors in

Washington the series of snowballing military defeats and morale fail-
ures that put the Japanese at the gates of Singapore. Enemy forces moved
with remarkable speed, driving Commonwealth units south on the Malay
Peninsula in a panicked retreat. They never gave the British an opportunity to pull an effective defense together and kept them harried and
on the run. The crumbling defensive lines proved the lie of the British
propaganda posters posted all over Malaya: "We are ready. Our preparations have been made and tested: our defenses are strong and our weapons
efficient."[12] In reality, one senior British official confided to his diary that
morale was "collapsing like a punctured tire."[13]

With Japanese forces rapidly closing the noose on Singapore, the US
Navy decided to pull out its contingent of naval observers. Bob Price
received his orders on January 9 to leave the city by whatever means possible. The rush of people trying to flee made it impossible to secure a berth
on a ship, but on January 15—a month before the city's surrender—Price
managed to obtain a seat on the last outbound commercial airliner. While
even today an eighteen-thousand-mile airline journey is unusual, in the
1940s it was practically unheard of. Price's narrow escape from Singapore made the newspapers back in his home state of Missouri. It took
him eight days to reach Cairo, via stops in India, Iran, and Iraq. In Cairo
he transferred to a US Army B-24 bomber, and flew an indirect route
across northern Africa and then across the Atlantic to Belem, Brazil. His
bomber developed engine problems while en route to Puerto Rico, forcing
an emergency landing in Trinidad. He made the remainder of the trip on
a Pan-American Airlines clipper, arriving in New York City on January
28. In the confusion of war, the British Overseas Airline Company did
not receive the US government's payment for the flight, and some months
later Price received an indignant bill from the airline, demanding an over-
due sum of $496.91.

CHAPTER 3

The *Cowpens* Crew

Cowpens' officers and crew gathered in Philadelphia in the spring of 1943, where she began her fitting out to make her ready for sea. A ship's first crew is called her plank owners, a reference to an old naval tradition where those men who were with the ship when she was commissioned are entitled to a plank from the deck when she is retired. *Cowpens'* plank owners assembled at the old redbrick Welsbach building in New York Ship's facility in Camden. The newly promoted Capt. Robert McConnell arrived there in January 1943; after nearly losing his life and career in the Java Sea, he undoubtedly was grateful for a second chance at command. *Cowpens* was a major step up from the *Langley*—and he was lucky to get her. Every single one of the prestigious full-size fleet carriers was captained by a Naval Academy graduate, as were five of the nine light carriers. But aviators with sufficient seniority to command a flattop were scarce, and so McConnell got the job.

The greenness of *Cowpens'* personnel presented a major challenge for Captain McConnell. Teaching any crew to operate and maintain a complex and untried ship is a difficult task, and in *Cowpens'* case these problems were compounded by the fact that most aboard were as new to the Navy as the ship itself. Men who had already served at sea were few and far between; most had only the basic skills taught in the Navy's boot camps and training centers. Only weeks before, they had been civilians from all walks of life—countless Americans from small towns and big cities, factory workers and farmhands, or kids fresh out of high school.

This was not unique to *Cowpens*; each one of the CVLs departed for the Pacific with more than 70 percent of their complement having no seagoing experience. The old Navy saying was that it took six years to make a sailor, but McConnell had only a matter of months to take this green mob of men and forge them into a combat-ready team.

Youth was one thing that the officers and men of *Cowpens* had in common. The bulk of the enlisted men were only seventeen or eighteen years old, while most of the ship's junior officers were only slightly older, with two to four years of college under their belt. There were only a few men aboard who were in their thirties or forties, mostly Captain McConnell and his senior staff. One of the ship's newly arrived Marines, George Terrell, was seventeen and described his shipmates as "just a bunch of green kids." In his estimation, 90 percent of the crew was as young as he was. "A man got to be twenty-one [and] he was looked up to as a senior citizen," Terrell explained. "Even the pilots that flew these hot fighter planes were kids. By the time they got to be twenty-five they were veterans...most of them were between twenty-one and twenty-two."[1]

The first thing that struck new arrivals when they reported to the shipyard was the smell. The Delaware River was the drain for all the industrial plants in Philadelphia, and it was a slurry of waste and filth. The odor was similar to that of a paper mill, a stench of rotten-eggs sulfur. Silver coins turned green from the vapors, and chrome and braid on uniforms quickly tarnished. Adding to the sensory overload were the sights and sounds of a shipyard working at full tilt; new arrivals made their way along the pier amid crowds of workers hurrying in every direction, and the air was filled with the blue flashes and sparks from welding torches and the hammering of riveters.

Proceeding farther along the Delaware River, *Cowpens'* berth finally came into view, and the nearly universal reaction from all who saw her for the first time was disappointment. One newly arrived junior officer expected the *Cowpens* to look like the long, graceful flattops that he had seen in the movie newsreels. But when he saw "what had to be *Cowpens*, my heart sank." He likened the homely little carrier to a "horizontal factory-like building with four short smokestacks in a row on the roof."[2]

Another man recalled his first reaction when seeing *Belleau Wood*, one of *Cowpens'* sister ships. "You could have knocked me over with a feather. All this time I had thought [she] was one of the big *Essex*-class carriers, but there she was, a little ugly flattop and a starboard list to boot. For a moment I'd wished I'd joined the Army."[3]

Junior Officers

Only a handful of the Moo's complement of 107 officers had prewar experience or Naval Academy degrees. Instead, most were reservists—fresh out of college or civilian employment, and recent graduates of the Navy's three-month crash course officer training program, earning them the moniker of "ninety-day wonders." The number of reservists so significantly outnumbered the career officers that it sometimes seemed to them that they were strangers in their own Navy. More officers were in training in 1943—120,472—than there were total personnel in the Navy in 1938.

One of the few trade school boys assigned to the Moo was Lt. Frank Griffin "Grif" Scarborough. He graduated in the Academy's class of 1942 and served one cruise aboard *Enterprise* as an ensign. He was a rarity aboard the Moo, as he was one of the few who had actually fired a weapon in combat. Although Scarborough started the cruise commanding a gun crew, the *Cowpens'* senior assistant engineer was suddenly reassigned, leaving a position that needed to be filled. This wasn't just a matter of a gap in the organizational table. The ship's senior engineer was a thermodynamics professor from Penn State with no experience operating a ship's power plant. McConnell and his executive officer, Cmdr. Hugh Nieman, wanted a seasoned officer to help him grow into the role. Given Scarborough had a degree in engineering, and the bulk of his fellow officers were either aviators or ninety-day wonders, Grif recalled, "Suddenly I was the man of the hour—I became senior assistant engineer of the *Cowpens* by default!"[4]

In contrast, Ens. Sam Sommers, a native of Selma, Alabama, joined the Navy Reserve as a young Harvard student in the fall of 1939. The war had begun in Europe on September 1, the US began a peacetime draft by midmonth, and Sommers knew that "we would be in it sooner or later."[5]

Like many of his classmates, he thought it best to take some control of his destiny before the powers that be decided it for him. Volunteering allowed him to pick his service, become an officer, and avoid the draft. While Sommers didn't know much about the Navy, he had some sailing experience in the Gulf of Mexico. He also recalled the recruiting poster—"Join the Navy and see the world!" Even after the outbreak of the war in December 1941, the Navy allowed Sommers to continue at Harvard, graduating in June 1943. He reported to *Cowpens* that summer, not long before she sailed.

Enlisted

The bulk of the men aboard *Cowpens* were enlisted, more than 1,300 in all. A ship is like a small city, and the enlisted aboard did the physical work of running and maintaining it. Known collectively as "bluejackets" in reference to the US Navy's historical uniform during the age of sail, the sailors ran its boilers, operated its equipment, repaired its aircraft, manned its guns, fed and sustained the crew, and performed the hundreds of other vital but thankless tasks required to operate a warship. While the ship's pilots and even its captain served aboard only a few months before rotating to new assignments, the sailors were in for a lengthy stay aboard *Cowpens*. Many of its plank owners who came aboard in Philadelphia remained until the ship's refitting in the spring of 1945. Others were with her for the duration, up until the Japanese surrender in Tokyo Bay or even longer.

These were the men of the Depression generation, raised in some of the country's most difficult economic times. In many ways, they were perfectly suited to the war they were about to fight. Used to little in the way of outside help, they had a hardscrabble "make do and get the job done" approach to life that served them well aboard ship.[6] Like Sam Sommers, most sailors joined the Navy to avoid getting drafted into the Army. They had heard the tales from their fathers from the First World War and understood what being an infantryman was like. Rather than living in a muddy foxhole, all realized that service at sea meant a clean place to sleep, a roof over your head, and three meals a day. "I joined the Navy when I was seventeen because in the Second World War when you turned eighteen, you were connected to the draft board," said *Cowpens* sailor Bill Kuntz. "If you wanted the branch of service of your choice you enlisted early."[7]

Once in the tender embrace of the Navy, the service was determined to turn them from civilians into sailors as rapidly as possible. One such recruit was Art Daly, from Dorchester, Massachusetts. Daly was a firebrand of a teenager who had wanted to enlist immediately after Pearl Harbor, but he had a good job with the Army Corps of Engineers that supported six of his siblings at home. It took almost a year until he could convince his family to let him enlist, signing up in November 1942. Daly was shipped to the enormous naval training center at Great Lakes, Illinois. Recruits were stripped naked and their civilian clothes thrown into a box to mail home. Then they were marched through the processing line, measured for a uniform—which never fit regardless of the measurements written in red pen marks on their bodies. The recruits each received a mattress cover and the quartermasters threw all their issued clothing and equipment into the cover. And finally, the Navy's barbers sheared the recruits like sheep, leaving only an inch on top, and bare on the sides. Daly wrote in his journal, "We all have baldies and look like a pack of assholes. My uniforms do not fit at all. My dress blue shirt is down around my legs. When I tie it around my middle, it hangs around my waist!"[8]

Daly and his fellow recruits endured endless drilling and marching, while also learning to speak Navy. In that dialect, rooms became compartments, floors became decks, walls became bulkheads, and beds became racks. Daly was one of many men tripped up by confusion over terms. Given an order to "clean the ladder," he dashed outside in the midst of an Illinois winter to clean the only one he could find—which went up to the roof. "I went outside, froze my ass off, and cleaned the snow and ice off the ladder," he said. Returning inside, Daly's officer was waiting for him, demanding to know why he had not followed his order. Daly said of the moment that he was "cold and ripping mad. I told him I cleaned the ladder outside. He pointed to the stairs and said, 'Mister, that is the ladder in the Navy.' So I had to clean the stairs too!"[9]

At the outbreak of war, George Terrell was a seventeen-year-old Bosto-nian, who by his own description was "full of piss and vinegar."[10] Terrell had dropped out of school to help support his father, who was disabled from a serious lung infection that kept him bedridden for the better part of a year. This left George as the only breadwinner, and he went to work so his family could eat. The attack on Pearl Harbor enraged Terrell, and he was eager to join up. "I already had a good mad over on Herr Adolf. I was convinced that it was vitally necessary for me, personally, to do everything in my power to bring that bandit to justice," he recalled.[11] Ter-rell was sworn into the Marines just before Christmas 1942 and shipped down by train to boot camp at Parris Island.

For many servicemen, the great melting pot of national mobilization was their first exposure to other Americas besides their own. This first encounter was not always a pleasant one, as future *Cowpens* fighter pilot Lee Nordgren discovered while traveling by train to Pensacola for flight training. He was from small-town Minnesota, and when the train stopped in New Orleans he took the opportunity to get a shave in a local barber-shop. He later recalled that he "really didn't understand how southerners felt about northerners, but when I was done with my shave I was bleeding all over, like a stuck pig."[12]

George Terrell's first exposure to Americans from other places and cultures went better than Nordgren's. Terrell described the Marine boot camp at Parris Island as "a strange new world populated with an incred-ible collection of aliens." Terrell had never been out of New England before, but "my compatriots in this crazy place were hillbillies from West Virginia, farmers from Missouri and Ohio, and rebels from Louisiana and Texas. It turned out alright though. They all thought I was a little funny too."[13] Terrell recalled that despite their differences, they all had some-thing in common. "No matter how badly things were going on the vari-ous fronts of the war—and they weren't going too well at that time—we knew we were going to win, eventually. Never any doubt about it."[14]

Terrell suffered through seven weeks of physical training and drills at Parris Island, before receiving orders for sea duty aboard the *Cowpens*. All major US Navy warships had a complement of Marines—aboard the

Moo there were forty-two in all—a tradition that they took from the British Navy. These men were, in the words of Rudyard Kipling, "soldier and sailor too."[15] During the age of sail a ship's Marines manned some of the ship's broadside guns, served as snipers on the topmasts, and led the boarding parties to capture an enemy vessel. They also maintained order aboard ship, an important role when the bulk of the crew were forced aboard by press gangs. In the modern US Navy, the Marines had a variety of duties aboard, including operating some of the ship's antiaircraft batteries, manning all gangways while in ports, and guarding the brig while at sea.

Messmen

At the bottom of the ship's social hierarchy was the ship's contingent of African American mess attendants, known after 1943 as steward's mates. The Navy—and the *Cowpens*—was a microcosm of 1940s America, demonstrating its injustices as well as its virtues. One such injustice was the Navy's policy on racial integration. Since 1932, African Americans had only been able to serve as enlisted men on Navy combat vessels, and only as steward's mates, where they were effectively domestic servants. They did a variety of menial tasks, including cooking, waiting on officers' tables at meals, and doing their cleaning and laundry.

It had not always been this way. The Navy was integrated throughout much of the nineteenth century, and during the Civil War as much as 20 percent of its sailors were Black. But in 1919, Navy Secretary Josephus Daniels closed the door to any recruitment of African Americans. FDR had served under Daniels as assistant secretary of the Navy, and as president he sought to strike a middle ground between the demands of White segregationists and civil rights activists. Under his watch, the Navy allowed African Americans in only noncombat roles such as messmen, shore workers, dockhands, and in construction battalions, and like the other armed services it remained racially segregated.

It was not until 1944, when James Forrestal became secretary of the Navy, that the service began shifting toward integration. But in the meantime, the Navy came down hard on any resistance to segregation. In the so-called Philadelphia Mutiny of 1940, fifteen African American messmen aboard the cruiser *Philadelphia* wrote to one of the leading Black newspapers—then a powerful voice in the fight for racial equality— warning other African Americans not to join the Navy, for they were little more than "sea-going bell hops, chambermaids, and dishwashers."[16] All fifteen were dismissed from the service, which denied them any veterans' benefits.

Cowpens had a contingent of twenty-eight steward's mates aboard under the supervision of a White officer, but unfortunately no account of their experience survives. The account of one messman on *Independence* gives us some idea of what their life aboard the Moo might have been like, however. Willie Thomas was an eighteen-year old from Cincinnati, Ohio, who volunteered for the Navy because he saw little opportunity to contribute to the war at home. Willie's primary responsibility was taking care of the pilots' ready rooms and officers' quarters, making sure coffee and donuts were available after every mission. But like many steward's mates across the Navy, he also volunteered for additional tasks that pushed the boundaries of the racial restrictions that prohibited him from combat duty. When the ship was under attack, he carried clips of 40mm ammunition from the ship's magazines to its antiaircraft guns so they could maintain a steady rate of fire. Despite working in a system that was biased against him, Willie was upbeat about the relationship of the steward's mates with the majority-White crew, saying that "we were all on this big ship together."[17]

While Willie was chartiable about the state of race relations aboard, George Terrell thought there was some room for improvement. He wrote in his journal about how shocked he was to encounter overt segregation and racism for the first time. "I was young and impressionable and terribly innocent about these things," he recalled years after the war. "Many of the older career officers on the ship were natives of the Deep South...they really believed that these black boys were inferior human beings."[18] Terrell gradually learned that the prejudice was not universal, saying how it was "not shared by all the officers, not even by all the southern officers. And it was certainly less prevalent among the lower ranks." For example, the enlisted Marines' berthing compartment was right next to the steward's mates, and the two groups got to know each other and often socialized. Getting to know each other, Terrell concluded, taught him how "screwed up" segregation really was.[19]

CHAPTER 4

Air Group 25

The Pilots

As the ship's officers and men were gathering in Philadelphia, her pilots assembled at nearby Willow Grove airfield, just to the north. After his escape from Singapore, Bob Price reported there in late January as commander of *Cowpens'* fighter squadron, known as VF-25. One of Price's former squadronmates from Jimmy Thach's VF-3, Lt. Cmdr. Mark Grant, led both the composite squadron (VC-25)—which included its torpedo and dive bombers—and was in overall command of Air Group 25. The two men were friends but polar opposites. Grant was a social and outgoing Naval Academy graduate, whose fondness for hard drink and a good time undercut his gravitas as a commander. Price, in comparison, was modest and restrained, with a civilian education—and grew into a natural leader that inspired the faith and confidence of his men. Price chose as his deputy an old friend from flight school, Lt. Gaylord "Brownie" Brown. The two men complemented each other well. Price had all the qualities of a good squadron leader: excellent judgment, a talent for administration, and the ability to win the support of superior officers. Brownie, in contrast, was an expert pilot who helped polish the squadron's flying and tactics.

The bulk of Price and Grant's pilots were reservists fresh out of flight school. While the Navy required two years of college education to qualify for flight training, most were only twenty or twenty-one years old with an associate's or a bachelor's degree. They came from wildly different backgrounds; one of the later squadrons aboard the Moo had among its pilots bankers, newspapermen, a toolmaker, a chemist, a science teacher, a draftsman, a wool businessman, an assistant attorney general, a mortician, and a soap salesman.[1] Despite their different backgrounds, many pilots arriving at Willow Grove found the squadron filled with familiar faces. Most of the brand-new ensigns assigned to the squadron had passed through Jacksonville as trainees, where both Air Group Cmdr. Mark Grant and some of the squadron's more seasoned hands had been instructors. Joining the air group, said one pilot, "was just like coming home again."[2]

Another thing the pilots had in common were their motivations for volunteering to fly. First, they wanted to fight. Pilots are confident by nature, and most wanted to take it to the Japanese for the attack on Pearl Harbor. One *Cowpens* pilot, Robert Soule, said, "We couldn't believe that anybody would have the guts to attack us like that, and certainly we were anxious to get into the fight." Soule explained how his generation took a no-nonsense approach to the challenge. "It was...like every generation before you, each one had their own tasks, and we just figured this was ours," he said years after the war.[3]

Second, many of Price's pilots shared a childhood fascination with aviation. Powered flight was still relatively new and exciting; Hollywood movies glamorized pilots as courageous daredevils, and record-setting aviators like Charles Lindbergh or Amelia Earhart were some of the most famous people of the day. This made flying irresistible to many young men, who wanted to see if they were up to the challenge. One such *Cowpens* pilot, George Ayers, said he wanted to fly a fighter because "it was the hottest thing...and I wanted to fly the hottest thing."[4]

Left unsaid was that flying the hottest thing carried with it a substantial risk. At the peak of the war, US planners assumed that a carrier lost 10 percent of its aircraft a month to either combat or accidents, and pilots' fatality rates from all causes were as high as one in three. Aviators' mindsets were sometimes inexplicable to their shipmates, who saw the risks of carrier operations. Sailor John Ingraham, who served aboard *Cowpens* late in the war, said, "I remember feeling so sorry for these pilots, you know [because of] the terror of landing on that damn ship. Then I got to know a couple of them, and the reality was they loved it... they were having a ball."[5]

One pilot who served in Price's squadron was fighter pilot Ed "Stump" Haley. While Haley was a replacement pilot who did not report to *Cowpens* until later in 1943, his background and experience was representative of those men who reported to Willow Grove at the squadron's formation. While the training bases varied from pilot to pilot, the system was the same—a five-phase process teaching increasingly difficult skills in steadily more capable aircraft. It was a sink-or-swim system; there was no time to make sure each man was ready to advance, and as a result accidents and fatalities were common. More than fifteen thousand aspiring pilots from all services died in training accidents in the United States over the course of the war.

Haley, a native of Beverly, Massachusetts, had always dreamed of flying—his high school yearbook motto was "I can run, I can fly!"[6] After graduating from high school in 1940, Haley studied mechanical engineering at Northeastern University and earned a civilian pilot's license there. By the time Haley completed two years of college, the United States had entered the war, and Haley joined the Naval Reserve as an aviation cadet. He described how his father, a First World War veteran, saw him off as Haley was boarding a train at South Station in Boston. "He told me that I was about to begin an awesome adventure, to do my best and that God would see me through the great and rugged times ahead."[7]

Haley reported to preflight school in Chapel Hill, North Carolina, and he had been told only to "pack a change of underwear and a toothbrush and that the Navy would take care of all my needs from then on."[8] Preflight was military indoctrination and ground school. Those expecting excitement grumbled that they learned more about washing airplanes and cleaning heads (toilets) than they did about flying. But washout rates were still one in three, earning preflight a reputation as an elimination school. The trainees studied math, physics, Morse code, aircraft identification, navigation, and other key skills related to flying. The program also included physical fitness training, hand-to-hand combat and self-defense, long marches, and close order drill.

The final period was recreational sports; each training unit fielded teams to compete with the others, with the winner earning a four-hour liberty on Sunday afternoon. Injuries were so common that preflight was infamous for it; one aspiring pilot arrived in Chapel Hill to be greeted by a dozen or so aviation cadets in casts from broken legs or ankles, who warned him: "Welcome to Chapel Hill. You'll be sorry!"[9] Ed Haley got off light—suffering only a broken nose in a boxing bout that left a permanent slight bend to the top of his nose.

The next stop for Haley was basic flight school at Olathe, on the outskirts of Kansas City. During his time in the "prairie Navy," Haley and his fellow cadets learned to fly the Stearman Model 75 biplane—known to the trainees as the "yellow peril" for its canary-yellow paint scheme and the number of cadets who failed this phase of training. Flying in the open-cockpit Stearman in the depths of a Kansas winter was no walk in the park. Ed Haley bundled up against the cold with a face mask, a wool-lined flight suit, boots, and helmet over multiple layers of heavy clothing. But even with those precautions, after two hours or so in the air Haley said that "even your eyeballs still got stiff with the cold!"[10]

Haley soon completed all requirements for primary flight training and was reassigned to Naval Air Station Corpus Christi, Texas, for additional training—where the milder weather was a welcome change. Corpus was the largest US naval air station in the world at that time, and there the cadets learned more difficult techniques in more advanced aircraft, including aerobatics and formation and night flying. The first training aircraft was the Vultee Valiant, affectionately known to the cadets as the "Vultee Vibrator" for the way it rattled at high speed. It was a much heavier aircraft than the Stearman; it was an all-metal monoplane with a 450-horsepower radial engine, fixed landing gear, and enclosed cockpit. There was night flying and instrument training in the North American SNJ (also known as the T-6 "Texan"). The SNJ had a 600-horsepower engine, and upgrading from the Vultee to the SNJ, Haley commented, "was like changing from a Ford Model A to a Buick."[11] With a more advanced plane came more difficult exercises, including practice carrier landings on a runway painted with the outline of a flight deck, dive-bombing practice with dummy bombs, and then shooting at a towed sleeve to practice aerial gunnery. With these tests behind him, Haley's only remaining task before joining a combat squadron was learning to fly the Navy's previous-generation fighter aircraft, the F4F Wildcat.

Haley got through training without much trouble, but some of his future squadronmates had to fend off the bullies among the instructors. Future *Cowpens* torpedo bomber pilot Robert Soule found himself in just that situation. During his training, Soule—who already had a civilian pilot's license—received only one "down check," a failing grade on a flight exercise. It was from a Marine major who routinely flunked his students, earning him the nickname "Down Check Garrison." Soule had the rotten luck to be assigned to him during one exercise in an open-cockpit Stearman, and after they had completed the training requirements, Garrison signaled he wanted control of the airplane. Soule described how Garrison then tried to get him airsick in an attempt to fail him. "He was doing all kinds of maneuvers, and I was down there holding onto the bottom of my seat just trying to stay in the airplane, and getting madder and madder."[12] After Garrison finished his aerial hazing routine, Soule popped his head up and said, "I'll take the airplane." He then turned the tables on Garrison, doing his own set of acrobatics—during which the weld on the oil tank ahead of the cockpit failed and dumped about twenty gallons of hot oil on Garrison's lap. "He was fit to be tied," Soule recounted with glee. Garrison's only comment was: "What are you trying to do, cadet, kill me?"[13]

Naturally, Garrison down-checked Soule for the exercise, and he had to go back and fly it again with the commander of the training squadron to avoid expulsion. Soule had no trouble at all passing under an impartial instructor, and on coming back for a landing saw that all the cadets were cheering his arrival on the flight line because they thought that old "Down Check Garrison" had finally gotten what he deserved.[14]

Meeting the Hellcat: "If This Plane Could Cook I'd Marry It!"

At its formation, Grant, Price, and Brown were the only men in Air Group 25 with experience in the fleet, and they made sure the junior men got as much time as possible in the squadron's SNJ trainers while waiting for their F6F-3 Hellcat fighters to arrive. Neither Price nor Brown had ever seen the Hellcat, which was the Navy's newest frontline fighter. They made arrangements to travel to the Grumman plant in Bethpage, Long Island, to learn to fly the F6F and then return to Willow Grove with two planes. To their surprise, on the morning of their trip the duo discovered Grumman's pilots had delivered a pair of brand-new Hellcats the previous evening. The squadron's mechanics spent the morning checking out the two aircraft while Price and Brown read the technical manuals and familiarized themselves with the cockpit. Then, "with all hands on the air station watching us from the ramp, we roared into the sky," recalled Brown.[15] After about an hour in the air, Price and Brown declared themselves Hellcat instructors and set to work teaching their men how to fly it.

The Hellcat became the mainstay of frontline US carrier fighter squadrons in the Pacific, and more American fighter aces flew it than any other aircraft. By V-J Day Hellcats had shot down more than 5,200 enemy planes while losing only 270 of their own, a kill ratio of more than 19:1. It was more than a match for the Japanese Navy's frontline fighter, the Mitsubishi A6M, known in the West as the Zeke. US naval intelligence gave each type of Japanese warplane its own name; fighters had male names and bombers female. But the Zeke more commonly became known as the Zero, for the last numeral in the year of its introduction—the Imperial Year 2600, or 1940. The Zeke was nimble and deadly; its design combined lightweight construction, excellent thrust-to-weight ratio, low wing loading, and high lift—traits that made it capable of out-climbing and out-turning every Allied aircraft in service early in the war. The Zeke's lightweight construction also made it highly fuel-efficient, and it routinely flew missions of more than 1,000 miles, and with a drop tank could manage as much as 1,900—far greater than comparable Allied fighter aircraft.

But in order to achieve its maneuverability, the Zeke was lightly constructed, without self-sealing fuel tanks and with little armor—making it highly vulnerable to gunfire.

In contrast, the Hellcat was fast and sturdy, with 2,200 horsepower and a supercharger to improve its high-altitude performance. It featured the largest wing fitted on an American wartime single-seat fighter, making it stable and well-behaved at low speeds. It was considerably faster than the Japanese Zeke, capable of 375 mph. Below fourteen thousand feet it could climb just as fast as the Zeke, it was faster at higher altitudes, and could always out-dive it. Like all Grumman products the Hellcats were rugged and heavily armored, built with self-sealing fuel tanks to guard against fire and explosion. The Hellcat had six Browning .50-caliber machine guns with four hundred rounds of ammunition each, enough for thirty seconds of sustained fire. The six Brownings were devastatingly effective against lightly constructed Japanese aircraft; a two-second burst loosed 160 rounds toward the target, a total of sixteen pounds of metal traveling approximately 2,800 feet per second. A well-aimed burst could slice off a Japanese fighter's wing or shred its fuselage. The Hellcat could also carry six rockets or a one-thousand-pound bomb, making it a capable ground attack aircraft and all-around utility infielder for the US Navy.

The Hellcat was a good match for Price and his squadron of inexperienced pilots, and in the coming months they learned to master it. The normally restrained Gaylord Brown positively gushed about the plane, exclaiming, "What a jewel the Hellcat was to fly!"[16] Ed Haley, too, raved about it, calling it "a monstrous beauty."[17] After his initial shock over its size, Haley grew to love its handling characteristics. "It was very stable, had wide landing gear, easy to handle on the ground, it was just a wonderful airplane all around," he recalled. "It didn't have any bad habits."[18] Naval aviator Gene Valencia summed up most pilots' enthusiasm for the F6F after returning from a mission over the Japanese stronghold of Truk, where he shot down three Zekes: "I love this airplane so much that if it could cook, I'd marry it."[19]

Avengers, Turkeys, and Torpedoes

The Air Group's Grumman TBF Avenger torpedo bombers arrived at Willow Grove shortly after the Hellcats. The Avenger was the fleet's general-purpose bomber and patrol plane. Originally designed to haul the 2,200-pound Mark 13 air-dropped torpedo, the Avenger did most of its wartime work as a conventional bomber, dropping bombs or depth charges. The TBF was a classic Grumman design—tough and simple.[20] It was a large single-engine plane, with a three-man crew, a fifty-four-foot wingspan, and a spacious internal bomb bay. It was easy to handle for even an inexperienced pilot, well-behaved at low speeds, and offered good visibility from the cockpit. All the controls on the aircraft operated either hydraulically or electrically, including the plane's folding wings, meaning that the Avenger's forty-foot-long bulk was economical on deck space aboard a carrier. It had two rear-facing machine guns for self-defense; a .30-caliber "stinger" belly gun located in the aft part of the radio compartment, and a .50-caliber gun in a rear-facing dorsal turret.

The Avenger was not without its faults. It was not a graceful aircraft; other aviators derided it as the "turkey," hardly one of nature's inspiring fliers. Its controls were heavy and the plane was underpowered. Moreover, it lacked a reliable torpedo, usually the most effective weapon for sinking ships. At the onset of the war, the Navy's Mark 13 aerial torpedo was so fragile that the Bureau of Ordnance recommended it only be released at 140 feet and 140 knots. This "low and slow" combination made torpedo bombers sitting ducks to enemy fighters and antiaircraft fire. At the Battle of Midway, forty-two out of fifty-one TBD Devastators—the Avenger's predecessor—attempting to drop torpedoes were shot down without scoring a single hit on a Japanese warship. Worse yet, *Hornet*'s Torpedo Squadron 8 lost all of its aircraft with only one survivor, Ens. George Gay Jr.—and the loss of an entire squadron in battle made a deep impression on the American public. Even when the Mark 13 was dropped within the specified parameters, it only rarely functioned as intended. In mid-1943, a study of Mark 13s found only 31 percent ran hot, straight, and true. The rest suffered from one or more problems, such as dud exploders, sinking or deflecting before reaching the target, or running at the wrong depth or on the surface. It wasn't until 1944 that the Navy ironed out the weapon's problems and turned it into an effective ship killer.

Despite the torpedo problems, *Cowpens'* pilots were enthusiastic about the Avenger given its advantages over the Devastator. Robert Soule described how "we were very happy to get the airplane because it was much faster than the TBDs [and] carried a much bigger bomb load."[21] That being said, there were still considerable reservations about torpedo bombers given the losses suffered at Midway and Torpedo 8's experience in particular. Many believed that an assignment to a torpedo squadron was especially hazardous duty, and Robert Wright said some of his squadronmates spoke "half seriously of being assigned to a 'death squadron'" when they received orders to join VT-25.[22] Reservations aside, *Cowpens'* pilots still had to learn to fly the new plane. While the TBF had been in service since August 1941, Wright recalled that few of the squadron's pilots "had seen one up close, let alone had an opportunity to fly one." And so, like their fighter pilot counterparts, it was up to them to self-educate on the aircraft.

The Weed-Out Process

Pilots and aircraft gradually arrived at Willow Grove throughout March and April 1943 to begin their predeployment training. There were twenty junior pilots competing for fifteen slots aboard the carrier, and it was up to Price, Brown, and Grant to select the most capable and reassign the rest. The leap from the SNJ to the Hellcat was considerable, and as a result this was a risky time for the young ensigns. The pilots were eager to prove themselves and earn a spot aboard ship, but they were often not experienced enough to fully handle the more powerful F6F or to understand the limits of their capabilities.

Crashes and fatalities were common in many squadrons' predeployment workups. This was particularly true among reservists who did not plan to stay in the Navy and were therefore often undeterred by the threat of disciplinary action for unauthorized "flat-hatting" or "hot-dogging."

Each of the three other air groups that followed Air Group 25 aboard *Cowpens* lost one or more pilots or aircrew—and in one case, a squadron commander—to training accidents even before leaving the United States. Price and Brownie's steady leadership and the threat of transfer to nonflying assignments or to cargo or patrol planes managed to keep their pilots in line, and Air Group 25 suffered no casualties before shipping out to the Pacific.

Air Group 25's pilots described the training as fun—playing at war usually is. But it all had a purpose, teaching the deadly serious skills they needed to survive in combat: flying, strafing, navigation, carrier takeoffs and landings. And all the while, Price, Brown, and Grant were closely watching each man's performance. One of the best accounts of this training period was from Anderson "Dick" Bowers Jr., an aspiring Hellcat pilot in VF-25. Bowers was twenty-one years old, from Pilot Knob, New York. He kept up a steady stream of letters back to his father—a World War I naval aviator and Navy lieutenant commander—detailing his experiences throughout the spring and summer of 1943.

That spring Air Group 25 completed several training rotations from Willow Grove to other naval air stations on the eastern seaboard, such as Atlantic City, New Jersey, and Quonset, Rhode Island. Small groups of pilots from the squadron then rotated down to Norfolk in June to cut their teeth on carrier landings aboard the escort carrier *Charger*, with eight successful "traps" (landings) needed to qualify. Bowers wrote to his father describing how he had the highest gunnery score in the squadron and was enjoying the mock strafing attacks as well as some dogfighting. Bowers had only fifty hours of flight time in the Hellcat but he liked it more with every passing day. In May, he wrote that he "had the best hop yesterday I have had since I have been in the Navy. We did [mock dogfights] with some P47s, and then made [practice attack] runs on a Liberator [bomber], it was really fun."[23] A month later, Bowers was upbeat after practicing his landings aboard the *Charger*. The Hellcat "is the best plane for carrier landings I have ever flown, it really handles fine at slow speeds, which makes it very easy to fly."[24]

A lengthy training period stateside allowed Bowers and other junior pilots to learn from rookie mistakes that might get them killed in the Pacific. Aerial navigation was a critical skill for survival; once in combat pilots would need to navigate from a moving ship to the target, often a small speck of land in the Pacific, and return to point option—the spot where the carrier expected to be at the appointed time. There were no computerized navigation systems or GPS; pilots had to find their way with dead reckoning—using their compass, watch, and airspeed indicator to track course and speed on a board each carried on his lap. Especially tricky was correcting for wind speed that could blow a plane off course, which sometimes pilots could estimate by watching the sea below to note the effect of wind on the waves. It is not an exaggeration to say that a pilot's life often depended on his ability to navigate. Search-and-rescue capabilities were primitive at the time, and many pilots who landed at sea were never heard from again.

Bowers had not yet perfected his navigation skills and wrote to his father in mid-June about how he had gotten lost off the New Jersey coast, an incident that could have gotten him killed in combat. Taking off from Atlantic City, Bowers described how he "went out over the ocean and the weather was no good and I proceeded to get myself lost." While uncertain of his precise location, he knew he had enough fuel to reach Norfolk and so set out in that direction, hoping to find a field before he had to ditch. But to his relief Bowers made landfall on the southern tip of New Jersey. "I landed in Cape May, gassed up, and flew back here," he ruefully admitted. "Everyone makes mistakes, but this was a rather stupid one."[25]

When the air group was not flying, the pilots, like many men about to ship out for combat, did their best to live life to the fullest—keeping a busy schedule of parties, dances, and trips to neighboring cities. Price, Brownie, and Grant encouraged socialization because it helped build squadron cohesion, although sometimes that came at the cost of operational effectiveness. On May 3, Anderson Bowers wrote his father that "last night they had a big dance here and I don't think I ever saw such a washed out crew as we had this morning, they had to secure flying because everyone was knocked out."[26] Captain McConnell attended one of their last predeployment parties, and all the pilots were heartened by his approachability and sincere attempt to get to know them.

Single men like Anderson Bowers did their best to paint the town red before shipping out. He was unhappy about the crowds of servicemen in Atlantic City, which he described as "a town for soldiers, it is full of salutes."[27] But it was an easy train ride to Washington, DC, and some of the pilots made the trip on the weekends. Bowers wrote his father that he had gone there in his tropical white uniform and "really knocked the town cold. I was the only one in whites."[28]

CHAPTER 5

Cowpens Takes Her First Steps Toward the War

The ship's fitting out was completed in record speed, with inspections beginning on April 28, 1943. Over the next month, the Navy checked and rechecked all the ship's systems to ensure they were functioning as designed while she was at the dock. Her commissioning came a month later, on May 28, when the *Cowpens* was officially turned over to the Navy and Captain McConnell assumed command. Due to wartime pressures, the Navy and New York Ship curtailed much of the pageantry that normally accompanied a commissioning, such as invocations, speeches, and the symbolic first manning of stations. There were only a handful of naval officers and shipyard officials present to oversee the formal passing of authority from the shipyard to the Navy. Also in attendance was a delegation from the Cowpens chapter of the Daughters of the American Revolution, who donated a Bible for the ship to carry on its journey into harm's way. But with the completion of this brief ceremony, the Moo's commissioning pennant—a single red-and-white stripe against a starred blue field—was soon fluttering from her masthead.

Over the next four months, the Moo endured her shakedown process, a series of steadily longer journeys intended to identify any remaining problems and give the crew a chance to learn their seagoing roles in safe waters—starting with the Chesapeake Bay and then culminating in a short seagoing cruise to the Gulf of Paria, off Trinidad. After that, it was off to the Pacific, to join the fleet at their anchorage in Pearl Harbor. While the ship's officers and men quickly took to their new conditions, roles, and responsibilities, the ship demonstrated an early streak of bad luck that would soon come to be known as the "*Cowpens* jinx."

The Moo Earns Her Name and Cramped Quarters

Sometime before leaving Philadelphia, *Cowpens* acquired her nickname "the Mighty Moo." History does not record who coined it, but almost everyone latched on to it with enthusiasm. The ship's history said that the name "was a strange mixture of pride and derision. Only a great ship could have such a nickname; even to take pride in the element of nonsense. If you weren't a *Cowpens* man, you had to smile when you said it."[1] Soon, the logo of a stamping, snorting, and heroically well-endowed bull appeared on the ship's island to cement the name. Captain McConnell wasn't thrilled with the moniker, perhaps thinking it unbefitting of a serious man-of-war. Before leaving Philadelphia, Sam Sommers recalled, he directed the crew to begin pronouncing *Cowpens* as "cuppens." McConnell was the captain, but the order didn't take, and Sam Sommers said they "were soon back to 'cow pens,' then the 'Mighty Moo,' and finally, the just plain 'Moo.'"[2]

As *Cowpens* headed for the Chesapeake, the men were getting used to their accommodations aboard. Officers and men slept and ate in different areas, a product of what Sam Sommers described as the Navy premise that "familiarity breeds contempt, with an accompanying breakdown in discipline and efficiency."[3] Although many reporting aboard for the first time were impressed with the Moo's size, that changed to claustrophobia once they were packed into its maze of compartments and ladders. Berths for the ship's enlisted complement were often forty or more to a room, with lockers for each man along the bulkhead and hinged racks (beds) in the center of the compartment stacked three to six high. Packed floor to ceiling two deep and end-to-end, twelve men could sleep in a series of tiers about 60 inches wide by 140 inches long. *Cowpens* sailor John

Ingraham recalled how the racks had only eighteen inches of clearance between them, describing how "I could lie on my back and make a fist and then just put up a thumb and touch the bunk above me."[4] The vertical stacking also presented some hazards when all the occupants exited their racks at once, such as when general quarters was sounded. Avenger aircrewman Herbert Todd recalled that if your bunkmates didn't get out in the proper order, "you were gonna get stepped on by the one coming down from above."[5] It was not a restful arrangement; the number of bodies packed into such a small place meant it was often loud and the air stale. One CVL crewman described the environment as "lots of noise…farts, chatter, snoring, and air pumps."[6]

Food, too, was often rudimentary for the sailors. In port, the quality and variety was fair, with fresh vegetables and milk. At sea, however, conditions quickly deteriorated and everything that could be dehydrated was. The powdered milk tasted like chalk; the sailors poured it on cereal then drained it off, leaving just enough to moisten their corn flakes. The dehydrated potatoes and carrots were usually badly overcooked and came out like thick soup. One *Cowpens* sailor vividly recalled the powdered eggs: "Green in color at times, you think you're eating moldy stuff. Almost like a hardboiled egg, when you open it up, it's yellow in the middle, and getting greener around the outside when it's a little older."[7]

Radioman Art Daly recalled the endless repetition of some meals, such as beans and corn bread, Spam, or chipped beef on toast, the latter universally known as "shit on a shingle." There was also "some kind of stuff like Cream of Wheat that they cooked in pans until it hardened and got cold. Then they cut it into squares. We put syrup on it."[8] In the tropical heat and humidity, it was impossible to keep pests out of the dry storage, and many sailors found unwanted "raisins"—bugs in the cereal or cockroaches in the bread. Sailors didn't mind the cold cuts sandwiches on Sundays, but other meat was usually a disappointment. Art Daly recalled how they frequently ate some kind of stringy meat that no one could identify. "Some guy on the ship said he was a butcher back home and said he didn't know what kind of meat it was. When we would be on GQ, we would get a sandwich made of this stuff, coffee, and an apple."[9] Sometimes the men eagerly lined up for what they thought was steak, only to discover once it was on their tray that it was a slice of liver.

Equally primitive was the enlisted head (toilets). It was essentially an open sewer, with a gutter at one side of the compartment and a rack of wooden slat toilet seats over the top. Seawater pumped in with the ship's forward motion constantly flushed out the gutter, and the crew checked their rank and seniority as they sat cheek to cheek. One CVL sailor on *Cowpens'* sister ship *Cabot* described the environment: "The head is one hell of a place, no more than an open trough where one and all rub elbows now and then."[10]

Occupants needed to keep their wits about them. The rolling of the ship caused the filth and water to slosh over the metal deck—losing your footing could sully your pride as well as your uniform. Moreover, the head was sometimes the location for pranks by the ship's mostly teenaged sailors. "Every now and then some asshole near the end would make a big ball of toilet paper and light it on fire," wrote Art Daly. "It would float under the guys' asses while they were trying to take a crap. You had to keep your eyes open."[11] Sailor John Ingraham, who many years later was president of the American Society for Microbiology, thought it might be a good place to get an up-close view of oceanic bioluminescent organisms. "When I turned off the lights to make what I thought would be a microbe sighting, I was rewarded, along with the howls of some very angry shipmates, with the spectacular sight of the toilet troughs glowing like huge neon tubes in the pitch black compartment—a particularly gorgeous sight."[12]

But for all its tribulations, the ship's complement kept a sense of perspective about the conditions aboard, knowing that other servicemen routinely suffered far worse. Sailor Carswell Wynne thoughtfully observed that life aboard wasn't so bad, and that he "almost hated to talk to guys who had been on the battlefield given all the conveniences we had."[13] The ship's executive officer, Cmdr. Hugh Nieman, provided his own dose of context in the ship's newspaper. "The going is tough and the road is rough," Nieman advised, "but it's never so bad that it couldn't be worse. Think of Joe in wave one [of an amphibious landing] or Jungle Pete with leech feet. Our floating hotel is some classy way to go to war."[14]

Conditions for officers were luxurious by the crew's standards. They were entitled to better beds, regular showers, folded laundry service, and a steward to clean and keep their cabins in order. Officers' country was in the forward part of the ship, off-limits to sailors except those on specific business. Captain McConnell was even further isolated, with his own private office, mess, and orderlies. In addition to his personal staff, McConnell made sure that his Filipino steward from the *Langley* was transferred to the Moo—the two men were fished from the Java Sea together after her sinking. Senior officers such as Mark Grant and Bob Price also had singleton lodging far forward in officers' country. Price wrote to his wife in early July that "I'm really well fixed with a dandy cabin all to myself and a good lad to keep it clean."[15]

The junior officers were lodged two to four to a compartment near the ship's bow, some in bunks built into the bulkhead and others in racks suspended from chains. Ed Haley was lucky; his berth was far enough forward that it was distant from some of the ship's machinery. He was enthusiastic about the accommodations, saying years later that "it was a great way to fight a war."[16] Other pilots were less fortunate and found themselves bunkmates with the ship's catapult. Herschel Pahl, a *Cowpens* pilot who arrived aboard in the fall of 1943, said that "the big hydraulic ram of the catapult, with all the mammoth pulleys and heavy cable wrappings, was lined up exactly with my bunk." He recalled that the catapult made such an awful rattling and banging noise when it was in operation that he feared the piston would smash out and kill everyone there—and vowed to be elsewhere whenever it was in operation.

The food, too, was excellent for the officers, who paid part of their salary into a mess bill to keep the quality high. The Moo's wardroom was located forward on the main deck just aft of the open forecastle at the bow of the ship. It was the full width of the ship and had portholes on both sides, which brought in a cooling breeze when the ship was underway. Moreover, even among other carriers, *Cowpens* had a reputation for good food, although as with the crew, the overall quality and variety deteriorated the longer the ship was at sea.

The wardroom was much like an old-fashioned dinner club in protocols and standards of behavior. In advance of a meal, a mess steward made the rounds through officers' country, ringing a chime to signal assembly. The officers filed in—proper uniform and ties required—and by Navy custom stood behind their assigned seats awaiting the arrival of Executive Officer Hugh Nieman, who presided over each meal. Each was expected to stay until everyone was done eating and required to solicit the XO's approval if arriving late or departing early. Meals were on china, with real glasses for water or iced tea. Junior pilot Anderson Bowers wrote his father that "the food is wonderful and there is plenty of it."[17] After dinner many of the junior officers went out onto the ship's open forecastle to relax and socialize. Herschel Pahl described how "when the ship happened to be steaming downwind, it was very pleasant out there and it became a popular place for young [officers] to enjoy the fresh air and good after dinner conversations. It was quite natural for some of us Midwestern farm boys to dub it 'the front porch.'"[18]

A Rocky Start to Flight Operations

After months of training and preparation, VF-25 squadron commander Bob Price and Air Group Cmdr. Mark Grant completed their roster cuts, picking the pilots they would take aboard the Moo and reassigning the rest. Each of the air groups that made their home aboard *Cowpens* over the course of the war had their own personality—and not all of them got along, either with the ship's officers or each other. But Price and Grant had selected not only capable pilots but ones they knew could live and work together. Air Group 25 was well on its way toward becoming a tight-knit group of friends, with its officers collectively referring to themselves as "the squad." They were eager to get to work, and were upbeat about *Cowpens* and their commanding officer. In a letter home in early July, Bob Price told his wife that "the boys were raring to go" and ready to join the war.[19]

Price had been absent from the fleet for almost two years and was itching to get back to sea. He said of his first few days aboard *Cowpens* that it was "really good to be back...sort of like coming back to an old haunt of past years. New faces but same old feeling."[20] Anderson Bowers wrote to his father that he had narrowly made the cut to remain in the squadron, but only because someone else higher in the rankings flunked out at the last minute. "I am now on the task force for the carrier, I was not before," he wrote, somewhat sheepishly. But despite his close call, he reassured his father that all would be well. "Please don't worry about me for I have a good ship, skipper, and the best plane going. You can't beat that combination."[21]

Half the squadron flew aboard the *Cowpens* on August 3 when she arrived in Chesapeake Bay, while the rest went aboard by boat. Approaching planes entered what was known as the landing circle around the ship, ending in a descending turn over its wake to put themselves "in the groove" for landing. A quarter mile out, the pilot lost sight of the flight deck beneath the nose of the plane, and so the pilot looked to the landing signal officer (LSO), who stood on a platform extending out from the edge of the flight deck on the port side, aft. The LSO wore a bright yellow vest and carried two striped yellow paddles to guide the incoming pilot in for a landing.

The LSO was in the best position to gauge the incoming plane's position relative to the ship. Beginning each approach with his arms out horizontally, his peacock dance was the sole direction for a pilot on approach. If the pilot was too low, the LSO lowered his arms; if the pilot needed to slow down he did a rowing motion; and if the plane needed to level out he tilted his torso in the direction the pilot needed to bank. If the pilot was out of position for a safe landing, the LSO frantically waved his paddles over his head—the direction to "wave off" and gun the throttle to go around for another try. But if the plane was in the right position, the LSO slashed the paddles across the front of his body, the signal to cut power. When the pilot got the cut signal, he chopped the throttle, and his plane dropped onto the flight deck—hopefully catching an arresting wire and bringing him to an abrupt stop. But a failure to catch a wire was even more violent, sending the plane into the crash barrier at middeck—a cable fence about eight feet high that was always up while a plane was on approach.

Because her aircraft elevators were built into the center of the flight deck, *Cowpens* could not simultaneously land planes and move them below to the hangar deck. Accordingly, planes returning aboard were temporarily spotted (parked) forward of the crash barrier until all were aboard. After the arresting wire yanked the plane to a halt, one of the ship's deckhands sprinted out from the catwalk to disengage its tailhook. Then the barrier went down, and the pilot goosed his throttle just enough to get the plane across the barrier where it could be parked and wings folded. The barrier went up again just as soon as the plane rolled across it, as another plane was coming in close behind. It was a precisely choreographed series of steps, and when it was done perfectly, a carrier could bring an aircraft back aboard every thirty to thirty-five seconds. "On those days," one aviator said, when a flattop's flight operations are working at peak efficiency, "a carrier sings. She is a symphony of engine thunder and colored signals. She is a ballet almost."[22]

Bringing a fast-moving aircraft that is bobbing and weaving in the air back aboard a ship that is independently rolling and pitching with wind and waves is a difficult task, even without battle damage, pilot wounds, or fatigue. The CVLs, in particular, were an especially challenging type of ship to land on. In comparison to her seventy-three-foot-wide flight deck, a Hellcat had a forty-two-foot wingspan and an Avenger fifty-four-foot, meaning that a pilot had very little margin of error for a safe landing. It was so challenging that one experienced pilot likened it to "hitting a splinter with a bolt of lightning."[23]

Moreover, in rough weather the *Cowpens'* fantail at the stern might rise and fall as much as thirty feet. If the deck was coming up at the crucial moment the plane touched down, the hard impact could blow out tires or bounce the plane over the crash barrier into the planes spotted forward. Even a wave-off could be dangerous. A Hellcat on final approach was flying with gear and flaps down, just a few knots above stall speed. At this speed the controls were sluggish, and if the pilot got the wave-off all he could do was add power and pull away. If he was too slow to do so, he could pancake on the deck in a crash. If he added too much too quickly, the additional torque generated from the aircraft's eighteen-cylinder

radial engine roaring to life pulled the plane over into a snap roll to the
left. This put the plane over the side and into the drink, and if he hit
the water inverted that did not offer good odds for the pilot to escape
before the plane sank.

Aviators who made daily carrier landings aboard simply had to make
their peace with the risk. Hellcat pilot Lee Nordgren said that the ship's
unpredictable motions meant that each one of his one hundred landings
aboard the Moo was completely different, keeping him on his toes. Nordgren had a little more room at his wingtips than Robert Wright, who was
upfront about the stress resulting from bringing his larger Avenger back
aboard day after day. He said that landing aboard *Cowpens* was so difficult
that for his squadron "it was not surprising that there were a few gray hairs
in our heads after a lengthy stint of carrier duty."[24] But the pilots also took
a great deal of pride in the skill required to land on the Moo, and they
poked fun at other pilots who had a larger ship to land on. One CVL pilot
diverted to land on an *Essex*-class fleet carrier cheerfully inquired: "Which
runway?"[25]

Despite its enthusiasm for the work ahead, Air Group 25 did not put its
best foot forward on its initial landings aboard, the first indication of the
rotten luck that would soon befall the ship. The trouble started even before
the squadron left the ground, when Ens. Archibald "Big Mac" McIlwaine
collided with a stationary object while taxiing his Hellcat, rendering it
no longer airworthy. Adding to the trouble, the winds were erratic out in
the bay, and with Bob Price and Captain McConnell watching from the
bridge, the nervous and inexperienced pilots botched one landing after
another. Mark Grant was the first on approach; he came down on deck so
hard he burst two tires, and the pilot following behind did the same plus
collapsed his starboard landing gear. The third was a moderate improvement, with only one tire destroyed on impact. The fourth crashed over the
side; a Coast Guard cutter hovering nearby fished its pilot, Ens. Donald
Van Gordon, from the water unhurt. He earned the dubious distinction
of being the inaugural member of the ship's "Dunkee Club."

Given the mess on deck, McConnell sent the rest of the circling planes
back to Norfolk to try again the next day. It was an inauspicious start,

even though they completed their second attempt the following day without incident. Price wrote home acknowledging that he had some work to do to get his squadron into shape. "We have done some operating and things are going as well as can be expected for the beginning. There are a lot of things to straighten out, though, so we are having to put the old nose to the grindstone."[26] Clearly, the captain expected more in terms of performance from his pilots. Price told his wife that "Captain McConnell is right in form, although not a perfectionist, demands plenty and we're all doing our best to put out."[27]

The *Cowpens* Tangles with a Submarine Net

Captain McConnell soon had his own unforced error. After two weeks operating in the Chesapeake, the *Cowpens* headed into Norfolk to refuel and reprovision on July 12 before departing for Trinidad for the final leg of her shakedown cruise. It was a warm, clear day, and junior officer Sam Sommers recalled that without wind, the "bay was a sheet of gray glass."[28] With Captain McConnell on the bridge, *Cowpens* crawled toward the ship channel into Norfolk, marked on both sides with red and black buoys. The ship was out of position, however, in part because she had veered to avoid a tugboat in her path, but also because the inexperienced navigator had not taken enough locational fixes and the officer of the deck had compounded the problem by failing to keep an adequate record of the ship's course. The starboard buoy marking the edge of the antisubmarine net guarding the entrance to the harbor disappeared beneath the flight deck overhang and then dragged along the starboard side of the hull until it reached the outboard propeller on that side. The cables quickly tangled on the screw and the dead weight of about a half mile of underwater net pulled the ship to a halt. *Cowpens* was stuck. The ship's history ruefully described how she "hung there like a trapped fish" for three days until Navy divers cut her loose.[29] Even after she was freed from the net, the outboard screw had been so badly fouled that it had to be replaced. *Cowpens* went into dry dock in Norfolk while six tons of replacement propeller came down from New York Ship on a railway car.

It was a humiliating start. George Terrell summed up their collective embarrassment, saying "we didn't need any enemy to put us out of action…here the Pacific Fleet was waiting for us to get our act together and get out there and we get hung up on our own equipment."[30] As captain, McConnell was accountable for the errors of his men, and he received an official admonishment in his record—the last thing he needed after narrowly dodging Admiral Glassford's allegation of dereliction of duty the previous year. Although it cited his crew's errors, the Navy's scolding put the blame squarely on McConnell. "You are admonished for allowing the USS *Cowpens* to become fouled in the submarine net gate at Norfolk, Virginia, on 12 July, in that you, while conning the ship, failed to exercise proper foresight so that the ship could be maneuvered with precision and safety to transit the [net]."[31]

While the Navy cleaned up the mess, the pilots drowned their sorrows at the Norfolk officers' club. The *Cowpens*' pilots were no stranger to the bar while the ship was operating in the Chesapeake, but one particular incident while she was in dry dock became a squadron legend and set the stage for a related incident in combat more than two months later. Shortly before *Cowpens*' departure for Trinidad, a hungover Mark Grant reported to the airfield for an early morning flight after a hard night of drinking at the O club. Grant was scheduled to fly a racetrack pattern over the Moo so her crew could calibrate the ship's radar. The natural swaying and bobbing of the aircraft quickly made Grant nauseous, and not having a bag to vomit into, he opened his canopy and let fly into the slipstream. While this resolved Grant's immediate crisis, it created another, as he lost his upper and lower dentures in the process. A full set of teeth (real or artificial) were a requirement for sea duty, and so Grant had to rush to get replacements made before *Cowpens* departed for the Caribbean. Their commander's embarrassing mishap was the talk of the air group. Price wrote to his wife that "of course we all got a big laugh out of it and [Grant] took a beating about it."[32]

CHAPTER 6

Hawaii

Hawaiian Expectations and Reality—"Never Have So Many Pursued So Few..."

With her shakedown cruise complete, *Cowpens* transited the Panama Canal on her way to join the Pacific Fleet in Honolulu, arriving on September 19, 1943, on a clear tropical morning. As the Moo sailed toward its anchorage in Pearl Harbor, evidence of the December 1941 attack was still visible. The shattered hull of battleship *Arizona* lay in her grave on the east side of Ford Island, with her main guns and the twisted wreck of her superstructure having been stripped by salvage teams the previous year. Bullet holes were still evident in many buildings, and crewmen spotted the steel frames of several burned-out hangars. There was a tarry black stripe at the high tide mark all around the piers and pilings—a reminder of the flood of oil that gushed from shattered battleship hulls.

With a Navy band playing to welcome her arrival, *Cowpens* moored at berth F-10, next to the broken, overturned wreck of former battleship and then target ship *Utah*, sunk on December 7 and never successfully refloated. As soon as *Cowpens* tied up at the pier, Captain McConnell hurried ashore to receive his orders. The men were briefly allowed liberty, but there was a curfew in effect starting at 5 p.m. This, George Terrell remarked, was "the first real reminder we had since joining the *Cowpens* in Philadelphia that this was a serious business, that there was in fact a real war going on."[1]

The men were eager to explore the island; Hawaii had occupied a special place in the American popular consciousness since the 1930s. Even during the darkest days of the Depression, as much as half of the US population saw a movie every week, and "Hawaii Hollywood-style" was a staple of the films of the era.[2] A string of blockbusters romanticized it as a tropical paradise with a hula girl under every palm tree. The islands' exclusiveness also added to their popular mystique. In the prewar era, a Hawaiian vacation was well out of reach of the vast bulk of American society, affordable only for the very affluent.

Once servicemen arrived in Honolulu, it was difficult to reconcile the popular image of the place with reality. Rather than an idyllic paradise, Honolulu was just another crowded Navy town, "full of sunlight and sailors and bad liquor."[3] Pearl Harbor was a major shipyard, supply center, and way station for the Pacific Fleet, and from 1941 to 1945 more than a million servicemen and defense workers passed through it on their way to or from the war. Sam Sommers commented that with the huge volume of men, equipment, and supplies pouring into Hawaii, "the island could have fought a pretty good war by itself."[4]

Few servicemen said much good about it, however, dubbing it "the rock." Some of this was just a case of unrealistic expectations, although there were also plenty of legitimate gripes. These included overcrowding by fellow servicemen, high prices, a male-to-female ratio that most men swore was at least several hundred to one, and the seedy industries that sprung up to separate the sailors from their $50-a-month salary. The complaint that there were just too many servicemen was the most common. The men waited in line for everything—restaurant, movie theater, bar, or brothel. The crowds would reach their peak in December 1944, when 137,200 soldiers, sailors, and Marines were ashore, more than half of Honolulu's 1940 population. The islands had a tradition of hospitality, but many residents felt they had avoided a Japanese invasion only to suffer through a Navy one.[5]

Cowpens had six days at anchor in Pearl Harbor before putting out to sea for exercises, and during that time McConnell released the crew for liberty in rotating shifts. While the officers enjoyed time in the O clubs or playing golf and tennis, some of the sailors went sightseeing, or swam or sunbathed on Waikiki Beach, seeing for the first time that the iconic beach was marred with double lines of barbed wire and patrolled by sentries. Other popular destinations were the USO clubs, the largest being the Army-Navy YMCA in downtown Honolulu. At these clubs, A-list celebrities such as Bob Hope and Jack Benny put on lavish musical variety shows, which interspersed big band music with stand-up or dance routines. The Navy had its recreation center, the Breakers Club, on Waikiki Beach—Artie Shaw and his Navy band made it famous, and up to 4,400 men visited every day.

The Army's Maluhia Club, at the other end of Waikiki, had the best dance floor on the island. Many soldiers and sailors went there in hopes of meeting women, but the odds were skewed against them. Paraphrasing Winston Churchill, the men joked that "never have so many pursued so few, with so much, and obtained so little."[6] The Maluhia was staffed by a cadre of volunteer USO girls, many of them the daughters of socially prominent Hawaiian families, each accompanied by a watchful chaperone. Perhaps 250 or so were there on any given night to dance with 3,500 or so men. There was no cutting in until the whistle blew, which it did every 2.5 minutes. The female volunteers danced for three or four hours at a stretch just to make sure each of the lonely servicemen got their turn. One such group of patriotic women volunteers called themselves the "Flying Squadron," and in twelve months from 1942 to 1943 they attended 127 dances with more than sixty thousand men.

The most popular destination for the enlisted men in Honolulu was Hotel Street, the city's vice district—where they went to get "stewed, screwed, and tattooed." While the men had arrived looking for the Hawaii they had seen in the movies, on Hotel Street they found the Hawaii later depicted in *From Here to Eternity*. James Jones's iconic 1951 novel detailed the intersection between the island's servicemen and its seedy side, what one scholar of the period called "a small world of rough men and prostitutes, of drinking, gambling, sex, violence, and despair."[7] For countless enlisted men headed to the war zone, Hotel Street was their last chance to experience civilization's vices before departing for points unknown.

While memorable, the crowds and costs eventually put off most sailors. Crewman Robert Lee cheerfully recalled Hotel Street was "fun the first couple of times but not after that. The prices are high as hell."[8]

An average of thirty thousand servicemen and civilian defense workers descended on the vice district per day, and one officer recalled how it was filled with "white hats of sailors on leave as far as you could see."[9] After considerable liquid lubrication, some of these sailors joined the long lines for one of the district's second-story brothels. The gaudy neon left little doubt as to the wares they were selling, but the lines were so long and so difficult to keep track of out in the street that sometimes men joined one thinking it was for something else. Art Daly was one such man. He wrote in his journal that "one of the first things I saw was a long line of sailors going into this building. I thought it was a movie house or something, but an old salt soon set me straight. I headed away from there. My liberty was spent swimming on the beach. I want to know how to swim real good if the ship is sunk."[10]

Then it was back to the ship. Most commanding officers looked the other way when it came to the condition that their men were in when they returned aboard. The unwritten rule, explained one career sailor, was that "if a man was sober enough to somehow navigate the accommodation ladder, salute, and manage the words 'Report my return aboard, sir!'" the state of his intoxication and the condition of his uniform were of little consequence."[11] It wasn't just the enlisted men that came back to the ship drunk. An oft-repeated witticism was that "a naval officer never drinks. If he drinks, he doesn't get drunk. If he gets drunk, he doesn't stagger. If he staggers, he doesn't fall. If he falls, he falls flat on his face with his arms under him so no one can see his stripes."[12]

CHAPTER 7

A Dress Rehearsal at Wake Island

The arrival of a flood of new aircraft carriers to Pearl Harbor in the summer and early fall of 1943 gave the Navy the assets it needed to go on the offensive. *Essex*, first of her class, arrived in Hawaii on May 30, followed by two of her sister ships, *Yorktown* and *Lexington*, both named after ships lost in battle in 1942. The first of the light carriers followed soon after; beating *Cowpens* to Hawaii were her sisters *Independence*, *Princeton*, and *Belleau Wood*. This was just the bow wave of the surge of American shipbuilding that had been slowly gathering momentum for the previous eighteen months. The Navy's days of scarcity in aircraft carriers were over. From this point on, American shipyards delivered almost one flattop a month until the end of the war, when a total of 16 *Essexes* and nine CVLs were in action against Japan.

In advance of a general offensive, Nimitz concluded the Navy needed a practice operation. The *Essexes* and CVLs were untested, as were the Navy's Hellcats and its evolving strategy for fighter defense. For the first time it was fusing all its radar and radio into a single coordinating center aboard carriers known as the Combat Information Centers (CICs). Working from there, fighter director officers (FDOs) were the calm voice on the radio guiding Hellcats in to intercept "bogeys," or possible enemy planes, on their way to attack the fleet. Backstopping the FDOs in each CIC were a team of specialists, from the radar operators who interpreted the lines and blobs on their screens into determinations of distance, bearing, and altitude, to the sailors who transcribed the position of friendly and enemy planes backward onto a Plexiglas map grid, so the FDO sitting on the other side could absorb the information at a glance. In the summer of 1943, this system still needed refinement, and a test operation or two would allow these unproven crews, ships, and technologies to be debugged in a low-risk environment.

Navy planners selected Wake Island as the site for this practice operation; it was far enough away from Japanese strongholds that the task force could strike and withdraw without risking a confrontation with enemy carriers. In charge for the operation was Rear Adm. Alfred E. Montgomery. He was a tough, hard-driving, and impatient Nebraskan—too gruff to be popular but respected for his ability. He was also a rarity in naval aviation; a double-dipper who wore not only the golden dolphins of a submariner but also aviator's wings. He would have at his disposal the largest concentration of US naval aviation in the war so far, involving three fleet carriers and three CVLs, for a total of 372 aircraft—plus seven cruisers and twenty-four destroyers for escort. The plan called for a dawn attack to catch the Japanese planes on the ground and knock out the airfield, with subsequent waves of air strikes targeting gun positions and installations.

Felix the Cat Aboard the Mighty Moo

Cowpens' pilots worked furiously to ready themselves for combat. The air group transferred off the ship to the airfield at Barber's Point, Oahu, where they spent the week in a series of exercises and getting much-needed practice in night operations and landings. Bob Price wrote to his wife, "Everything is swell. We're working pretty hard but seeing plenty of results so don't mind. As for me...I'd just as soon work 24 hours a day every day and get the job done so there could be a bit of a homecoming. Actually I think everyone feels the same way but I'll bet no one wishes more earnestly than I."[1]

A last-minute change threw the air group's preparations into disarray. The Navy decided to retool the air complement aboard the CVLs, removing the dive bombers. They did not have folding wings and took up a great deal of space on the hangar deck; removing all nine SBDs made room for twelve Hellcats. The Navy reasoned that the additional fighters were a net gain in firepower, as they strengthened the CVLs' fighter defense and were capable bombers in their own right. Air Group Cmdr. Mark Grant, who had previously flown an SBD, hurriedly qualified to fly both Hellcats and Avengers so he could remain aboard.

Unfortunately, there were not enough excess pilots in Hawaii to fully staff the expanded twenty-four-plane fighter squadron aboard *Cowpens* and the other CVLs, and not enough time to train new ones. The Navy in its wisdom decided to take Price and Grant's old squadron of VF-3, now known as VF-6, and divide it up into three parts to go aboard three separate CVLs—*Cowpens*, *Princeton*, and *Independence*. It was a puzzling move to break up one of the most experienced squadrons in the Pacific, particularly since it was commanded by Butch O'Hare, a national hero and Congressional Medal of Honor winner. The Navy promised it was only a temporary measure; VF-6's home carrier *Enterprise* was under repair, and when it was ready Butch's pilots could be reassembled aboard, as by then as more pilots would be available to backfill the light carriers. Both Grant and Price were happy to be working with O'Hare again, even if the change caused some administrative chaos aboard the Moo. "We are in the midst of a lot of work so are mighty busy," Price wrote to his wife. "Mark just dropped in and we are going over to see Eddie ["Butch"] O'Hare which will probably take some time."[2]

VF-6 could not have been more different than Price's VF-25. While Price and his men essentially self-trained on the Hellcat, O'Hare and VF-6 were practically fighter pilot royalty. Despite the squadron's vaunted pedigree and reputation, its commander wasn't the typical Navy officer. His father, Edgar "EJ" O'Hare, was a dog track owner in Chicago who was an informant against Al Capone and later murdered in a gangland hit. In contrast, Butch emerged as the Navy's first wartime hero at a moment when the country badly needed it. He earned the Congressional Medal of Honor for shooting down five Japanese bombers in four minutes while defending *Lexington* off Bougainville in February 1942—although contemporary sources indicate he probably only shot down three and damaged the other two. Stout, aggressive, and a man of few words, O'Hare was indisputably the best marksman and pilot in VF-6. His men loved him for his leadership, courage, and commitment to their development—and to them he was both a mentor and a larger-than-life father figure. While his star burned bright, it would not burn much longer. By the end of November he would be lost off the Gilberts—probably falling victim to friendly fire during the Navy's first-ever nighttime intercept of enemy fighters.

One of O'Hare's recently arrived junior pilots in VF-6 was Herschel Pahl. Born the second son in a family of six children, Pahl grew up on his parents' farm in southern Nebraska during the dust bowl years of the 1920s and 1930s. Like many of his generation, he made do during tough times, working on neighboring farms, growing and selling vegetables, and trapping fur during the winter. An athlete as well as a scholar, Pahl played football on the scout squad at the University of Nebraska during the 1938–39 academic year and again at Kearney State College in 1940–41. Pahl worried his experience with farm equipment and two years of Army ROTC made him vulnerable for conscription in the Army and decided to volunteer for the Navy in hopes of avoiding it.

O'Hare took a personal interest in training his newly arrived ensigns, and Pahl described how "right away he started working out with us getting to know us in the air and teaching us his ideas on tactics and how to get the most out of the new plane...we tried to live every day to the fullest and scrambled for every minute in the air we could get."[3] Butch hammered into his new pilots not only the skills they needed to succeed in combat, but also the aggressive mindset of a fighter pilot. "This is no drill," he warned them. "We aren't playing funsies. You have to anticipate every move your opponent may make. If you sit there fat, dumb, and happy, you're dead."[4] The brisk pace and pressures of training meant that accidents were inevitable, and Pahl had a close call in September, surviving a midair collision with another Hellcat while practicing radar intercepts over the Pacific. Pahl never saw the other plane until they collided, and suffered a back injury bailing out of his stricken plane as it spiraled into the Pacific. Unfortunately, the impact killed the other Hellcat pilot, Bob Locker—who was the best man at Pahl's wedding mere weeks before.

Air Group 25 wasn't letting the grass grow beneath its feet, either. In the two weeks since they'd arrived in Hawaii, McConnell, Price, and Grant got their inexperienced fliers as much time in the air as they could. But Air Group 25 was nowhere near as polished as their counterparts in VF-6, given that squadron's combat experience and months of training under O'Hare's personal tutelage. The difference was on stark display on September 24, when both squadrons flew out to *Cowpens* for a three-day training cruise. Pahl and seven other VF-6 pilots completed the day's exercises and were ready to come back aboard ship. With *Cowpens* having turned into the wind to take aboard aircraft, Pahl was the first in the procession of planes out of the landing circle. When the LSO gave him the cut, the ship was still heeled over from the sharp turn, but she had enough wind across the deck to land planes, so Pahl came in anyway. "We put the whole flight aboard, bam, bam, bam, with no wave offs," Pahl noted with pride, "after which Captain McConnell put that squirmy little CVL through another sharp turn and ended up right in the *Cowpens'* assigned position in the formation."[5] It was an impressive show of airmanship and coordination, one that took Price and Grant's own pilots additional weeks of practice and training to equal.

CHAPTER 8

Cowpens' Baptism by Fire at Wake

Rumors about *Cowpens'* imminent departure for combat had been swirling for days, and finally she weighed anchor on September 29, 1943, bound for Wake Island. By long Navy tradition, the captain revealed her destination only after the ship was safely at sea, to prevent any loose lips ashore. Upon hearing the news, *Cowpens'* hands were enthusiastic about their first mission, with VF-25's squadron historian cheering that after months of training and preparation, "we are off to battle!"[1]

Wake Island is one of the most isolated atolls in the world, 2,300 miles from Oahu and 2,000 miles from Tokyo. A horseshoe of sand and scrub, it is V-shaped, with the open end to the northwest and a shallow lagoon between its five-mile-long arms. Its three islets, Peale, Wilkes, and Wake, comprise only about 2.5 square miles of surface area, no more than twenty feet above sea level. It was a desolate place, with no palm trees, no source of fresh water, and with a native population limited to flightless birds, hermit crabs, and rats.

While the operation was only a hit-and-run attack, Wake had symbolic importance. The Japanese had captured the island from the United States shortly after Pearl Harbor, and the valiant but doomed defense of its tiny garrison inspired comparisons at home to another famous lost cause in American history, the Alamo. While many aboard the Moo and across the task force savored the opportunity for a little payback, it was only a dress rehearsal for future operations. *Cowpens* for the first time was operating as part of a task force, divided into two cruising groups. The first group included *Essex* and *Yorktown* supported by two CVLs, *Independence* and *Belleau Wood*. The second cruising group included *Lexington* and the Moo. Admiral Montgomery had overall command of the task force from the flag bridge of *Essex*, and Rear Adm. Arthur Radford oversaw *Cowpens'* cruising group. Captain McConnell had reported to admirals in the Asiatic Fleet, but never in such close proximity, and the command arrangement effectively reduced him to the role of middle management. He commanded the Moo but operated within the confines of the admirals' overall strategy and plan.

Cowpens' pilots took up their share of the rotation of constant patrols involved with a multicarrier formation, which had them in the air at least every other day. The ship's fighter pilots took their turn flying combat air patrol (CAP)—where two divisions of four fighters each stood guard aloft against enemy attack, one at 20,000 feet and the other at 10,000. Having fighters in the air dramatically reduced the intercept time if radar detected inbound bogeys, but circling uneventfully overhead for three to four hours a shift was a dull assignment for pilots. About all they could do was alternate their direction or smoke cigarettes to break up the monotony. By the end of the assignment, most pilots, so the saying went, were "bored stiff and stiff as boards." The torpedo squadron—collectively and somewhat pejoratively known as "torpeckers"—also had their share of duties with antisubmarine patrols (ASPs). The Avengers, armed with either depth charges or bombs, flew search patterns out 150 miles from the ship, looking for subs on the surface or enemy ships. Like those of the fighter pilots, these three-hour patrols were typically dull, but occasional encounters with the enemy kept these fliers on their toes.

The outbound trip to Wake was uneventful, providing the needed time for *Cowpens'* complement to attend to all the necessary preparations. The ship's order of the day on the eve of battle instructed all hands to shower and wear clean clothing to reduce the risk of infection in case they were wounded. The sailors tucked the bottoms of their pants into their socks and wore gloves to protect against flash burns resulting from the ignition of gasoline or other volatile fuels. They kept their protective gear—a steel helmet, gas mask, and life preserver—stowed near their battle stations. And finally, the ship's chaplain conducted religious services so all hands could feel assured they were squared away with the Almighty in case the worst came to pass.

Down in the squadrons' ready rooms, pilots and aircrew were familiarizing themselves with the plan of attack and the anticipated enemy resistance. Part fraternity house, part workspace, and part locker room, the ready room was the squadrons' operational and social hub aboard ship. Air-conditioned and kept supplied with coffee, donuts, and cold cuts by the ship's stewards, the ready room was where the pilots prepared for missions, relaxed with their squadronmates, or just kept informed of goings-on with the teletype at the front of the compartment. As the mission approached, VF-6 pilot Herschel Pahl noted how the squadrons devoted themselves to "long study sessions and coordination discussions... the planners and briefers alike had really done their job and had everything organized to the last detail."[2] There were hours of briefings and the pilots committed the details of their individual briefing packets to memory, which included the radio call signs and frequencies, as well as the strike plans, ordnance loads, and the countless other logistical details required to orchestrate an attack involving multiple carriers and scores of aircraft.

By the eve of battle, the Moo's pilots and crew were prepared for the task they faced. Their work was not without reward; consistent with Navy tradition, the wardroom treated the pilots to a lavish precombat dinner the night before. Anderson Bowers described the feast in a letter to his parents that evening: "We had a marvelous dinner tonight; crabmeat cocktail, big steaks, peas, carrots, potatoes and desert. It was really good."[3]

A Snake-Bitten Operation

Cowpens' pilots projected confidence about the upcoming operation in front of their shipmates, but the reality was more complex. After the war, many aviators, regardless of age or service, observed that their youth and ignorance helped mitigate their fears. At eighteen or nineteen years old, many didn't really reflect on the possibility that they could be killed in combat. "There was a huge difference between men that were 19 and 25," said one combat aviator. "Kids thought 'nothing's gonna happen to me, it'll be the other guy.' The older men were more realistic."[4] Once in the heat of combat, most were too preoccupied with doing their jobs to really think about the situation they were in. "You're young. You were frightened—very frightened—but very excited at the same time," another flier explained. "You were well trained but everything is happening fast. There was an exhilaration to things that are sweeping by you."[5]

It was in the quiet moments before combat that some men wrestled with fear or doubt. One veteran flier said that "I was scared to death every goddamn mission I flew. Anyone who said they weren't was a liar."[6] But the social cohesion within units and determination not to let down friends and teammates motivated these men to push through. "The thing that keeps you going is how you look to your friends," said one combat aviator. "That's really important when you're young. You want their respect in the worst way. Your stomach may churn and your asshole might be tight but you pushed through it."[7]

The *Cowpens* came alive well before sunrise. Preparations for launch were made in the dark of the predawn hours so that the first wave of strikes would arrive over Wake just as the sun broke over the horizon. The Moo's planes were scheduled to follow in the second wave shortly after. The weather was lousy for flying, with poor visibility and fog and clouds all the way up to 12,000 or 14,000 feet. Regardless of the weather, Captain McConnell had a schedule to keep, and general quarters roused the men hours before dawn. In the officers' wardrooms, the pilots enjoyed a hearty breakfast of steak and eggs before assembling in the ready room for a final round of briefings. If some had not slept well the previous night, they didn't show it—and powered through on a mix of adrenaline and thick black Navy coffee, known as mud. One by one, they wrestled into their flight gear: soft helmet and goggles, oxygen mask, bright yellow "Mae West" life jacket, parachute harness, and .45-caliber pistol in a shoulder holster. Added to that was a bag of survival gear, including additional ammunition, knife, waterproof flashlight, and canteen.

Finally, just before 5 a.m., came the call they had been waiting for—
"Pilots, man your planes." The deckhands had spotted (parked) the now
armed and fueled aircraft at the aft end of the flight deck. Walking out on
the darkened deck through the closely packed maze of planes, the pilots
climbed into their cockpits and began their warmup procedures in the
predawn gloom. Plane captains helped get them adjusted and snapped the
buckles of their harness to the parachute and life raft package in the cockpit seat. Pilots went through their preflight checklist, waiting expectantly
for the order from the ship's loudspeaker: "Start engines!"

The plane captains inserted a blank shotgun shell into a port in the
engine as a starter, while standing by with a fire extinguisher in case of
emergency. Each pilot gave his plane a little throttle and primer, turned
on the ignition, and flipped the starter switch. Engines turned over, first
reluctantly, with a sputtering cough—and then catching and roaring to
life, with the exhaust belching fire and a cloud of blue smoke. The plane
captains listened to the roar of the engine for irregularities before signaling
approval to the pilot. The *Cowpens'* first strike package of twelve Hellcats
and six Avengers sat on deck with wings folded a few moments, letting
their engines warm up and the individual roar of each engine blend into
a thunderous, pulsing symphony of noise. The din was so overwhelming
that it drowned out all conversation on deck, forcing communication only
by hand signal or radio.

With a faint hint of dawn on the gloomy, cloud-covered horizon,
McConnell turned *Cowpens* into the wind to begin launching planes. The
ship briefly heeled over as she turned out of formation, steadily accelerat-
ing to thirty knots to put as much wind as possible over the flight deck.
The white fox flag with a red diamond went halfway up the yardarm,
signaling that flight operations were imminent. When the Moo was set
and ready, the flag soared to the top of the mast, and the launch officer
waved to each plane in turn to take off. With the horizon lost to sight and
the edge of the flight deck marked only by dim, hooded lights, the pilots
rolled down the deck guided at least in part by memory and feel. VF-6's
Ens. John Ogg was the first in line for takeoff, and he gunned his engine,
released his brakes, and rolled forward. He misjudged his direction or the

edge of the ship, however, and he and his Hellcat tumbled over the port side of the flight deck into the sea just forward of the elevator without ever taking flight. Ogg freed himself from his quickly sinking aircraft and was rescued unhurt by the plane guard destroyer *McKee*, which was trailing aft of the *Cowpens* for just such an occurrence.

Ogg's crash was an ill omen for the Moo, the first of a series of setbacks and losses to follow. The rest of the squadron took flight into the pre-dawn fog, where their carefully synchronized battle plan quickly began to unravel. Following orders, the Moo's pilots attempted to assemble into formation in the dark without using their running lights. In the months to come they would become adept at doing so, guided only by the red tail navigation light and blue flames of the engine exhaust from the plane ahead of them. But that morning they were still new to the practice and struggled to find each other in the dark and fog. Making matters worse was the arrival of a stream of Hellcats from the neighboring carrier *Lexington*, who blundered into *Cowpens*' rendezvous area with all their lights shining brightly. The end result was total chaos. The Moo's strike group was never able to coalesce, and its pilots winged to the target in small groups of whatever planes they could find in the murk, whether they were from the Moo or from *Lexington*. Moreover, sometime after takeoff two *Cowpens* pilots—Bill Stanton and Archibald "Big Mac" McIl-waine—disappeared and were never seen again. They might have collided in midair, or suffered vertigo and crashed into the dark Pacific. Five men from other carriers died the following day in similar circumstances; one Hellcat pilot developed vertigo and plunged into the sea, while two dive bombers collided in midair, killing four.

Small bands of *Cowpens*' aircraft made their way toward Wake. As they drew closer, the weather cleared somewhat and the fliers could hear the excited radio chatter of the first wave of Hellcat pilots engaging Japanese Zekes over the target. Tipped off by either radar or a patrol boat, the Japanese scrambled twenty-seven fighters into the air to meet the onrushing Americans. By the time *Cowpens* aircraft arrived over the island at 6 a.m., the first wave had either shot down or scattered many of the defending fighters and completed their strikes. To her fliers, the tiny island seemed covered with thousands of fireflies, not only the flares from exploding bombs and burning fires, but also the muzzle flashes of antiaircraft guns firing up at them.

As *Cowpens'* Avengers began forming up to drop their bombs, a flight of Japanese fighters—perhaps ten in all—appeared. Despite having an altitude advantage, they lurked just outside of gun range and appeared reluctant to pick a fight. The Moo's fighters turned to meet them and scored the ship's first aerial kills. Lieutenants George Bullard and Alfred Kerr teamed up to set one Zeke aflame, sending it spiraling into the ocean, while Lt. Benny Farber riddled another with gunfire, and it tumbled out of control into the sea.

With the enemy fighters gone, the Avengers focused on their target, a barracks on Peacock Point on the south end of the island. Unfortunately, just as the bombers began their bombing run, another air group—likely in a misguided attempt to be helpful—dropped magnesium flares over the target. The flares were so brilliant they completely washed out the pilots' view of the targets below. Squinting against the painfully bright light, the bomber pilots took their best guess and scattered their bombs in the target area between the runways, causing many fires but scoring no hits on the barracks itself. As the Avengers turned back toward base, the pilots and aircrew were unhappy about having their first mission sabotaged by friendlies, complaining that continued in the squadrons' ready rooms back aboard ship.

The returning planes approached the task group from a designated heading, sweeping wide into the landing circle so jumpy antiaircraft gunners would not confuse them with Japanese attackers. Still, their approach did cause some excitement. Radioman Art Daly recalled how the Moo's chaplain, Charles Hacherl, a Catholic parish priest from Massachusetts, was supposed to give the sailors down belowdecks a running account of events over the ship's loudspeaker. Most importantly, if he hollered "Here they come!" it signaled that the ship was about to be hit.

Sure enough, Father Hacherl was relaying reports of the action when he spotted *Cowpens'* returning aircraft and screamed, "Here they come!'" Nerves aboard ship were already on edge, and most sailors belowdecks who heard the overexcited chaplain braced for the explosion of a bomb or torpedo. "All our guys were shitting our pants," explained Art Daly. The ship's gunners squeezed off a few rounds at the incoming friendlies, but thankfully their officers quickly put a stop to it before they scored any hits. Adding insult to injury, a nearby ship signaled to *Cowpens*, congratulating her on the lousy shooting. That was the last time the chaplain was allowed to narrate events, and Daly later grumbled that the padre "was on my shit list from then on!"[8]

VF-6 pilot Herschel Pahl was relieved to touch down on the *Cowpens* and feel the solid tug of his tailhook catching an arresting wire. Pahl rolled his Hellcat forward of the barrier into a parking spot, and he hadn't even gotten unbuckled from his harness before his plane captain was on the wing, asking one excited question after another. They were the front end of the ship's gossip pipeline, spreading news so efficiently, Pahl remarked, that sometimes the ship's "cook and boiler-tenders learn about shoot downs and anything spectacular before the captain of the ship does."[9]

Once the planes were parked, the deckhands inspected each one for battle damage while the pilots hurried below to the squadron ready room to debrief. Pahl talked to the maintenance chiefs about the performance of his aircraft before describing his mission in detail to the ship's intelligence officers. These debriefers, typically lawyers or reporters in their civilian lives, always cross-checked pilots' claims against one another before drafting the after-action reports to identify any "gun decking," or exaggerated claims of success. Captain McConnell, too, wanted a debrief from each of the pilots who had scored aerial victories that morning, calling them each up to the bridge. He had been waiting twenty months for payback for the loss of the *Langley*, and he savored every detail.

The second day's strikes began on a much better note. The weather had improved, and after the previous day's debacle, Admiral Montgomery increased the spacing between the task force's carriers, so they wouldn't interfere with one another on takeoff. *Cowpens* contributed all nine of her Avengers and most of her Hellcats to the dawn mission, which lifted off at 5:45 a.m. With most of the atoll's fighters cleaned out the day before, and friendly squadrons having gotten the memo to refrain from using magnesium flares, the Avengers completed their bombing runs unmolested—and the results were much improved. One of the Moo's planes scored a direct hit on an oil tank at the center of Peale Island, while subsequent hits on a power plant and an ammunition dump resulted in satisfying secondary explosions.

With the Avengers safely on their way back to *Cowpens*, the Hellcats descended to make low-level strafing attacks. The previous day's raids had knocked out most of Wake's large-caliber antiaircraft gun emplacements, but as pilots came in low and fast, they encountered a hail of small-arms and machine-gun fire, particularly along the beaches. In the coming months *Cowpens'* pilots learned that against determined ground fire, making more than one strafing run was not worth the risk—the best approach was to make "one pass and haul ass." But at Wake, the fighter pilots' combination of inexperience and overenthusiasm led them to come back again and again, and the ground fire quickly began to take a toll.

At first, the Hellcats scored a few hits. Ensign Nichols set fire to an oil tank, while Ensign Seaver destroyed two twin-engine bombers on the ground, and Bob Price destroyed another. Others were not so lucky. A Japanese antiaircraft round exploded in the cockpit headrest of VF-6's Lt. (jg) George Rogers, peppering his right shoulder with shrapnel. He managed to make a safe landing on *Belleau Wood*; after getting his wounds bandaged he flew his own plane back to *Cowpens*. Additionally, Japanese gunners riddled Ens. Orson Thomas's Hellcat with fire—he managed to keep his plane in the air only long enough to ditch two miles out at sea. Thomas's plane sank almost immediately but he escaped from the cockpit. Other pilots observed him waving at passing US planes, apparently unhurt. Search aircraft went back to find him but by then he had disappeared and was never seen again.

Air Group 25 Cmdr. Mark Grant was another victim of the Japanese ground fire. With Anderson Bowers as his wingman, the pair made four separate low-level strafing runs against enemy positions. Bowers flew CAP the previous day and was eager to get in on the action for the first time. The "AA was terrific, it was still dark, and it was tough," Bowers later wrote in a letter home.[10] Grant and Bowers screamed in, machine guns blazing, skimming just above the ground the whole length of the island from north to south. They turned around to repeat the trick and, in Bowers's words, "flat-hatted the length of the island very low."[11]

On their third pass, the duo flew in over the lagoon; Bowers described how he was filling a water tower with .50-caliber holes when his plane was jarred with the impact of what he described as "a big hit in the right wing. I looked over, and could see them shooting at me on the lagoon side. So on the next run, I cleaned them out."[12] It was on this run that Bowers lost Grant, whose engine quit after multiple hits, forcing him to ditch just offshore. Undeterred, Bowers made a fifth strafing run alone and then, engine sputtering, found another Hellcat to escort him home. After landing back aboard, Bowers inspected his plane, which he described as having more holes than a piece of Swiss cheese. "My rudder tab had been shot off and I could put my head through the hole in the starboard wing," he later wrote. Deckhands also soon identified the cause of his sputtering engine; two of its eighteen cylinders had been shot out. Bowers concluded it was a "good indoctrination" to how dangerous enemy ground fire could be.[13]

Montgomery ordered *Cowpens* to participate in an unscheduled and final strike about midmorning, but the operation had exceeded the point of diminishing returns. Peale Island had already taken a pounding in previous attacks, but VT-25 went back as directed to finish off any remaining buildings or gun emplacements. The Avengers scored direct hits on a barracks that looked intact from the air, but on closer inspection at low altitude turned out to have already been gutted by fire. Moreover, the ground fire claimed another victim, Lt. Harold Kicker. He was a native son of Tuscaloosa, Alabama, and a graduate of the university there. He made a supporting strafing attack, but was so badly battered by ground fire that he ditched in the Pacific two miles west of Peale Island.

Lt. Kicker Inaugurates the Submarine Lifeguard League— "Dr. Livingstone, I Presume?"

The 311-foot-long US submarine *Skate* was waiting just offshore of Wake Island to pick up downed airmen. Rescuing aviators was a new role for

subs, but naval commanders realized that their pilots might be more willing to press the attack if they were confident they would be recovered if
shot down. The first test of the concept during a raid on Marcus Island
in August was unsuccessful, but the second try at Wake produced much
better results.

Skate arrived offshore prior to the raid and played hide-and-seek
with the enemy, repeatedly diving to evade enemy fighters and Wake's
coastal defense guns. On the morning of the seventh, she was searching
for downed aviators, staying low in the water, with decks awash in hopes
of avoiding drawing any unwanted attention. It was about this time that
VF-25's Harold Kicker ditched his damaged aircraft offshore. Kicker's
wingman, Lt. Relly "Raffles" Raffman, rushed to assist when he saw his
friend was in trouble. With the aid of two other pilots in Kicker's division and despite the heavy Japanese ground fire, Raffles located *Skate* and
then, using hand signals, directed her to Kicker's location. Following the
fighter pilot's direction, the sub came in so close to the atoll to recover
the downed pilot that they soon became a target of Japanese gunners.

The six-inch guns ashore seemed to have the sub's number, with the
shells splashing ever closer. One of the sailors on deck, looking right down
the barrel of that gun as it spat out round after round at them, later said,
"Believe me, when we looked down its muzzle, it looked like a sixteen-
inch!"[14] Thankfully, US dive bombers finally knocked the coastal gun out
of action just as *Skate* plucked Kicker from the Pacific. He was the first of
518 pilots and aircrew recovered by submarines over the course of the war,
in an effort informally known as the Submarine Lifeguard League. He
was not the only pilot aboard *Skate* for long; Raffman and the two other
Cowpens fighters circling overhead guided her to another pilot from the
Lexington who was floating nearby. That pilot, Murray Tyler, was fated to
be a repeat customer of the league; subs fished him from the Pacific three
times over the course of the war.

Skate remained in her patrol area offshore for the next few days, diving
several times to avoid enemy gunfire or marauding aircraft. On the ninth,
the sub picked up another aviator in his life raft, and the following day
discovered two more. Midafternoon the following day one of the sub's

lookouts spotted something bobbing on the waves three miles distant on the port bow. She drew in close to investigate and discovered a life raft with its cover flap closed to shield its occupant from the sun. With a yell of "Ahoy, the raft there!" *Skate's* officer of the deck awakened *Cowpens'* air group commander, Mark Grant, who by then had been adrift for three days. Suddenly startled awake, he flung back the cover, clearly surprised by the sub's appearance. *Skate's* captain described how Grant flung himself out of the raft with a whoop and "flew through the water to the vessel's side and up its steel ladder like a squirrel."[15]

Despite his long wait in the raft, Grant never lost confidence he would be rescued—as his luck at Wake had been so lousy that he thought it could only improve. Japanese gunners peppered his aircraft with hits on his last low-level strafing run with Anderson Bowers, and the skipper claimed to have seen the Japanese rifleman whose bullet finished off his already-damaged engine. While Grant was upbeat about his chances of rescue, after firing at seagulls and gooney birds in hopes of obtaining lunch, he had saved the final round in his pistol for himself just in case.

To pass the time, Grant amused himself planning his conversation with his rescuers, concluding that the correct opening remark was "Dr. Livingstone, I presume?"[16] Moreover, remembering the loss of his dentures off Norfolk, he removed his shoes and placed the teeth in one of them, thinking they would be safest there. But the *Skate's* sudden appearance caught Grant off guard; not only did he forget his prepared speech, he left his dentures in his shoes in his raft. He only realized his mistake when the sub's commanding officer ordered one of his deckhands to sink the raft with machine-gun fire, and Grant dove back into the water to retrieve them. In subsequent retellings of the story at the Honolulu O club, Grant claimed he was fully aboard and the sub submerged when he convinced *Skate's* captain to resurface and allow him retrieve his teeth.

Aftermath

Wake began for the Moo with a pilot going into the drink and it ended the same way. Shortly before 4 p.m., Ens. Eldin "Whitey" Arms was returning from CAP, the last *Cowpens* plane in the air before the ship turned for Hawaii. Arms misjudged his approach, came in too low, and caught his tailhook on the ship's ramp. The Hellcat hurtled over the port side of the flight deck and crashed into the sea. Arms never emerged from the plane, which quickly sank out of sight.

Arms's death was the final blow for what had been a bloody baptism by fire for VF-25, who accounted for all of the ship's losses—three Hellcats lost in accidents and three shot down, with four pilots killed. It was left to the surviving pilots and officers to try and absorb what they had learned in their first combat operation. "With no trepidation we had undertaken the operation, truly fledglings," noted VF-25's squadron history. "We got a taste of battle, enough to learn what we didn't know."[17] But they still had much to learn, and that same account defended the risky low-level strafing attacks that had cost them dearly, arguing that their impact justified the losses.

While accepting combat losses is always difficult, the unexplained disappearances of Stanton and McIlwaine were an especially bitter pill for the squadron to swallow. VF-25 was a tight-knit group, and the label of "missing in action" left many of its pilots lacking closure for the loss of their comrades. "We will never know, perhaps, whether they spun in, had a collision, or were shot down by the enemy," explained the squadron history. "All we know is that we lost two of our finest boys and friends."[18] Testament to the bonds that quickly form between men in wartime, McIlwaine's roommate, VF-25 pilot Don McKinley, years after the war gave one of his sons the middle name McIlwaine in tribute to his missing friend.

With Mark Grant aboard the rescue sub for the next two weeks, Bob Price stepped into the role of air group commander and went about notifying the casualties' families. As Stanton's wingman, explaining his disappearance must have been especially difficult for Price. His letter to Stanton's parents detailed the confusion on the first day of strikes, and put the best possible spin on his loss. "Because it was dark none of us were able to identify positively the other planes in the formation," Price wrote. "I feel quite sure, however, that Bill reached the target and gave an excellent account of himself."[19] Price went on to explain how much Stanton was missed in the squadron. "Bill's absence from the squadron has been a blow to all of us. He has been a real friend and one of the most popular ensigns in the outfit."[20] He also tried to put the loss in a greater context. "Fine men such as these do not leave this old world for no reason at all," he offered. "We like to think of them as still carrying on for us wherever they are."[21]

In a strategic sense, the operation was a success, validating US multicarrier doctrine and tactics. Over the course of two days, the fleet launched six strikes totaling 738 combat sorties, losing only 13 planes in combat and another 14 in accidents. US warplanes claimed to have destroyed 65 Japanese aircraft on the ground or in the air, although the reality was probably lower. *Cowpens*, in contrast, had not yet found her stride. Taking a ship of raw recruits and inexperienced officers and turning them into an effective ship-handling team is a slow process, accomplished only through constant practice and improvement. Despite Captain McConnell's best efforts, *Cowpens* had only just arrived in the war zone, and she was months away from reaching full operational effectiveness.

As with his experience aboard the *Langley*, Captain McConnell's immediate supervisor noticed *Cowpens'* difficulties and made his disappointment known. Writing in Captain McConnell's postoperational review, Admiral Radford indicated the captain still had considerable work to do in whipping his crew into shape. "The performance of the USS *Cowpens* was not altogether up to the standard which may be expected from the CVLs as a type," wrote Radford. But the admiral conceded McConnell had been given little time to prepare and noted that his ship showed steady improvement throughout.[22] Thankfully for McConnell, higher command took a different view, much as it had done after the *Langley's* sinking. Admiral Montgomery noted that McConnell "handled his ship with skill...I would be most pleased to have Captain McConnell serve under my command during war operations."[23]

CHAPTER 9

Back to Pearl: The *Cowpens* Jinx Strikes Again

*C*owpens returned to Hawaii on October 11, 1943, with her squadrons temporarily transferred to Naval Air Station Kahului, Maui. The subsequent weeks Air Group 25 spent on Maui were a delightful interlude between the squadron's bloodying at Wake and the operations to follow. The island was beautiful, the duties light, and everyone passed the time with luaus, sightseeing, athletics, and trips to a swimming hole beyond Lahaina. Maui was not the vacationer's paradise that it is today, and at the time was very rural. Kahului was hacked out of the tropical scrub and conditions were rustic. The barracks had open-screen side panels, which let the ocean breezes blow the volcanic dust in one side of the building and out the other. The pilots and their bunks were filthy, and Price in mid-October wrote his wife about showering off "about an inch and a half of red volcanic dust out of eyes, hair, ears, etc. Seems like I've eaten it for weeks."[1]

On October 19 he described to his wife an additional airborne enemy that rivaled the Japanese: mosquitos. Even though he doused himself in repellent, Price groused, the mosquitos hounded him, undeterred by "the bodies of their dead comrades on the floor." Price complained that the noise they made was terrific; "I can sleep through the bites but the continual buzzing drives me wild."[2] But by the end of the month, Price wrote how he and some of the other pilots had shaved off their hair for comfort and hygiene in the heat and dust and were finally acclimating. "We are getting used to eating and living with the dust and mosquitos. Thank goodness for a cool ocean and plenty of fresh water showers to wash it off."[3]

Price was perhaps the one man in the squadron whose workload increased while on Maui. Mark Grant's physical condition after several days in a life raft precluded his return to the ship for a few weeks, so Price retained temporary command of Air Group 25 in addition to his usual duties as commander of its fighter squadron, VF-25. He relished the additional responsibility and the opportunity to contribute. "It's all new and different but particularly satisfying to be actually involved in the job we came out here to do," he wrote to his wife in late October. While the censor prohibited specific mention of the air group's recent casualties, Price made a veiled reference to it, indicating that he, like many others in the squadron, was still feeling the losses of his friends and squadronmates. "Familiar faces fall by the wayside and that is the tough part about it but something we are to get used to and for the most part will become calloused."[4]

The only interruption in the relaxed Maui pace was a two-day training cruise in mid-October. *Cowpens* put to sea in company with destroyers *Abbot*, *Chauncey*, and *Coghlan* for night carrier qualifications and gunnery practice off the south coast of Oahu. McConnell, probably still stinging from his casualties at Wake and the recent rebuke from Admiral Radford, wanted to get his pilots and deck crew some much-needed training. The pilots flew in shifts of six at a time, with each getting three opportunities to take off and land in the dark. Captain McConnell recognized the inexperience of all involved and took the exercise slow and easy, gradually qualifying one group of pilots after another. McConnell and *Cowpens* successfully completed the first two cycles by 2:15 a.m. on the eighteenth, and were ready to begin the third.

During a routine rotation of *Abbot*'s position from antisubmarine guard ahead to plane guard astern, her officer of the deck evidently decided to slow his ship, let the *Cowpens* go by, and then make a turn to port to get in behind the Moo. But he misjudged the timing, and put

Abbot on a collision course with the Moo. McConnell ordered right full rudder and sounded the alarm, but the destroyer quickly closed the distance and knifed into *Cowpens'* starboard side, slashing through the hull from the main deck to seven feet below the waterline.

Those officers and men who were off duty at the time of the accident were first awakened by the clanging of the collision alarm—a sound that Sam Sommers said would wake the dead—and then by the impact itself. Crewman Robert Lee had just gotten off the midnight watch and was sound asleep when the collision occurred. His compartment was close to the point of impact and soon began to flood. He described how he woke up "with a wet ass and a lot of US currency floating around the compartment" from payday the day before. Thinking the *Cowpens* had been torpedoed, he scrambled for the exit, ignoring the money. "Self-preservation came first," Lee later explained. "You can't spend money at the bottom of the Pacific Ocean."[5]

Both ships were dead in the water, and as the early light of dawn broke over the scene, *Abbot* was visible off their starboard side with the forward thirty feet of her bow bent seventy-five degrees to one side, which George Terrell described as "folded back like a crushed beer can."[6] Three men were crushed to death in their bunks aboard *Abbot*, and another six injured, although no one was hurt aboard the Moo. The collision opened three of her compartments to the sea, flooding them with three to five feet of water. Immediately fore and aft of the point of impact were the chief petty officers' and enlisted men's berths. Had the impact been ten feet in either direction there undoubtedly would have been additional casualties.

Cowpens limped back to dry dock at Pearl Harbor for nine days of repairs. The ship and her squadrons had been scheduled to go south with *Essex* and *Bunker Hill* to raid Rabaul, the lynchpin of Japanese defenses in the Southwest Pacific. But with the ship out of action for a few days, the Moo's sister ship *Independence* took her place. In his official report, Captain McConnell noted that during the incident the conduct of the ship's officers and men was excellent, and "the only complaint voiced was that this unfortunate accident would delay us getting into action."[7] In reality, the universal reaction was more like disgust. The crew couldn't believe that their ship could be so unlucky, and some began talking of the "*Cowpens* jinx." "First a submarine net. Then this," grumbled George Terrell. "With allies like that, who needed enemies?"[8] Even the local sympathy for *Cowpens'* condition was short-lived. Initially, the bluejackets got a lot of attention from local women for what they thought was the ship's battle damage. But this evaporated just as soon as the word spread as to how the Moo came home with a hole in her flank. "It sure was a big letdown from being the hero one minute to the butt of a big joke," sailor Robert Lee groused.[9]

The *Cowpens* jinx wasn't quite done. During the repair work, someone attempted to drain an onboard water tank but instead turned the wrong valve and dumped several hundred gallons of aviation fuel into the dry dock, where it settled into a drain. A spark from the repairs above ignited the fuel, setting off a tremendous explosion and towering fireball that sent those present scrambling for their lives and then the fire hoses. Thankfully no one was hurt, and the only damage was a black scorch mark on *Cowpens'* newly repainted hull—another black eye for the ship's already wounded pride.

The explosion led the naysayers aboard to insist *Cowpens* was a jinx ship. What else would explain her recurring misfortunes? But the ship's rumor mill soon offered another interpretation. The "word"—unsubstantiated gossip spread as fact—in the shipyard was that *Independence* had run into trouble at Rabaul. Rumor had it she had been under heavy air attack, was torpedoed, and lost a quarter of her crew. While this was not the case, in believing the rumors of *Indy's* misfortune some sailors began to argue that the *Cowpens'* mishaps had allowed her to avoid a greater disaster in battle. Sam Sommers said that "we started to think that the Moo was a lucky ship, if the luck would hold."[10]

CHAPTER 10

GALVANIC and FLINTLOCK: The Marshall and Gilbert Islands Campaigns

Cowpens' Air Group 25 closed out their time on Maui with a homecoming party for Mark Grant and Harold Kicker, returning from the rescue submarine *Skate*. The pilots gathered at the officers' club and the festivities quickly grew rowdy. Ever the responsible commander, Bob Price departed at about 10 p.m. when things, in his words, "began getting pretty hot."[1] Anderson Bowers, however, wrote to his father the following day about how "we had a squad party last night at the O-Club. We had steaks and all the trimmings (I had 3) and all the drinks we wanted. Even the bartender passed out!" Price wryly noted to his wife afterward that things had gotten out of hand at least in part due to the absence of the stabilizing influence of the pilots' wives and girlfriends. He then inquired whether she could "gather all the gals and start out [for Hawaii]?"[2]

Another factor driving the pilots' enthusiasm for a party was the understanding they would soon return to combat. *Cowpens* was out of dry dock on October 28 after her unfortunate run-in with the *Abbot,* and with Pearl Harbor packed with ships and the nearby airfields crammed with planes it was clear that the Moo wouldn't stay at anchor long. General MacArthur needed the Navy to open a second front to divert Japanese attention away from his northward advance through New Guinea. In its prewar plans, the Navy had always envisioned an advance westward across the Central Pacific. The Japanese had reached the same conclusion about US strategy, staking out a spiderweb of installations there, with the first major defensive line being the Marshall Islands.

The Marshall Islands are composed of thirty to thirty-five low-lying coral atolls, each with scores of smaller islets and reefs. Of modest size and with few natural resources, their only strategic value was their location. The Japanese had built a series of airfields and anchorages there that would allow them to strike a US force advancing westward across the Central Pacific. The problem for US planners was how to neutralize these bases so far distant from friendly territory—some 2,300 miles from Hawaii, well beyond the reach of land-based US aircraft that the Navy's planners wanted to support the carrier strikes.

US planners concluded that the only solution was to take a closer target—the Gilbert Islands—as a springboard for attacks into the more heavily defended Marshalls. Once the US had a foothold in the Gilberts, it could bootstrap its way westward across the Marshall Islands. The next target would be Kwajalein, the world's largest atoll—a boomerang-shaped ring of land about sixty-five miles long. It has a lagoon of 839 square miles, large enough to host hundreds of ships, and the Japanese had constructed several bases there. Afterward, US planners looked to seize Eniwetok, the midway point in the long air route connecting the Japanese home islands with their other strongholds in the Central and South Pacific. It was a good plan, but for *Cowpens* the march across the Gilberts and Marshalls over the following six weeks was a frustrating string of missed opportunities and close calls.

On November 10, *Cowpens* and the fleet weighed anchor from Pearl Harbor, exiting single file through its narrow channel. VF-6 pilot Herschel Pahl and his squadronmates were on deck counting and identifying ships as each departed in turn. There were so many leaving all at once, Pahl later wrote, "that it was like watching a cold front move—difficult to see it all at one time."[3] Soon after the *Cowpens* was underway, Captain McConnell went on the ship's loudspeaker and announced her destination and explained the outlines of the GALVANIC plan. After the Moo's long string of bad luck, everyone was eager for action. "We are going to take the Gilbert Islands," radioman Art Daly wrote in his diary. "The whole Pacific Fleet is in on this…here we come Tojo!"[4] Once at sea, the pilots were disappointed to learn that their role would be primarily defensive. The Moo and the rest of Task Group 50.1 were to cruise northwest of the Gilberts along the line that Japanese planes might take from the Marshall Islands, preventing air attacks that would interfere with the landings. The fighter pilots were unhappy and groused that GALVANIC "looks like a lot of CAP—and not much else!"[5]

Cowpens and Task Group 50.1 arrived in their assigned operating area on November 19, in advance of the scheduled landings. Bob Price and the rest of VF-25 spent the next six days holding up their share of the CAP rotation, but it always seemed that the Japanese only appeared en masse when another carrier was on duty. For example, on the twenty-third, Hellcats from the *Lexington* pounced on a formation of 21 Zekes from above, scoring 17 confirmed kills and 4 probables—and the very next day bagged 19 more. *Cowpens'* pilots had to settle for the leftovers; at dawn on the twenty-first, the Moo's VF-6 commander, George Bullard, splashed a Japanese Betty bomber that lingered too long in the area after its overnight search for the task force. Bullard made one firing run on the Betty and, judging from its lack of evasive maneuvers, caught it completely by surprise. Subjected to a stream of fire from Bullard's guns, it caught fire and plunged into the sea.

Air Group 25's only offensive operations were three strikes on Mili in the Southern Marshall Islands. The missions were dogged by mechanical gremlins—persistent hydraulic problems that made it difficult for the Avengers to drop their bombs. On their first strike on the nineteenth, a frustrated Mark Grant made four runs on the target before he was able to dislodge his bombs, while his three wingmen took two tries each. On a later mission, these same issues grounded four of seven planes scheduled to go on the strike—and a fifth made it halfway to the target before leaks forced him to return to the ship. With the Avenger pilots besides themselves in frustration, *Cowpens'* repair teams identified the source of the problem: their hydraulic fluid was eating away at the rubber gaskets in the planes' systems. A quick change to a different type of fluid put these problems behind them.

While combat proved to be a disappointment, an accident aboard ship garnered the Moo national press attention. Lt. Alfred McGee had just taken off from the Moo on November 24 when a fuel leak in his belly tank forced him to return to the ship. He was on final approach when the spray of fuel dripping out from his Hellcat ignited into a huge fireball trailing out behind him. McGee could smell the fumes but did not know his aircraft was on fire until he touched down and the flames enveloped his plane. He scampered to safety across the wing as the ship's firefighters swarmed in to extinguish the blaze. Fearing that the fire might still be burning inside the fuselage, the firefighters pushed the smoldering Hellcat overboard. The ship's photographer captured the incident in a series of photos that appeared in the December 4, 1944, issue of *Life* magazine.

A follow-up raid on Kwajalein Atoll on December 4 gave the crew their first real taste of combat. *Cowpens* again drew the short straw to the big deck flattops in flight assignments, with her planes conducting CAP and antisubmarine patrols while other squadrons went on the attack. But the fleet carriers turned in a mixed performance, due to poor intelligence on enemy positions and lackluster coordination. They swept the sky of fighters, wrecked planes on the ground, sank several cargo ships, and torpedoed an ammunition ship, which blew up in spectacular fashion. Only as their planes were withdrawing, however, did they spot an additional sixty or so Bettys that they missed camouflaged in revetments.

The Japanese counterattacked soon after; a flight of three Kate torpedo bombers came in low and fast with the sun at their backs. Circling shortly after launch, George Bullard spotted the low-flying Japanese planes, whose olive drab camouflage stood out against the blue sea. With Herschel Pahl on his wing, Bullard dove on the Kates, rapidly closing the distance. *Lexington*'s gunners downed one Kate as the duo pressed home their attack on a second; it flew directly into a stream of tracers and burst into flames. By then, friendly antiaircraft fire had grown quite intense, and Bullard pulled up to avoid being the next victim as the burning Kate cartwheeled down into the Pacific. Lex's furious barrage of defensive fire knocked down the remaining enemy plane, but she managed to loose a torpedo before being downed. *Lexington* threw her rudder hard to starboard, and the Japanese fish passed harmlessly one hundred yards astern.

A second wave of four Kates sneaked in low from the opposite side to get *Yorktown*. Cruiser *San Francisco* and destroyers *Taylor* and *LaVallette* bagged two; one crashed into the sea so close to the stern of *Yorktown* that her flight surgeon later said he could have evaluated the Japanese pilot's teeth. The third enemy plane, discouraged by the thick clouds of antiaircraft fire, broke and ran, while its remaining wingman passed down the center of the formation between the *Cowpens* and several other ships who were all furiously attempting to shoot it down.

The Moo's gunners joined in with a barrage of 20mm and 40mm shells. Sam Sommers vividly recalled the attack. "A single engine Japanese plane headed directly for us, to starboard, about 100 feet above the water. He had been hit and was trailing a thin stream of dark smoke... all of our starboard guns were firing at him, tracers going right by, and it seemed right into him, but still he came on... I was saying to myself for somebody to get him, get him, boy somebody GET HIM!"[6] Finally, some rounds connected, and a burst of smoke and flame erupted from a wing root. The wing tore off the fuselage, and the tumbling, burning remains of the plane crashed into the sea.

The Japanese attack crystallized Rear Adm. Charles "Baldy" Pownall's reservations about lingering in the area. He was in overall command aboard *Yorktown* but had gained a reputation for timidity in an August 1943 raid on Marcus Island. Although he knew that several dozen enemy torpedo bombers remained on Kwajalein, he believed that his pilots had not yet recovered from the exhausting GALVANIC campaign, and he wanted to get out of range of the Japanese bases as soon as possible. *Yorktown*'s captain, James "Jocko" Clark, was dumbfounded at Pownall's decision. Flying into a rage, he badgered Pownall to reverse it, warning, "You'd better get back there and knock out those Bettys, or they'll come and get you!"[7] Pownall refused, and the enraged Clark stormed off to fume. In contrast, Pownall was upbeat, sending to the fleet the listing of enemy assets destroyed on Kwajalein and offering his CONGRATULATIONS ON A FINE JOB WELL DONE.[8]

As Clark and Pownall were crossing swords aboard *Yorktown*, a tragedy was about to unfold on *Cowpens*. Shortly after 1 p.m., a Hellcat from *Lexington* attempted an emergency landing aboard the Moo. After several weeks of operations, the crew had grown used to emergency landings; as explained by Marine George Terrell, "We'd done it so often now that it wasn't even interesting anymore."[9] But the situation quickly went bad. The pilot was wounded and his aircraft damaged by flak, and he likely had little experience landing on the narrow flight deck of the CVLs. He came in too low and got a wave-off; he opened his throttle to pick up speed to go around for another try. Terrell watched in horror as the disaster played out. "When the engine roared up to full speed, the propeller torque pulled his nose over to the left and his left wing dropped. The plane flipped over on its back, and, engine roaring, plowed upside down right through the amidships gun blister where my buddies were on duty."[10]

Four men were cut to pieces in the accident, including Ted McKay, the ship's second-ranking Marine. Another ten Marines and sailors were injured. While the pilots had taken casualties at Wake, these were the first losses among the crew and they had a tremendous impact, particularly on the Moo's small and tight-knit complement of Marines. The crash with its aftermath was traumatic for everyone who witnessed it, and Art Daly noted in his journal that one of the Marines, Oscar Mealor, confided in him that the only time he cried during the war was after the accident that day. Sailor Robert Lee likely spoke for many aboard when he observed, "It sure was a hell of a mess and I hope I never have to see anything like it again."[11]

The task force beat a hasty retreat with the enemy hot on their trail. Everyone expected trouble that evening, and the Japanese did not disappoint. They were expert at night attacks, with a robust playbook of tactics. A little before sunset, one or more snoopers—usually Betty torpedo bombers—would trail the American formation just out of range, radioing the ships' position to their squadronmates ashore. When darkness fell, the snoopers dropped a string of float lights marking the direction the ships were traveling. When the striking planes arrived, the snoopers flew over the fleet at high altitude, dropping parachute flares to illuminate the ships for torpedo attacks. Getting spotlighted or backlit by brilliant flares produced a profound sense of vulnerability even among the most grizzled sailors. Capt. William Tomlinson, who commanded the Moo's sister ship *Belleau Wood*, likened it to one of his recurring bad dreams where he was naked in a bathtub under the bright lights of Times Square—except in this case it was real.

Sure enough, a Japanese snooper shadowed the force in the late afternoon, and as Clark had warned, after dark it guided in the Bettys that the day's strike had missed. Starting at 7 p.m. and continuing for the next six hours, *Cowpens* and the fleet were under almost continual attack, with small groups of one to four bombers at a time trying to break through the outer edges of the formation to torpedo the carriers at the center. When the Bettys were not attacking, they were circling or ganging up for a fresh strike, so that bogeys were constantly on US radar screens. The moon was dangerously bright, and sailors aboard the Moo could easily see the formation of ships around them, illuminated further by the fiery, hissing parachute flares that descended from high above.

Tracking the bogeys on radar, Pownall ordered frequent and sometimes radical changes of course to throw off the Japanese and present them the least favorable angle for a torpedo attack. While the maneuvering frustrated most attacks, there were many close calls. One of the Moo's flight deck firefighters, George McIntyre, described how the water was "lousy with torpedoes."[12] One passed just astern of *Cowpens*, while *Yorktown* had two near misses of her own. *Lexington* was not as lucky, and took a torpedo to the stern, wrecking her steering gear and killing nine.

Just before 11 p.m., the enemy started to come in with more determination, and Admiral Pownall signaled his ships, ANYONE WITH A GOOD SETUP LET 'EM HAVE IT![13] Aboard the Moo, those topside watched the fireworks as the task group's outer cordon of ships lit up the sky with muzzle flashes, orange tracers, and the bright flares of hit and burning Japanese planes. *Cowpens* and the other CVLs—unlike the larger ships in the fleet—had no radar-guided guns, and so to avoid giving away her position at night she usually did not fire unless the target was brightly illuminated and at close range. The crew, watching the action from the center of the fleet's battle formation, quipped that what the Moo needed was a big neon arrow on the flight deck with the words: "The big carriers are over there."[14]

The Japanese planes withdrew just before 1:30 a.m. as the moon set, and soon after the task force's radar scopes were clear of enemy aircraft. Pownall signaled to the fleet: CONSIDER PRESENT EMERGENCY OVER. ALL HANDS RELAX AND BE READY TO GO FIRST THING IN THE MORNING.[15] *Cowpens* had survived her first real determined enemy attack, and everyone was satisfied that they had successfully faced what the Japanese threw at them. But their survival did not translate into bravado; they had sweated out their close calls that evening, and they recognized how lucky they had been to escape unharmed. As sailor Robert Lee succinctly put it: "We were really scared and I am not ashamed to admit it. We all had the same thing running down our legs."[16]

By the next day, the task force was out of range of Kwajalein and the ship buried her dead from the landing accident. The weather was clear and warm, and all men not on duty assembled on the hangar deck on the forward elevator, with sunlight streaming through from the flight deck. The bodies were sewn up in weighted canvas bags and covered with American flags with the blue field of stars placed over the fallen's left shoulder. A Marine honor guard stood at attention. The men sang a hymn, and the chaplain, wearing his black vestments over his khaki officer's uniform, read the rite of Christian burial, which states in part: "Unto Almighty God we commend the soul of our brother departed, and we commit his body to the deep, in sure and certain hope of the resurrection unto eternal life, through our Lord, Jesus Christ, Amen."[17] The bugler sounded taps, and as he played the final notes, the pallbearers lifted one end of the planks holding the bodies. With an order to "Present Arms!" from the Marines, all hands snapped to a farewell salute as the remains slid out from under the flag at the opposite end into the passing sea. Volleys of rifle fire from the Marines offered the final tribute. Sam Sommers described the ceremony as "quick, final, and moving,"[18] while George Terrell, who was one of the pallbearers, described how the mood aboard ship that evening was somber.

On the long cruise back home to Hawaii, *Cowpens'* pilots vented their frustration over the string of second-tier assignments and missed opportunities—although their contributions to GALVANIC hadn't gone entirely unrecognized. Captain McConnell's hard work and persistence in hammering his ship into fighting form was paying off, and he received the first uncaveated praise in his new command. In a performance evaluation dated December 31, Vice Adm. John Towers wrote of McConnell, "USS *Cowpens* has been well handled and has proven herself an effective unit of the task force, to the great credit of her commanding officer. I consider Captain McConnell a very good carrier commander who will continue to improve as he gains experience. His personal and military character are exemplary."[19] In turn, McConnell nominated Bob Price both for promotion to lieutenant commander and for the Navy Cross for his leadership at Wake. McConnell had grown to rely on Price, who in turn developed a great respect for his commanding officer. True to form, the humble Price kept his expectations low that either nomination would be realized. Price remarked to his wife it was only "scuttlebutt as far as I'm concerned until somebody pins the oak leaves on."[20]

CHAPTER 11

Passing the Hours

It is often said that war is long periods of boredom interspersed by moments of sheer terror. This was certainly true aboard the Moo, especially early in her career, when her days in combat were a minority of her total days at sea. During this time, there were watches to stand, patrols to fly, and all the endless routine work needed to keep a ship functioning. It was during these long periods—such as the seven-day cruise back from the Marshalls to Pearl Harbor—that the monotony was the most numbing, and the crew began to feel like it was not living multiple days, but a single day multiple times.

With the days seemingly repeating without end or variation, the ship's complement of officers and men found ways to try and pass their off-duty hours. Recreation was largely self-supplied and often dependent on the skills and interests of those who were stationed aboard. In addition to endless bull sessions about the war, the Moo's next target, and women, card games and gambling were popular, as well as reading books and magazines. There was also the occasional movie, music, and exercise or athletics.

Movies were the great escape for the Depression generation, but aboard ship conditions were less than ideal for cinema. Although in port movies were shown on the hangar deck, at sea the enlisted men saw films in their mess and the officers in their wardroom. Neither was air-conditioned, and when the ship was buttoned up to maintain light discipline the heat was stifling with all the bodies packed inside. Moreover, while at sea replacement films were hard to come by. The men saw the same movies over and over, and soon knew every line just as well as the actors on screen. Carswell Wynne said that the endless repetition took a toll, and that they saw the same few films "so many times we almost couldn't bear to see them anymore."

Although officially forbidden, gambling was widespread in the fleet and commanders often turned a blind eye to the practice. One young Marine described how he was in a makeshift bar in New Caledonia watching a craps game when Admiral Halsey and his entourage walked in. Halsey dressed down everyone in attendance for gambling in defiance of regulations, and then he pulled a $20 bill from his wallet and joined the game. The history of Torpedo Squadron 50, the ship's last Avenger squadron, detailed how all hands aboard *Cowpens* hid the gambling that everyone knew was going on. The enlisted men played their poker games out of sight of the officers, who purposely avoided finding them because they had their own games that they were trying to conceal from the executive officer. Naturally, everyone suspected the XO had poker games of his own and wondered where they might be.

Ed Haley described how the dinner tables in the officers' wardroom and the squadrons' ready rooms (the latter had the added benefit of being air-conditioned) were the natural venue for the officers' card games. Almost every night there were a couple of poker games going on, plus bridge, acey-deucy, and gin rummy. He and his roommate Willie Reed "settled into a marathon game of gin rummy and at one time I think I owed him somewhere in the neighborhood of $1,500; some months later he owed me. That's how much of our spare time was spent playing cards as we travelled over the vast ocean west of Hawaii."[1] But these were friendly and just intended to pass the time, and they agreed to just waive the balance when they got home.

Not all of the games were as good-natured, and some squadrons discovered that the Pacific was shark-infested in more ways than one. Poker was serious business for Air Group 50 while they were traveling from San Diego to Hawaii to join the *Cowpens* for the first time in mid-1945. The fighter pilots considerably lightened the wallets of both the air group commander and the torpedo squadron's administrative officer. Of the torpedo squadron, only its Texas cow roper, John "Pecos" Atkins, managed to uphold their collective honor and come out ahead. The officers never knew how their enlisted aircrewmen fared, but it was rumored "that one of our radiomen banked his wallet to over-flowing in the games back aft."[2]

Reading was another popular form of entertainment. The most immediately available source of reading material was the ship's newspaper, naturally entitled the *Mighty Moo*. More of a pamphlet than a full-size paper, it was a combination of shipboard news, inspirational talk from the chaplain, sophomoric jokes and cartoons, and pin-up girls. In addition to the ship's newspaper, paperbacks were also commonly available. During the war, a coalition of publishers gave away nearly 122 million paperbacks as Armed Services Editions. There were more than 1,300 titles in all, each in a compact form designed to fit into a cargo pocket or backpack. The campaign was a huge success, and the books, reported one serviceman, "were as popular as pin-up girls."[3]

Passed from hand to hand between servicemen, they were read and reread until they were tired and dog-eared. They ran the gamut in terms of subject matter: American classics, westerns, mysteries, collections of poems, or serious history. Some books, such as F. Scott Fitzgerald's *The Great Gatsby* or Betty Smith's coming-of-age novel *A Tree Grows in Brooklyn*, found their first real audience and success in these servicemen's editions. Bob Price wrote home to his wife about his reading habits, noting, "I'm doing quite a lot of reading now and there appears to be enough material on board so that I can keep well occupied for a long time to come."[4] Price worked his way through *The Robe*, a 1942 novel about the crucifixion of Jesus, and *The Disputed Passage*, a 1939 medical romance-drama set in wartime China. But he especially enjoyed *30 Seconds Over Tokyo*, a serialization of Jimmy Doolittle's 1942 bombing raid on the Japanese capital. Noting that he had read the first two installments and was on the lookout for the third, Price wrote that "I just gave it to Brownie and the rest of the boys to read because I think it's pretty swell."[5]

The most popular books aboard were the most risqué. One favorite that made its way through the ship was *Forever Amber*, a 1944 historical romance set in seventeenth-century England. Although on the surface an odd choice for servicemen, the mammoth book—it was 972 pages as originally published—was the first of the "bodice ripper" style of trashy popular novels, a distinction that got it banned in fourteen states as pornography and condemned by the Catholic Church. Naturally, that only helped the book become one of the bestselling novels of the 1940s. In listing his reasons for banning the book, the Massachusetts attorney general—who apparently gave it a very close reading—counted 70 references to sexual intercourse, 39 illegitimate pregnancies, 7 abortions, 10 descriptions of women undressing in front of men, and more descriptions of bosoms and other portions of the female anatomy than he could count. Other favorites aboard ship included *The G-String Murders* by famed burlesque dancer Gypsy Rose Lee. In that book, Lee cast herself as the detective investigating the deaths of several dancers in her troupe who were strangled with their own thongs. The men aboard appreciated its witty dialogue as well as the vivid descriptions of life in a burlesque show. Finally, and perhaps most relevant to the pilots, there was Frederic Wakeman's *Shore Leave*, a semibiographical account of aviators filling their leave in San Francisco with heavy drinking and freewheeling sex. Bob Price wrote to his wife about the book, describing the buzz among his men about it—and jokingly suggested she give the novel to his mother-in-law just to scandalize her. "Why don't you let your mother read it? I'd sure like to watch her face as she did!"[6]

Shifting from the profane to the sacred, the Navy also made sure the sailors had the opportunity for religious services. Over the course of its wartime service, the Moo had two chaplains aboard, both Catholic priests. While little information is available about the first, the second, Lt. Ralph Handran, arrived in March 1944. Handran was a colorful character, a self-described "crotchety old buzzard" whose salty, down-to-earth style worked well with officers and men alike.[7] Handran inherited a desire to serve at sea from his father, the captain of a tramp steamer. He quit his assignment at Villanova University to join the Navy in 1943, and he described his time aboard *Cowpens* as the highlight of his career. Handran wrote that in general he found an amazing response to religious services aboard ship, though he conceded that was perhaps in part because the men "had no place else to go."[8]

Usually services were held in one of the enlisted messes, where the noises from a ship at sea were more subdued, but at anchor the faithful often assembled on the hangar deck. For Catholic Mass, Handran did everything: He preached, led prayers, and played a wheezy waist-high organ scrounged from the wreckage of the Japanese garrison at Kwajalein. He also oversaw services for other faiths. The Protestant services included hymns, prayer, and Bible readings, and Handran made sure to find a chaplain to lead them whenever the ship was in port. He also arranged a Jewish service on Friday nights, but relied on the attendees to lead it, as his Hebrew was poor. There were also a handful of Mormons aboard, and their services were led by an elder in the church who worked on the flight deck.

No matter the denomination, attendance usually increased in advance of missions; Chaplain Handran reported that "constant danger makes us a good church-going ship and the men are not ashamed to pray."[9] While many aboard credited Handran for successfully easing their nervousness in advance of combat, in their view the chaplain's most important duty was securing the ship's protection with the Almighty. Handran relayed how in advance of each combat operation the officers and men urged him to "get to work on this one," and afterward credited him for "coming through." Although the spiritual authority aboard ship, Handran was humble about his pull with the Lord, saying that the "amazing good fortune of the ship is, surprisingly enough, sometimes attributed to a watchful Providence."[10]

Music also helped sustain morale aboard ship, and both officers and men indulged in it every chance they could. One source of music was Radio Tokyo, and sailors knew its variety of English-speaking female announcers by a single name: Tokyo Rose. She played popular American music leavened with often ludicrous propaganda. The selection was better than any comparable US program, so the crew listened in without taking her narrative seriously; often the Japanese were hilariously off base on US culture and geographic distinctions. Daly remembered listening to a broadcast with "two Japs who were supposed to be from Brooklyn, talking about their 'pappy.' We all knew she was full of shit, but she did play good music."[11]

The Moo often had a big band drawn entirely from members of her complement. It came out to play for special events, when the ship was in port, or sometimes even when the Moo refueled from an oiler, serenading the men hauling lines. Fighter pilot Raffles Raffman led the first iteration of the band starting in mid-1943, playing alto sax and writing and arranging all their numbers. After his arrival in March 1944, Chaplain Handran took up the job. He was an accomplished musician with a master's degree in music from Catholic University, and had helped manage Villanova University's band. Aboard the Moo, his musicians included a former Artie Shaw guitarist, a trumpeter who had his own big band on the East Coast, and a top-ranking college pianist. Departures of personnel from the Raffman era left them in need of a bass and some trombones, however. Recorded music was almost as welcome as live; many officers aboard had record players that they kept playing to set the soundtrack for their downtime. On slow days Father Handran connected his Victrola to the ship's loudspeaker and hosted impromptu concerts. Torpedo Squadron 50 went so far as to haul their own jukebox aboard in mid-1945, placing it right outside their ready room. The pilots contributed three hundred records, enough to keep the music selection from getting stale. "It was nothing unusual to hear it playing from early morning until late at night," the squadron history noted, and "everything was available, cowboy, jazz, swing, classical, piano recitals, or Harry James trumpet."[12]

Men smoked and sometimes drank to relieve the boredom and stress. Most American men at the time were smokers, and packs of cigarettes were available in the ship's store for sixty cents a carton. Most warships only carried a single brand, and the Moo was a Camel ship. "Everybody aboard seemed to smoke Camels," recalled Sam Sommers. "You couldn't give a carton of Luckys or Chesterfields away."[13] In addition to imposing segregation, Navy Secretary Josephus Daniels banned alcohol in the Navy in 1914—and nearly thirty years later, bluejackets still cursed him as a self-righteous Puritan.[14] There was an exception for medical alcohol, which the ship's flight surgeon kept under lock and key. Across the fleet, flight surgeons typically dispensed a shot of liquor, usually brandy or bourbon, after combat missions to calm pilots' nerves. This allegedly medical alcohol often made other appearances, such as on pilots' birthdays or other holidays, making the flight surgeon one of the most popular men aboard ship.

Enforcement of the ban against alcohol eroded over time, and most ships had some kind of arrangement for obtaining libations for the officers, which aboard the *Cowpens* was a cost-sharing pool conducted with the full knowledge of the captain and executive officer. Each bought a share with prices based on rank; Captain McConnell paid $100, while the ensigns and lieutenants paid $30 and $40, respectively. Participation wasn't mandatory, but Sam Sommers observed that "if you hadn't bought in you'd have been thought curiously square."[15] Each share bought thirty fifths of your poison of choice, issued only one bottle at a time, and only when the officers were going ashore on liberty. The rules were intended to keep alcohol out of reach when the ship was at sea, but no one could drink a whole fifth in a single day ashore. Ed Haley described how this arrangement suited everyone, as "we always managed to smuggle a fifth back aboard and kept one available in our desk safe for an emergency... [and] we did have an emergency now and then."[16]

As for the source of supply, rumor had it that someone aboard the Moo was connected to the Schenley Distilling Corporation in New York, which wanted to support the morale of the nation's fighting men. One day while the Moo was preparing to leave Philadelphia, six of the torpedo squadron's Avengers flew to New York "off the books," loaded their bomb bays with wooden cases filled with bottles, and flew home. Sam Sommers described how armed Marines guarded the pile of boxes—30 feet by 8 and 5 high—on the hangar deck until it was secured in locked storage rooms belowdecks.

Alcohol was harder to come by for the bluejackets. There was a prewar cartoon of a sailor unimpressed with a hobbyist putting a ship into a bottle, saying: "That's nothing. Ever try getting a bottle into a ship?"[17] While the enlisted were theoretically dry at sea, the Moo carried a supply of beer for beach parties and special occasions. But beer was not the only alcohol available, and *Cowpens* sailor John Ingraham described how down in the belly of the ship "there was always somebody trying to ferment something."[18] One common home brew among the sailors was raisin jack, made from yeast and raisins. After ten days fermenting in the South Pacific sun it was a tolerable moonshine.[19] Moreover, the ship's rarely used Mark 13 aerial torpedoes were fueled with seventeen pounds of 180-proof grain alcohol. This torpedo juice could not be drunk straight from the source, but had to be filtered or distilled to separate it from the croton oil the Navy had spiked it with to make it indigestible. One of the Moo's shipfitters, Robert Boyd Riley, described how this filtered hooch, if cut with orange juice, made "a damn good highball."[20] Riley was transferred off the ship due to recurring stomach problems, perhaps the cumulative effect of this industrial-strength alcohol on his digestive tract.

Exercise and sports were another way to pass the long days at sea or in port at remote atolls. Throughout much of the war, there were dumbbells and bench presses on the hangar deck, but in 1945 the ship's executive officer, Cmdr. Frederick Brush—a notorious disciplinarian—declared them "excess weight" and had them thrown overboard, infuriating Art Daly. Both Bob Price and VF-6 commander George Bullard required their pilots assemble for calisthenics on the flight deck, although Price's preference for early mornings generated a great deal of grumbling among his men. George Bullard, in contrast, got his pilots out in the afternoon to toss around a heavy medicine ball. Herschel Pahl usually came back limping from these workouts; his back still hurt from his midair collision off Maui, but he didn't dare tell Bullard about it for fear he would be sent ashore.

The capabilities of the Moo's organized sports teams ebbed and flowed with the talents of the men aboard. The Moo had its own basketball league, which played in the ship's aircraft elevator—and late in the war their matches against other ships benefitted from the help of Lt. John Dick, who was a member of the University of Oregon's 1939 national championship team. There were occasional boxing matches, although VF-46's Ens. Pete Kooyenga had a hard time finding someone to get into the ring with him. He was Chicago's heavyweight contender in the 1939 Golden Gloves Tournament.

The ship's two later air groups, 46 and 50, had excellent baseball teams for both officers and enlisted men. The VF-46 squadron history noted that the skills common among fighter pilots—coordination and timing—are helpful in baseball, and that the squadron "more than held [its] own in the Atlantic Coast league and later in the South Pacific League."[21] In addition to the amateur talent in the squadron, VT-50's executive officer, Skip Connors, played A-League professional baseball before the war and "caused his opponents a lot of trouble with his fast, shrewd ball handling."[22] Other sports came and went: tennis, badminton, and even wrestling. One writer for the ship's newspaper felt sufficiently insulted by criticism of his writing that he issued a challenge: "For a derogatory remark directed at this column . . . a wrestling match with the loser to apologize for the aforementioned slur!"[23]

Interlude and Pearl Harbor

Cowpens returned to Pearl, where she remained until mid-January 1944, giving all hands nearly a month of light duty and shore leave punctuated by occasional short training forays to sea. Captain McConnell had often served as ship's morale officer in previous assignments and knew that Christmas was a hard time to be away from home and family, especially for a green crew such as his. Homesickness and separation from loved ones was a recurring theme in many of the holiday songs of the era. For example, in 1943, Bing Crosby's "I'll Be Home for Christmas" wistfully promised, "Christmas Eve will find me / Where the love light gleams / I'll be home for Christmas / If only in my dreams." The song went on to be a number three hit in the United States and the most requested song at Christmas USO shows—although the BBC banned it because they feared it might lower British troops' morale. Similarly, Judy Garland's 1944 hit, "Have Yourself a Merry Little Christmas," was featured in the movie *Meet Me in St. Louis*, where she sang: "Someday soon we all will be together / If the fates allow / Until then we'll have to muddle through somehow."

(Frank Sinatra made the lyrics more cheerful in a 1957 version that is now a Christmas staple.)

Mindful that his men might be pining for home, McConnell made sure that the Moo's Christmas festivities did not disappoint. It was a full-day event including dinner with all the trimmings and then a USO show on the hangar deck. There was also a series of shipboard competitions, including a treasure hunt, a quiz, and a song contest. Sailor Robert Lee represented his division in the ship's pie-eating competition. "I guess I looked like I had the biggest mouth and stomach but I only came in third," Lee recalled. "There were bigger mouths and stomachs in the contest than mine...anyway, the party was a grand success."[24]

For the pilots, the biggest thrill was receiving a backlog of several weeks' mail, which was waiting for them ashore. Price wrote on December 11 that they "all found our letters and packages piled in our quarters when we arrived and couldn't resist the temptation of opening them. As you can imagine it was quite an evening. After having undergone a period of about a month with no mail, it was really a treat that has no close equal."[25] Despite the merriment, Price grappled with his own dose of homesickness. Writing home on Christmas Day, he mused to his wife that "little did I expect last year at this time that I'd be spending the day in this particular spot, although I guess we both realized that our chances of being together were pretty slim. This actually doesn't seem like Christmas at all...I wonder how many service men have said or are saying the same thing. I'm quite sure now—there is only one Christmas and that is the time when we can all be together again."[26]

Mail Call: A Double-Edged Sword

Nothing more directly affected sailors' morale than mail, or the lack thereof. Written correspondence was the primary way to stay in touch with home, and one veteran described how the simplest of letters could make all the difference for sailors' psychological well-being. "Everything you've ever read about mail or seen in the movies is absolutely true. It was crucial for good morale...A letter could make your day. It didn't have to be much of one; maybe just some chit-chat from someone you loved or a friend from home. It would lift your spirits."[27] In the best-case scenario, letters took about three weeks to get from the United States to the Moo. But conditions were rarely best case, and when the ship was at sea, deliveries were erratic, and most commonly letters were just forwarded to the ship's next port of call. The result was sometimes long periods of no mail at all, followed by a deluge of letters—exerting a roller-coaster effect on morale. The same was true for outbound mail; opportunities to send letters were often limited to those times when the ship was in port or near one. Outgoing letters also had to pass the censor's review to make sure they did not disclose any operationally sensitive information.

The irregular mail service was sometimes a frustration to those at home as much as those on board. In March 1944, Captain McConnell fielded a letter from a sailor's wife complaining that she did not receive regular correspondence from her husband. Only McConnell's response survives, so it is not clear whether she blamed the Navy mail system, the captain, or her husband. In his response, McConnell patiently explained how mail service to the ship had been irregular for months, and that opportunities to send a letter were few and far between. McConnell made sure to personally look into it, and the closing paragraph of his response identified the real source of the problem:

Your husband admits to a certain amount of negligence in anticipating outgoing mails and also to a certain amount of laziness about writing. For that I hope you will forgive him. He really does appreciate you, and now that his thoughtlessness has been pointed out to him you may expect to receive mail a little more frequently. Very truly yours, R.P. McConnell, Captain, US Navy.

In addition to letters, the sailors often received packages from home, and books or magazines to help vary the available reading on board were especially welcome. It took far longer for packages to arrive than letters, and so food from home was usually stale and moldy by the time it arrived. The ship's newspaper in September 1944 pointed out that "from the smell of things, the forty-odd sacks of second class US mail recently received, someone is importing cheese. In fact we suspect pre-war stuff."[28] Another problem with packages was that the Navy searched them for contraband. One crewman, Frank Martinich, told his mother that while he appreciated her sending him cookies, candy bars, and gum, she should not bother doing so. "By the time I get it, [the Navy] had gone through so much trouble finding out what's in there it looks like a bunch of rats got at the box."[29]

The Replacement Pilots—Ed Haley Smushes His Hellcat

VF-6's days aboard the Moo came to a close, and its pilots departed *Cowpens* for the carrier *Intrepid*. With VF-6 gone, the Navy needed a dozen replacement pilots to fill out the Moo's complement of fighters. One of these pilots was Ens. Ed Haley, who had finished his training and made his way to Pearl Harbor. He was eager to join the squadron and recalled how VF-25 commander Bob Price and his executive officer, Gaylord Brown, "were very friendly and welcomed us like family…It gave us a warm home-like feeling right from the start."[30] Privately, Brown was frustrated with what the Navy dumped on them. He grumbled that VF-25 got "12 brand new pilots and 12 beat up old F6Fs. We would have preferred it the other way around."[31] In contrast, Price put a characteristically positive spin on the situation, writing on December 15 that "everything is going along nicely and we are taking it easy for a bit. The next few days will see us quite involved, however, we've just received a flock of new boys and lost some old ones to another outfit so we've got a lot of work on our hands."[32]

The amount of work the replacements needed became clear during a three-day training cruise. On the first day, three of *Cowpens'* replacement pilots, including Haley, crashed their Hellcats on deck attempting to land. Their inexperience was certainly the largest factor in the accident, but fireman George McIntryre, watching from the catwalk, also thought that anxiousness to make a good showing was a contributing factor.[33] Although Haley was eager to nail his landing, his primary problem was his small size. The diminutive Haley—who soon earned the nickname "Stump"—sat low enough in the cockpit that he lost sight of the landing signals officer (LSO) under the nose of his aircraft on final approach. He poured on the power and tried to wave off, but caught a wire anyway— and after briefly taking flight, the arresting gear slammed Haley's Hellcat back down onto the port catwalk. His propeller chopped into the deck, killing the engine, and one of his landing gear struts partially collapsed. Haley was stunned by the impact, while his aircraft "hung teetering over the port side, pretty well smushed."[34] After one of the deckhands helped him from the plane, Haley watched in shame as a deck tractor pushed his damaged Hellcat over the side. Haley was beside himself with embarrassment, thinking he hadn't been in combat yet and had already lost a plane.

Lt. R. P. McDonald, the ship's LSO, had seen this problem before and recommended that Haley stick his head out of the left side of the canopy on final approach so he could keep the LSO in view. The solution worked—Haley was soon back in the air and over the course of the day made six successful landings using that technique. That being said, Haley did not escape ribbing from his shipmates. McDonald later joked with Haley that his head-out-the-window technique reminded him of a railroad engineer, and he always knew when Stump was on approach because there was always a white blob hanging out of the left side of the cockpit.[35]

Cowpens made two more such brief training cruises, from December 29 to January 2, 1944, and again from January 10 to 14. McConnell knew the crew would bellyache about missing New Year's Eve parties in Honolulu, but his green replacement pilots desperately needed some training time. During one of these short cruises, Ens. Wilbur "Steve" Steven disappeared after takeoff on a predawn flight. Steven was one of the original fifteen VF-25 pilots who joined the squadron at Willow Grove; his friends never learned whether he was lost due to mechanical failure, vertigo, or some other cause. McConnell kept the ship at sea on New Year's Day to search for him, without success. Steve, noted the squadron history, "is sorely missed."[36]

Steven was not the only loss over *Cowpens'* break in Hawaii. The combination of the burdens of command and his hard-drinking lifestyle proved too much for Mark Grant. He was relieved from duty in early January and sent to a hospital ashore. This left Bob Price again in charge of the air group, while command of VT-25 passed to the squadron's executive officer, Dick Cottingham. Initially in letters home, Price was unwilling to criticize his commanding officer, describing Grant's problems as nothing serious, "just run down, a bad cold, and in need of a good long rest." Some days later, when Price received his orders as *Cowpens'* air group commander, Price allowed himself a rare bit of criticism of his friend. Grant's struggles with "demon rum" contributed to his worn-out condition, Price wrote, and he hoped Grant's reassignment home and a long period of recovery would provide the opportunity for a fresh start.[37]

CHAPTER 12

Strikes in the Marshall Islands

All good things come to an end, and by early January the Moo's time at anchor was growing short. There were many rumors about her imminent return to the war, as the signs of her departure were impossible to ignore. Repair parties were working overtime, while Captain McConnell had those sailors not on liberty loading stores and ammunition. The Moo fueled for the outbound voyage, taking on more than 235,000 gallons of bunker oil and almost 30,000 gallons of aviation fuel. Soon, the ship's official history noted, *Cowpens* was "ready to take the next steps on the long road to Tokyo."[1]

The scuttlebutt was right: The fleet was scheduled to depart for an ambitious operation in the Marshall Islands. Nimitz's plan was to strike deep into the heart of that island chain and take the Japanese base at Kwajalein. Time was of the essence; the December raid had spotted an additional bomber base under construction there, while intercepted Japanese radio chatter indicated that the Japanese had neglected its defense in favor of other islands in the Marshalls. Accordingly, Nimitz concluded there was an opportunity to take Kwajalein before the Japanese corrected their mistake.

In charge of the operation were two men who would lead the Navy to great success in 1944—Vice Admirals Raymond Spruance, commanding Fifth Fleet; and Marc "Pete" Mitscher, commanding its carriers, known as Task Force 58. Spruance, the man behind the victory at Midway in 1942, was widely regarded as one of the brightest officers in the US Navy.

He was rational and methodical, a meticulous planner with a steely composure. Spruance managed naval combat as an analytical exercise, saying "that making war is a game that requires cold and careful calculation. It might be a very serious thing if we turned the wrong way, just once."[2] He was spartan, modest, and cautious—almost monkish in temperament. He was careful with his fitness and diet, equating physical fitness with mental acuity. He never smoked, rarely drank, and made sure to exercise every day and get a full night's sleep. Moreover, he avoided publicity, and after once making the cover of *Time* magazine—which dubbed him "the mechanical man"—Spruance put his copy facedown in his quarters and never looked at it.

Mitscher was bald, slender, and wrinkled, with a leathery face that he often hid under a long-brimmed cap while at sea. He had decades of experience with aviation, and looked far older than his fifty-seven years—his friends joked that he "didn't look a day over 80."[3] His voice was often barely above a whisper, leaving his staff to interpret the substance of his mumblings from the variation in the scowl upon his face. A fellow admiral once described him as "one of the few men I've known who could give an order with a glance."[4] Mitscher was a fighter, a seeming contradiction to his soft-spoken nature—what his biographer called a man "who had a Sunday punch in each hand and knew it, and was willing to take a blow to get in two."[5] He was also a natural leader who routinely got the most out of his men. He fostered a culture of competitive performance among his carrier commanders, telling them what he wanted, but giving them the space to figure out how best to accomplish it.

Cowpens Enters the Realm of Neptunus Rex, Ruler of the Raging Main

Cowpens cast off on January 16 with the rest of Task Force 58. After the disappointments of the past few operations, the pilots were hopeful for "a big show and plenty of Jap opposition."[6] This was the last time the Moo was based from Hawaii, which given the Pacific Fleet's westward advance was now too far from the front lines. Price, like many others, made sure to get his latest batch of letters to his wife in the mail before the ship sailed—describing their departure in the broadest of terms to avoid the censors. "A few things have come about," he wrote, "which will probably mean this will be my last real letter for awhile."[7] Across the ship, there were all the usual jitters about a return to combat, particularly given the Moo's close calls in GALVANIC. "The Gilberts had been rough," wrote Art Daly. "We wondered what the Marshalls would be like."[8]

The Moo's southbound course put her across the equator for the first time some seventy miles west of Baker Island on January 22, an occasion that the ship marked with a line-crossing ceremony. In this centuries-old tradition, sailors who have never crossed the equator before—known as pollywogs—are initiated into the "Ancient Order of the Deep" by their more experienced colleagues, known as shellbacks. Filled with farcical ritual, harmless pranks, and old-fashioned hazing, the festivities were a welcome distraction from daily routines and worries about the upcoming operation. In the days before the ceremony, the crew had received occasional warnings from the ship's loudspeaker system: "Beware all you pollywogs!"[9] On the nineteenth they received a legal summons from King Neptune himself, warning the *Cowpens* was approaching his royal domain:

Whereas the good ship USS *Cowpens* is bound southward for parts unknown...and is about to enter our domain...and the aforementioned ship carries a large and slimy cargo of landlubbers, beachcombers, sea lawyers, hay tossers, and all other living creatures of the land, and last but not least he-vamps and liberty hounds masquerading as seamen...be it known that we hereby summon and command you to appear before the Royal Court...disobey this summons under pain of our swift and terrible displeasure. Our vigilance is ever wakeful and our vengeance is swift and sure...[signed] Davy Jones, Royal Scribe, and Neptunus Rex, Ruler of the Raging Main.[10]

In advance of King Neptune's arrival, his shellbacks relieved Captain McConnell in a bloodless coup and took command of the ship. The air group's senior officers were forced to serve lunch in the enlisted men's mess, while many of the junior officers were assigned meaningless tasks, such as calling the bridge every five minutes to report on temperature. For his part, newly arrived pilot Ed Haley was stationed on the forecastle with a pair of beer bottles for binoculars and ordered to scan the horizon for the Royal Party.

Streaming seawater and festooned with seaweed, Neptune and his Royal Court—all of whom bore a suspicious resemblance to several of the Moo's saltiest chief petty officers—planted themselves on the flight deck and bid the lowly pollywogs to do them homage. A group of Royal Bailiffs rounded up the pollywogs and herded them to the flight deck. Some did not go quietly; Art Daly and some cohorts ambushed several shellbacks in advance of being dragooned, engaging in a bare-fisted skirmish with officer and enlisted alike. There was nearly a large brawl on the fantail between the two groups before a passing officer warned them to knock it off. In another instance, some mutinous pollywogs roughed up a couple of Neptune's royal cops, and shellback reinforcements restored order by spraying down the melee with fire hoses.

George Terrell described how the pollywogs were rounded up and then led single file up to the flight deck by a group of shellbacks that he called the "Judas Battalion." Once there, "we were beaten to our knees with blivets by our merciless captors, formed into creeping columns," and, with further whacks with wooden paddles, encouraged to move forward."[11] With Captain McConnell watching the proceedings from the bridge with a bemused look upon his face, the pollywogs were force-marched to the Royal Court's red carpet. This was a target sleeve, a fabric tube thirty inches in diameter and thirty feet long, normally towed behind an airplane as target practice for the ship's gunners. Unfortunately, the pollywogs were not to walk on it, but crawl through it, and the sleeve had been loaded with stinking garbage and slop from the ship's galley for the occasion. With further encouragement from the paddles, the pollywogs dove headfirst into the sleeve and crawled through thirty feet of muck. "Do you know how fast you can move on your hands and knees?" wrote Terrell.

"Would you believe thirty feet in 15 seconds? Records were set and broken in rapid succession."[12]

Finally, the pollywogs were introduced to King Neptune and his entourage, bedecked in robes, wigs, and gold-painted cardboard crowns. The most colorful member of the court was the Royal Baby, a fat, balding, half-naked chief petty officer in a diaper and covered in axle grease. Each pollywog was forced to his knees in front of the baby, who took a handful of lubricating grease from a drum at his side and rubbed it all over his sweaty abdomen. Then came the order: "Kiss the baby's belly!" If the pollywog hesitated, a shellback bailiff delivered a whack to his backside. "I closed my mouth and eyes," recalled Sam Sommers. "I wish I could have held my nose."[13] Accepting the kiss as tribute, the Royal Baby haughtily waved on the pollywog, with his paddle-wielding bailiffs making sure he cleared out quickly to make room for the next victim.

The final stop was the Royal Barbers and their merciless clippers. Each pollywog ended up with a highly unconventional buzz cut that left his hair in tatters. "They were real artists," said Marine George Terrell. "A thousand haircuts to be given and no way were any two going to be alike."[14] Some sailors emerged with a Mohawk or bird's nest (bald on top, with a fringe around the bottom), but the barbers also sometimes amused themselves by spelling C-O-W-P-E-N-S or V-I-C-T-O-R-Y on successive heads. Sailor Robert Lee attempted to evade the royal clippers with a pre-emptive head shaving, but soon found out "it doesn't pay to be smarter than King Neptune. For punishment I had my head and body smeared with a combination of oil and eggs and had to stand on the bow of the ship for one hour in the sun. Did I have fun taking the oil and eggs off my head and body with cold salt water. I learned my lesson."[15]

A good time was had by all, more or less. Afterward, Bob Price described the mayhem in a letter home. "Fraternity initiations are nothing compared to what we went through...did you ever try to get a combination of raw eggs, graphite grease, and garbage out of your hair? Anyway I'm now a trusty shellback and sure happy I'm one of the clan."[16] Ed Haley enjoyed himself as well, but with a bruised backside from the shellback gauntlet it was painful sitting on his parachute for his three-hour CAP the following day. Similarly, Art Daly was unhappy about the abuse with the paddles. He grumbled to his journal that "this captain is bullshit."[17]

Return to Kwajalein: "Somebody Had to Watch the Back Door"

The initiation was a welcome break, but there were still some worries about the Moo's green replacement fliers as their first operation approached. "We have had some rough landings among the new pilots and are a bit concerned for them," explained the squadron history, "but everyone is anxious to get going."[18] The evening of the twenty-eighth, the Moo's pilots received their operational briefs for attacks the following day. *Cowpens* and Task Group 58.3 were scheduled to arrive off Kwajalein seventy-two hours before the landings to destroy aircraft and airfield facilities. The force would then shift to working over Eniwetok in the Western Marshalls to prevent the Japanese from bringing in reinforcement planes via that route. VF-25 drew the short straw, and its pilots again flew escort duty plus CAP. There was much bitching in the squadron ready room about the assignment; although Ed Haley was more stoic, noting, "Someone had to watch the back door."[19]

The Moo's task group launched several waves of attacks that day; the initial fighter sweep found no Japanese planes in the air, and follow-up waves of dive and torpedo bombers left the island a shambles, destroying scores of aircraft on the ground and ensuring that the airfield wasn't operable before the amphibious landing. The Moo's fighters escorted waves of bombers from other carriers to their targets, and then descended to cut up a small fuel lighter and two junks with almost ten thousand .50-caliber rounds. Upon returning to the ship, the pilots were upbeat about the overall lack of resistance. "Apparently we caught them flatfooted again," cheered the VF-25 squadron historian. "It's getting to be a habit!"[20]

Late in the day the Moo cleared out for Eniwetok in the Western Marshalls for strikes the next morning. The atoll's importance was its location as a midway point in the long chain of airfields connecting the Japanese home islands to their bases in the Central Pacific. Kwajalein was only 326 miles away, Saipan 1,017, and Truk 669, all well within range of the long-legged Betty bombers. There were many enemy planes on the airfield at Eniwetok, and the task group's job was to destroy them and wreck the airfield so it could not be used to attack the landing forces on Kwajalein, scheduled to arrive on January 31. A lack of intelligence on their target kept everyone on edge, and the pilots brooded that "nobody knows much about the place."[21]

Cowpens' green replacement pilots finally saw their first real action at Eniwetok. Twelve VF-25 Hellcats participated in the early morning fighter sweep over Engebi Island; their mission was to clear the way for the bombers, knocking down any aerial opposition and then destroying any aircraft on the ground. The squadron's veteran fliers took the news in stride, but the junior pilots were thrilled they were finally going into combat. Ed Haley described his reaction and those of his fellow replacements: "We were on cloud nine as we were finally going to see some real action!"[22] After the initial excitement faded, the jitters set in. Haley was likely not alone in sleeping poorly the night before the mission, and general quarters blared seemingly louder than normal at 4 a.m.

Soon, the entire flight was airborne and heading to Eniwetok right on schedule. It was a beautiful morning, and the initial broken clouds gave way to an excellent view of the string of sandy white islets strung like pearls in the sapphire sea. Despite the view, Ed Haley was a ball of nerves, and years after the fact described himself as maturing a great deal on the forty-minute flight to the target. "In those few minutes I shed all past thoughts of hoping the war would last long enough for me to get into action. I was in it for sure and now had to focus on doing the job for which I had been trained and not making any stupid mistakes."[23]

Haley needn't have worried; the mission was a success, with the pilots describing it afterward as "a good show."[24] The antiaircraft fire was manageable, conditions were ideal for strafing, and the pilots found two neat rows of Bettys lined up on the airfield. Over the course of twenty-five minutes, the pilots worked their way up the field setting many of them afire. Moreover, it was satisfying to see an aerial photo of the burned-out Bettys on the cover of *Life* magazine a few weeks later. Ed Haley's father wrote to him and asked if he had been involved in the attack. Haley responded that "I had a particular interest in the second Betty from the end of the runway shown in that picture."[25]

Air Group 25 made several return trips to Engebi over the next two days, but Japanese resistance quickly petered out. The Avengers continued their bombing of the runway and buildings, while the fighter pilots amused themselves with more strafing and looking for aircraft hidden in the coconut plantations nearby. By day three, *Cowpens'* pilots described the island as a "hell of a mess,"[26] while task group commander Ted Sherman noted that "everything above ground had been obliterated and the island looked like a desert waste."[27]

Sleepy Lagoon

With their work on Eniwetok complete, Task Force 58 pulled out for the nearby atoll of Majuro on February 2. After several days of operations, all hands enjoyed the interlude offered by routine air patrols and a refueling from oiler *Saugatuck*. Bob Price wrote home, trying to describe the welcome return of monotony: "The old days are more or less routine except they are a little more filled with time in the air—and I must say seem awfully short, which isn't bad at all. The only trouble is—as always—that the nights are too short and I find myself continually wishing for more sleep."[28]

Cowpens' crew was surprised on February 4 when the Moo and the rest of the fleet steamed in to Majuro Atoll and dropped anchor in the lagoon, only ninety to one hundred miles from Japanese-held bases at Mili, Maloelap, and Jaluit. It was a remarkably pretty place, untouched by fighting, with sparkling white beaches, swaying palm fronds, and gin-clear waters.[29] George Terrell described it as "a dreamy kind of tropical atmosphere. I think everybody spent the first night on deck drinking it all in. Imagine balmy breezes and the moon rising, silhouetting the palm trees against the sky."[30] Sailors quickly dubbed the idyllic atoll "Sleepy Lagoon" after the popular 1940 song of the same name. "A sleepy lagoon, a tropical moon, and two on an island," sang crooner Harry James. "A sleepy lagoon and two hearts in tune in some lullaby land..."

Aesthetic virtue notwithstanding, the Navy's interest in Majuro was entirely pragmatic. With Task Force 58 pushing ever westward into Japanese waters, the Navy needed a forward anchorage and supply depot. Launching offensives from Majuro rather than Pearl avoided the long cruise back to Hawaii to reprovision, giving the fleet more range and allowing them to stay on the attack for weeks at a time. Majuro was perfectly situated to serve as an operational hub, lying almost equidistant between Hawaii and the Japanese strongholds in the Marianas Islands. At 114 square miles, the lagoon was large enough for the entire task force, and with only a single channel in and out it was easily guarded against roving enemy submarines. Moreover, fuel and vital supplies could come directly from the US West Coast to Majuro; skipping Hawaii cut nearly two thousand miles out of the voyage. In the coming months, Task Force 58 often returned to Sleepy Lagoon between missions. "It was a perfect setup," wrote George McIntyre. "At twilight this evening there must be over 200 ships here and there is room for 200 more."[31]

Cowpens spent a pleasant week anchored at Majuro Atoll as plans for the next operation came together. All hands caught up on "sack drill" (missed sleep) and had the opportunity for some drinking and recreation on the beach. The bluejackets had their own party, with each man issued two beers; the sailors enjoyed sunbathing, playing sports, and swimming in the warm tropical waters. The *Cowpens* air group and ship's officers had a steak cookout ashore that was especially memorable. Most dipped into their stash of alcohol for the occasion; according to Ed Haley, "We had a ball and there were more than a few bombed out souls before the day was over." One of the ship's LSOs made his own landing attempt out of a palm tree and in the subsequent crash suffered a mess of cuts and scrapes on his face that lingered for weeks. "Everyone managed to survive," Haley recounted. "It was a good change of pace and a relaxing time."[32]

CHAPTER 13

Truk: Operation HAILSTONE

Her island interlude over, *Cowpens* hoisted anchor at Majuro late in the day on February 12. One by one, the Moo and three of the fleet's four task groups filed out of the narrow channel and spilled into the Pacific. The raid on Eniwetok had revealed the extent of the weakness of the Japanese defenses in the Marshalls. It was initially scheduled to be captured in May, but now US planners realized that it was vulnerable and its garrison was rapidly strengthening its defenses. Eniwetok, it seemed, was low-hanging fruit and might not stay that way if the United States waited to strike. The US already had the forces needed to stage an immediate landing, and the invasion, designated Operation CATCHPOLE, was pushed forward to February 17.

The problem was Truk, the Japanese stronghold approximately seven hundred miles to the west of Eniwetok in the Caroline Islands. It was the main southern anchorage of the Japanese Combined Fleet and the hub for aircraft ferry routes to Eniwetok and Rabaul; the latter was the major obstacle to General MacArthur's advance in New Guinea. As a result, its neutralization became a priority for both lines of US advance. Task Force 58 scheduled its attack against Truk to coincide with the Eniwetok landings; a raid there would both distract from CATCHPOLE and help gauge whether Truk could be bypassed or had to be captured.

The intelligence officers said Truk was pronounced "trook, as in spook," although the pilots called it "Truck."[1] Regardless of how you said it, the atoll was a very different type of island than the US had encountered before. Rather than a low-lying coral atoll of the type seen in the Gilberts and Marshalls, Truk was what eminent historian Samuel Eliot Morison—the author of the Navy's official history of the war—called "a drowned mountain range inside a coral ring."[2] A circular barrier reef approximately forty miles in diameter sheltered a calm, deep-water lagoon of approximately five hundred square miles—the best fleet anchorage in the Central Pacific. Within the reef were six large islands, the remnants of a large volcano—as well as seventy-eight smaller islets. Truk's natural geography was its best defense; there were only four easily guarded passages through the reef into the lagoon, and unless US warships ventured inside, the atoll's biggest islands were out of range of their guns.

In early 1944, the name Truk was an ominous one for naval pilots. Very little about it was known in the West, since the Japanese closed off their Pacific mandate territories to outsiders in 1920. Rampant speculation in the fleet only added to its sinister mystique. Rumor was that Amelia Earhart's disappearance in her attempted 1937 round-the-world flight was because she had been shot down trying to take pictures of Truk, or that prewar spies sent there disappeared without a trace. In the absence of real information, Truk developed a reputation as an impregnable island fortress—the "Gibraltar of the Pacific." Truk's reputation was so ominous that as word of their destination spread throughout the *Cowpens*, as the Moo's history described it, "almost immediately a feeling of apprehension spread throughout the ship."[3] With the understanding that the air group would bear the brunt of the risk for the Moo, Ed Haley noted that "many of the ship's officers got very respectful of us."[4]

HAILSTONE in Action

Task Force 58 arrived at its launching point some ninety miles from Truk Atoll just before dawn on February 17. The initial fighter sweep lifted off in the dark, and the seventy-two Hellcats crossed Truk's barrier reef at thirteen thousand feet just as dawn broke. By the time the Hellcats arrived, perhaps eighty Japanese fighters were airborne, and the melee that followed was the largest dogfight most of the American pilots had ever seen. Herschel Pahl, the former *Cowpens* VF-6 pilot now on *Intrepid*, described it as "a great scrap, more than a dogfight." Instead, he likened it to a "big cloud of bees all trying to shoot the tail off each other."[5] While the Japanese pilots were both aggressive and competent, the mismatch in numbers and element of surprise was too much for them to overcome. The fight quickly turned into a rout, and soon black smoke from the funeral pyres of downed Zekes dotted the lagoon.

The bombers moved in after the fighter sweep. Some air groups worked over the shore installations and airfields, while others went after the fifty or so cargo and auxiliary ships moored in the lagoon. *Cowpens* and Task Group 58.3 had as their targets the airfield on Moen Island. It was on the west side of a one-thousand-foot peak, and with the morning sun still low in the eastern sky, it was cloaked in shadow when the *Cowpens* aircraft arrived overhead. Despite the poor visibility, the Moo's aircraft and their friends from *Bunker Hill* wreaked havoc on a long line of closely parked planes under camouflage netting on the runway apron. As many as ten enemy planes were burning fiercely, and the entire field was covered with thick black smoke by the time the last *Cowpens* Avenger turned for home. As the bombers plastered the field, the Hellcats went after antiaircraft batteries in an effort to suppress the ground fire, facing what Gaylord Brown called the most intense flak he'd seen. He said Japanese batteries started firing at them just as his planes went into their attack runs at eighteen thousand feet, and kept shooting at them all the way down to 2,500 feet as they dropped their bombs and pulled away. Although several aircraft suffered hits—one Avenger was battered by eight probable 25mm rounds—all the Moo's planes landed safely back aboard.

Cowpens' fighters made a return trip to the atoll at midmorning, again with planes from *Bunker Hill*. The fighters stood guard on the bombers, who showered Eten airfield with bombs and then turned for home. The Moo's Avengers, flying separately, received instructions from the target director to pursue a light cruiser, *Naka*, spotted fleeing the battle twenty miles outside the barrier reef. *Naka*, which by chance had put to sea before the task force arrived, was capable of more than thirty-five knots and was a difficult target to hit. *Cowpens*' Avengers were the first to try their luck, but *Naka* wriggled away from their bombs, which fell more than one hundred feet wide. *Bunker Hill's* dive bombers fared no better; but in avoiding the falling bombs, *Naka* set herself up for a torpedo attack, and one of *Bunker Hill's* Avengers put a fish into her side while she was in a high-speed turn. The hit cast a ball of orange flame into the air, and the cruiser slowed to a crawl. Soon, she was afire, and a large oil slick pooled astern as she settled by the bow.

Some contemporary sources suggest that *Naka* sank after her torpedo hit that morning, but *Cowpens'* official account of the battle claims she was still afloat that afternoon and trying to limp back to Truk, trailing an extensive oil slick behind her. The Moo launched all nine of her Avengers to finish the job, and they peeled off one by one from twelve thousand feet on their bombing dives. Three struck home: Lt. (jg) Jim Douthit from Columbus, Georgia, scored a glancing miss, with his one-thousand-pound bomb bouncing off the hull on the starboard side and exploding alongside. Coming in close behind, Lt. Dave "Peeb" Peebles placed his bomb on *Naka's* aft gun turret, and the blast hurled fire and debris several hundred feet in the air. But it was Robert Wright, from Mobile, Alabama, who likely delivered the killing blow. His two-thousand-pounder struck the cruiser just aft of her third stack, engulfing much of the ship in fire and smoke. The cruiser was soon dead in the water as the Avengers circled overhead, her fires spreading from bow to stern. Japanese sailors scrambled into their lifeboats as their ship started going down. *Cowpens'* pilots were worried about their lack of fighter cover and did not stay to observe her final moments, but after their departure she broke up and sank, taking with her 240 of her 450-man crew.

Cowpens participated in the last strike of the day, placing delayed-action bombs on one of Truk's airfields. The bombs were set to explode at random times throughout the night, to make it difficult for the Japanese to repair their fields or organize an overnight strike on the task force. "It was a tough assignment," the pilots recalled. "A large cloud lay right over the field, and the Jap anti-aircraft had its aim calculated to a T. Every time one of our planes stuck its nose below the cloud the Japs would open up with everything they had."[6] The Hellcats managed to plant two of their three bombs on the runway, but antiaircraft fire found its mark. Lt. Relly "Raffles" Raffman's Hellcat was hit in the engine; he nursed it away from the atoll but could not make it home before it quit entirely. Raffles successfully ditched at sea some thirty-five miles from the task force; he only narrowly escaped the cockpit of his sinking plane and became momentarily tangled on its tail fin. He popped to the surface after swallowing a mouthful of seawater and green survival dye.

Raffman's wingmen reported his plight to the task force and within minutes an OS2U Kingfisher floatplane from the battleship *Massachusetts* took off to pick him up. Pilots typically dubbed any rescue seaplane a "Dumbo"—in honor of Disney's ungainly flying elephant—for their slow speed and awkward appearance, but the Kingfisher was an especially unlikely savior. The underpowered, two-seat floatplane was designed to serve as a spotter for naval gunfire from battleships and was pressed into service in the search-and-rescue role. The OS2U had little space to carry downed airmen, and usually the rescued pilot crammed into the back seat with the tail gunner. Moreover, the underpowered OS2U often struggled to take to the air again with the weight of an additional person on board. That being said, no downed pilot ever complained when an OS2U trundled over the horizon. Three of Raffles's wingmen circled overhead, dropping green dye packets to mark his position in the choppy sea for the incoming OS2U. The Dumbo, piloted by one Lt. Charles Ainsworth, made a beautiful landing in the rough sea and picked up Raffman. As described by the anxious *Cowpens* Hellcat pilots watching overhead, they "somehow got off again in that overloaded crate."[7] The squadrons' pilots were listening to the radio in the Moo's ready room as the rescue unfolded, and when they learned Raffles was safe everyone there "yelled like hell... as far as we are concerned, that pilot rates a Navy Cross."[8]

The last drama of the day came with the return of the day's last shift of CAP. The Moo's fighters had a good day providing air cover for Spruance's warships, bagging a Val dive bomber and a pair of Jake seaplanes. But they were released to return to the Moo well after dark and there was some white knuckles on the bridge and in the squadron ready room as the fighter pilots lined up for their approach. Five of the eight had never completed a night landing before, and the task force's radars were beginning to register Japanese snoopers out looking for the fleet. Captain McConnell feared that turning on the ship's landing lights to guide his pilots in could invite enemy attack. To make matters worse, turning into the wind to take the planes aboard put the Moo on a collision course with a coral reef some fifteen miles ahead. The endless hours of training that McConnell and Price had demanded of the air group paid off; all eight planes landed aboard safely, with the last one touching down just as the ship needed to turn to avoid the reef. It all went so smoothly that Admiral Hanson, commander of Task Group 58.3's battleship screen, signaled his congratulations. CAPTAIN MCCONNELL IT WAS A PLEASURE TO WATCH THE SKILL OF YOUR PILOTS LAND AFTER DARK X YOU HAVE A VERY SMOOTH WORKING OUTFIT XX GOOD LUCK.[9] After the long months of training and frequent criticism of his ship's performance, the praise must have been especially gratifying for Captain McConnell.

Cowpens, with her strike role completed, grudgingly returned to CAP and ASP duty on the second day while the task force conducted another two-hundred-aircraft strike. Smoke was still rising over the lagoon when the US aircraft returned, and no Japanese fighters rose to challenge them. The task force's pilots bagged a few additional targets that morning, including sinking two destroyers, but in many cases were just piling on damage inflicted the previous day. Spruance, aware that he had hit the point of diminishing returns, recalled his planes, and Task Force 58 set off for Majuro.

The importance of the victory at Truk was exaggerated by its fearsome reputation. The raid bolstered the confidence of the Moo's green air group and helped reassure them that they could take on any Japanese base with carrier airpower alone. Sailor Robert Lee related how the Moo's pilots had "really raised hell and had a field day" against surprisingly feeble opposition.[10] Moreover, HAILSTONE achieved its primary strategic objective, as Eniwetok's capture went off without a hitch. With its huge lagoon anchoring the US presence in the Western Marshalls, the American reach in the Pacific—as measured by the maximum range of search and carrier planes—was now 2,400 miles closer to Japan. Enemy strongholds such as the Marianas Islands and Palau were now within reach.

Another Enemy: Heat

After weeks of operations in the Central Pacific, the heat and humidity were making the already trying living conditions aboard ship even more difficult. The US Navy did not have a fully air-conditioned surface ship until 1949, and aboard the Moo only a handful of compartments had the benefit of climate control. For the rest of the ship, the bath-warm equatorial waters added to the heat emanating from the oil-fired boilers in her belly. In another one of New York Ship's design compromises, the air intakes for ventilation were inside the hangar deck, away from the cooling breezes topside. Even worse, during general quarters these vents were closed and all hatches dogged down to control fires or flooding.

Sleeping in these conditions was a challenge. With the ship buttoned up to maintain light discipline at night, ventilation was poor and it was hard to get any restful sleep. The hot, stagnant air made breathing difficult, and sailors often woke up in a pool of their own sweat. Crewman Ray Williams noted how the men in the compartment fought over the fan all night long. He described how "you'd wake up and move the fan so it would blow on you, and you would wake up two hours later, and it was pointed at some other direction."[11] Other sailors sought to improve airflow by cutting holes in the ducts, which improved their ventilation at the expense of other compartments.

After several weeks in the equatorial waters of the Pacific, miliaria, also known as "prickly heat" or heat rash, was endemic around the ship and made everyone miserable. Caused by constant sweating, it was worst around the waistline, crotch, and armpits, where damp clothing chafed the skin—and the continual itching made sleeping even more difficult. In severe cases, pus-filled blisters grew a quarter inch high. The only treatment was to get out of the heat and stop sweating. "It was bad," said sailor

Ray Williams. "I've never itched so much. There wasn't anything they could do for you."[12]

To escape the heat, many men took to sleeping on the flight deck, catwalks, gun tubs, or anyplace else topside where there was a breeze. It wasn't so bad up there, Williams recalled, but when you woke up in the morning "you felt like you had a salt water bath."[13]

CHAPTER 14

"We'll Fight Our Way In!"

Task Force 58's abrupt departure from Truk fueled endless scuttlebutt aboard the Moo that Spruance had another target in mind. Sure enough, the word came that HAILSTONE's success had inspired the admiral to seek an encore in the Marianas Islands before Task Force 58 returned to Majuro for rest and refit. The Marianas stretch in a rough arc north to south starting 250 miles north of the Caroline Islands. The four biggest of these islands—Saipan, Tinian, Rota, and Guam—are all on the southern end of the chain and the only ones of any military value. Fleet intelligence thought Saipan was a fighter training base and an important stop on the airplane ferry route from the Japanese home islands to Truk. A quick strike could help gauge the real strength of its defenses before the fleet returned to capture the islands in earnest later on. The Marianas' proximity to Japan raised some eyebrows aboard the Moo—they were only 1,200 miles away from the enemy's home islands, practically in their backyard in view of the size of the Pacific. But the successful Truk raid gave *Cowpens* confidence to face the challenge. "Big, bad Truk wasn't so bad after all," noted the VF-25 squadron historian with pride, "and we feel we can take 'em again."[1]

Japanese snoopers dogged Task Force 58 as it made its way northward, and on February 21 a Betty cased the fleet and made a successful escape. The likelihood that Task Force 58 had been located so close to the target put all hands on edge, and soon the crew was seeing the enemy everywhere. The ship went to general quarters when one of her 40mm gunners spotted an alleged periscope and opened fire, although it was probably only a school of fish. Adding to the tension, one of the Moo's veteran pilots was killed coming aboard just before dusk on the last CAP of the day. Lt. Benny Farber was on his final approach to land when the LSO gave him a wave-off. Farber jammed his throttle forward in an attempt to regain altitude, but his Hellcat, engine roaring, struck the gun gallery on the port quarter and crashed into the sea, sinking immediately out of view. Farber was charismatic and well-liked, and the VF-25 squadron history eulogized him by noting that "his death was a blow to everyone on the ship. We miss him."[2]

Up until this point, every operation in which the *Cowpens* had been involved started with the element of surprise in its favor. But now the fleet had been spotted, turning the advantage to the Japanese. All hands aboard the Moo knew they were in for a long night of attacks, but Mitscher was undeterred, declaring to the fleet, "We'll fight our way in!"[3] The first enemy torpedo bombers appeared on US radar screens just after 9 p.m., and from then until dawn the task force was hounded by perhaps forty enemy planes. The night was darker than it had been in the last major night attack off Kwajalein, without any moon. But as they had before, the Japanese snoopers hunted the fleet by following their wakes and, when they found ships, dropped parachute and float flares to mark them for the torpedo bombers. "The Japs threw everything they had at us," the pilots recalled. "All night, it seemed, the blackness was broken by gunfire."[4] One Betty drew close enough to *Cowpens* that those topside could hear the sound of its engines, which they described "as a cheap, tinny sound, not healthy and full throated like ours."[5] It flew by the Moo and into a stream of gunfire from an escorting heavy cruiser. The Betty burst into flames and crashed into the darkened sea nearby while those on deck cheered like their team had just scored a touchdown. "These night attacks are beautiful, if dangerous," stated the VF-25 squadron history. "The tracers from ship's guns exceed any fireworks display in memory."[6]

The fighting continued as dawn broke. As the fleet reached its launching point west of Saipan, radar showed a flight of enemy planes only twenty miles away, still searching for American ships. *Cowpens'* Hellcats were first in the rotation for the day's CAP. While in the past this meant the Moo missed more glamorous missions elsewhere, for once her fighters were in the right place at the right time. "For a change, we profited," noted the squadron historian with satisfaction.[7] Don McKinley scored the first kill of the day; he torched a Betty flying low on the water, and it rolled over and crashed into the sea. Later that morning, Horace "Bug" Bolton spotted two Bettys coming in toward the rear of the task group, perhaps one hundred feet off the water. He and his wingman, Paul "Papo" Parker, chased them down and splashed them both.

Around 4 p.m., Task Force 58 had its planes back aboard and beat a hasty retreat. All hands aboard the Moo were exhausted; the action had gone on for almost forty-eight hours, and officers and men alike were relieved that the Japanese opposition was surprisingly feeble despite the advance warning of their approach. "Them bastards won't fight in the daytime," wrote fireman George McIntyre in his journal. "All they want to do is come out at night and hope they can see our trail so they can sink a pickle into us."[8]

Staying at Chris Holmes's Place

On the three-day journey back to Majuro, there was endless speculation aboard ship about the Moo's next stop. "The scuttlebutt reached new heights," the pilots recalled. "The yarns had us going back to Pearl for a month, going back to the States, getting ready for another strike on Truk, going up to the Aleutians for duty, and what-have-you. Even money and take your choice."[9] Secretly or openly, though, most aboard hoped for a return to Pearl Harbor. Even the normally dedicated Bob Price was ready for a longer break. "It sure seems like we've covered an awful lot of ocean (which we have) and it would be nice to see something else for a change," he wrote. "We are all hoping for it like nobody's business and are anxious to find out what is in store for the future."[10]

As they hoped, *Cowpens'* orders sent her back to Pearl Harbor for a much-deserved midcruise break—almost two weeks in Hawaii plus a six-day journey each way. It was a lazy journey there, and the Moo dropped anchor at Pearl on March 4, with plenty of liberty for all. Everyone was thrilled to discover a large pile of their mail was waiting in anticipation of their arrival. Bob Price had the happy duty of handing out a huge stack of letters to the air group, and noted that each of his pilots was as eager as a child on Christmas morning to receive them.

The air group spent several days aboard the Moo before they transferred ashore to the Navy's rest home on Waikiki. This gave Price time to mull over the state of his pilots and their performance. In a letter to his wife, he described how Air Group 25 had jelled as a unit, growing from a bunch of green pilots into a confident group of veterans. "My biggest thrill is the feeling of pride I get when these compliments are thrown in our direction and what is more the air group personnel, which at one time was a conglomeration of personalities is now a fighting unit, welded pretty well together by continual successful operations against the enemy and the mutual feeling of pride that comes from such success."[11]

Price downplayed his own role in the group's improvement. But in a subsequent letter he highlighted how his willingness to trust his men and delegate responsibility contributed to the group's development. Price noted that "the boys have stumbled onto a certain group spirit that has done wonders for morale and is in no small way responsible for the close coordination and team work so necessary for a good organization. I've actually done little personally except to place responsibility into the hands of more people and it has had a very gratifying reaction. But largely I think the reason behind it all is found in the old quotation of 'success breeds success.' When the lads are successful they're naturally happy and a little bit cocky—and you can't beat a condition like that."[12]

Once released to go ashore, the air group discovered the Navy's pilot rest home was no mere government facility. The house was one of the most luxurious residences in Hawaii, a three-story Art Deco estate in white stucco under towering palm trees, just yards from Waikiki Beach. It was the Hawaiian residence of Chris Holmes, the heir to the Fleischmann's Yeast fortune who accumulated substantial wealth on his own as a Hawaiian tuna packing magnate. Holmes was a playboy who had been a household name in the 1930s. His family history described him as "a fun-loving man with nearly unlimited resources."[13] He purchased the Waikiki mansion soon after his arrival in the islands in 1933; the estate and its outbuildings occupied some of the best real estate on Oahu. Holmes named the mansion "Queen's Surf" in tribute to the beach house of Hawaiian queen Lili'uokalani, which once stood nearby. After Pearl Harbor, Holmes evacuated his valuables and loaned the house to the Navy for the duration of the war. The Navy installed bunk beds upstairs at Queen's Surf to provide sleeping arrangements for about three dozen pilots, and began rotating through combat-weary air groups for stays of several days at a time. A charming Honolulu matron and her husband lived in one of the guest houses, and their sole job was to make sure the pilots' stay was as relaxing as possible. Unfortunately, Holmes did not live to see Queen's Surf again; Air Group 25's stay came roughly a month after his death. He had decamped to New York and died of an overdose of sleeping pills in a posh hotel.

VF-25 got the pick of the litter, moving into Queen's Surf while the Avenger pilots stayed down the beach in another home. For once, Hawaii seemed like paradise to the air group, and the experience was one of the high points of their war. "This is the life!" the pilots thought. "A sumptuous, big house right on the ocean. It's difficult to decide whether to stay in the sack, go for a swim, start drinking, or try to round up a female. There is all the liquor, beer, or wine one wants... a welcome respite!"[14] Ed Haley looked back fondly on the time at Queen's Surf, recalling it as a "wonderful, relaxing week. We were wined and dined, all on the Navy. We swam, tried to ride surfboards, and in the evening there were dances, movies, and all the good stuff that we hadn't seen in awhile."[15] But all good things come to an end, and the air group returned to the Moo on March 15, just as it pulled up anchor for Majuro. "We had a marvelous time at the rest home and it was just what the doctor ordered in the way of relaxation—mental mostly," Bob Price wrote in summation. "The war seemed a million miles away—but now we're back in it again and you'll have another gap in your mail for awhile."[16]

CHAPTER 15

Palau, Hollandia, and Truk

Operation DESECRATE: The Great Dry Run at Palau

After the excitement of Pearl Harbor, the ten-day steam south was a boring one, with the monotony only broken by routine air patrols and gunnery drills. Bob Price wrote to his wife on March 17, 1944, of returning to their shipboard routine. "We are again in our old familiar spot—at sea—and the good times had by all during our short stay on the beach seem very remote—but certainly not forgotten because we are all looking forward to another visit as soon as the fates decide."[1]

The task force's next objective was Palau, where the Japanese fleet withdrew from Truk in advance of HAILSTONE. Palau is the westernmost cluster of islands in the Caroline Island chain, farther west than Tokyo, just over one thousand miles southwest of Truk, and only seven hundred miles northwest of New Guinea. It was a hub of Japanese and naval air activity and within striking range of MacArthur's next objective of Hollandia on the north coast of New Guinea, and the general wanted the potential threat to his operation removed. *Cowpens'* pilots were upbeat about the possibility of action, noting that "there should be plenty of planes, aircraft facilities...and shipping to work on."[2]

Enemy snoopers spotted the fleet during its run-in on the twenty-fifth, and once alerted, the Japanese did not stick around for a fight. They withdrew their warships to Singapore, Borneo, and the home islands. A US sub lurking outside the harbor radioed news of their departure, leaving all aboard the Moo disappointed that their quarry escaped for the second time in two months. With the major warships having left town, the Moo's pilots were forced to accept shooting up cargo ships and bombing the ground facilities and parked aircraft. The pickings were so slim that some of the ship's comedians dubbed it the "great dry run."

Despite the absence of the enemy fleet, land-based planes from Palau and nearby islands remained to menace the US carrier task force. By 8 p.m. on March 29 Japanese torpedo bombers were massing at the edges of the Moo's radar screens. Two divisions of Hellcats led by Al Morton were flying the last CAP of the day; faced with encroaching darkness and imminent enemy attack, Captain McConnell ordered Morton to bring his planes home. Seven of the eight got aboard, but the last man in the formation, Ens. Anderson Bowers, ran into trouble when the plane in front of him went into the crash barrier. By the time the plane handlers cleared the wreck out, McConnell had put the Moo into its evasive maneuvers to throw off enemy attacks, which put her out of the wind and unable to land planes.

Admiral Reeves ordered Bowers to ditch his plane alongside a destroyer, and Bowers, who had little experience in night operations, took the order literally. He made a perfect water landing near one of *Cowpens'* escorts, but did not remember that standard procedure was to land one thousand yards ahead of a rescue ship—and the destroyer steamed off ahead looking for him. Bowers floated in his Mae West life vest for fifty-five minutes in the bath-warm Palauan waters before finally attracting the attention of another ship with gunfire from his pistol. Bowers did not keep his gun for long, however; the destroyermen extracted a ransom for every carrier pilot they recovered. Usually they stripped the pilot of every possible souvenir—flight jackets, silk survival maps, knives, and pistol—and then demanded in trade from his home ship a GI can full of ice cream, perhaps thirty-five to forty gallons in all. While grateful for the rescue, one pilot observed that "you don't come out with a thing except your life."[3]

Over the course of the evening, Japanese aircraft made nine separate attempts to get inside the destroyer screen for a torpedo shot. The task force's skillful maneuvering frustrated each attempt, and when the enemy planes drew too close heavy antiaircraft fire from the accompanying cruisers and destroyers shot down two and drove the rest off. While the task force as a whole took no damage from the attack, *Cowpens* suffered one loss from a senseless accident. As some gathered on deck to watch the enemy attack unfold, replacement pilot Ken Dye was knocked overboard by the wing of a parked Hellcat. The plane's wing was upright in the folded position but not locked in place, and it came down suddenly, striking both Dye and fellow pilot Lee Adams, who was standing next to him. Adams received some nasty cuts about the face and only narrowly avoided following Dye over the side. The destroyers looked for Dye but were unable to find him. "It was a miserable thing," explained the VF-25 squadron history. "A little like an acrobat being killed by slipping on a banana peel. Everyone was greatly depressed by Dye's loss."[4]

Paradise Loses Its Charm

Cowpens returned to Majuro for a week, reprovisioning and refueling before setting out for Hollandia, New Guinea. Recreation parties on the beach helped pass the time, but the *Cowpens* had not received much mail for a month, and Majuro's tropical charm was beginning to wear thin. "This certainly is a big ocean and it seems to me I've seen every nook and corner of it," groused Bob Price in early April. "Strangely enough it all looks pretty much alike. Coral reefs and palm trees don't have nearly the fascination for us that they used to."[5]

In addition to the mounting boredom, the week was marred with a swimming accident that cost the lives of two crewmen. During a beer party on April 7, Seaman Second Class Donald Sealey swam out too far into the lagoon; some said he was trying to reach another island where the Majuran women were living. The tide was going out to sea and so the current was fierce, and soon Sealey was in trouble. An African American steward, James Martin, went to his rescue, and the pair were swept into the channel and drowned. Unfortunately, the bodies weren't found for four days and were, in sailor Robert Lee's words, "a horrible sight" when they were finally recovered.[6] Majuro was not a good place for a burial; the Marines had trouble digging a grave in the coral rock, and there wasn't enough wood available for two coffins—so the pair were buried together in a single casket. Despite the primitive conditions, there were full military honors at the funeral for the two fallen sailors, with an honor guard and three volleys of rifle fire in salute. George Terrell recalled how Chaplain Handran, presiding over the ceremony, spoke of the "fitting way in which they were being laid to rest together, in one common grave, as a symbol of their common humanity."[7]

While the novelty of pristine tropical beaches had faded, the return of movie nights aboard ship was a welcome relief. The Moo's hangar deck doubled as a makeshift theater, but when crammed with men the ventilation left something to be desired. Describing the moviegoing experience to his wife on April 8, Bob Price wrote that "the old hangar deck gets crowded, uncomfortable, and awfully hot, but we all sit there and sweat and get a big kick out of the corniest western. Tonight though we had a swell one—*Du Barry Was a Lady*." This 1943 musical comedy included Red Skelton, Lucille Ball, and Gene Kelly, with music by the popular big band act Tommy Dorsey and his Orchestra. And best of all was that the movie was set in a nightclub, offering a vision of scantily clad showgirls that was racy by the standards of the day. Price described their collective reaction, saying there was "more girls, legs, and bare flesh than we've ever had and of course the bluejackets ate it up ... the officers sat there all calm, cool, and collected, but I still haven't gotten over it." Then, shifting gears back to the role of responsible commander, Price mused that an occasional bit of titillation was necessary to keep the crew sane and prevent them from becoming a "bunch of wild men."[8]

Operation RECKLESS: The Invasion of Hollandia, New Guinea

The days on Majuro seemed to go on forever, but on April 13, *Cowpens* put to sea as part of Task Group 58.1 under Rear Adm. James "Jocko" Clark. Accompanying the Moo in 58.1 on her eighth sortie were carriers

Hornet, Belleau Wood, and *Bataan,* along with their ever-present escort of cruisers and destroyers. With Palau effectively neutralized as a Japanese naval base, Task Force 58's mission was to directly support MacArthur's landings in northern New Guinea. They were to hit airfields along the coast to keep the Japanese grounded during the operation; *Cowpens* and Task Group 58.1 were assigned the three airfields in Hollandia and its staging airfields, one hundred miles to the west. Afterward, the task force was scheduled to linger offshore for a few days in case of a Japanese counterattack.

Per the usual practice, the Moo's pilots endured days of briefings and preparations in advance of the strike. For the Moo's now-veteran flyers, these briefs had become thoroughly routine, but this time the survival briefings were sobering. Hollandia was not the place you wanted to make a forced landing; it was some of the most hostile jungle in the Southwest Pacific, with rugged mountain ranges and malarial swamps infested with crocodiles. It was also inhabited by tribesmen who were hostile to both sides and reputed to be cannibals and head hunters.[9]

On the twenty-first and twenty-second the Moo's pilots hit primitive airfields at Wakde, Sawar, and Sarmi, braving tropical rain and mist that made accurate bombing difficult. Encouraged by the lack of serious ground fire, the Avengers and their escorting fighters sometimes came in so low to drop their bombs that one plane was hit by flying lumber from a building destroyed by the preceding aircraft. By that evening the pilots were telling the ship's intelligence officer that the target airfields were "thoroughly wrecked" and that no further strikes were needed.[10]

There weren't enough enemy planes to keep the fighter pilots busy, and so a race to the kill developed anytime one made an appearance. One such race occurred during a mission to Sawar on the twenty-first. The Hellcats were circling overhead at approximately nineteen thousand feet when two pilots, Harold Kicker and Ed Haley, spotted a Japanese Helen bomber that was skimming along the shoreline at treetop height. Seeing a potentially easy target, Kicker, followed by Haley and two other Hellcats, dove in pursuit. Ed Haley recalled the hectic dive down to wave-top level. "I rolled over on my back and dove at maximum speed. The F6F-3 was redlined at 415 knots. But in that dive, after about 15 seconds, I was well over that speed."[11] As the fighters descended from the cool high-altitude air to the humid jungle air, their windshields fogged up, and all four pilots had to open their canopies and put their heads into the slipstream to see their quarry.[12] With his head out of the plane and unable to use his gunsight through his fogged windshield, Kicker came in from astern, guns blazing. Trying to fly and shoot in this manner nearly proved fatal; Kicker missed the Helen completely and almost crashed into a line of trees. Ed Haley and the other Hellcats also made firing runs on the Helen and fared no better. Finally, on Kicker's second pass, he managed to score a few hits, and the fleeing Helen crash-landed on the beach and skidded to a halt. Haley thought his fire might have forced the Helen into the ground, but the ship's intelligence officers credited Kicker for the kill.

After the strikes on April 22, Task Group 58.1 worked their way back down the coast toward Hollandia, where MacArthur's troops were going ashore. Word came from the brass that US troops encountered only slight opposition. Most of the eleven thousand Japanese defenders fled into the hills, and not a single enemy plane appeared overhead. Nimitz offered his congratulations to Task Force 58, but the Moo's sailors were unconvinced the effort had been worth the trip. Art Daly complained to his journal that "the landing was a joke... very little opposition."[13]

Task Force 58 withdrew from the landing zones and cruised the northern coast of New Guinea until MacArthur finally released them on the twenty-fourth. The pace was relaxed; the squadron historian recalls that "during this period we loafed around off Hollandia, flying CAP, fueling, and generally bothering the hell out of the Japs."[14] The only enemy activity *Cowpens* encountered was recurring snoopers. Nearly every morning the Japanese sent one down from the north, and whoever had the CAP shot him down. Don McKinley splashed the first Betty at 10:10 a.m. on the twenty-fourth, and Ensigns L. J. Eckhardt and Donald "Danny" Rouch bagged another on the twenty-fifth, also at 10:10. After that, it became a joke on board—who would get the 10:10 Betty? Everyone tried to get their division scheduled for that rotation of CAP. Ed Haley jokingly noted, "I don't imagine the pilots in that Japanese squadron looked forward to that patrol."[15]

With the Army's landings finally secured, the fleet refueled for the long voyage back to the Central Pacific and set off the next day. What started as a welcome break from operations transitioned into the mind-numbing monotony of a long sea cruise as the Moo returned north to its usual stomping grounds in the Central Pacific. Bob Price wrote home trying to put words to his Groundhog Day experience: "All our days are characterized by a standard pattern of flying, eating, and sleeping," he told his wife. "A little sun and exercise thrown in regularly, and of course, constant talk of home and families." It was both encouraging and dispiriting, Price wrote, to know that while each day got them closer to home, they still had a long way to go.[16]

A Bloody Return to Truk

Cowpens and Air Group 25 had not seen the last of Truk. While the success of the HAILSTONE raid proved that an invasion of Truk was unnecessary, the Army Air Corps continued its bomber raids against the island to keep it neutralized. For weeks, these raids met little resistance, but on March 29 they ran into trouble. Arriving over Truk, the B-24s were swarmed by dozens of Japanese fighters. The sudden increase in enemy activity meant that Truk had been reinforced and now it was back in business. Nimitz passed the word to Mitscher that the island needed to be hit again.

For the pilots, "this Truk affair is a piece of news nobody cares for particularly."[17] While Truk had not been as fearsome as its reputation had suggested, everyone remembered the ferocity of the antiaircraft fire, and now intelligence suggested the Japanese had reinforced it with even more guns. The intelligence was right; the ground fire soon proved to be, in the words of the squadron history, "as deadly as it was numerous."[18]

The Moo's pilots spent two days hitting airfields and shore installations at Param and Dublon Islands on Truk, braving a buzzsaw of enemy fire.

The Japanese in some cases had lugged their antiaircraft guns up to the top of their islands' volcanic peaks, and so as the Moo's fliers came out of their bombing dives they faced red streams of tracers coming up at them as well as from the side or above. The Moo's Avengers suffered a particularly heavy toll. Ground fire ripped through Lt. William "Pop" Watson's plane on his bombing run over Param airfield, tearing off part of its elevator and damaging one of its wings. Despite the damage, Watson continued his dive and dropped his bomb before nursing his plane back to the Moo. Pop came back to Param on a second mission that afternoon, and scored direct hits on buildings below with his four 500-pound bombs. As he pulled out of his dive at low altitude, a shell pierced the radio compartment behind the cockpit and exploded. The shell mortally wounded radioman Anthony Limpinsel and shredded the plane's hydraulic lines. Watson immediately turned for home and managed to get his wheels and flaps down for an emergency landing on the closest carrier, *Belleau Wood*. As he flew the plane home, Watson coached his turret gunner on how to administer first aid to his dying friend.

At Dublon the following day, Japanese gunners hit Lt. Richard Peters's low-flying Avenger twice after it dropped its bomb. One round tore off the entire starboard stabilizer and elevator, and in an echo of the previous day, the second mortally wounded the Avenger's radioman, John Chmura, and started a fire inside his compartment. Chmura was unconscious and covered with hydraulic fluid from the plane's shattered lines when tail gunner Arnold Olson came to his aid. Olson, adrenaline pumping, didn't think to use the onboard fire extinguisher and beat out the blaze with his hands and feet. He then turned to help his friend. While the onboard first aid kit had been blown to bits, Olson did the best he could to patch Chmura's wounds. By that point, Peters had gotten their battered plane out to sea and was heading toward the nearest carrier.

With his hydraulics out, Peters was only able to get his landing gear partway down—which made a ditching extremely risky, as most planes in that state flipped over and sank when they hit the water. As a result, Peters was determined to get his gear locked into place. With coaching from Peters, Olson managed to patch the hydraulic line with lens paper from the onboard camera. "I was so damned scared," said Olson, "but I did what Mr. Peters told me without knowing what was going on."[19] Reaching the *Hornet*, Peters got a wave-off on his first landing attempt but caught a wire on the second. Once safely aboard, Olson did a walk-around of his damaged aircraft and "got scared all over again" when he saw that the armor plate around his turret was badly dented from shrapnel. Olson received the Air Medal for his heroism, but unfortunately his friend Chmura died of his wounds soon after.

The Moo's Hellcats took their own losses. On a bomb run over Param, Ed Haley was flying behind Brownie along with his wingman, Danny Rouch. They began their dive on the target into what Haley described as a solid sheet of flak bursts. He later detailed what happened next: "We got closer to those flashes by the second and just before we reached it I looked over at Danny and threw him a salute and to my horror he disappeared in a gigantic ball of fire."[20] Haley, despite his grief, managed to complete his bombing run and then pull away. Decades later, Haley still keenly felt his wingman's loss. "There is a special bond between flying buddies," he said. "It left an ache that took a long time to heal...I continue to think of him often."[21]

A later strike against Param brought still more tragedy. The moment the Moo's planes came out of the clouds to begin their attack run they flew into a storm of intense and accurate ground fire. Five *Cowpens* planes were hit. One was piloted by Ens. Albert "Satchel" Sanchez, who despite the fierce flak, made several low-level strafing runs on antiaircraft batteries, guns blazing, in an attempt to suppress the fire that was hammering his fellow fliers. The Japanese gunners caught up with him; his squadronmates last saw Sanchez lining up in a dive on another target, and he never returned to base.

Cowpens' air group was exhausted and relieved when Task Force 58 finally withdrew the night of April 30. The VF-25 history described the operation as the "toughest job the squadron ever has undertaken."[22] They lost two pilots, both technically classified as missing but certainly dead. The torpedo squadron was hit just as badly, losing two aircrewmen while six of its nine Avengers were damaged by flak. While the losses were grievous, the number of aircraft that took hits and returned to base testified to their sturdy construction, a trait that Bob Price praised in his after-action report. "Too much emphasis cannot be placed upon the ability of the TBF-1C and F6F-3 airplanes and engines to absorb enemy gunfire."[23] Haley, too, was grateful for the ruggedness of the Hellcat and relieved they had made it through in one piece. He and his roommates "broke out a fifth of scotch that night and had a few pops to toast the Grumman Ironworks and the indestructible Hellcat. None of us were scheduled to fly the next day and the task force was heading back for re-supply so we had quite a party."[24]

Fighting the Bore War—a New Captain

Cowpens pulled in to Majuro Atoll on May 14, and its wait there was a long one, lasting almost three weeks, until June 5. "We pilots played cards, read, exercised, slept, and ate and slept some more then went through the same routine all over again," described Ed Haley. "It got boring awfully fast."[25] Over the following month, everyone aboard looked for ways to break up the monotony. "We've had a stretch of awfully good movies so we had one more or less from one evening to the next," Price wrote in early June. "Plenty of music and girls—and that helps to pass the time away."[26]

Captain McConnell concluded his service aboard the *Cowpens* while she was swaying at anchor. The captain had received his orders for his next assignment on the Joint Logistics Plans Committee in Washington—and had finally prodded the Navy bureaucracy to promote Price and Brownie to lieutenant commander. The duo shared their good fortune with the squadron—with Price wryly noting that "it looks like all the boys are going to do a lot of cigar smoking for awhile."[27] But he spoke for many aboard ship when he described his disappointment over "Captain Mac's" departure. "We are all sorry as can be to see him go. This has been a very pleasant home for us while he has been at the helm...regardless of how tough the sledding got he always came through 100 percent. And believe me we've been in some mighty ticklish situations."[28]

Captain McConnell's replacement was Capt. Herbert Watson Taylor.

From Newark, New Jersey, Taylor was the son of a former US senator and a 1921 graduate of the US Naval Academy. He earned his aviator's wings in 1924 and was a specialist in aerial photography, twice serving as chief of the Bureau of Aeronautics' photographic section. A father of three, Taylor served at sea as the navigator of the carrier *Ranger*, and immediately prior to arriving on board the *Cowpens* he commanded the escort carrier *Coral Sea*. Taylor was a quiet man; his US Naval Academy yearbook (known as *The Lucky Bag*) commented that "the phrase 'still waters run deep' was never more applicable to anyone than it is to [Taylor]."[29] Despite his disappointment over McConnell's departure, Price committed to building a relationship with his new commander. "The new skipper looks like a good sort so [we] will have to start getting used to his particular likes and dislikes."[30]

Cowpens celebrated her first birthday at Majuro on May 28. A Moo-centric birthday bash broke the monotony of time at anchor and rallied the ship's morale. "Today is the ship's birthday...she is one year old and plenty salty," noted George McIntyre in his journal with pride. "We had a big feed and holiday routine."[31] Art Daly, too, got into the spirit of the day. "This was a big day for us," he wrote in his journal. "Races on the flight deck. Boxing matches. Movies. A case of beer for the winners."[32] The day's feast did not disappoint; cream of potato soup, ripe olives, sweet relish, roast chicken and giblet gravy, creamy mashed potatoes, pie and ice cream, rolls and coffee. The ship's big band headlined the talent show, while best of all, the night's movie was *Up in Arms*, the 1944 musical comedy about a misfit soldier embroiled in a love triangle with his best friend and an Army nurse. The movie was another round of the occasional titillation that Price regarded as helpful to keep his men sane. He was enthusiastic about the movie, describing it as "Dinah Shore, Danny Kaye, and a bevy of the nicest looking young things I've seen in a long time. Wow!"[33]

CHAPTER 16

Operation FORAGER: The Invasion of the Marianas

As *Cowpens* began June 1944, all hands were happy to learn that Task Force 58 would soon go back into action. "The fact that we are to be the advance guard of an amphibious attack designed to take the Marianas does not remain a secret long," noted the VF-25 history. Most important to the air group was the news that it would be their last operation before heading home, and the pilots observed that "everyone is anxious to get it over with."[1] As had been the pattern in previous operations, the task force's next sortie was bigger and more ambitious than those before. A steady flow of ships kept arriving at Majuro, and soon even this normally spacious lagoon was, according to Ed Haley, "bulging at the seams."[2]

The rumor mill was right: The task force had orders to set off for the invasion of the Marianas, Operation FORAGER. This operation had two major objectives—first, the capture of that island chain would put US forces in a better geographic position to threaten the flow of oil, rubber, and other raw materials from Southeast Asia to Japan. The Empire imported almost everything it needed to sustain the war, and the 3,500-mile-long sea route from its captured territory to the home islands was its logistical jugular vein. Secondly, the Marianas were the ideal launching pad for the Army Air Forces' B-29 Superfortress heavy bomber. At the time, it was the largest plane to have ever been put in production; developed at twice the cost of the Manhattan Project that produced the atomic bomb, it could carry ten thousand pounds of ordnance to targets 1,600 miles away. In addition to being long-ranged, it was also fast, capable of almost three hundred miles per hour, and bristling with .50-caliber guns in defensive turrets. The Marianas were close enough to Japan that bombers flying from there could strike Tokyo and the industrial centers of the Kanto Plain surrounding the capital.

The US Fleet had been the aggressor in every operation throughout the *Cowpens'* short service life. Task Force 58 attacked one target after another, and in each case the enemy fleet displaced to avoid battle. But intelligence indicated that for FORAGER there was a risk that the Japanese fleet might come out to fight. Filipino guerrillas had captured a copy of a Japanese strategy document known as the Z-Plan and handed it over to their US advisors, who smuggled it out by submarine. Although more of a general outline than a detailed operations order, it made clear that the Japanese planned to challenge the next American landings in hopes of engineering a decisive naval battle that they hoped could shift the balance of the war back in their favor.

Task Force 58's primary mission during FORAGER was to protect the beachhead for the landings, but also to seek out and destroy the enemy fleet should it appear. To accomplish this task Admiral Spruance had at his disposal the largest US fleet yet assembled. It included fifteen aircraft carriers—seven fleet carriers plus *Cowpens* and seven of her light carrier sisters, carrying more than nine hundred aircraft. Joining them were 7 fast battleships, 4 heavy and 13 light cruisers, and 53 destroyers. The fleet's leadership had been reorganized into two teams, the first led by Admiral Spruance, and the second by Adm. William Halsey. Under this arrangement, one command staff executed the current operation while the other planned the next. While the fleet remained the same, its name changed depending on who was in charge. Under Spruance, it was Fifth Fleet and Task Force 58, and under Halsey, Third Fleet and Task Force 38. For FORAGER, Admiral Spruance and Fifth Fleet were up to bat, under the watchful supervision of Admiral Nimitz in Hawaii.

Cowpens and the rest of the task force sortied from Majuro on June 5 under leaden, rainy skies. In a grim parade the fleet transited Majuro's narrow channel into the Pacific one at a time, a process that took more than five hours. To the sailors standing on the *Cowpens*, the size of the fleet assembling around them was awe-inspiring and filled them with confidence about the task they were about to embark on. "The sight of this force is enough to dispel any fears that the Japs can stand against it," declared the ship's history.[3] Once at sea, Captain Taylor announced the news of the June 6 D-Day Normandy landings, provoking a roar of satisfaction from the men, and fueling their hopes that in a few days they would make their own headlines for the home front.

Cowpens was part of Task Group 58.4 under Rear Adm. William Keen Harrill, a genteel Tennessean and member of the Naval Academy class of 1914. He was an experienced aviator and earned the Navy Cross in World War I, but in recent years he had grown indecisive and timid. His was the smallest of the four task groups under Spruance's command in FORAGER; along with *Cowpens*, it included fleet carrier *Essex* and fellow CVL *Langley*. While their task force was more modest in size, the formerly green Air Group 25 was now one of the most experienced in Task Force 58. Rotations of air groups home had thinned the task force's number of veteran squadrons, and Price's pilots were among only a handful remaining who had participated in the first raid on the Marianas in February.

It was a five-day cruise from Majuro to Saipan, and the days at sea offered the first opportunity for *Cowpens'* officers and crew to get to know Captain Taylor before FORAGER kicked off in earnest. Bob Price spoke well of Taylor in his letters home, writing, "I've had an opportunity during the past few days to get to know the new skipper quite well and he's pretty OK. A different type than Captain Mac but I think he's going to be just what the doctor ordered."[4] Ship's officer Sam Sommers took to Taylor immediately. He described the captain as relaxed and competent and that "when he was on the bridge, he said little but you know every move was being observed . . . if a correction was needed, he let you know it, quietly."[5] Taylor's hobby was shooting his .22-caliber target pistol. "On fine days during routine steaming, the captain would stand on the outboard wing of the bridge and shoot at flying fish when they were flushed by the ship's bow," Sommers recalled. "I don't believe he ever hit one, but when we heard the pop-pop of the skipper's pistol, all was right with the world."[6]

A Costly First Two Days at Saipan

The next month of combat operations was the most intense of Air Group 25's combat tour. Bob Price and his pilots would get their long-hoped-for opportunity to break free of their second-tier assignments and tangle with the Japanese in earnest. The air group maintained a blistering pace of operations, putting the pilots' endurance to the test with sometimes three or four missions a day. And while they shot down twenty enemy planes in combat, along the way they lost five pilots and an aircrewman.

For FORAGER's first two days, the Moo's pilots split their efforts between targets on Saipan and Pagan, an uneven barbell of an island two hundred miles to the north. They hit airfields on both, showering bombs on runways and revetments, and strafing any planes they found parked on the field. While destroying enemy airfields was a necessary step toward preventing the Japanese from attacking the landing fleet, many pilots aboard *Cowpens* weren't thrilled with the assignment. The airfields were typically thick with antiaircraft guns, and raids were often risky. Moreover, it was difficult to knock an airfield out of action for good, sometimes requiring multiple strikes on the same target. In one example of the risks of these types of missions, while attacking Aslito airfield on June 12, W. J. Day's Avenger was riddled by ground fire; he managed to nurse his battered aircraft back to the fleet before he ditched. Day and his radioman, Daniel Kirschner, managed to escape their plane before it sank, but tail gunner James Maddox never emerged from the plane and went down with it. At Pagan later that day, the Moo's Hellcats demolished an airfield hangar and set fire to a nearby barracks. VF-25 pilot Ens. Robert Wright disappeared after a strafing attack; no one saw what happened to him, but pilots from the *Essex* spotted a body in a lifejacket in the ocean just offshore from where he was last seen. They saw the body sink, and the Moo's pilots feared it was Wright.

Lt. Norman Petersen also had a hard time of it over Pagan, but unlike Wright he lived to tell the tale. Petersen was flying one of *Cowpens'* two camera-equipped Hellcats and made a single pass over the airfield taking photos. The trouble started when he decided to get in on the action and follow up his photo run with some strafing. On his first pass over the field, he took an antiaircraft round in his engine, which quickly began to sputter. Petersen managed to get his plane approximately five miles offshore before it gave out completely and he was forced to ditch. His wingmen circled overhead until an OS2U Kingfisher arrived, strafing several small Japanese boats that came out to try and capture the downed US pilot. Finally, the OS2U landed and recovered Petersen, but with his additional weight the scout plane couldn't get airborne and crashed on takeoff. Now there were three men in the water—Petersen and his two would-be rescuers. A second Kingfisher soon arrived and hauled the three waterlogged fliers aboard. Knowing he could never take off with all five men, the pilot of the second rescue plane radioed the fleet for help. Soon, destroyers *Charles Ausburne* and *Thatcher* steamed over the horizon and took all of them aboard.

There were more enemy planes on the ground than in the air, but they appeared in ones and twos and VF-25 shot down six over the course of the day. It was in one of these dogfights that the squadron lost veteran pilot Paul "Papo" Parker. He pursued one Zeke in a steep climb before stalling out a moment before his quarry did. The enemy fighter turned the tables on Parker, taking position on his tail in a diving chase. With Ens. William Kinkaid firing from long range to try to shake the Zeke off, the enemy fighter fired a long burst into Parker's Hellcat and tried to make a run for it. He did not get far; Kinkaid caught up to him and splashed him. Unfortunately, the Zeke scored a fatal shot on Parker or his Hellcat. Papo dove out of view; he did not return to base and was never seen again. That evening, Ed Haley and Willie Reed mourned Papo's death. "We lost a Hellcat and a good friend," Haley recalled. Papo was the second roommate they had lost on the deployment; Haley later explained, "Willie and I were very lonesome that night and for many nights to follow."[7]

Bob Price's Fateful Encounter with a Japanese Convoy

As the Moo's fliers worked over Saipan and Pagan, a Japanese convoy was attempting to flee the area. The previous day it had left Tanapag Harbor on Saipan just before US planes arrived; it numbered twelve cargo ships plus a mix of escorts and patrol craft. Once reports of the convoy reached him, Admiral Harrill ordered his planes to cut off their escape. *Cowpens* mustered a dozen Hellcats and seven Avengers to the effort, and the carrier aircraft swept in low and fast on the convoy. The Hellcats were first, strafing the hulls and superstructure with their machine guns, and the Avengers followed behind with five-hundred-pound bombs. Of the seven *Cowpens* Avengers, five scored hits or close misses—sinking one ship and crippling two others.

While the attack was a great success in terms of damage inflicted, the intense antiaircraft fire exacted a toll. Ed Haley's roommate Willie Reed had a very close call; an antiaircraft shell went through the arc of his propeller and punched a hand-size hole in his engine. With his engine sputtering and spewing oil, Willie managed to fly 150 miles back to the Moo for a successful landing. Ed Haley was watching in the catwalk when Reed brought his Hellcat back aboard. After he touched down, Haley gleefully related how all he could see of his roommate's face "was two big white eyes when he pushed up his goggles and a bigger white grin, everything else was covered in black oil."[8] The deckhands shuffled the plane below for an overnight engine change. Haley had the poor luck to fly the newly repaired plane the following day and described how he got "greasy all over."[9]

The most devastating loss for the Moo that day was Bob Price. He was making a strafing run on one of the cargo ships when his Hellcat took an antiaircraft round head-on. Its engine sputtered to a halt within sixty seconds; Price radioed to his men he was going in and made a hard water landing right in the middle of the enemy convoy. As his pilots watched from overhead, Price's Hellcat sank so quickly that he was unable to free his survival raft from the plane. This left him floating in the Pacific in only his Mae West life jacket, although he waved repeatedly to the planes circling overhead to signal he was OK. Price was beloved by his men, and once back on board the Moo they pleaded with Captain Taylor and Admiral Harrill for permission to go back to find him. Some five hours later—late in the afternoon—the approvals came through, and twelve Hellcats went back to the site of the convoy to locate their commander. They found Price still floating in his Mae West. Al Morton dropped him a raft and a note: "Will bring OS2U in the morning." Knowing Price would be worried about the fate of Lt. Petersen, who was shot down earlier that day, Al added: "Pete has been picked up. Good luck!"[10] Back at the ship, Brownie and the rest of the pilots continued to lobby for Price's rescue. Harrill relented and signaled to *Cowpens*: AT 0630 LAUNCH RESCUE SEAPLANE WITH PILOT ONLY TO RESCUE COWPENS PILOT LAST REPORTED IN RUBBER BOAT.

Brownie and Lt. Bolton, accompanied by an OS2U from *Vincennes*, took off to look for Price right on schedule the next morning at 6:30 a.m. All three aircraft soon reached the site of the previous day's attack. The two badly damaged cargo ships were still nearby; one was only barely underway and the other was dead in the water. The pilots searched the area and found no sign of Price, but a Japanese Betty soon arrived and began circling over the enemy ships. Brown and Bolton chased it down and flamed it. The pair searched the area for another two hours, at which point the OS2U was low on fuel and they had to escort it home.

Brownie, now acting commander of the air group and VF-25, complained to Captain Taylor that with only three planes he had not been able to thoroughly search the area before having to return to base. Taylor signaled to Harrill: PILOTS REPORT NEGATIVE GROUP COMMANDER PRICE X MORE PLANES NECESSARY TO COMPLETELY COVER DRIFT OF RAFT.[11] With *Cowpens'* planes assigned to CAP and ASP that day, Harrill did not want to thin his air cover, and so he assigned *Essex* to the job. Unfortunately, *Essex*'s planes had no more luck than the Moo's, and they reported back: SORRY TO REPORT RESULTS NEGATIVE X CTF 58 ADVISED.[12] This was not satisfactory to Brownie and the Moo's pilots, who believed *Essex*'s search had not accounted for Price's drift on the currents. Asking for permission from

Harrill for another search, *Cowpens* sent back Price's estimated course and DO NOT BELIEVE ESSEX SEARCH COVERED DRIFT X REQUEST CTF 58 BE INFORMED.[13] Unfortunately, Harrill or his staff chose not to authorize another search, leaving Price to the mercy of the sea.

Harrill and Clark Run North

Spruance knew from intercepted Japanese radio chatter and the captured draft of the Z-Plan that the Japanese were likely bringing additional planes from the home islands to the Marianas with a refueling stop at Iwo Jima or Chichi Jima in the Bonin Islands. To cut this flow of reinforcements, Spruance directed Mitscher to send two task groups north to attack airfields there. Mitscher selected James "Jocko" Clark's Task Group 58.1 and *Cowpens'* 58.4, under the command of Admiral Harrill. The two admirals were an odd pair for the mission; Harrill was cautious and indecisive, while Clark was aggressive to a fault, always spoiling for a fight. While neither one was thrilled about diverting to a secondary target, Mitscher manipulated Clark into accepting it by describing it as difficult and dangerous, knowing that would fan the flames of his enthusiasm. Clark, in turn, shamed Harrill into participating. He batted aside the reluctant admiral's excuses why his task force could not participate and threatened to complete the mission alone if 58.4 did not accompany him. Harrill crumpled, but in the coming days did as little as possible to support Clark. He later confided in one of his officers, "I must be getting old. I find I can't make decisions like I used to."[14] This would cost the lives of more of the Moo's pilots in the days to come.

As the admirals argued, *Cowpens*, along with the rest of Task Groups 58.1 and 58.4, refueled and prepared for their seven-hundred-mile run north to the Bonins. Pilots went through their intelligence briefs for the coming missions; Iwo Jima was the main target, for it had the best airfields, hosting probably about one hundred planes. While Mitscher convinced Clark the mission was dangerous, *Cowpens* pilots came to believe it all on their own. "Nobody knows what is there," commented the VF-25 history, "but its proximity to Japan keeps everyone on edge."[15]

The two task groups had not traveled far before Spruance learned that US subs had spotted the Japanese fleet putting to sea and they were likely on the way to the Marianas. He directed Clark and Harrill to cut their strikes to one day to give them time to return to the Marianas before the Japanese arrived. Clark, playing fast and loose with his orders to get the two days of strikes he thought he needed to accomplish the objective, raced north with Task Group 58.1 to get there early, with Harrill reluctantly following along. The weather did not cooperate, and a large front moved in between the two task groups and Iwo Jima. As dawn broke the next morning, conditions had soured into fifteen-foot seas, twenty-five-knot winds, squalls, and a thick overcast. Historian and aviator Barrett Tillman described the day's weather in aviation terms as "dogshit"—causing even "enthusiastic pilots to doubt their calling."[16]

There were brief openings in the weather over the following forty-eight hours, enough to get *Cowpens'* planes into the air for attacks against Iwo. On the first day, the Moo's pilots struggled to find targets to bomb through the rain and clouds, but they had more luck on the second. Finding enemy aircraft lined up in rows on Iwo Jima's airfield, they descended to strafe in such close formation that the expended .50-caliber shell casings from one Hellcat struck the windshield and leading edge of the plane following immediately behind, resulting in damage that the repair crews back on the ship initially thought was from ground fire. The Avengers followed behind, with bomb hits on the runway, barracks, and support buildings.

The weather worsened at night, bringing towering seas and green water breaking over the *Cowpens'* flight deck. Conditions were treacherous, with the gathering darkness and the wet and pitching deck making the already challenging task of landing on the narrow CVL deck that much more difficult. The VF-25 squadron history described the conditions as "probably the worst ever experienced by this outfit in the Pacific."[17] All hands were used to the warm tropical waters near the equator, and the combination of cold weather and high seas was an unpleasant shock. "Half the ship's crew was sick," wrote Art Daly in his journal. "The weather was brutal, sleet at times. I froze my ass off. Some asshole stole my blanket. Our quarters were as cold as hell. I slept with my pea coat on."[18]

Overall, the raid destroyed more than one hundred enemy planes that could have been used in the upcoming Marianas battle, but it was a costly exchange, with twelve downed US aircraft. Despite these losses, the ship's history concluded it was a "highly profitable target," reducing the Bonins to "a poor condition to stage flights into the Marianas."[19] Regardless of the results, Harrill was eager to get out of Dodge, and he recovered his planes as soon as he could. Clark, in contrast, was determined to spend every possible minute on the attack, and did not turn south toward Task Force 58 and Saipan until nearly dark.

Where the Meatballs Grow Thickest

By June 18, battle with the approaching enemy fleet was looking increasingly likely for the following day. *Cowpens*, Clark, and Harrill rejoined Task Force 58 that morning, giving Spruance and Mitscher the full force they wanted to fight the Japanese. Although their fleet was beyond the reach of US scout planes, an enemy slipup betrayed their position. Japanese commanders made a brief radio transmission to Tinian to arrange supporting attacks from land-based planes. American intelligence intercepted the transmission and triangulated the Japanese position to approximately four hundred miles from Task Force 58—data that soon made its way to Spruance. Based on the enemy fleet's location, Spruance and his staff concluded that the enemy was preserving its advantage of range. Japanese planes had longer legs than their American counterparts, and at that distance they could attack the US task force while remaining out of reach of US counterattacks. Additionally, the US submarines tracking the Japanese approach had not spotted the whole enemy fleet, and their periodic, incomplete sightings left Spruance uncertain whether they were seeing parts of one big formation or multiple smaller groups. Complicated, multipart attacks were a hallmark of Japanese naval strategy, and

Spruance worried that trying to close the distance to the enemy left the landings vulnerable to an end run attack by a secondary Japanese force. His primary responsibility was to protect the beachhead, and as long as there was uncertainty about the location and disposition of the enemy he concluded that the best response was to stay put and let the Japanese come to him. Spruance's decision ran contrary to the accumulated lessons learned in the last three years of war, which said that victory in carrier warfare typically went to the side that struck first. His defensive approach meant that Task Force 58 would just have to take the enemy's punches the next day. As Mitscher's chief of staff, Arleigh Burke, expressed it, "We knew we were going to have hell slugged out of us in the morning."[20]

On the evening of the eighteenth, *Cowpens'* executive officer, Cmdr. Hugh Nieman, informed Gaylord Brown, the acting air group commander, that battle was imminent. The task group's air plan called for continuous CAPs from dawn to dusk; the Moo had orders to keep eight Hellcats in the air at all times and another fourteen ready to launch at a moment's notice. Based on this information, Brown assembled his pilots and briefed them on the situation. Many of the Moo's pilots were excited to learn of the potential battle ahead. Japanese resistance in the *Cowpens'* previous operations was uneven, and the ship's fighter pilots were eager to take on the Japanese carriers. Referring to the red rising sun emblem on the side of enemy planes, the pilots quipped, "The Jap fleet is where the meatballs grow thickest."[21]

Brownie also claimed for his own use the *Cowpens'* only F6F-5 Hellcat, which had arrived on board not long before. This improved version of the Hellcat had been in production only since April 1944 and had just started to reach the fleet. The F6F-5 soon proved to be Task Force 58's utility infielder of a fighter, excelling not only at fighter sweeps but also ground attack. The -5s were on the surface similar to the earlier F6F-3, but they were better armored, slightly more maneuverable, and fifteen knots faster. Most important, the F6F-5 had a water-injection system in its engine that provided 250 extra horsepower for as much as fifteen minutes at a time—a brief burst of power that one of the Moo's pilots likened to "a catapult shot all the way."[22]

The Marianas Turkey Shoot: A Battle to Write Home About

June 19, 1944, was a beautiful day for a battle. The Pacific sunrise put on a magnificent display that morning, starting with shades of deep red gradually turning to pink and orange over the azure sea. It was warm and clear with excellent visibility; perfect weather for flying. Down at sea level, the 9 carriers and 450 planes of the Japanese fleet and 15 carriers and 900 planes of Spruance's Task Force 58 were separated by less than four hundred miles of ocean. By the end of the day these two forces would fight to conclusion the fifth and final fleet battle in history where the opposing ships never once saw one another. The day's action was to be bigger than any of those previous clashes; the twenty-four carriers at sea on this day were more than the combined flattops employed in the previous four.[23]

General quarters sounded at 3 a.m., and *Cowpens* and the rest of the fleet prepared for action. Hatches and portholes were dogged down, life vests and helmets donned, and all men were at their battle stations. Down in the VF-25 ready room, the Moo's fighter pilots were nervous and eager, waiting for the enemy to appear. Fighter pilot Don McKinley likened the mood to a locker room before a big football game—"[nervous] butterflies and little conversation."[24] Each man was alone with his thoughts, preoccupied with the battle ahead or wishing that lost comrades and friends like Bob Price or Papo Parker could be there to fight alongside them. While some pilots on other carriers relaxed their guard when an attack did not materialize at dawn, the Moo's fighter pilots stayed put in the ready room and anxiously waited for the order to fly. "We were ready to go," McKinley recalled.[25]

Mitscher, too, was on guard. Guam was abuzz with enemy activity that morning, with Hellcats from other carriers downing almost three dozen enemy planes. But it was the radar tracks of the approaching first wave that convinced him that the long-awaited Japanese attack was at hand. At his direction at 10:15 a.m., all fifteen carriers swung into the wind and accelerated to twenty knots to launch aircraft. Mitscher instructed his FDOs to issue the recall order for the twenty-three fighters circling over Guam—with the old circus call of "Hey, Rube!"[26]

While the dozens of Hellcats already in the air on CAP—including those from *Cowpens*—streaked toward the enemy, the rest of the flattops launched their ready fighters. The Moo's pilots' vigilance paid off; the ship distinguished herself by being the first carrier from Task Force 58 to get her planes in the air. Only two minutes passed between Mitscher's order to launch planes and the first of *Cowpens*' Hellcats lifting off the deck. Ed Haley recalled that it was a true scramble, with no preflight briefing—just the order "Pilots, man your planes." Haley sprinted up the ladder to the flight deck, climbed into the first unoccupied Hellcat, and was airborne a few moments later.[27] After launch, Haley joined up with another Hellcat piloted by Lee Adams, and they turned to the west and climbed at full throttle.

Don McKinley must have been slightly more fleet of foot than Haley; he was third in line off the flight deck. He recalled how instructions to the pilots were not to waste time joining up as a squadron or with designated wingmen. "If any vectors [from the FDO] were given I did not hear them," McKinley recalled years after the battle, and described how planes all around him were just pointing their noses west toward the enemy and "hanging on their propellers" to gain altitude as fast as possible.[28] As the planes rushed toward the enemy they formed into groups with whoever was nearby. As McKinley headed west, another *Cowpens* Hellcat formed up on his wing, and McKinley was relieved to see it was one of his roommates, Fred "Stinky" Stieglitz. Haley, McKinley, Stieglitz, and their wingmen were only a few of the scores of Hellcats leaping off carrier decks across Task Force 58 in those first few minutes, bringing the total number of fighters facing the Japanese to more than 230.

On the long flight to Task Force 58, the Japanese pilots fell out of formation and spread out into a drawn-out line. When the first wave's leading elements drew to within seventy-five miles of the perimeter of the American formation, their flight leaders circled to allow their lagging aircraft to catch up and to issue final instructions. It took the Japanese fifteen minutes to regain their tactical cohesion, during which time the Hellcats gained valuable altitude and distance toward them. Their briefing finally over, the Japanese airplanes broke out of their circle and started again toward the task force. By this time, American fighters had closed the distance. Eight Hellcats from *Lexington*'s VF-15 were the first to join battle at 10:35 a.m., followed by fighters from *Cowpens* and others from *Bunker Hill*, *Princeton*, and *Enterprise* minutes later.

Eight *Cowpens* pilots joined the melee at about twenty thousand feet and within twenty miles of the task force. "The interception is marvelous," the Moo's pilots enthused, "and the next hour is one huge dogfight, with Jap planes literally falling like flies."[29] The air was filled with fighters, and the radios crackled with instructions from the FDOs and chatter from the pilots. The *Cowpens'* radar screen was confused with friendly and enemy contacts as the battle devolved into a series of individual dogfights; given the Americans' greater numbers, often multiple Hellcats were chasing a single Japanese plane. In the swirling melee, the Moo's pilots became separated and afterward found themselves flying wing on whatever US fighter they could find.

Gaylord Brown and his division were guided to the attack by the Task Group 58.4 FDO, who brought them within five miles of the enemy and instructed them to "look sharp" when the Japanese should be in sight. Sure enough, Brownie spotted a formation of enemy planes above and just off his bow, called out the tally-ho—the traditional call upon sighting the enemy—and turned his division to attack. As Brownie closed in, the group of twenty-five to thirty enemy aircraft were beginning to break out of formation. "By this time it seemed there were hundreds of F6Fs in the air," Brownie recalled, and under their attack "the enemy formation was scattering. The bombers were diving away and only the fighters remained at our altitude."[30] Two Zekes closed in on Brownie's division as he entered the fray. Brownie and his wingman, Raffman, turned into the lead plane, and McKinley and Stieglitz took the second.

As soon as Brownie turned into the leader, the enemy plane broke off and made a climbing turn in an attempt to evade, with Brownie behind and just out of gun range. Brownie hit his F6F-5's water injection for a burst of speed and closed to within two hundred feet. He fired a long burst from behind and below, knocking pieces off the Zeke. As Brownie pulled away, Raffman caught up and with his own burst set the Zeke afire, and it plummeted down to the sea. Both men could still see aircraft below them, and with the broken cloud cover it was difficult to distinguish between US and Japanese fighters until they drew close. The pair headed back in the general direction of the task group, when through a break in the clouds Brownie spotted a lone airplane circling about two miles ahead. Brownie closed in for the attack; as he later explained, "If one of our planes had gotten separated from its leader, it would have headed for the carriers, and would not be circling."[31] Closing in to a mile from the aircraft he confirmed it as a bomb-carrying Zeke and jumped on its tail. "I splashed him in flames with one burst," he recalled.[32]

Meanwhile, McKinley and Stieglitz had lost their first Zeke and were looking for other targets. "The sky was full of planes at all altitudes, some burning and falling," McKinley described. The pair were climbing through 7,500 feet when McKinley saw a three-plane section of Jill torpedo planes with torpedoes attached. They were painted a brownish gray with red meatballs on their wings and fuselages, and were flying a tight V formation 1,500 feet below, heading toward the task force. McKinley was having less luck on the radio than his boss Brownie. As he later described it, there was so much "garbage chatter" on the airwaves that there was no way he could communicate with Stieglitz, who was flying close formation on his port side. He got Stieglitz's attention by waving from the cockpit and pointing at the Jills, and Stieglitz nodded to acknowledge he also saw them. The pair swooped in behind the formation of torpedo bombers and closed rapidly. As McKinley and Stieglitz closed in, the Jills split up. McKinley followed the pair that dove away to the right and Stieglitz the single that broke off to the left.

Stieglitz dove on the single Jill and quickly dispatched it. He called the FDO on the radio to report "scratch one fish," pulled away from the fight in a climbing turn, and was never seen again.[33] McKinley pursued his pair of Jills into a shallow dive toward the water at high speed. The Japanese pilots took little evasive action, so McKinley closed to within one hundred yards and opened fire. Under his guns, the lead Japanese aircraft rolled over and went into the water without burning. McKinley stayed to make sure it hit the water before sprinting after the second Jill. When McKinley resumed his position on the enemy's tail, the Jill had descended to fifty feet in altitude, just above the waves. McKinley recalled, "I was directly behind him and his [tail] gunner was firing at me. I noticed splashes in the water at that time, but was so intent on that plane that I did not see we were approaching the American task force and the splashes were coming from friendly antiaircraft guns trying to get the Jill before it dropped its torpedo."[34] After McKinley hit the Jill with several bursts of fire, it began to smoke, then nosed over and hit the water with a tremendous splash. McKinley finally looked up from his gunsight to see an *Essex*-class US carrier about a mile away, with its antiaircraft guns blazing away at him. McKinley pulled away so the gunners could see the profile of his Hellcat, and the fire stopped almost immediately. Now alone, McKinley regained altitude and was quickly jumped by two Zekes, but he managed to lose them in the clouds.

Haley and Adams fell behind the rest of their division while climbing toward the dogfight. Arriving on the scene, they found several friendly Hellcats at eighteen thousand feet and were looking for their division leader when they saw suspicious planes low on the water. They dove down to investigate and joined a melee of five Hellcats trying to corner a single Zeke, who expertly evaded their attacks. "Each time one of us would get on his tail or in a position to fire he managed to roll inside our turn," Haley later said.[35] After several unsuccessful firing passes, Adams's guns began to cut out, and Haley suspected the Zeke was having his own problems or was out of ammunition. The enemy pilot turned directly at Haley and made a close head-on pass. "He came right at me and I was sure he was trying to ram my fighter for the red spinner on his prop got larger and larger as he closed. At the last second I belted my control stick forward and he flashed over my head so close I could see the rivets on the belly of his aircraft."[36]

Finally, after failing to connect with a few bursts of his own, Haley broke off the fight when his guns overheated. He was one thousand feet above the Zeke when it somehow eluded the other American fighters and fled westward. Haley jammed the throttle forward and went in pursuit; after forty miles he closed the distance and rolled in behind him. Haley fired a short burst, anticipating a left break in a climbing turn, as the Zero was sluggish to the right at that speed. "Sure enough he rolled left," Haley recalled. "I cut inside his turn blasting his wing root and cockpit with a long burst from all six guns. The wing burst into flame and he rolled over on his back and went straight in from about 1,500 feet."[37]

With his quarry gone, Haley looked around to assess his situation. "There was no one in sight, even my wingman had left me, which made me very unhappy. I was at about 1,000 feet with nothing but Pacific Ocean in all directions. It was time to go, so I headed for home, climbing to the east."[38] Much to Haley's relief, after about twenty minutes the Fifth Fleet drew into view. Years later, Haley vividly recalled that moment. "It was an awesome sight, the whole Fifth Fleet steaming west, stretching to the limit of my visibility from horizon to horizon."[39] Meanwhile, Haley's wingman, Lee Adams, had lost contact with the enemy. While looking for other planes, a lone F6F appeared, pursued by three Zekes, and Adams made a high side run, firing at the leading plane. At this the Zekes scattered. The other Hellcat joined up on Adams, and together the pair pursued one of his former antagonists, which was low on the water. He made a firing run from behind and to the side; the Zeke hit the water with its wings and fuselage level, bounced once, and landed in the sea, apparently intact.

Lt. Kicker approached the melee at fifteen thousand feet with his three wingmen when they sighted many planes fighting below and dove to investigate. By the time they reached three thousand feet there were no enemy fighters left, although they could see several descending toward the water, trailing smoke and flames. Kicker circled to evaluate the situation and spotted a lone Jill some distance away from the other planes; jamming his throttle forward, he easily closed the distance and swung in behind the enemy plane, which did not take evasive action. He fired a short burst and it caught fire and dropped straight into the sea. When Kicker peeled off to dispatch his Jill, Ensign Jim Nourse spotted another two flying low on the water. Having too much speed from his dive, he dropped his flaps to avoid overrunning, got on the tail of one of the pair, and smoked it with one burst. Nourse temporarily lost sight of the second

Jill, and was climbing away when he saw five F6Fs diving after the enemy plane. Nourse dove ahead of the other friendly fighters, and fired a long burst into the Jill from above and astern, downing it.

Ensigns Eckhardt and George Massenburg became separated from their division in a dive from altitude to sea level to investigate the same dogfight that had drawn the attention of several of their squadronmates. Discovering that fight was largely over, the pair were climbing back to altitude when they stumbled onto more enemy planes. Massenburg's engine had not been running well since he took off, but he managed to get in a small deflection burst at a Zeke. At that moment, he lost power completely and the Zeke pulled in behind him. Eckhardt shot the Zeke off Massenburg's tail, drawing smoke (a probable kill), but at that moment his wingman radioed to say his engine had quit and that he was going in. Eckhardt opted not to pursue his wounded Zeke and followed his wingman down. He confirmed that Massenburg made a successful water landing and got into his survival raft, then radioed his downed friend's position to the fleet—approximately fifty miles west of the task force. He circled overhead until his fuel ran low and he had to return to base. The request to recover Massenburg went up the chain of command from *Cowpens* to Harrill and his staff aboard *Essex*, but either by omission or decision no rescue was ever forthcoming, and Massenburg was never seen again.

Dénouement

Thus ended the Moo's contribution to the greatest carrier battle of the war, an experience that its pilots described as "something to write home about."[40] Task Force 58's fighters blocked every attack the Japanese threw at them that day, probably destroying somewhere between 250 and 294 enemy planes for a loss of approximately 22 Hellcats—with the Moo accounting for 9 sure enemy kills and 3 probables. The pilots received two celebratory bottles of beer or shots of medicinal brandy to toast the day's victories. *Lexington* pilot Ziggy Neff famously summed up the mood; after shooting down four fighters, Ziggy exuberantly claimed that "Why, hell. It was just like an old-time turkey shoot down home!" His squadron commander overhead the comment and passed it up the chain, and the name stuck. And so, aviation historian Barrett Tillman observed, "did the air battle pass into history as 'The Great Marianas Turkey Shoot.' "[41]

Aboard the *Cowpens*, the exuberance over the day's victory was dampened by the squadron's two losses, and especially Massenburg's abandonment at sea only fifty miles from the Task Force. The pilots were furious at Admiral Harrill for leaving their colleague to die; "the failure of our admiral to rescue Massenburg," explained the squadron history, "is another nail in the coffin in his reputation as far as we are concerned. Morale was never lower than now as a result of the admiral's indecisive policy regarding rescue."[42] Even the ship's official reports of the day's action diplomatically criticized Harrill and his staff. "It is strongly recommended that every effort be made to rescue aviators who are forced down at sea. Failure to provide adequate rescue is very injurious to morale."[43] Receiving condolences for their losses from an admiral the squadron blamed for Massenburg's death only rubbed salt into these wounds. I JOIN WITH YOU IN DEEP REGRETS FOR THE LOSSES YOU HAVE SUFFERED, Harrill signaled to Task Group 58.4 on June 22. THE OPERATIONS OF THE CARRIERS AND THEIR GROUPS HAVE BEEN EXCELLENT X TURNING BACK THE ENEMY AIRCRAFT BY ANNIHILATION WAS SUPERB X I AM VERY PROUD TO BE YOUR GROUP COMMANDER.[44] The feeling was not mutual as far as Air Group 25 was concerned.

CHAPTER 17

Left Behind

Spruance's victory in the Turkey Shoot was by nature a defensive one. While the Japanese air strength had been shattered, it had been US submarines, not the carriers, who inflicted the only losses on its ships, sinking two enemy flattops as the aerial battle raged. As a result, the admiral wanted a crack at the enemy fleet, some 320 miles away and running for home. As before, every mile Spruance chased the enemy fleet to the west took him farther away from his primary responsibility of guarding the landing beaches, and he was looking for a way to accomplish both simultaneously. Admiral Harrill failed to fuel his destroyers before the battle and afterward he requested an opportunity to do so. This gave Spruance and Mitscher a way to guard the beaches and prevent their least aggressive admiral from slowing them down. Harrill was ordered to stay behind to refuel and cover Saipan.

As the rest of the task force went off in pursuit of the enemy fleet—managing one mass air strike in the dark before it escaped out of range—Cowpens, Harrill, and Task Group 58.4 lingered off Saipan until July 6. After the excitement of the day before, and the disappointment of missing the strike against the Japanese fleet, the Moo's pilots, in their words, settled down to the "drudgery of daily patrols and strikes on Guam and Rota."[1] Pickings were slim, as days of air strikes had cleared these islands of most worthwhile targets. The fatigue of several days' near-constant operations had worn out pilots and crew alike, while the oppressive summer heat led to widespread heat rash, worsening already frayed nerves.

Admiral Harrill was not through neglecting downed fliers, and pilot Jim Nourse was the final beneficiary of his slipshod treatment. On June 24, the Moo launched a routine strike on Rota along with planes from *Langley*. The mission itself was successful; the Moo's eight Hellcats and four Avengers scored fifteen direct bomb hits on the runway and four others on some nearby buildings. While the antiaircraft fire had been paltry, Nourse's Hellcat picked up a round in his engine, and the plane dumped him in the Pacific five miles offshore. Despite requests from the *Cowpens*, Harrill or his staff did not organize a rescue, passing the buck to the landing forces to pick him up. The unfortunate Nourse spent a long night in his survival raft, paddling with his hands to keep from washing ashore on Japanese-held Rota. His luck did not get much better the following day, June 25. The seaplane that arrived to pick him up crashed while landing, and it was not until a friendly minelayer arrived an hour later that Nourse was finally recovered. "Believe me," Nourse later recalled, "that was a thriller."[2]

To the relief of everyone aboard the Moo, Admiral Harrill did not remain in command much longer. His health quickly deteriorated, and by the end of the month he was bedridden and underwent surgery for appendicitis. Harrill's poor performance during the battle had cost him Mitscher's confidence, and his illness was the perfect excuse for his face-saving removal. Harrill was relieved of command and sent back to San Diego; he never commanded at sea again.

Price's Saga

Admiral Jocko Clark was never one to leave a job half done, and his rushed sortie to the Bonin Islands left him eager to go back and give them a more thorough working over. Clark received permission from Mitscher to head back to Iwo Jima, and so his Task Group 58.1 turned north.

Meanwhile, one of Bob Price's friends, Tex McCrary, who was working on Clark's staff aboard *Hornet*, had a dream that Price was floating in the Pacific, waiting for somebody to pick him up. McCrary had the eerie feeling it was true. He shared his vision with the admiral's flag lieutenant, who in turn shared it with Clark. McCrary feared Clark would think him nuts, but Jocko was eager to help.

Unlike Harrill, Clark's policy was to try and rescue all fliers no matter how slim the chances, and all three men sat down with the charts to figure out where Price might be. Taking into account the winds and currents, they estimated Price might be about one hundred miles out of the task group's way, and Clark approved the detour. Their estimates of time and drift were right, and late that afternoon destroyer *Boyd* found Price floating in his life raft, severely weakened from hunger and dehydration. The admiral personally greeted Price when he arrived on *Hornet* and pinned a Purple Heart on him.

Being lost at sea is the fear of every naval aviator; some five years earlier, in February 1939, Price had put words to this sentiment while a junior pilot aboard *Saratoga*. "Sometimes I wonder why I didn't get in the Army Air Corps!," he wrote in his journal. "At least when they have a forced landing they don't have to swim! I'd much rather be stranded on some lonely mountain or something than on the water in a flimsy little rubber boat!"[3] But that was exactly the situation Price found himself in, and he did the best he could in his difficult situation. The continuing rain squalls kept him supplied with water, and while he had no great desire for food, the fish and gulls were abundant.

After a couple of days, Price still wasn't hungry but decided to try and eat a gull as a preemptive measure. He had no problems grabbing one, then cut off its head with his survival knife and skinned and cleaned it. The meat was unpalatable, very salty and fishy, and it seemed to make Price thirstier, so he threw the rest overboard. Instead he found the birds useful for another purpose—company. As a diversion, Price often engaged in one-sided conversations with the gulls, which he likened to talking to a pet dog. The practice seemed silly in retrospect, but he said it kept him engaged and occupied during the long, uneventful days. For food, underneath his raft were a variety of small fish who were sheltering in the shade. He wasn't able to catch one with an improvised lure, but on day six, two fish leapt into the raft—one about four inches long and the other about six. "I immediately cleaned and ate both, finding them very tasty and refreshing," Price described. "They were quite juicy and helped to alleviate my thirst to a great extent."[4]

By June 23—his eleventh day adrift—dehydration was really beginning to take a toll on Price. The inside of his mouth was dry and covered with a salty scale, and his tongue was swollen and prickly. But the day was his son's fourth birthday, and Price tried to stay positive with thoughts of his family. Late that afternoon, he was bailing out his raft when he spotted a destroyer closing fast from behind, about three hundred yards distant. As the ship pulled in closer, a deckhand yelled to Price, asking if he could take a line thrown to him. Price described it as "one of the most beautiful sounds I had heard in many a day."[5]

He waved affirmatively, caught the line thrown from the ship, and pulled himself and his raft alongside the cargo net that the crew threw over the side. Three sailors climbed down the net to help Price from his raft and get him aboard. Price couldn't walk, so sailors hustled him below to the sick bay where he received a quick exam; he was found to have lost almost thirty pounds in his eleven days at sea. The medics gave him "a half glass of water at intervals that seemed too long," Price said, and also "a small cup of soup but water was the big attraction. The relief and gratification felt after having been rescued was almost indescribable and I immediately began to feel better physically."[6]

On the Way Out, for Keeps

Air Group 25 learned of Price's rescue on June 24; the news considerably lifted their morale. While their new task group commander, Rear Adm. Gerald Bogan, was a marked improvement over his predecessor, all hands had been run ragged by the hectic pace of operations since they'd begun supporting FORAGER on June 11. Finally, the pilots received the news they had been waiting for. *Cowpens* received its orders to depart for Pearl Harbor, where Air Group 25 would be relieved and sent stateside. "When directed by the Commanding Officer, USS *Cowpens*," the orders instructed, "Air Group 25 will regard itself detached and will report to the Commandant Fourteenth Naval District for transportation to a port in the United States."[7] "It is over!" cheered the VF-25 historian. "We are on the way out, for keeps... everyone is proud of the way the gang has held together and done its stuff despite losses, a killing schedule, and the lowering of morale attendant upon our admiral's indecisive and ineffectual rescue policy."[8]

A review of the air group's performance in FORAGER demonstrates they had something to be proud of. The air group, and particularly VF-25—which did the bulk of the flying—kept up a punishing tempo. From June 6 to July 3, *Cowpens* flew 959 sorties, and her Hellcat pilots on average over that period had more than ninety hours in the air. Upon their return to the States, the Navy trumpeted their endurance in press releases as a record for sustained combat flying for carrier-based aviation, with each pilot spending at least four hours a day in the air for twenty-three days straight. During the peak days—the first three days of FORAGER and a three-day stretch around the Turkey Shoot—some section and division leaders were flying as much as twelve hours a day, and the ship's after-action report noted how the air group was badly fatigued by the time they shipped home.[9]

The Moo's pilots had 37 confirmed aerial victories, 20 of them during FORAGER, and claimed another 83 aircraft destroyed on the ground. VF-25 took the heaviest losses in the air group; of the 15 original pilots who joined the ship in the summer of 1943, 6 did not come home, a loss rate of 40 percent. In addition, the squadron lost 7 more replacement pilots before its tour was complete. In contrast, the torpedo squadron fared better, losing no pilots but three aircrew.

Cowpens made two stops on her way back to Pearl, first at Eniwetok and then Majuro, just long enough to transfer supplies and passengers and replenish and refuel for the long trip back to Pearl. A stop at Majuro also provided the opportunity for some much-needed celebration. The ship held a recreation party on the beach for half the crew, while the pilots and officers trooped ashore to, in their words, "take the edge off a big thirst" at the island's O club.[10]

Bob Price was waiting for the ship when it arrived at Eniwetok, with what the pilots described as "a story to knock our ears off about those

11 days in the raft."[11] Price was thrilled for the opportunity to rejoin his men on their way home, and the pilots were delighted to have their commander and friend returned to them. The squadron history describes how the pilots were "pleased with him for his good fortune and the stuff it takes to live that long on eight ounces of water, and he with us for carrying on as always while he was communing with Davy Jones."[12] Price was rapidly regaining his lost weight and took the opportunity at Eniwetok to write home to his wife, reassuring her that he was OK. He had already been interviewed by several reporters and worried that his wife would first hear of his experience from the newspaper. Price described his physical condition and his subsequent recovery, noting, "I won't attempt to go into all details except to say that I don't recommend such a procedure as a steady diet."[13] Price commented only half in jest that the opportunity to take his squadron home "no doubt had a lot to do with my quick recovery!"[14]

It was a five-day cruise back to Pearl Harbor, and the VF-25 squadron history for this period recorded "no flying, thank God."[15] A day out from Hawaii, Captain Taylor ordered a general muster and presented awards and commendations. Writing that evening, Price described how the recognition fueled his men's eagerness to return home. "We had a nice little ceremony today at which the Captain presented...awards to pilots and gunners of the group. That has further elated the boys and believe me they're a bunch to handle!"[16] Nine men received air medals, while Taylor pinned the Distinguished Flying Cross on Bob Price, plus a gold star in lieu of a second air medal. The text of his commendation cited Price's "heroism and extraordinary achievement...while leading a fighter squadron in many successful attacks...his tactical handling of his own or combined groups evidenced a superb grasp of the fundamentals of combat aviation, and his personal conduct was an inspiration for those who flew with him."[17]

Cowpens pulled into Pearl Harbor on July 16, and the Moo's complement were astounded to see all the workers at the yards cheering her arrival while the Navy band played the traditional "Aloha" in welcome. With the earnings from four months at sea burning holes in their pockets, everyone was eager to get ashore and enjoy all that Honolulu had to offer. Captain Taylor quickly obliged them, releasing the crew for liberty in rotating shifts. As for Air Group 25, they were officially detached from the *Cowpens* the following day and secured berths for the West Coast on an Army troop ship. Ed Haley had fond memories of the journey, recalling how "we slept a lot, played cards a lot and just plain loafed a lot. It was a happy time. We were going home and were a very, very relaxed group."[18]

CHAPTER 18

The Recapture of the Philippines

A New Moo Crew: Air Group 22

Cowpens' new squadrons from Air Group 22 arrived on board on July 30 as the ship readied for sea. Each of the air groups that came aboard the Moo had their own personality; in contrast to Bob Price's genial band of brothers in Air Group 25, their successors in 22 were a hard luck crew. They would have a difficult tour aboard the Moo; with the task force now operating out of the Western Marshall Islands, they were much closer to their primary targets in the Philippines. Accordingly, Air Group 22 spent less time in transit and more time in combat. The relentless pace of operations and steady casualties throughout the fall diluted its cohesion, while its pilots' overconfidence and uneven performance put them on a collision course with Captain Taylor.

Lt. Cmdr. Thomas Jenkins's Air Group 22 was a combat-experienced group when they arrived aboard *Cowpens*. Their introduction to combat happened aboard the Moo's sister ship, *Independence*, as well as a brief stint aboard another light carrier, *Belleau Wood*. Either separately or together, the fighter (VF-22) and torpedo (VT-22) squadrons fought at Baker, Howland, and Marcus Islands in August 1943, followed by Wake in October. After the Moo's collision with the *Abbot*, *Independence* took her place at Bougainville and Rabaul in the Solomon Islands in November, and then joined Task Force 50 at Tarawa later that month—where a torpedo put an end to her first combat tour.

While Indy went into drydock, Air Group 22 was ordered to California for thirty days' leave before re-forming for a second cruise. It gathered to begin their predeployment training in pleasant Watsonville, California, outside Monterey. Accommodations for the officers were so luxurious there that some among the air group suspected that Indy's misfortune at Tarawa was a blessing in disguise. One VT-22 pilot, Robert Soule, described how "all the big shipping magnates and so forth in San Francisco had this gorgeous club and all these houses on the beach." The residents were worried about a Japanese invasion, and so most rented the houses to the Navy for the duration. It was easy living; each pilot had his own mansion on the sea, and he sunbathed and swam in the morning and flew in the afternoon.[1] The air group was genuinely sorry to leave Watsonville when they shoved off from Alameda for Pearl Harbor on June 27, 1944.

The Deputy Commander: The Ace Pilot

The most detailed account of Air Group 22's time aboard the *Cowpens* comes from Lt. Clement Craig. Clem was the deputy commander of Air Group 22's fighter squadron. He was a stern man, devoted to duty, and fated to be the ship's highest-scoring fighter pilot. Born in 1914 in Indianapolis, Clem was the son of the local fire chief. He was serious even as a young boy; his father joked that his middle initial—M, for Melvin—actually stood for "morbid." Clem worked his way through high school during the Great Depression, earning a bachelor's degree in journalism in 1936 from Butler University. At the time, the nation's unemployment rate was more than 14 percent, and even a college graduate like Clem struggled to find meaningful work.

Clem had been interested in aviation since college, when a local barnstormer took him up in a two-seat JN-4 Jenny biplane. The Jenny was the first mass-produced American warplane, a fragile construction of wood, fabric, and wires. But it didn't matter to Clem; at some point in the flight the pilot turned the controls over to him, and he was hooked. With civilian employment turning out to be one disappointment after another, joining the Navy as a pilot seemed like a good alternative. Clem earned his wings in Pensacola in April 1941. With the threat of war growing ever more real, the Navy was rapidly expanding its pilot training program. At least in part due to his age and maturity—at twenty-six, he was several years older than most trainees—Clem's first assignment in the Navy was teaching others to fly. He liked to say that he was "too old to fight, so they made me an instructor."[2] Clem spent more than eighteen months in that role, and by the time he joined VF-22 in September 1942, he was one of the most experienced pilots in the squadron, with almost 1,100 hours in the air. Clem's experience complemented his natural aptitude as a combat pilot; by the time he arrived aboard *Cowpens* with the rest of VF-22 in the summer of 1944, he had already scored two-and-a-quarter aerial kills. He shot down a Dave during the raid on Wake Island and a Val dive bomber at Rabaul, and he shared the downing of a Betty with three other pilots off Betio.

Air Group 22's Early Stumbles

The Moo's training and departure schedule did not allow much time for the new air group to settle in. *Cowpens* was due at Eniwetok by mid-August, and Captain Taylor had only a few days in the safe waters around Oahu to gauge the capabilities of his new pilots and help them shake off the rust from several months away from the war. *Cowpens* made two short training cruises from Oahu in late July and early August—and the air group spent the time in between relaxing at their favorite watering hole, a tennis club close to Pearl Harbor.

In their first exercises aboard *Cowpens*, not much went well. The pilots were out of practice, and their landing technique, practice intercepts, and torpedo drops showed considerable room for improvement. Moreover, the air group suffered its first fatality of the cruise when a malfunctioning catapult put Lt. John C. Maxey from Jackson, Mississippi, and his Hellcat into the Pacific, where he drowned. Destroyer *Halligan* recovered his body, and the young pilot was buried in Honolulu when the ship returned to port. The ship, too, had her own teething problems. One of her newly rebuilt boilers lost pressure, adding another item to the ship's predeparture repairs punch list. Then it was back to Pearl Harbor on August 8, where, according to Clem: "Liberty commenced at once. Muster at tennis club."[3]

Cowpens weighed anchor on August 10 for the seven-day cruise to Eniwetok, where the fleet was gathering. As the journey began, Clem and his fliers settled into the routine of shipboard life. "Most notable thing so far this cruise is the complete change of attitude from that of the *Independence*," Clem noted in his diary on August 11. "This really is a happy ship."[4] The routine of CAP and antisubmarine patrols helped both pass the time and provide some much needed practice for the air group. And from Clem's perspective there was still considerable work to do—a case in point being the dramatic crash of Ens. Newton Streetman on August 15. He made a hard landing, bounced over the barriers, and smashed into the mass of planes parked forward. While no one was injured, three planes were damaged so severely that they never flew again. Clem delivered his verdict in his journal: "Poor technique was responsible for damaging planes."[5]

Halsey and McCain

Vice Admiral William Halsey relieved Raymond Spruance as part of the two-platoon system of rotating fleet command. While the ships remained the same, the former Fifth Fleet and Task Force 58 under Admiral Spruance became Third Fleet and Task Force 38 under Admiral Halsey. While Halsey was a legend in the fleet and his daughter was the Moo's sponsor at her christening, this was *Cowpens*' first encounter with the admiral, whom the press dubbed the "Bull."

Halsey was the polar opposite of his predecessor. Where Spruance was a calculating, analytical strategist, Halsey was brash, sometimes operating by the seat of his pants. One naval officer summed up the difference between the two men. "When Admiral Spruance was in command, you knew precisely what he was going to do. But when Admiral Halsey was in command, you never knew what he was going to do."[6] Halsey was a blunt instrument when it came to strategy; he simply threw everything he had at the enemy. Where Spruance was fastidious about his health, Halsey powered through his duties with ten cups of coffee and precisely forty cigarettes a day. Quick with profanity and with a healthy appetite for scotch, Halsey professed that "I never trust a fighting man who doesn't smoke or drink."[7]

Halsey also had a magnetic charisma and desire for publicity that Spruance lacked. He didn't rein in his aggressive nature in his press conferences or communiqués; in one breath he would offer thanks to God for the safety and success of his men and in the next promise the death and destruction of his enemies. Typical of his bombast was Halsey declaring of the Japanese, "We are drowning and burning them all over the Pacific, and it is just as much pleasure to burn them as to drown them."[8] He frequently signed off his communications with the slogan that made him famous: "Kill Japs, kill Japs, and keep on killing Japs."[9] Halsey's take-no-prisoners demeanor was especially effective among the enlisted, who appreciated his blunt manner and desire for a fight. The admiral once overheard a conversation between two enlisted men where one said to the other, "I'd go to hell for that old son of a bitch," and Halsey broke in to scold them, stating he was "not so old, young man."[10]

Cowpens soon met her new task group commander, Vice Adm. John "Slew" McCain, recently arrived from Washington. McCain was slight of build, with a shambling gait and a visage that some sailors thought resembled Popeye. McCain came from a distinguished line of soldiers stretching back to the American Revolution. One forebear served on George Washington's staff, and others fought in the War of 1812 or with the Confederacy in the Civil War. Slew was the first McCain to attend Annapolis rather than West Point, graduating in 1906. In subsequent decades, his descendants carried on the McCain military legacy in the Navy; his son commanded the Pacific Fleet during the Vietnam War, while his grandson was a naval aviator turned prisoner of war turned senator from Arizona and presidential candidate.

McCain had long hoped to command Task Force 38, but he lacked experience with multicarrier formations, and so needed to apprentice first. *Cowpens'* Task Group 38.1 was his training assignment, and as part of this learning process, McCain made the rounds of his flattops, visiting *Cowpens* to meet Captain Taylor. This allowed the ship's officers and men to see firsthand one of McCain's eccentricities: his hat. McCain always wore a shabby fatigue cap that his wife had embroidered with the scrambled eggs (gold braid) of an admiral. Even the tolerant Halsey called it the most disreputable hat he'd ever seen on an officer. *Cowpens'* executive officer, Hugh Nieman, made sure everyone on board was forewarned not to react when they saw it to avoid embarrassing either the admiral or Captain Taylor. "His cap is said to be a knock out," wrote Clem. "The executive officer warned everyone not to laugh at the cap. Well, RHIP [rank has its privileges]."[11]

The happy ship vibes Clem described in his journal soon began to diminish, with Task Group 38.1's brief training sortie on August 21–22 fueling Captain Taylor's dissatisfaction with his pilots. McCain wanted to get his five carriers—*Wasp, Hornet, Belleau Wood, Monterey,* and *Cowpens*—operating together for the first time. Not surprisingly for a first exercise, there was plenty of room for improvement, with Clem calling it a "very poor exhibition from my view point."[12] VF-22's performance was especially lackluster; as a result of their amateurish showing in front of Admiral McCain, the Moo's air officer and executive officer, presumably at the direction of Captain Taylor, called the entire air group together and dressed them down. Clem seemed to approve, noting in his journal that the lecture was "well deserved and well given, maybe it will make a difference when we go to work again."[13]

Cowpens and Task Force 38 departed Eniwetok early on the morning of August 28. The preparations for the Philippines campaign were massive, far outstripping what the Navy had assembled for the Marshall and Gilbert Islands. Its planners had sketched out an ambitious timetable for the fall, with landings scheduled on Morotai and Peleliu in September, Mindanao in the Southern Philippines in November, and Leyte in the Central Philippines in December. Halsey had ten weeks to eliminate the 650 Japanese planes on sixty-three airfields in or near the Philippines before the first landings there.

Once at sea, Captain Taylor kept his gunnery crews busy with drills and the underperforming air group on routine patrols, practice intercepts, and bombing and strafing practice. Clem must have thought the previous week's talking-to had made a difference, because on the first day at sea he wrote in his journal that his fighter pilots' "landings [were] much better than previously," and the next day stated that "air operations [were] quite smooth."[14] But the improvement was short-lived, and over the next five days, the squadron suffered four separate deck crashes—with even VF-22's commander, Lee Johnson, going over the side. The uninjured skipper managed to extract himself from his sinking plane, and the destroyer *Cowell* retrieved him and returned him to the Moo.

Cowpens crossed the equator on September 1, complete with all the pomp that normally accompanied a visit from King Neptune and his court. Clem was shocked by the severity of the hazing and put in a word with Neptune's entourage to take it easy on his pilots. "The ship's company seems carried away with the rough stuff for King Neptune," he wrote later. "Did get them to lay off pilots as we have a lot of flying to do."[15]

CHAPTER 19

Lackluster Strikes in Palau: Captain Taylor's Decision

*C*owpens and three of Task Force 38's four groups arrived off Palau on September 6 for three days of strikes intended to eliminate any Japanese planes that could threaten the upcoming Mindanao landings. The Moo's Hellcats were stuck on patrols for the day, and it was not until the seventh that her planes got in on the action—or what passed for it. Over the course of two days *Cowpens* and Task Group 38.1 hit three separate Palauan islands—Ngesebus, Angaur, and Malakal. With the exception of a single mission to Malakal, where the squadron set fire to several warehouses, the rest were a washout. The pilots could not find any targets of value on Ngesebus, which the Army Air Corps had already bombed; the squadron described it as "one group of overlapping craters."[1] Additionally, *Cowpens* hit Angaur all three days and each mission proved more unproductive than the last. Each time, the Moo's planes put down the few antiaircraft batteries they found and then went looking for anything of any military value. As a result they kept hitting the best—but still only marginal—set of targets day after day, including a lighthouse, phosphate plant, and boat piers.

By the time Task Group 38.1 refueled and pulled out for Mindanao on the night of the eighth, the pilots were frustrated and disappointed with a series of missions that they felt were a waste of time. The squadron's after-action write-ups clearly convey this frustration, rather pointedly noting that "one photographic mission over the island would have disclosed the absence of suitable targets."[2] They cited the law of diminishing returns, bluntly stating that "there comes a time when targets do not justify the use of carrier based aircraft in large striking groups," and argued in cases like these that a naval bombardment could do a better job with less risk to personnel.[3]

Air Group 22 was far more willing to criticize their leadership in their after-action reports than their predecessors in Air Group 25, who diplomatically conveyed them up the chain of command. This outspokenness likely did not help their case with Captain Taylor, who had his own set of gripes about the missions. In an unusual rebuke of his own pilots in the ship's official record, Captain Taylor criticized their decision to dump their bombs on the already-destroyed airfield on Ngesebus Island on the first day. "It is felt that an individual strike leader should carefully inspect the area...and decide on a pin-point target for the planes he is leading, rather than blindly throw bombs in an open area, as intimated herein."[4]

This was not just an isolated criticism. Unbeknownst to Lee Johnson, Clem Craig, and the rest of the air group leadership, their standing with Captain Taylor was already at rock bottom. We can only speculate as to why; Taylor left no record of his time aboard *Cowpens*, and the only account of events comes from Clem Craig, leaving us with only one side of the story. It's possible that the series of deck crashes in late August led Taylor to question the air group's abilities or leadership, or perhaps he perceived there was an attitude problem with his pilots that in his mind justified a shakeup. Pilots by nature are a confident, sometimes cocky bunch, and the frequency of their complaints in the after-action reports could suggest they came aboard the Moo with a chip on their collective shoulder. Indeed, some of Clem's later journal entries hint at a disdain for ship's personnel. For example, in early October, Clem described in his journal a "slight collision [confrontation] with a ship's officer who has been to war for a year and probably has not seen the enemy yet."[5]

That is not to say that Captain Taylor's conduct was praiseworthy. Air Group 22 had been aboard less than a month, and in contrast to Captain McConnell's steady, constructive development of his men, Taylor never personally spoke with his air group commander to address his concerns before openly criticizing them in the official record. The August 21 scolding that the executive officer and air officer delivered on Taylor's behalf was the only warning that we know about that suggested the captain was unhappy with his pilots' performance. Undoubtedly, Captain Taylor would have justified his actions, stating that as the commander of a warship heading into combat, he had the responsibility to get his air group up to par. In this he was correct; but his quiet, "still waters run deep" style of leadership won him no respect among the pilots. The mood aboard ship was descending into a vicious cycle; Taylor's antagonism fueled his pilots' unhappiness, which reinforced Taylor's antagonism.

Taylor wanted a trusted ally between himself and the pilots to whip them into shape. The Moo's current air officer—whose job it was to serve as the intermediary between the ship's senior officers and its pilots—was due to rotate home, and Taylor pulled strings to get the right man to replace him. The assignment came as a complete shock to Bob Price, who had just arrived in Jacksonville on September 7 to start his new assignment and almost immediately received new orders. "You will proceed to San Francisco...and report to the Commandant, Twelfth Naval District for first available air transportation to the USS *Cowpens* (CVL-25) and upon arrival report to the commanding officer of that vessel for duty involving flying."[6]

Mindanao and Visayan Islands: Building Sampans into Ships

Despite their initial rocky start at Palau, Air Group 22 started to find their sea legs in the coming weeks. Halsey kept Task Force 38 on the move, striking targets across the full length and width of the Philippines. *Cowpens* flew missions as far west as Panay and Negros, as far north as Manila, and as far south as Davao—plus a standalone raid by its task group to Morotai, the formerly Dutch-controlled (now Indonesian) island of Sulawesi. Halsey had several objectives in these operations; he wanted to diminish overall Japanese strength in the area in advance of the scheduled landings, as well as facilitate the capture of Morotai, which was MacArthur's halfway stop between New Guinea and the Philippines.

Although technically successful, the first mission in the Moo's Philippines campaign proved to be a point of contention for weeks to come, angering the captain and sparking a nasty dispute within VF-22. On September 9, *Cowpens* struck Digos airfield and Sarangani Bay, just to the southwest of Davao City on the south end of the Philippine archipelago. Her Hellcats provided high cover for the first wave of bombers while her Avengers participated in the second wave of strikes. VF-22, as the lead element in the fighter sweep, had pride of being the first Navy carrier squadron over the Philippines since the beginning of the war. It was, in the words of the pilots, a "big day for the group."[7] They had to be satisfied with the honor, because they encountered no enemy fighters and orbited overhead while the strike package from carriers *Hornet* and *Wasp* did their work. Heading home, they spotted six small ships—the pilots later debated whether they were sampans or actual cargo vessels— at the mouth of the bay. Lee Johnson's fighters took turns strafing these boats; one exploded and sank on the spot, three more went down shortly after, and the remaining two were afire and beached themselves to avoid sinking.

VF-22 squadron commander Lee Johnson would be dogged by accusations that he had been insufficiently aggressive on this mission, and that he had kept his pilots on high cover—rather than descending to strafe the airfield—once it was clear that there would be no Japanese aerial opposition. But the controversy did not break out into the open for some time, and that evening Air Group Cmdr. Tom Jenkins offered some constructive criticism of the day's missions. Lee Johnson, in Clem's words, "paid no attention as he was building sampans up to ships," insisting that the small, two-masted sailing vessels he strafed that morning were actually enemy cargo vessels.[8] Clem was skeptical of the claim but Johnson seemed to prevail in the end, with the ship's after-action report describing the ships in question as one-thousand-ton freighters.

With the dispute lying dormant for now, the squadron busied itself with their next missions in the Visayans, in the Central Philippines. On

September 13, the Moo launched a series of long-range strikes against Panay Island. It was at the outer limits of carrier aircraft range, and the ambitious effort cost the Moo dearly. On a mission to Dumaguette, on the southeast coast of Negros, the nearly hundred-plane strike showered their bombs on the field, a hangar, and the adjacent Japanese Army bivouac area. During this attack, antiaircraft fire struck the Avenger of Smithville, Utah's Lt. Paul Reeder. His plane caught fire, rolled over, and plummeted into the ground. Only one man—probably Reeder—managed to escape, while the other two, probably crewmen William G. Stevens Jr. and Joseph A. Brunson Jr., died in the impact. Unfortunately, Reeder's parachute dropped him near the airfield and the burning remains of his aircraft. His squadronmates hoped that he would be held as a POW, but Filipino guerrillas reported that Japanese soldiers bayoneted him to death on the spot. It took a month for word to reach the *Cowpens*, and his squadron eulogized him by noting that "his loss was strongly felt."[9]

Another bitter loss for the group was the death of one of the ship's reconnaissance pilots, Lt. Robert Ashford. During a strike on Mactan airfield, on an island just offshore of Cebu City, he released his wingmen to descend to the field to strafe and was last seen doing his photo runs through heavy bursts of flak. No one saw him go down, and there was no indication he had bailed out or ditched at sea.

Manila: "The Best Audience in Asia"

Halsey was surprised by the lack of Japanese resistance in the Central Philippines, and by late September was eager to press his luck. *Cowpens* and the task group steamed north to the nerve center of Japanese power in the region, Luzon and Manila. It was a target-rich environment, with nineteen airfields capable of hosting more than one thousand planes— and likely better defended than anything the air group had seen. Halsey, as always spoiling for a fight, signaled the fleet: BECAUSE OF THE BRILLIANT PERFORMANCE MY GROUP OF STARS HAS JUST GIVEN, I AM BOOKING YOU TO APPEAR BEFORE THE BEST AUDIENCE IN THE ASIATIC THEATER.[10] The Moo's fliers weren't nearly so confident; even the normally stoic Clem Craig noted in his journal that they were "heading for Manila and rather expect it to be a hot place."[11]

Flying from a launch point off the east coast of Luzon, the Moo hit Manila on the afternoon of the first day of strikes. The Moo's bombers struck targets on opposite sides of the Pasig River, which bisects the city's central port area. When they arrived, there were fifty ships of various sizes in the harbor. Sherwin Goodman was a nineteen-year-old Avenger tail gunner from Charleston, Virginia. He described how earlier strikes had already worked these ships over, and he recalled how some "were already afire, and pillars of smoke were rising up several thousand feet."[12] As the Moo's planes closed in on their targets in the central port district, the city's antiaircraft batteries put up a spirited defense. As Goodman later described it, "All the way down our glide bombing path the AA bursts were bracketing our plane. I couldn't hear the bursts but the thick, greasy smoke was everywhere."[13]

The Moo's planes made good drops on the port facilities on the edge of Manila Bay and machine shops on the other side of the river. Goodman's pilot put his bombs right on target, a large tool and machine plant, and it went up in a flash of smoke and fire. Given the intensity of the flak, the pilots and aircrew counted their blessings that they returned home safely. Seeing planes from other squadrons going down in flames, Sherwin Goodman thought to himself, "There but for the grace of God..."[14]

The weather soured the following day, September 22, but Halsey, not to be deterred, followed through on his planned strikes. *Cowpens* mostly had the CAP and ASP duty for the day, although VF-22 provided high cover for the day's raid on Manila. It was engine failure, not enemy fire, that caused the day's only loss. One *Cowpens* Avenger went into the drink twenty-five miles from the task group, and destroyer *Dortch* rushed to the scene to look for survivors. She fished crewmen D. G. Knight and Donald Robie from the stormy seas, but pilot Ens. Earl Snell, from Columbia, Missouri, was never found.

Halsey ordered Task Force 38 to retire from the area at sunset and steam toward a refueling rendezvous 250 miles to the east of Samar.

Despite the miserable weather, Halsey was pleased with the results of the raid, signaling the fleet: ALTHOUGH THE CAPACITY AUDIENCE HISSED THE MAGNIFICIENT LUZON PERFORMANCE THE GATE RECEIPTS WERE GRATIFYING AND VERY LITTLE WAS THROWN AT THE ACTORS X THE SHOW GOES ON THE ROAD AGAIN SOON AND KEEPS GOING AS LONG AS THE AUDIENCE HAS A SPOT TO HISS IN X ADMIRAL HALSEY.[15]

A Brief Respite at Manus

With its last round of strikes complete, the task force dispersed. Task Group 38.1 and the *Cowpens* headed to Manus, in the Admiralty Islands off the northern coast of New Guinea, to reprovision, while the other three task groups scattered to other targets or anchorages across the Central Pacific. After the brisk pace of operations in the Philippines, all hands were ready for a break and hopeful for the opportunity to receive their mail. "Well, we are on our way to Manus and maybe we will catch up on our mail there," Clem wrote on the twenty-fifth. "We had another delivery yesterday but we are still missing a lot of first class stuff—cigars, magazines, etc."[16]

Cowpens and Task Group 38.1 arrived at Manus's Seeadler Harbor at dawn on the twenty-eighth, anchoring the Moo in the midst of a heavy rain squall. They spent four days there, but it was not one of the idyllic tropical atolls that the Moo's crew was used to. Seeadler Harbor played the same support role for MacArthur's forces in the Southwest Pacific that Majuro did for the Navy, but the hot, rainy, and humid New Guinea weather that the Army routinely endured came as a shock to everyone aboard. The torpedo squadron history summarized conditions at Manus as "malaria...rain, and mud," and no matter how much it rained the precipitation never managed to cool the heavy air.[17] With the oppressive humidity, condensation began to drip from the Moo's interior bulkheads. The problem was especially bad in compartments adjacent to one of the ship's climate-controlled spaces, as Clem's cabin was. As a senior squadron officer, he rated an air-conditioned room, which he shared with another officer, but the climate control had been out of commission for weeks. With another air-conditioned space directly above, the condensation on the ceiling resulted in artificial precipitation, a situation Clem described as a "really a bad state of affairs."[18]

The lengthy stay at Manus also gave the repair crews an opportunity to try and address the ship's growing list of mechanical problems. By this point, *Cowpens* had steamed more than 108,000 miles, and it was beginning to take a toll. Even after their rebuild at Pearl Harbor in the summer, her boilers were growing steadily more unreliable and inefficient. The Moo's top speed had fallen below thirty knots, and anything over twenty resulted in a persistent vibration in the aft part of the ship that hadn't been there before. The engineers were reduced to temporary fixes for enduring problems that required a full overhaul to fix—which would take the ship out of action for weeks. But there was no time; the first wave of soldiers were scheduled to hit the beach at Leyte in mere weeks, and the ship would remain in action at least through then.

CHAPTER 20

Operation KING II:
The Buildup for Leyte Gulf

Like every operation that had preceded it, KING II, the invasion of Leyte, was the largest and most ambitious operation in the war to date, employing practically all available US military forces in the Pacific. Leyte is the eighth largest island in the Philippine archipelago, located immediately to the west of Samar in the Eastern Visayan Islands. It is 115 miles long and 45 miles wide at its broadest point; much of its 2,800 square miles is rugged and mountainous, with thick jungle blanketing knifelike volcanic ridges. But on the northeast corner of the island is the Leyte Valley, a broad and fertile plain that empties into Leyte Gulf. Lacking a coral reef, the bay offered the best landing beaches in the region—plus deep-water anchorages right offshore. From the Army's perspective, it was the perfect place to establish a springboard for the coming attack into Luzon. The air distance from there to Manila was only 295 miles, and the Army's planners thought the broad valley was an ideal spot to construct bases and airfields.

The opening stages of the invasion of the Philippines started a period of unprecedented activity that exhausted both the Moo's crew and her air group. From October 6, 1944, to January 26, 1945, Task Force 38 was at sea and on the attack thirteen of sixteen weeks. This frenetic period of activity started with the preparatory work for the landings on Leyte. The first target was the Ryukyu Islands, the string of islands along the coast of mainland Asia connecting Japan with the Philippines; any Japanese aircraft from the home islands would have to pass through there to refuel. Halsey's plan was to start at the north end of the Ryukyus, nearest Okinawa, and work his way south along their three-hundred-mile length to Formosa, neutralizing as much of the Japanese air strength as he could along the way. Intelligence believed the Ryukyus were a transit area and not likely to be heavily defended, but Formosa was a Japanese stronghold, with fifty airfields and several hundred aircraft. From there, Task Force 38 would turn south to the Philippines, hitting Luzon and the airfields in the Visayans, arriving at Leyte at the same time as MacArthur's invasion fleet. Halsey had under his command eight *Essex*-class carriers, *Enterprise*, and *Cowpens* and six of her *Independence*-class sisters, with more than one thousand aircraft between them.

Cowpens weighed anchor from Manus on October 2 in the company of the rest of Task Group 38.1, all under Admiral McCain. Many aboard were happy to be rid of Manus and its oppressive weather, including Clem. "Shoved off about 1040 and no regrets," he noted in his journal that evening.[1] Conditions did not improve after their departure; *Cowpens* and Task Group 38.1 passed through an area recently traversed by a typhoon, and the strong winds and rough seas made landing aircraft difficult.

Air Group 22's poor performance in the first few days at sea aggravated the already troubled waters between the air group and Captain Taylor. While we have few details, the Moo's pilots made a lackluster account of themselves in drills and exercises, with Clem noting on the first full day at sea, "more practices, still N.G. [no good]."[2] A series of minor accidents and deck crashes certainly didn't help matters, either. But given how badly the Moo was being shaken up by the rough seas, Clem was sympathetic to the pilots, noting: "All hands having trouble with landings and blowing tires... Not all pilot trouble. The sea has been rather rough with swells... really pitching and rolling."[3]

During this period, Captain Taylor communicated his displeasure with the air group's performance via a series of overt slights and petty insults against its senior officers. While we have only Clem's account of these events, if they transpired as he described, Captain Taylor's leadership had strayed from the unproductive to the toxic. Soon after pushing off from Manus, either Captain Taylor or one of his senior staff ordered the reassignment of some of the air group's senior officers' compartments, ignoring the rank and seniority ratings by which they were normally assigned. In the shuffle, Clem and his roommate were forced out; it was probably not coincidental, he noted bitterly in his journal, that the repairs to the air-conditioning in his former cabin took place immediately after a ship's officer moved in. The air group commander, Lt. Cmdr. Tom Jenkins, also was forced to give up his berth to a lieutenant, junior grade—a far-lower-ranking officer. From Clem's perspective, this was a "deliberate humiliation attempt made on air group by senior ship's officers. Things are rapidly coming to a head."[4]

By the second day at sea, Captain Taylor was openly insulting his flyers in front of some of his subordinates, a significant breach of professional decorum. "Now Captain [Taylor] making cracks at air group," Clem wrote on October 3. "I wonder if he thinks he is doing us a favor."[5] The situation was bad enough, he concluded, that some confrontation was inevitable. An initial skirmish followed soon after; on the fifth, Clem noted that "we finally got the room assignments straightened out and also a gripe session with the air officer which settled nothing but should relieve the pressure somewhat."[6]

Task Group 38.1 joined the rest of the task force 375 miles west of the Marianas on the afternoon of the seventh, and they proceeded together to the fueling point. But despite Halsey's attempts to find a calmer patch of ocean to refuel, seas were heavy, and the Moo rolled and pitched in the heavy swells and gale-force winds of up to forty knots. All flight operations were canceled for the day, and the ship's deck handlers moved every plane they could fit into the hangar bay and lashed to the flight deck all those that remained above. Weathering a storm at sea is always an unpleasant experience, but the Moo's poor sea-handling characteristics made everything worse. "The weather and seas are getting rougher if possible," Clem wrote in his journal that day. "We can expect trouble if this keeps up. Very uncomfortable."[7] With the howling winds and the ship's high center of gravity, the Moo was soon rolling twenty-six to twenty-eight degrees to port and starboard, and junior ship's officer Sam Sommers remembered how it continued "until one wondered if it would stop."[8]

Down in the squadron ready rooms, tail gunner Sherwin Goodman described how the aviators were dodging flying furniture. The furnishings were set into sockets in the deck to keep them in place, but as conditions worsened, chairs, desks, and furniture broke free and went careening across the room. At times, the fliers were forced to grab on to the overhead beams and pull their legs up to avoid being hit, a sight Goodman likened to "monkeys hanging from trees."[9] The heavy seas also helped the crew's mess live up to its name. "Getting fed in the mess hall was a challenge," Goodman recalled. "The tin food trays slid right off the table . . . the decks were an unsightly mess."[10] The situation down in the enlisted men's head was even worse. The rolling of the ship caused the filth and water to slosh out of the drainage gutter and across the deck. Art Daly described conditions there as more and more men became seasick from the churning seas. "One guy would be heaving his brains out in one hole, the guy next to him taking a crap. Water and turds running and splashing all over the deck."[11]

That evening, one of the Moo's Hellcats broke free of her lashings during a twenty-five-degree roll and began sliding around the hangar deck. While the deckhands tried desperately to lash it down, the Hellcat bounced back and forth off several other planes with each roll of the ship, destroying itself and six others nearby. It bashed in one of the roll-up hangar bay doors, and about a foot of seawater topped with gasoline from the battered planes sloshed across the deck. The fumes from the gasoline were overpowering, and by some miracle there wasn't a spark from the colliding planes to set it ablaze. The crew scrambled to close and dog nearby hatches to contain the fumes, while the loudspeaker kept screaming, "The smoking lamp is out! The smoking lamp is out!"[12] After a brief period of utter chaos, the deckhands finally managed to get the deck under control, and by the time Clem arrived on the scene, the broken fighters were "lashed down in a heap."[13]

"We Didn't Expect to Get Any of You Onboard"

Cowpens battled through heavy seas on October 8 as Task Force 38 steamed north toward its launching point near Okinawa. Despite the bucking of the flight deck, Captain Taylor was determined to get his patrols in the air, and they took off in the afternoon. As the day wore on and dusk drew near, *Cowpens'* planes returned home from their patrols. Conditions were still difficult and the ship's deck was wallowing in the heavy seas. The first plane in the pattern—a Hellcat piloted by Ens. Arthur Watts—missed the arresting cables entirely, took out the crash barrier by the roots, and smashed into the ship's island. While Watts was uninjured, the wreck closed the flight deck for quite some time. Three more Hellcats and four Avengers circled overhead while the deckhands tried to repair the barricade and clear the debris. One of them was Avenger pilot Bob Soule, who was worried about his rapidly dwindling fuel. He kept radio-ing the Moo: "You know, we're getting low on gas, and it doesn't look to me like you're gonna get that repaired. How about sending us to one of the other ships?"[14] By the time Captain Taylor threw in the towel and ordered them to divert to the *Wasp*, it was an hour after sunset and Soule was running on fumes.

Like the Moo, *Wasp* was bobbing like a cork in the heavy seas, and it took Soule five tries to get his landing gear and the deck in the same place at the same time. Finally, on the fifth attempt, he touched down but missed the wire. His Avenger careened into the crash barrier, and the impact sparked a blaze aboard his plane. He and his crew bailed out as the *Wasp's* deck handlers pushed the wreck over the side to clear the way for the four other *Cowpens* aircraft coming in. Soule and his gunner and radioman were hustled below to sick bay, where the flight surgeon handed them a snifter of medicinal brandy. "Boy, you've had a rough one," he said by way of sympathy.[15] Soule was downtrodden for having crashed his plane, but *Wasp's* captain called down to offer his condolences. "Don't feel badly," he told Soule. "We didn't expect to get any of you onboard."[16]

Back aboard *Cowpens*, the drama precipitated yet another clash between the ship and air group leadership. Captain Taylor, likely unhappy with that evening's crashes but unwilling to talk to his pilots directly, informed Air Group Commander Tom Jenkins by way of the executive officer that he did not consider the air group—and presumably Lee Johnson and Clem's VF-22 in particular—well led. "This topped it off," wrote Clem angrily.[17] Again we have only Clem's account of the argument, who fumed in his journal about the accusations. He claimed the only evidence Taylor cited was the infamous September 9 mission to Mindanao where the *Cowpens* Hellcats were assigned high cover and "didn't fire a round." Clem dismissed that argument, countering that the whole point of high cover was to stand guard in case of a Japanese aerial attack. "Captain Taylor certainly stepped over the bounds that time, as well as exposing abysmal ignorance."[18]

Moreover, Clem made his own counteraccusations in his journal, although he did not say whether he or Jenkins had made them to the XO and the captain. Clem argued the weather that day was too rough for flying; most of the Moo's CVL sisters suspended operations for the day or only flew the dawn patrol. But Taylor was determined to get his planes in the air that afternoon, an attitude Clem described as "pig-headed pride."[19] Even after Watts crashed and it became clear that the rest of the planes would have trouble returning aboard, Taylor was still reluctant to ask the larger carriers for help. By the time he broke down and did so, it was well after dark and his planes were running on fumes. The crashes, Clem concluded, were "predictable on takeoff."[20]

CHAPTER 21

Raid on Formosa: The Moo Rides Herd on *Houston* and *Canberra*

The raid on Formosa proved to be a challenge for both the task force and the Moo.[1] The objective was to knock out Japanese air strength on the island to prevent those planes from threatening the landings on Leyte. This was no small task; Formosa was a Japanese stronghold, thick with enemy planes and antiaircraft guns. The original plan called for only two days of strikes, but it became what Admiral Halsey called a "knock-down drag-out fight," and one of *Cowpens'* most notable actions of the war.

The Moo arrived at her launching point off Formosa on October 12. It was a big day; the task force flew 1,378 sorties, primarily against airfields and rail yards. The first fighter sweep over the island met clouds of enemy fighters, perhaps two hundred in all. Most of the inexperienced enemy pilots did not survive the encounter; only sixty planes rose to contest the second wave of US attacks, and only a handful for the third. US losses were still heavy, largely because of the murderous flak. The Japanese downed forty-eight planes on the first day alone, and rescue subs recovered two dozen fliers at sea over the course of the following week. Ditching at sea was far preferable to parachuting ashore, where chances of rescue were virtually nil. The Japanese held the valleys and coast, there were hostile tribes in the mountains, and eleven species of poisonous snakes made no distinction between Formosan native, Japanese soldier, and American pilot.[2]

Cowpens lost two pilots on the first mission of the day. Nine Hellcats set out just before dawn for a fighter sweep and reconnaissance mission to Reigaryo airfield, near Takao on the southwest coast of Formosa. The pilots had just completed their first strafing run on the parked planes on the airfield when they spotted twelve to sixteen enemy fighters circling wide around the field at about eight thousand feet. With VF-22 commander Lee Johnson in the lead, the Moo's fliers sprinted to thirteen thousand feet and turned to engage, sparking a melee.

The Moo's fliers bagged as many as nine enemy planes in the brief dogfight that followed. The skipper plowed into the enemy formation and scored two quick kills; one on his first pass and then dispatching a second that turned directly in front of him. Lt. (jg) Bob Richardson and his wingman, Ben Amsden, lost each other in the melee while trying to intercept a pair of Zekes firing at one of their squadronmates; Richardson recovered by flaming one Zeke that crossed his path, while Amsden pounced on another that was on the tail of a friendly fighter. He fired a burst directly into its cockpit, and his prey fell off on its port wing, tumbled into a flat spin, and exploded when it hit the ground. Ens. Mike Roche made a head-on pass at another Zeke. Roche was a native of Kansas City who worked for the local power company; his squadron biography described him as a demon behind the Hellcat's six guns. He scored several engine hits on the opposing plane for a probable kill without being hit himself and then peppered the engine of another passing dead ahead. Meanwhile, Lt. Ormond Higgins and Ens. Francis Kelly teamed up to dispatch a Japanese Oscar fighter who got a little too close to the Moo's Avengers, which had just arrived over the airfield on their own bombing mission. Higgins raked the enemy plane with .50-caliber fire as he attempted a split-S to get away, while Kelly got in two bursts of his own. The Oscar spun out of control and cartwheeled down to the ground.

The Japanese got in their own hits, claiming two of the Moo's pilots. Lt. (jg) Donald Stanley was last seen with a Zeke dead to rights; he was credited for a probable kill, but he never returned to base. Separately,

Roche's wingman, Max "Doc" Frellsen, made a head-on run at a Zeke, with the pair trading shots. He did not fare as well as Roche did, and both planes went down shortly thereafter with smoke and fire pouring from their engines. At the conclusion of the firefight, the remaining Zekes scattered and the remaining Hellcats spotted four parachutes descending to the ground, giving them hope that Frellsen and Stanley had survived. Both *Cowpens* pilots had indeed bailed out, but were captured and became POWs. They spent the rest of the war at the notorious Ofuna prison camp outside Yokohama, where they endured considerable torture and abuse.

The Avengers returned to the ship, refueled and rearmed, and were back in the air within an hour for a midmorning strike against Takao (now Kaohsiung City). A senior pilot from *Hornet* was in command, but the whole affair was a disorganized mess. After arriving over the city, *Cowpens'* planes circled for a half hour waiting to be assigned a target while Air Group 22 commander Tom Jenkins pestered the strike leader for direction. When that didn't work, Jenkins requested fighter cover for his planes to conduct their own attack, and when that was not forthcoming, he and his Avengers set out on their own for the shipyard and warehouses at Takao Harbor. The eight planes made their initial bomb run against heavy, accurate, and intense antiaircraft fire, which battered them on their dives toward the target. Tail gunner Sherwin Goodman described how the bursts of enemy flak blanketed the area, and "as we dove, the enemy fire descended along with us, tracking our path."[3]

Goodman's pilot, Lt. Leo Meacher, spotted one of the antiaircraft batteries contributing to the barrage. He adjusted his dive and dropped his bombs squarely in its midst, and the blast flung pieces of wreckage high into the air. The rest of the Avengers blanketed the harbor with their bombs, sparking numerous fires. Tom Jenkins scored a direct hit on an ammunition warehouse, and the secondary explosions sent up a sheet of flame more than two thousand feet. The fireball towered over the bombers, which had just pulled up from their attack runs at low altitude. The pilots were stunned by their good fortune, with only one *Cowpens* plane lightly damaged. In leading an attack against a heavily defended target with no fighter escort, Jenkins earned the Distinguished Flying Cross for the mission. His award citation described how "the attack was carefully planned and pressed home in the face of an extremely severe concentration of accurate, heavy, and automatic anti-aircraft fire... his courage and disregard for his own safety were at all times in keeping with the highest traditions of the United States Naval Service."[4]

Bogeys were out in force that evening after sunset as Tokyo Rose bragged on the radio that the mighty Third Fleet had been destroyed. After 7 p.m., perhaps fifty to seventy-five planes flew down from the Japanese home islands to challenge the task force. They were an unorganized mob of different types of aircraft, leaving Halsey's staff to wonder if Japanese air strength was depleted and they were just pulling together whatever aircraft they had available. Other task groups were the focus of their attention, and those topside on *Cowpens* watched as the attacks played out in the distance. "The sky was filled with tracer shells, creating cobwebs in all directions," Sherwin Goodman recalled. "Whenever a hit was scored, there would be a large flash, followed by a ball of fire falling into the sea."[5] Clem offered a similar but more subdued observation about the action that evening, noting that it was a "very impressive display of ordnance."[6]

Canberra and *Houston* Take a Fish

Task Force 38 returned to Formosa the next day, October 13, following the same pattern as the day before. The weather had soured, with a thick cloud cover down to two thousand feet, and scattered fog and mist below that. Snoopers lurked at the fringes of the fleet throughout the day, usually a good indicator that the Japanese intended to attack in force after dark.

At 6:30 p.m., the task force was only one hundred miles offshore, recovering the day's last patrols. The sky was thick with overcast, and the twilight was rapidly fading into night. Suddenly, lookouts and gun crews in the *Cowpens'* task group reported a large group of twin-engine planes approaching at wave-top level from the south, below radar coverage. As Admiral McCain ordered all ships to commence an emergency turn to port and ring up twenty-two knots, perhaps ten to twelve twin-engine

Fran torpedo bombers broke through the outer destroyer screen. Several planes attacked *Wasp* but only two or three made it past the concentrated antiaircraft fire from the inner ring of cruisers, only to fall to *Wasp*'s own guns. Meanwhile, a group of four planes approached *Cowpens* on her starboard quarter and were taken under fire by the cruiser *Canberra*, steaming in formation just port and aft of the Moo—and she managed to down three of the four. The fourth plane, under continuous heavy gunfire, stubbornly pressed home its attack and dropped its torpedo before crashing into the sea in flames. This torpedo passed just aft of the Moo and struck *Canberra* beneath her armored belt, eighteen feet below the waterline. It blew a huge, jagged hole in her hull and killed all twenty-three men in those spaces and wounded fourteen others. About 4,500 tons of water rushed into the ship before her damage control teams managed to seal the flooded compartments. With both her engine rooms out of action, *Canberra* coasted to a stop. As her escorts clustered around the wounded ship to shield her from additional attacks, fleet tug *Munsee* put her under tow.

Canberra's plight forced Admiral Halsey to consider his options. The wounded cruiser was less than one hundred miles from the coast of Formosa, and it would be days before she could be towed out of range of Japanese attacks, much less make it to the closest US base at Ulithi, some 1,300 miles distant. Guarding her retreat required the fleet to linger offshore, exposing more ships to enemy attack. Meanwhile, intercepted Japanese communications indicated enemy reinforcements were headed to Formosa. Halsey later described his dilemma as "we were squarely in the dragon's jaws and the dragon knew it."[7] Although the normal procedure would have been to evacuate *Canberra* and scuttle her, Halsey made the opposite choice. He informed Nimitz that he wanted to cover the wounded cruiser's retreat, and ordered a dawn fighter sweep the next morning to keep the Japanese air threat suppressed as long as possible.

The following morning, October 14, *Cowpens* and Task Group 38.1 stood by to cover the wounded *Canberra*'s withdrawal. The Moo joined the morning's fighter sweeps over Formosa but, with snoopers dogging the task group all day, preserved the bulk of her fighter strength at home on CAP. It was a lousy day for flying, with heavy overcast and periodic squalls and showers, perfect for concealing the approach of enemy planes. The continual reports of bogeys kept the Moo at general quarters. There were usually one or two on radar screens at any given time, probing for gaps in the fighter coverage. Fighters from other carriers kept shooting them down, but much to their frustration the Moo's pilots were never in on the action and often arrived too late to join in the fight. Clem grumbled into his journal: "Seems that everyone else is knocking them down around us but we have not done any good at all. Had a good sized raid about 1700 and we finally scrambled everything after everything was all over. We came back without seeing anything and landed at dark."[8]

The day's action was not over yet. By 6:30 p.m., with night beginning to fall, the task group's planes were all back aboard. It was dark and overcast, with a choppy sea and visibility less than eight thousand yards. Radar again picked up a group of bogeys closing in on Task Group 38.1, and in a repeat of the day before, nine to sixteen Fran torpedo planes came in fast and low, no more than fifty feet off the wave tops. Immediately, ships in the formation opened fire with their antiaircraft batteries, including the *Cowpens* and the light cruiser *Houston*, which only shortly before had taken *Canberra*'s former position in the formation just to the port and aft of the Moo. One of *Houston*'s officers, Cmdr. William L. Kirkland, described how in the postdusk gloom, the Frans were "almost invisible against the mauve-colored clouds on the horizon. Any quail hunter would understand when I say you would almost have to squat down to catch the silhouette of the bird against the sky."[9]

Cowpens' gunners also had trouble spotting the low-flying enemy planes in the near dark, due to the brilliant streams of tracer fire and the flash and flame of two planes that *Wasp* downed close by.[10] They did not see one of the Frans until she flew down the ship's starboard side at close range. All the gun batteries on that side of the ship opened up, scoring multiple hits on the enemy plane, which flared up and crashed into the sea some three thousand yards away. The Moo's gunners checked their fire twice to avoid hitting *Wasp* and *Monterey*, who were in formation nearby, but not everyone in the dense formation of ships was that careful. Eager gunners from across the task force blazed away at the enemy planes, and some of these rounds rained down on *Cowpens*. "Everyone was in a crossfire," Sherwin Goodman stated. "The shells were screaming over our head, so I headed to the bridge to get behind some steel. Flak was falling like rain on the deck."[11]

Despite the heavy antiaircraft fire, the task group could not prevent a repeat of the prior night's tragedy. *Houston* successfully dodged two torpedoes launched at her from the port side, but her gunners did not see the third Fran until it was practically on them. Although her gunners landed a series of punishing hits on the enemy plane, it managed to stay aloft, drop its torpedo, and pass over *Houston*'s bow before crashing into the sea. She was heeling hard to port as she attempted to turn away at twenty-six knots, but her list exposed her vulnerable underside. The torpedo struck the cruiser, blasting a 32-by-24-foot hole in her hull, breaking her keel, and killing everyone at the primary point of impact in her number one engine room.

With both of her engine rooms out of action, *Houston* lost all power, and soon she was dead in the water. With thousands of tons of water pouring into her wounds, she soon began to wallow, rolling as much as thirty-seven degrees to either side—only four degrees short of her threshold for capsizing. With her decks awash, *Houston* was at death's door, and Capt. William Behrens reported she was on the verge of breaking up. He ordered all nonessential personnel to abandon ship, and nearby destroyers evacuated 750 souls.

Bait Division One: "Now I Know How a Worm on a Fishhook Must Feel"

On Halsey's flagship *New Jersey*, *Houston*'s torpedoing rekindled all the debate of the previous day. The admiral paced nervously on his flag bridge, chain-smoking and cursing up a storm. His first reaction was that defending the two wounded cruisers just risked throwing good ships after bad, and he should "scuttle and skedaddle" before the Japanese massed for a counterattack that inflicted additional casualties.[12] Halsey's staff had a different view, arguing that the wounded ships were valuable as bait.

Under tow less than one hundred miles from Formosa, the two cruisers could make only four knots, presenting a tempting target for the Japanese. A few fake distress calls could help reinforce the impression they were wounded and vulnerable, and lure more enemy ships and planes into range of Task Force 38's still considerable firepower. Halsey agreed; while the rest of the task force moved off to the east, three cruisers and seventeen destroyers remained to escort the two wounded cruisers, under air cover from *Cowpens* and *Cabot*. Now that they were split off from Task Group 38.1, Halsey designated them Task Group 30.3—but the group soon accumulated a number of other, less charitable names. These included the "Streamlined Bait Unit," "Bait Division One," and, worst of all, "Cripple Division One" (CripDiv1).

The ruse worked, or at least partially. At first, a Japanese striking force of several cruisers and a destroyer division sortied from the Japanese home islands to investigate the wounded ships, but after an attack from *Bunker Hill*'s planes they realized the American fleet was not as weak as they'd hoped and turned for home. The Japanese had no problem committing waves of aircraft to the fight, however. *Cowpens*, *Cabot*, and the small formation of ships under their protection suffered near-constant air attack in the coming days as they withdrew to safety. For the men of the *Cowpens* and the rest of the CripDiv, the excitement of being front and center of the action was undoubtedly leavened with the understanding of the potential consequences of being in the crosshairs for repeated attacks. *Birmingham*'s Captain Thomas Inglis said it best when he observed, "Now I know how a worm on a fishhook must feel."[13]

Fleet tug *Pawnee* arrived at the CripDiv at midmorning on the fifteenth to take over the tow on the *Houston*. The two tugs, *Munsee* towing *Canberra* and *Pawnee* towing *Houston*, steamed abreast at 3.5 knots one mile apart, while *Cowpens* and *Cabot* interposed themselves between Formosa and the two wounded cruisers fifteen to twenty miles away. The weather had not improved much, with brisk winds and low, ragged clouds. Conditions were ideal for concealing a Japanese attack, which was not long in coming.

The first raid of the day started lighting up US radars at 8:15 a.m.

Wasp had the rotation of CAP, and under the direction of the Moo's FDO her fighters charged toward the bogeys while the task group went to general quarters. *Wasp*'s planes bagged half of the dozen or so attackers in one dogfight and then finished off the rest when they attempted to form up again for another try. About 9:45 a.m., the Japanese again tried to get their torpedo planes through the fighter screen to get to the damaged ships. One group came in from the southwest and the other from the northwest. By then, the CAP had turned over to *Cowpens* and *Monterey*, and their Hellcats dashed toward the inbound attackers. "This time we were waiting for them," noted the ship's history.[14]

Wasp's FDO put four *Cowpens* Hellcats right into a flight of four Bettys and three Zekes, and Ens. Mike Roche spotted the enemy aircraft dead ahead. The Bettys were in formation with the Zekes spread out loosely above them, and when they spotted the Hellcats, the Japanese formation made a 180-degree turn to try and escape. Lt. Richardson, leading the division, directed Roche and his wingman, Jack Roop, to go after the three Zekes, while he and his wingman, Ben Amsden, attacked the four bombers. Richardson and Amsden made firing runs on the trailing two Bettys, with Amsden's hits sparking his target's engine to burn. Meanwhile, Richardson shot away part of the control surfaces on his Betty, causing it to zoom upward into the path of the third. The two aircraft collided in midair and disintegrated into a cloud of tumbling, burning debris. Richardson and Amsden teamed up on the final Betty, which was diving for the wave tops in a vain effort to escape. Firing bursts from above and behind, the two pilots knocked out the bomber's tail gunner and then set its starboard engine afire, sending it arcing down to the ocean below.

The three Zekes tried to make a run for it, although trying to flee the faster Hellcats was an exercise in futility. The enemy fighters were flying in a two-plane formation with the third lagging behind. Roche, with Roop flying on his wing, made a pass from above and behind at the straggler. Roche's gunfire knocked chunks off the cowling and fuselage, forcing it to peel off; it was later judged a probable kill. On the same run, Roche hit the wingman, firing bursts into the engine and cockpit, and the Zeke soon burst into flames. The final Zeke tried evasive action to shake his two assailants; Roop followed him through a split-S down to three thousand feet and then through a loop, where Roop peppered him with fire in the wing and fuselage. Finally, the Zeke pulled out low over the water with the determined Roop still on his tail. He managed to score a final few hits, and the Zeke went straight in.

Cowpens accounted for eight enemy planes that day. Richardson splashed two Bettys and Amsden another pair, while Ensigns Roop and Roche shared three Zekes and Jim Ean bagged a single Japanese Irving fighter in a separate fight at about the same time. Clem was upbeat about the performance of his men, although slightly cynical about their luck as of late. Writing that evening, he called the day's dogfighting "really a darned good exhibition," but cynically joked that "only by some mistake" had the *Cowpens* fighters been sent to intercept.[15]

The Japanese waited a day before attempting their next major attack. The first CAP of the day on the sixteenth went up before dawn, but it wasn't until early afternoon that the Japanese made their play, what the ship's history called "a strong bid to finish us off."[16] *Cowpens* was expecting trouble, with her fighters on alert. Just before 1:30 p.m., *Cabot's* radar picked up two large groups of enemy planes. The northern group was headed straight for the CripDiv, while the other group was on the same course, but fifty miles farther south. Two divisions of *Cabot's* Hellcats streaked toward the first group, and *Cowpens* launched all available fighters to meet the second.

Clem Craig was in the lead for *Cowpens*; his two divisions followed the vector out to seventy miles, where they observed nine Jills armed with torpedoes several thousand feet below, heading toward the task group. They were laid out like a flock of geese, in a V formation with one plane trailing behind. As the Hellcats wheeled in behind them, the Japanese formation made a slow turn to port and nosed down to just above the water. Clem made four rapid kills; he hit the trailing plane and the last plane in the formation with a controlled series of shots that set them afire and down into the sea. A moment later, he bagged a third with a burst into the port wing, and then got his fourth with a series of well-aimed shots into an enemy Jill from seven o'clock high. Ensign Gordon Cumming was flying on Clem's wing, and targeted the last plane in the short side of the V, hitting him in the starboard wing and engine from above and behind, exploding him in the air. Lt. (jg) Edward Dale and Ens. Newton Streetman mopped up the remaining two. It was a bit like shooting fish in a barrel; none of the Jills attempted to dodge the Hellcats' fire, and their rear gunner positions were unoccupied, either because they lacked trained aircrew or because they anticipated the mission was a one-way trip.

As far as the air group was concerned, the day's engagement was a "grand slam," and even Captain Taylor offered some rare praise for his flyers.[17] "The pilots of Air Group 22 did an excellent job of covering and protecting Task Group 30.3, which was engaged in the safe retirement of the damaged *Canberra* and *Houston*," Taylor wrote in the ship's after-action report. "Their courageous engagement of enemy attacking planes is in keeping with the highest traditions of the US naval service."[18] The engagement earned Clem the Silver Star, while the wounded *Canberra* added her thanks to the praise, sending to both *Cowpens* and *Cabot* the message CANBERRA IS VERY GRATEFUL FOR THE WORK YOUR CHICKENS AND FDO'S DID TODAY.[19]

Although the two carriers wiped out the bulk of the attackers, the Japanese were not through yet. Three twin-engine Fran torpedo bombers found a gap in the fighter coverage. Spotting the fifty-mile-long oil slick that the two damaged cruisers were trailing, the trio of enemy planes followed it in. *Houston* and several of her escorts caught sight of them approaching from astern and opened fire. She dropped one Fran into the sea, while cruiser *Santa Fe* bagged a second, cutting it neatly in two right off her bow. In contrast, the third Fran came in low and fast and loosed a torpedo. With multiple ships' guns blazing away, it flew up *Houston*'s starboard side, and her crew could see the pilot slumped dead or unconscious over his controls before the plane crashed into the sea a few thousand yards ahead.

For a moment it looked like the torpedo would pass *Houston*, but it impacted on her stern on the starboard side. The torpedo tore a large hole in the bottom and side of her hull and flung debris hundreds of feet in the air. The starboard gasoline tank, containing 2,500 gallons of aviation fuel, exploded through the stern, catching much of the now-floating debris on fire. The shock wave from the blast flung ten men on deck into the burning seas, while falling debris killed one and wounded six others. Damage control teams extinguished the fires within fifteen minutes, but the blast split so many of *Houston's* already damaged bulkheads that another 6,300 tons of seawater poured into the ship, and she settled much lower in the water. Naval historian Samuel Eliot Morison summarized the severity of her wounds by noting that "no ship had ever been so flooded and survived."[20] Damage control teams restored enough power to keep the pumps working while her crew worked desperately to lighten the ship, throwing overboard ammunition, topside wreckage, and whatever metal pieces they could pry or cut loose. All but two hundred of her sailors transferred to *Santa Fe* or neighboring destroyers, to reduce the death toll in case the ship were suddenly to go under.

That day's attack was the last major Japanese attempt try to sink the CripDiv, although over the following two days a handful of singleton snoopers tested the CAP and were splashed for their trouble. Clem wrote in his journal on the evening of the seventeenth, "We had no excitement today although it is said there were several large groups of bogies which did not close. Had our usual snooper during [the] night but no raid."[21] *Cowpens* remained on guard until the twentieth, however, when the wounded cruisers were safely beyond striking distance from Formosa and well on their way to Ulithi. The Moo then turned around and returned to her task group.

With the danger of further Japanese attack successfully averted, the brass offered their congratulations to all hands who helped the two wounded cruisers escape. Halsey signaled: FOR SKILL AND GUTS THE SAFE RETIREMENT OF THE DAMAGED CANBERRA AND HOUSTON FROM THE SHADOW OF FORMOSA COAST UNDER HEAVY ATTACK...X TO ALL HANDS WHO CONTRIBUTED TO THE JOB 'WELL DONE' X HALSEY.[22] The two senior commanders in the cruiser screen also both sent their praise to *Cowpens* and *Cabot*, with one signaling to the carriers GOOD WORK X YOUR PILOTS HAVE ACCOMPLISHED WHAT WOULD SEEM

TO BE IMPOSSIBLE,[23] and the other, WE HAVE GREAT ADMI-
RATION FOR THE GRAND INTERCEPTION AND FIGHT-
ING YOUR PILOTS DID YESTERDAY X WE WILL ALWAYS DO
EVERYTHING WITHIN OUR POWER TO GET THEM BACK IF
THEY GET IN TROUBLE X THEIR SUPERB FIGHTING SAVED
US SOME SHIPS YESTERDAY.[24]

Santa Fe's Capt. Russell S. Burkey expressed his appreciation for
Cowpens and *Cabot*'s air cover by printing up award certificates for the
CripDiv that made a humorous nod to how they lured the enemy in. The
certificates were decorated with drawings of all kinds of bait—worms on
hooks, cheese in traps, and fish lures. The text stated that "special trust
and confidence had been emplaced in the holder's superficial qualities,"
and that the holder "has been appointed fall guy in the streamlined bait
group of the battered remnants of the Blue Fleet."[25]

CHAPTER 22

The Battle of Leyte Gulf

With Formosa temporarily neutralized, and *Canberra* and *Houston* safely on their way back to base, Task Force 38 turned its focus back to the Philippines to soften up the beachhead at Leyte in advance of the landings. While Halsey and his staff were as always both worried and hoping that the Japanese fleet might sortie to oppose them, fleet intelligence reported it was spread across several anchorages in Southeast Asia and the home islands. Believing he had a little breathing room, Halsey decided to rotate his exhausted carrier task groups one at a time back to the fleet's new supply depot at Ulithi for rest and replenishment, while the rest kept up attacks off the Philippines. First to go were Admiral McCain, *Cowpens*, and the rest of Task Group 38.1.

While the Moo sailed for Ulithi, two divisions of the US Sixth Army splashed ashore on Leyte on October 20 under the protection of the Seventh Fleet's air cover and a naval bombardment. The landings were initially unopposed, the weather cooperative, and by evening the Army had a solid foothold. The Japanese had not given up, however. For the second time in four months, they would try and engineer a decisive naval battle with the US Fleet, although their odds were even more desperate than before. The plan was to use their aircraft carriers as bait to lure Halsey away from the beachhead—and use the diversion to bring in their cruisers and battleships to attack the defenseless troop transports from the west and south.

Through a series of highly improbable events—which Adm. Ted

Sherman said would be discussed by critics for the next one hundred years—the Japanese snookered Halsey and made it practically to the Leyte beachhead. Halsey's initial waves of air strikes forced the Center Group approaching through the San Bernadino Strait to turn around to regroup—a move that the Bull interpreted as a retreat. Believing that these warships were no longer a threat, that evening Halsey set off to the north in pursuit of the bait group, despite numerous warnings from his senior subordinates that the Center Group had resumed its course toward Leyte. A breakdown in communications between Halsey's forces and Adm. Thomas Kinkaid, the commander of the Seventh Fleet landing forces, concealed the fact that the San Bernardino Strait was unguarded— as much of the naval strength in the area had moved south to block the Japanese advance through Surigao Strait.

The end result was that the Center Group sailed through the San Bernardino Strait unimpeded and fell upon the escort carriers guarding the beachhead off Samar on the morning of October 25. The Japanese had all the advantages; the six American "baby flattops" (escort carriers) and their accompanying destroyers and destroyer escorts there were outnumbered, outgunned, and not even fast enough to run away. But in yet another improbable turn of fate, after a brief battle Adm. Takeo Kurita turned his force around without eliminating the token American force before him. He was exhausted, not having slept in three days, suffering from the lingering aftereffects of a case of dengue fever, and interpreting the desperate American counterattacks on his force as an indication they were stronger than he knew. It was a miraculous reprieve for the much weaker US force, one which Kurita described to American interrogators after the war as a "judgement of exhaustion."[1]

Cowpens Rushes Back to the Action

Cowpens and Task Group 38.1 were steaming back to Ulithi on October 24 when they received word from Halsey that the Japanese fleet was on its way to Leyte and battle was imminent. Admiral McCain ordered an about-face and the task group turned back for Samar. By the morning of the twenty-sixth, the Moo and the rest of 38.1 were within range of the fleeing Center Group, which was withdrawing after the previous day's battle. The ship's master-at-arms roused pilots and aircrew before dawn for the traditional prebattle fare of steak and eggs. This was the first time since Air Group 22 had been aboard that steak was on the menu; Avenger tail gunner Sherwin Goodman was not one to turn up his nose at the food, but he wondered why everyone was suddenly being so nice. He concluded that it was almost like "they really didn't expect us to come back or something."[2]

The day's first scouts located Kurita's fleeing ships off the northwest coast of Panay, reported as three battleships, three heavy cruisers, two light cruisers, and ten destroyers. McCain committed more than a hundred aircraft to the attack, all scheduled to lift off by 6 a.m. Air Group Commander Tom Jenkins personally led the Moo's five torpedo-armed Avengers, while Clem Craig commanded the ship's four rocket-armed Hellcats. The senior pilot from *Intrepid* had the difficult job of target coordinator, and despite his attempts to herd cats and keep the formation together, several groups peeled off to attack targets of opportunity they spotted along the way. By the time the formation arrived at the Center Group's location, only twenty planes remained: three dive bombers and eight Avengers from *Wasp* and *Cowpens'* complement of four Hellcats and five Avengers.

Coming out of the low-hanging clouds, the pilots spotted the Center Group in formation ten thousand feet below, laid out like something out of a Hollywood movie. For Sherwin Goodman, the formation of closely packed warships far below was "a sight I'll never forget." He recalled how "the sea was dotted with islands all around, the sun shining brightly, some clouds casting shadows on the blue sea below."[3] From his altitude, the Japanese fleet below looked like models on a large map. They were steaming at high speed, with white wakes trailing out behind them, and Goodman easily identified the massive bulk of the superbattleship *Yamato* in the line of warships.

The Moo's planes circled, gathered into formation, and descended to attack, with the Hellcats in the lead and the torpedo bombers following close behind. As the formation closed on the Japanese ships, they opened

up with everything they had, from large-caliber guns to automatic weapons belching tracers. As the planes drew closer and dropped down in altitude, the fire picked up in volume and intensity until it was like nothing
the pilots had ever seen. At five miles, rounds from large-caliber guns
started hitting the water around the speeding planes, soon joined by a
blizzard of tracer fire. "The flak was the heaviest I had ever experienced,"
Goodman stated.[4] He turned his turret forward so he could see what was
going on, and there were so many guns firing at him from the Japanese
ships, Goodman recalled that their hulls were ablaze with the muzzle
flashes. Unnerved by the sight, he put the turret back in the rear-facing
position, but still, he later said, "All I could see was there were tracers
going by. It looked like we were in a tunnel with stuff going by us."[5]

The plan was to concentrate torpedo attacks on the giant *Yamato*, but
just as the carrier planes approached, the entire Japanese formation made a
coordinated 180-degree turn, presenting the narrow profile of their sterns
to the attackers—a much more difficult shot. But light cruiser *Noshiro* was
slow to do so and presented a perfect broadsides to the *Cowpens'* attacking
planes. The Hellcats were in the lead, and they peppered *Noshiro's* superstructure with several five-inch rocket hits. These did little damage, and
some skittered across the cruiser's armored deck without exploding. Even
still, the rockets forced the gun crews on her port side to take cover, reducing the amount of antiaircraft fire against the Avengers following close
behind. The Moo's Hellcats made one pass on *Yamato* and a heavy cruiser
before clearing out, scoring a few hits but again causing little damage.

As the Hellcats pulled away, the Avengers came diving out of the sun to
launch their torpedoes. In his turret, Sherwin Goodman "recited a quick
prayer and hung on for dear life." His pilot, Lt. Leo Meacher, was a ram-
bunctious former UCLA fullback known as "Mad Dog" Meacher. On their
attack run, he screamed over the intercom, "OK, you yellow SOBs, here we
come!"[6] The radioman, Ed "Lefty" Clark, called out the range to the target
until it reached one thousand yards. Lieutenant Meacher loosed his fish,
and with a sharp jolt the 2,200-pound torpedo dropped away. He yanked
his now-lightened turkey away from the Japanese cruiser and made a run

for it, giving Goodman a good angle for his rear-firing gun. He estimated the range at six hundred yards, close enough to clearly see the Japanese sailors manning its antiaircraft guns. Goodman blazed away at them with his .50-caliber machine gun, shooting "darned near all the ammunition I had."[7] As his Avenger made its escape, Goodman saw what he described as one torpedo hit on *Noshiro*, followed by two others in rapid succession.

With their attacks complete, and three of their five torpedoes apparently finding their mark, the Moo's planes made for home. Goodman was not alone among the pilots in thinking that it was a miracle they escaped being hit. Another miracle was that all planes returned safely back aboard. By the time they returned to the task force they were desperately low on fuel. One of the Moo's Hellcats diverted to the nearest carrier, the *Wasp*, because he feared his engine would quit at any moment, while the engine on Goodman's Avenger sputtered to a halt for lack of fuel after they landed and were taxiing forward of the barrier. Relieved to have made it home safely, "I got out of the plane and thankfully touched the deck with both hands," Goodman recalled.[8]

The *Noshiro* Controversy

By late afternoon, *Cowpens* and Task Group 38.1 had all their planes back aboard and for the second time in a week were released for rest and replenishment. The Moo, the ship's history recorded, returned to Ulithi "proud of its part in the crushing defeat of the Japanese fleet and the scotching of its attempt to liquidate the Leyte landings."[9] Not everyone was convinced that the *Cowpens* played such a proud role in the battle, with her captain being first among the skeptics. The antagonism between the ship's officers and the air group hit a new high over whether VT-22 had hit *Noshiro* and sunk her. In their postmission debriefings, several *Cowpens* pilots and aircrew reported seeing one or more torpedo hits on the cruiser. In addition to Sherwin Goodman, one Avenger pilot who crossed over the bow of the ship after dropping his fish said he observed two near-simultaneous hits amidships and then a third on the starboard quarter a moment or two later. Similarly, Clem recorded in his journal that night that they scored "three sure hits," but it is unclear if he was repeating someone else's claim or observed the hits firsthand.[10]

Captain Taylor and his senior officers were skeptical to the point of hostility of the fliers' eyewitness accounts. Again we have only Clem Craig's diary to go on, but he fumed that none of them received any recognition from the ship's senior staff—who in the intelligence debriefings practically accused them of lying about their torpedo hits on *Noshiro*.[11] The hard feelings festered until the twenty-eighth, when Admiral McCain reported back to *Cowpens* that Air Group 22 had sunk the light cruiser. Clem was exuberant. "It was reported as sunk previously but this clinched it. Also should almost call for apologies from the captain and exec. We all feel well vindicated."[12]

As can best be determined, the air group and the captain were both a little wrong and a little right. In postwar interviews, the *Noshiro*'s captain, Kajiwara Sueyoshi, stated only one torpedo struck his ship, which left her dead in the water with a dangerous list. According to Sueyoshi, it was a second strike from *Hornet* sometime later that delivered the death blow. A bomb hit near her number two turret worsened her flooding, and she sank bow first within an hour, leaving 328 survivors in the water. Based on this testimony, it seems likely that the air group did indeed torpedo the ship but probably did not sink her, and despite the pilots' claims might not have hit with all three fish. Captain Taylor and the ship's executive officer were right to question the squadron's claims, particularly if they were aware of the *Hornet*'s subsequent attack. But how Taylor and his staff chose to express that skepticism was another indication that the leadership climate aboard the *Cowpens* had grown toxic.

Perhaps the Navy's final word on the controversy was the medals it awarded, which seemed to reflect the pilots' claims rather than Taylor's doubts. Both Clem Craig and Tom Jenkins earned Navy Crosses; Jenkins's citation specifically stated that "he led his squadron in pressing home an attack which scored three definite torpedo hits on an enemy cruiser leaving her in a sinking condition."[13] Even Captain Taylor was decorated for the mission; his Navy Cross citation specifically mentioned that the

Cowpens' air group "was brought to bear against the enemy resulting in heavy damage to and the sinking of capital ships of the Japanese Fleet."[14] While Taylor had moved on to his next assignment by the time word of his award made its way back to Air Group 22, the fact Taylor was decorated in part for a sinking that he denied ever happened was an irony not lost on Clem and the Moo's other pilots.

Respite at Ulithi: Price's Return

Cowpens tied up at Ulithi Atoll on October 29. The atoll was on the far western end of the Caroline Islands, southwest of the Marianas. Vaguely resembling the outline of the Italian peninsula, the string of islets created a 209-square-mile natural harbor spacious enough to host in excess of seven hundred ships, more than enough for the Third Fleet. The atoll was a new acquisition for the US Navy, captured without a fight on September 23. Like Majuro before it, Ulithi had been largely bypassed by the war. Under US control, it became the major American fleet anchorage in the Western Pacific, replacing Majuro and Eniwetok, which were now too far to the east.

By the time *Cowpens* arrived, there were over one hundred ships in the harbor, including nearly forty from Service Squadron 10, which just that month had arrived from Eniwetok, some 1,400 miles away. The squadron rapidly transformed the idyllic Pacific lagoon into a major logistical base, bringing with it specialized ships for repair, salvage, supply, fueling, and medical assistance. For the Moo's officers and men, Ulithi's primary draw was Mog Mog, the small islet that the Navy set aside for recreation. After weeks of unending shipboard life, anything that got them ashore was a welcome break. Although it baked under a fierce tropical sun that varied, in the words of one sailor, from "the infernal to the merely intolerable," Mog Mog offered the opportunity to relax on the pearl-white sands, swim in the crystal clear tropical lagoon, or play baseball, basketball, or volleyball.[15]

The Moo's officers and men did not have it to themselves. Most of the ships in the harbor were releasing a third of their complement at a time to go ashore, meaning that as many as fifteen thousand sailors and one thousand officers were on the island on any given day. Arriving on the beach for a four-hour liberty, the sailors were given two cans of warm beer, sometimes Iron City beer from Pittsburgh or Rupert's from New York City. Naturally, the bluejackets soon developed a barter system so those who wanted could drink their fill, with the sailors trading cash and smokes for others' ration of beer. Unfortunately, the beer was spiked with formaldehyde to keep it from spoiling in the tropical heat. While this deterred few sailors, overindulgence resulted in what Clem described as a "walloping" hangover.[16]

On the officers' side of Mog Mog the engineers constructed a series of thatched huts that served as a makeshift O club and recreation area, known as Crowley's Tavern. The officers sipped beer or whiskey at a yards-long bar constructed of crushed beer cans or enjoyed grilled steaks or a game of horseshoes. After the wear and tear of weeks of flying and the strain of on-again, off-again clashes with Captain Taylor and his staff, Air Group 22 went to Crowley's to blow off some steam. Several of its fliers returned to the ship drunk and belligerent, and only the quick intervention of the air group's senior pilots averted a confrontation with the ship's officers. "Some of the boys went ashore in p.m. almost resulting in trouble aboard at night," Clem wrote sympathetically the following day. "Not that they can be blamed too much as we are still taking a beating about the last attack. Both *Houston* and the *Canberra* are here and so we are supposed to be heroes."[17]

Captain Taylor's preferred choice for dealing with Air Group 22 finally caught up with the ship at Ulithi. Bob Price, who commanded VF-25 and then Air Group 25 before surviving eleven days adrift in the Pacific in a life raft, returned aboard the *Cowpens* on October 30 after more than a month in transit. He made the long journey from Jacksonville to Ulithi by train, ship, and finally by air. Stopping briefly in San Francisco, he began his first letter back to his wife: "Well, here we go again on our usual—and all too frequent—round-go-roundy of letter writing."[18] Price was upbeat about his return to the Moo, commenting in letters written along the way,

"Believe me, it will be awfully good to catch up to the old familiar bucket of rivets."[19]

Once Price arrived on board, he was shocked when Captain Taylor laid out for him the reasons for his return. Writing on the day of his arrival, Price was dismayed to learn that what he hoped was a coincidental reassignment had actually been engineered by Captain Taylor. "I might just as well tell you now about how I happened to be here," Price wrote his wife. "It seems that I was asked for [specifically requested by name, and] . . . the Captain admitted to me last night and apologized all over the place . . . I fooled myself into believing that it just happened." Price's orders taking over as the ship's air officer were dated October 25, but he agreed to first serve as the deputy, a position that the good-natured Price likened to an apprenticeship. Many of the Moo's plank owners were happy to have him back, and were apologetic about the circumstances of his return—particularly the ship's executive officer, Hugh Nieman. "Everybody has been swell and of course feel that I've had a dirty deal," Price wrote. "Nemo's conscience bothered him so much that he had a wash basin installed in my room."[20]

CHAPTER 23

Black November

*C*owpens and Task Force 38 could not rid themselves of Leyte and General MacArthur. The Filipino monsoon season had deposited thirty-five inches of rain on the island over the previous forty days, slowing the construction of the airfields the Army needed to provide their own air cover there. The flooding and mud was so bad that one of MacArthur's field commanders described conditions in some areas as "a swamp and a mud hole and nothing more."[1] With only two of Task Force 38's four groups present, and the Army airfields not yet fully operational, the Japanese had secured air supremacy after dark and were bringing reinforcements in by ship to Ormoc, on the island's west coast. Meanwhile, kamikazes were taking a heavy toll on US ships in Leyte Gulf—inflicting grievous hits on *Intrepid*, *Franklin*, and *Belleau Wood*, to the tune of more than 150 dead, and dozens more wounded. Seventh Fleet commander Adm. Thomas Kinkaid warned MacArthur that the situation in Leyte Gulf was critical; enemy air strength had dramatically increased and threatened to strangle the Army's supply lifeline to the beachhead.

With the battlefield balance beginning to swing back in favor of the enemy, MacArthur turned to Halsey to provide the air cover he lacked. In turn, the Bull kept Task Force 38 on the move for the next three weeks, trying to choke off the supply of enemy planes and ships flowing into Leyte. The pattern of strikes repeated seemingly without end; two or three days in action, followed by a day or two to refuel, then rinse and repeat. By the end of November, the Moo's pilots joked they had made so many trips to Luzon that they could find the target blindfolded—but the humor masked the difficulty of the situation. Combat fatigue was mounting, and the Moo and her fliers took more losses that month than they had in any other in the war to date—eight dead, with four more shot down and on the run behind enemy lines.

First stop was Luzon, for two days of strikes starting on November 5. The Moo's planes scoured nearby airfields, wrecking hangars and destroying parked planes. Off Lingayen Gulf, near Santa Cruz, the Moo's fighters rocketed and strafed a fat convoy of twelve transports, setting two on fire and damaging two more. *Cowpens* in the past had poor luck attacking convoys of ships, and this was no exception, with enemy fire claiming two of its fighter pilots. A barrage of fire from one ship found Ens. Thomas Gunther of Houston, Texas. His plane took a hit and went straight in. Ens. Joel Bacon, of Chester, South Carolina, was also badly mauled by the antiaircraft fire, but he managed to fly his plane twenty miles back toward the carrier before ditching. Later strike planes passing through the area spotted Bacon's empty and deflated life raft but there was no sign of him, and he was never seen again. Clem offered his own assessment in his journal: "Bacon possibly picked up by sub, Gunther, no hope."[2]

The weather worsened on the eighth and ninth, and the *Cowpens* had a drink from the oilers in heavy seas. The seas were so rough, the ship's history recounted, that the flying spray drenched the deckhands on the catwalks—seventy feet above the water in normal conditions. The task force churned northeast to avoid the worst of the storm, but it didn't ease the ride. The Moo's history recorded how *Cowpens* "pitched and tossed all the time, the ship tripping a mad fantastic."[3] Clem was typically low-key in his own account. "Ran into a typhoon last eve and continues all day," he wrote. "Really something."[4]

Then it was a thirty-six-hour sprint back to Leyte, where scouts had spotted a large convoy of warships and troop transports heading for Ormoc Bay to reinforce Leyte's beleaguered Japanese defenders. The fleet did an about-face and increased to twenty-six knots, straining the Moo's weary power plant—and two of her four boilers temporarily dropped offline in apparent protest. "Turned around and making all possible speed in view of heavy seas towards Leyte," Clem wrote. "So here we go again."[5] The ships battered through the raging seas at high speeds, resulting in an even wilder ride than before. The ship's history recorded, "Standing on the flight deck was reminiscent of riding a giant snow plow as the waves burst into great clouds of dazzling white spray."[6]

The task force's planes arrived just in the nick of time on November 11, finding the enemy convoy when it was only a few miles off Ormoc Beach. Most of a Japanese infantry division had made it ashore by the time the carrier aircraft began their attack, but they sank the ships carrying the enemy's heavy weapons and most of their supplies, leaving the enemy soldiers with only what they were carrying on their backs. There were so many friendly planes in the air that several of the Moo's fliers had trouble putting bombs on targets because of the risk of midair collisions. Returning to the ship with no hits—and probably anticipating criticism from Captain Taylor—Air Group Commander Tom Jenkins sounded somewhat defensive in his after-action report. He attributed the poor results to the "extremely large number of our own planes all attacking at the same time resulting in distraction of the pilot's attentions from bombing to preventing collisions with other planes."[7]

Flying back and forth from the carriers to Ormoc gave the Moo's planes an opportunity to survey both the beachhead and the Army airfields around Tacloban. Sherwin Goodman looked down from above and was grateful he was not in the infantry; he could clearly see "the shell holes, the mud, the men struggling through it, ships in the harbor unloading supplies, and an airfield crammed with US Army planes, but unable to get airborne."[8] Clem was less charitable, noting that "it is a mystery to us why the Army do not attack the remaining shipping without yelling for help. Their fields were full of planes and we had to come 800 miles to help them out. Surely does not speak well for them."[9]

With the enemy convoy sunk or scattered, Halsey turned the task force back for Manila for strikes on the thirteenth and fourteenth. The feeling aboard the Moo was that the task force had left the Japanese there alone long enough for reinforcements to arrive, which meant "more business for us."[10] The strikes focused on Manila Bay, targeting shipping that the

Japanese could use to reinforce Leyte. US casualties were heavy, particularly from antiaircraft fire, with twenty-five planes lost across the task force. While costly, Halsey regarded the strikes as essential, for every Japanese ship sunk in Manila Bay was one less that the Japanese could use to move their soldiers to Leyte.

For once it was the Moo's torpedo squadron, not the fighters, that saw the lion's share of the action. Lt. Eric Rellis from Chicago, Illinois, was flying one of her Avengers in a large formation of planes as it approached Manila. Coming out of the clouds, Rellis saw that Manila Bay was "filled with light warships, freighters, and transports—ample targets for everyone."[11] Since the task force's last visit to Manila, the Japanese had significantly increased their antiaircraft defenses, however. As the guns opened up on the arriving bombers, Rellis thought it looked like a "hail storm was coming up at us."[12]

Of *Cowpens'* five Avengers on the strike, two went down in the bay and a third returned to the ship riddled with holes. Rellis's Avenger took multiple hits, forcing an immediate water landing. He and his tail gunner, Alan Pray, escaped their sinking plane into life rafts, but his radioman, Charles Stewart, never emerged and went down with the plane. Friendly aircraft circling overhead reported that Filipino fishermen picked up the duo and hustled them to shore. Similarly, Lt. Silas "Si" Johnson's Avenger, with crewmen Ralph Bridges and Robert Jones aboard, was also hit, ditched in the bay, and Si and Jones were picked up by civilians—although again the radioman, Bridges, was lost. All four men spent the next five weeks on the run with Filipino guerrillas, playing a deadly game of cat-and-mouse with the Japanese Army. Enemy informants were everywhere, and the men were sometimes only a step or two ahead of their pursuers. Si described one particularly close call where the Japanese raided the village where he and Jones were hiding. The Japanese officer commanding the raid demanded the residents surrender the Americans, identifying them by name, rank, and squadron, but the villagers would not give them up.[13]

On the fourteenth, the Moo went back to the bay to mop up any survivors from the previous day's attacks. The ground fire was as determined as ever; Sherwin Goodman described the docks along the bay as "as a solid sheet of anti-aircraft fire; the ships were firing and the shore batteries throughout the city were blasting away."[14] Several ships were still burning when Air Group 22 arrived, and under the pall of smoke the Moo's Avengers planted six bombs on two cargo ships that had escaped the previous day's onslaught. As they pulled out of their attack dive, they spotted an additional cargo ship dead ahead and proceeded to strafe it. It must have been an ammunition lugger, because once hit by gunfire it went up in a tremendous explosion. "We paid dearly for it," the pilots recounted, as one of the Moo's Avengers was right over it as it detonated.[15] Ens. Steven Korus's Avenger disintegrated in the fireball, and no sign was ever found of him or his two aircrewmen, Richard Eschbach and Joseph Budak.

The task force retreated back out to sea to refuel. But on the eighteenth it was back to business, with another trip to Luzon. The pattern of near-continual strikes had finally thinned out Japanese strength there, and targets were hard to find. *Cowpens'* Avengers hit two airfields in midsize towns north of Manila, Tarlac and Cabanatuan, but found few planes, and so the bombers mostly wrecked hangars and repair shops before heading home. Meanwhile, ten of VF-22's Hellcats set off on a sweep by themselves further to the northwest, investigating Lingayen Gulf and the nearby town of San Fernando, where Japanese shipping had often concentrated in the past. In town they used their rockets and gunfire to good effect on dock installations and set two oil tanks afire, and strafed three of six small cargo ships anchored nearby.

With the smoke from the burning oil tanks settling like a blanket over the town, the Hellcats moved out into the harbor, where they spotted two gunboats and two cargo ships heading to port. The Moo's pilots set upon the larger of the two ships and put the rest of their rockets and a great deal of .50-caliber into it. It was soon ablaze, and by the time the planes left the area, the pilots said the fire aboard "had spread from the stern amidships and was truly a noble bonfire."[16] The pilots then gave the works to the second freighter, which exploded under a hail of bullets. The defending gunboats did not give up easily, and knocked down Lt. James Bryce. His wingmen circled overhead for an hour until lifeguard submarine *Ray* arrived and recovered him. Bryce and two other rescued "zoomies" from the *Wasp* spent almost a month of quality time aboard *Ray* before they returned to Pearl Harbor on December 3. Despite the cramped living conditions and occasional depth charging, Bryce voiced his support for the silent service, noting that he and his fellow pilots aboard the sub "got back OK and we are really 100 percent for these submarine men."[17]

With the strikes on Luzon providing diminishing returns, *Cowpens* and Task Group 38.1 withdrew to Ulithi on the twentieth, where they finished out the month. All hands were grateful for the breather, as well as Thanksgiving dinner at sea. Turkey wasn't available, but there was roast chicken and ham, plus shrimp cocktail, mashed potatoes and all the trimmings, and pumpkin pie, cigars, and cigarettes afterward. But November had one last life to claim; on the twenty-second Ens. Kenneth Strandt of Everson, Washington, was returning from a routine CAP. He had just been waved off for landing when his engine quit, and his Hellcat crashed into the sea two hundred yards off the port bow. Observers on deck did not see him get out of the plane before it sank; destroyer *Collett* searched the area but did not find him.

Taylor's Replacement—Indoor Rainstorms

The interlude at sea in late November gave all hands an opportunity to catch up on their mail. One man aboard who was doing so was Bob Price, who wrote his wife about his new role as deputy air officer. "Things are going along well and I'm learning something new every day. As far as I can see, I'll have to keep on doing just that for a good long time yet as this new job has plenty of angles."[18] Price broke to his wife another important bit of news that was making its way through the ship's grapevine. Captain Taylor had received his orders for his next assignment in Washington, DC, "so it probably won't be too many days before he leaves." True to form, Price was charitable to the captain, even though Taylor had engineered his return to the Moo. "I hate to see him go—even though he did play a dirty trick on me, he's a swell gent."[19]

Capt. George DeBaun arrived aboard ship on November 15, serving in observer status alongside Taylor until the formal change of command

ceremony two weeks later. DeBaun was a definite change from his predecessor; where Taylor's withdrawn personality fueled his poor relationship
with his pilots, the pipe-smoking DeBaun was good-natured, outspoken,
and salty. His cheerfully profane outbursts and humorous asides to all
those around him soon endeared him to the crew. DeBaun was a native
Kansan from the tiny town of Bushong; his uncle had been a general officer in the Army during the First World War. DeBaun's uncle convinced
him that a career in the Navy was preferable to that of the Army, since
you took your bunks and chow with you wherever you went. DeBaun
transferred from Kansas State University to the Naval Academy, graduating in the class of 1921, and then flight school in Pensacola in 1923.
DeBaun had more time at sea than his predecessor—experience that soon
proved invaluable for the Moo. He served on four fleet carriers and a seaplane tender, helmed Torpedo Squadron 6 on the eve of the war, and then
commanded his first ship, the seaplane tender USS *Tangier*, from 1941
to 1942. After several months of tension with Captain Taylor, Clem was
guarded and cynical in his evaluation of the incoming commanding officer. "New captain flew aboard today, hope he has a better understanding
of his job than Taylor—but also find that it actually does not make much
difference."[20]

Cowpens limped into Ulithi lagoon the day after Thanksgiving, November 24, with one boiler again out of commission. The ship's wooden flight
deck, too, was showing its age. After more than seven thousand takeoffs
and landings the Douglas fir planking was seriously worn, and the growing gaps between boards allowed water to drip down into the hangar deck
below. "It is believed that this ship is the only carrier in the US Navy that
finds it necessary to put the hangar deck crews in foul weather gear during rainstorms," one after-action report grumbled. "Numerous leaks in
the flight deck are the cause."[21] Moreover, the report described how the
planks had worn down so much around some of the formerly flush tie-
downs in the deck that they now protruded above the planking, posing
a safety risk. Referencing an August 30 crash that totaled one Avenger,
the report noted that one serious accident had already been caused by an
aircraft tailhook catching on a protruding tie-down. The deckhands were

using grinders to keep them flush, but another accident was only a matter of time. In his accompanying memo, Admiral Montgomery recommended that *Cowpens* and her sisters be redecked before the safety risk worsened. Admiral's endorsement or no, the Moo had several months to go before her next overhaul, and she would just have to suffer through her problems.

The change-of-command ceremony between Taylor and DeBaun took place soon after the ship moored that afternoon. Whatever his differences with his air group, Captain Taylor left the *Cowpens* with a Navy Cross for *Noshiro*'s sinking and a Legion of Merit for the rescue of *Houston* and *Canberra*. Writing for Taylor's personnel record, Admiral McCain noted, "At all times his leadership and ability was demonstrated by the efficient manner in which the ship and air group under his command performed. I will be happy to have him serve with me at any time in the future."[22] In contrast, Clem and the rest of the pilots were relieved to see Taylor go. In his journal, Clem noted how Captain Taylor departed without ever having directly spoken to the air group while on board.[23]

A Wave of Kamikazes

The last few Task Force strikes in support of the Leyte landings occurred while *Cowpens* and Task Group 38.1 were back at Ulithi on November 25. Task Groups 38.2 and 38.3 netted more enemy planes and ships, but losses from kamikazes were heavy. The unlucky *Intrepid* took two hits—one wiping out a gun crew and the other crashing through her flight deck and exploding in the hangar deck below. Kamikazes also found *Essex* and *Cowpens*' sister ship *Cabot*; total losses were more than 120, with dozens more wounded. The carriers weren't the only target; in subsequent days, kamikazes hit battleships *Colorado* and *Maryland*, light cruiser *Montpelier*, and picket destroyers *Saufley* and *Aulick*.

Halsey was appalled by the losses and canceled the remaining strikes in the Visayans. Nearly one in four kamikazes found their target, and the list of damaged ships was growing by the day. With such a significant threat, Halsey concluded that "further casual strikes did not appear profitable; only strikes in great force for valuable stakes at vital times would justify exposure of the fast carriers to suicidal attacks—at least until better defensive techniques were perfected."[24] He recalled the remaining task groups to Ulithi and turned over responsibility for Leyte's defense to the Army Air Corps.

It was impossible for the sailors not to notice when the wounded *Essex*, *Hancock*, *Intrepid*, and *Cabot* limped into Ulithi lagoon, with some of their scars still smoldering. The sight fueled sailors' fear, dread, and fascination about suicide attacks; a press correspondent based in the fleet at the time described how the bluejackets were obsessed with kamikazes and spoke of almost nothing else.[25] It seemed at the time that the Japanese had finally devised a strategy that could hurt the mighty Third Fleet, and there were many aboard the Moo who did not look forward to heading back out to sea to face them. Art Daly remarked in his journal that the Moo was going out to help fill in for the wounded ships, and probably spoke for many aboard when he wrote, "I'm not too happy with this. I thought we would get a little respite."[26]

Clem, too, heard through the commanders' grapevine that kamikaze damage was really beginning to chip away at the task force's strength, and that the current defensive tactics had proved inadequate. "All big shots conferences have indicated that situation regarding carriers is desperate," he wrote. "The Banzai boys [kamikazes] really have them scared."[27] Both officers and men turned to trips to Mog Mog to ease their minds; but with three task groups anchored in the lagoon, there were more men trying to get ashore than there were whaleboats to carry them, resulting in sometimes hours-long waits. Clem groused to his journal early in their stay, "Went ashore and transportation so bad I do not believe I will go again."[28] At least there were still movies on board every night; Bob Price wrote his wife on the night of their arrival on the twenty-fourth that "we had a pretty fair movie tonight—*The War Against Mrs. Hadly*."[29] It was cookie-cutter patriotic wartime fare, following the somewhat improbable voyage of discovery of a spoiled society matron who realized her unwillingness to sacrifice her material comforts was hurting the war effort.

Cowpens and the rest of Task Force 38 weighed anchor from Ulithi on the morning of December 1, heading to support the invasion of Mindoro, which was scheduled to begin four days later. They were at sea only twelve hours when the fleet received new orders to turn around and head back to Ulithi. Everyone was perplexed by the turn of events. "Provisions is the best guess as we had been unable to get any fresh stores aboard," Clem wrote that evening.[30] It was a good guess, but the real reason was the continuing kamikaze threat and the Army's inability to tamp down Japanese air activity in the Central Philippines, which was a precondition for the Mindoro landings. MacArthur reluctantly agreed to delay that operation to December 15, and the subsequent Lingayen Gulf landings on Luzon until January. Halsey learned of the decision only once his ships were at sea, and sent them back to harbor with orders to make the best of the delay for rest, recreation, and repairs.

Ten days was the longest the fleet had been at anchor since August, and all hands were grateful for the break. The time passed quietly and slowly on board, which in addition to regular deliveries of mail helped take the edge off from the past few weeks and ease worries about kamikazes and the next round of operations. Bob Price used the time to acclimate to his new job as air officer and to Captain DeBaun, telling his wife that "it seems funny to have a new skipper. He is a swell gent, however, and I know we will get along. He is the third one now. Wonder how many more I'll have to wear out?"[31] Price was characteristically upbeat about his circumstances, and his only complaint was that his sudden return to tropical climes had come with a bad case of the prickly heat. The XO, perhaps still feeling guilty for Price's recall to the *Cowpens*, offered Price the use of his air-conditioned cabin to try and ease the itching. Describing himself as "playing the role of the plutocrat" sitting in air-conditioned ease, Price could avoid the itches only so long as he remained inside. Writing to his wife, he longed for cooler climes that would resolve his problem for good, thinking longingly of a "big snowball fight" outside of his home in Missouri."[32]

CHAPTER 24

The Mighty Moo Faces Typhoon Cobra

Eternal Father, strong to save,
Whose arm hath bound the restless wave,
Who bid'st the mighty ocean deep
Its own appointed limits keep;
O hear us when we cry to thee,
For those in peril on the sea.
—The Navy Hymn

The Big Blue Blanket—A New Threat Emerges

The stillness of Ulithi's cerulean waters was broken early on the morning of December 10 as the fleet put to sea. The destroyers were first, followed by the capital ships and carriers, each moving through the channel in single file a few hundred yards apart. The task force numbered seven fleet carriers and five CVLs loaded with more than eight hundred aircraft, with eighty-five escorts. *Cowpens* remained in Task Group 38.1 under Rear Admiral Montgomery, along with fleet carriers *Yorktown* and *Wasp* and sister ship *Monterey*. After a long break at Ulithi, all hands had caught their breath and were braced for action, and they commented how the "game seemed to be such that we could expect some excitement" in the next Philippines landing.[1] While MacArthur's forces stormed ashore on Mindoro, *Cowpens* and Task Force 38 had orders to smother airfields on neighboring Luzon starting on the fourteenth, destroying aircraft that could pose a threat to the landing ships or the fleet. Halsey and McCain hoped that by keeping a "constant CAP" over enemy airfields they could reduce the number of kamikazes that made it into the air. The tactic soon acquired another name: the "Big Blue Blanket."

This was Captain DeBaun's first time at the helm of the Moo, and as the ship put to sea his stomach was churning. DeBaun took seriously his responsibility to safeguard the nearly 1,500 souls aboard—and his thoughts must have been occupied with the looming kamikaze threat and the knowledge that they often went for the carriers first. The burden of command is a heavy one, and the bridge crew pretended not to notice when DeBaun discreetly stepped into his sea cabin to vomit, returning as if nothing had happened. But Clem and the others needn't have worried about DeBaun's mettle; in the coming weeks he would prove to be not only an expert commander and sailor, but possessed of a steely resolve that would get them through some of the Moo's most difficult days. The captain's tendency to puke every time the ship put to sea was noticed but never commented on, to avoid embarrassing him.

Dawn on December 14 found the *Cowpens* and Task Force 38 off the coast of now-familiar southern Luzon. The Japanese had seemingly grown overconfident after their kamikazes had driven the Third Fleet from Philippine waters. As a result, many airfields on Luzon were crowded with planes; over the course of the day, carrier air strikes wrecked as many as 270 and then imposed the Big Blue Blanket overhead. Relieved at four-hour intervals, the umbrella of air cover successfully prevented the Japanese from flying the planes already there or bringing in reinforcements. For their part, *Cowpens* searched three airfields in Southeast Luzon that morning, destroying ten or twelve planes on the ground. A second raid that afternoon was intended to pile on the morning's results, but the Japanese gunners had improved their aim since the first round of strikes. They hit Ens. George Whitehouse of Newport, Rhode Island. Apparently wounded, Whitehouse flew his Hellcat for several miles back toward the ship before it suddenly plummeted from the air and crashed into a small island. Clem offered his grim prognosis: "No hope of survival."[2]

The success of blanket coverage over Japanese airfields meant little business for *Cowpens'* planes flying CAP. "The operations during this period have been conspicuous for the absence of bogies," stated the ship's official account. The Big Blue Blanket, the report concluded, "spelled bad business for fighter direction but produced excellent protection [for the carriers]."[3]

Unbeknownst to *Cowpens* and the fleet, as they wrapped up their strikes on Luzon, a new enemy was beginning to grow. Approximately six hundred miles southeast of Ulithi, and just north of the equator, a meteorological disturbance was taking shape. An embryonic storm had emerged from the intertropical convergence zone, an equatorial belt of warm, humid air known to sailors as the Doldrums. Sailors for centuries had known that the Western Pacific was often storm-crossed, earning it the nickname "typhoon alley." Pacific typhoons are more frequent than either Atlantic hurricanes or Indian Ocean cyclones; in any given year an average of twenty cross the Philippine Sea. They can grow into some of the fiercest storms on the planet, with dense walls of clouds rising to fifty thousand feet, and at their core some of the lowest barometric pressures ever recorded. They are most common from July to October, but can still occur in November and December.

While Americans in the twenty-first century take for granted accurate meteorological forecasting drawn from satellite imagery, in 1944 those technologies were decades away. All Third Fleet carriers had aerologists aboard, but their equipment was primitive by modern standards and not capable of delivering long-range forecasts in that part of the world. In the Navy's westward rush across the Pacific, it was slow to establish a comprehensive network of weather stations that could track storms; and to maintain radio silence, even a friendly ship passing through a storm would not broadcast its location to avoid alerting the Japanese to US naval movements. As a result, the Navy warned, "all the scientific methods available to modern meteorology are not sufficient to forecast accurately the movement and intensity of the frequent typhoons in this area."[4]

As *Cowpens* and the fleet set off to meet their oilers several hundred miles to the east, the storm soon to be known as Typhoon Cobra cruised an empty patch of ocean north of Ulithi and southwest of Guam. As late as sunset on December 16, it covered an area of eight thousand square miles but had not yet been sighted. It was not until the morning of the seventeenth that the storm began to betray its presence in the area. The day broke dark and gloomy, with churning seas and a stiff wind, and the southeastern horizon marked by a threatening wall of multicolored storm clouds with a dark red tinge on their upper edge. Despite the worsening conditions, the task force urgently needed to refuel. The last three days of high-tempo operations had drained its fuel reserves, and now many of its destroyers' tanks were nearly empty. Some were at only 15 percent capacity, perhaps only enough for another day or so of steaming.

As sullen gray clouds thickened overhead, Third Fleet turned due east into the wind and attempted to refuel. The fuel-starved warships lined up next to the fat tankers, and the deckhands began working the lines to link them together. But the wind and waves had other ideas; the tankers and warships heaved and rolled, and the lines and hoses snapped and then parted. The sea was just too rough to refuel; Capt. Jasper Acuff, the commander of the replenishment squadron, assessed that the day's conditions were the worst he had ever seen in the Pacific. There had been foul weather in the Aleutians, Acuff noted, "but nothing as dirty as this."[5]

Cowpens fared better than most, managing a successful linkup with tanker *Aucilla* and successfully topping off to 95 percent capacity. By noon, while the Moo was still drinking from her oiler, the winds picked up to thirty knots, heavy rain began to fall, and a series of heavy swells arrived from the southeast, nearly one hundred degrees out of kilter from the direction of the wind. The difference between the direction of the wind and the seas put an end to the Moo's refueling before she could fully top off her tanks, as it became impossible to keep the two ships in position. Noting that the barometer had dropped 0.14 inches over the previous twenty-four hours, the ship's log recorded that all of these indications suggested the "possible existence of a tropical disturbance approaching from the southeast, although aerological information from the area showed none."[6]

Admiral Halsey claimed he had a "destroyerman's nose," a mythical skill where a sailor could stand in the wind and predict the weather. But neither he nor his aerologist realized that a typhoon was only 135 miles to the southeast and bearing down on the task force. They had virtually no weather data from the vast, empty swath of Pacific Ocean where the growing storm currently lurked. Its winds had increased to 70 to 80 knots, with gusts over 120, but it was still compact. Its winds did not reach out more than one hundred miles from the eye, not yet enough to be felt in earnest by the task force.

Third Fleet's aerologist erroneously concluded that the rough seas they were seeing were the result of a tropical disturbance some four hundred miles distant that was likely to merge with an approaching cold front and move off to the northeast. Based on this assessment, Halsey moved Third Fleet's refueling area two hundred miles to the northwest—steaming at a right angle to the estimated course of the storm in order to gain distance from it. Conditions continued to worsen over the course of the day, and by that afternoon, the admiral was worried he was still in the storm's path. He turned the task force to the south at approximately 2:30 p.m., and then, when that didn't work, back to the northwest at 10 p.m.

Back aboard the *Cowpens*, Eugene Corde, an enlisted man assigned to the ship's aerology department, had the watch the afternoon of December 17, and he prepared the daily forecast. Working from the same data as Halsey's staff, he concluded the heavy weather was likely to worsen and distributed his forecast to all the ship's department heads. The ship's chief aerologist, a young lieutenant, junior grade, who had just reported aboard, read Corde's work and disagreed—issuing a new forecast that predicted improved conditions the following day.[7]

In contrast, Captain DeBaun was an experienced sailor who also thought heavy weather was coming. He cross-examined the young lieutenant, who insisted the foul weather they were seeing was only a small disturbance and definitely not a typhoon. DeBaun regarded the lieutenant with considerable skepticism, explaining later that he thought the man lacked any meaningful seagoing experience and had "never seen a good line squall or any kind of heavy weather."[8] DeBaun opted to keep his own counsel and ordered the ship battened down for a storm.

After the Moo's two previous experiences with a Pacific gale, no one aboard took the power of a major storm lightly. At DeBaun's direction, each plane in the hangar deck was secured with multiple ropes and steel lines, as were the ship's tractors, jeeps, and mobile cranes. The ship's account of the storm recorded how by the time the deckhands were finished, "the place looked like a vast spider's web."[9] In anticipation of extended operations in support of MacArthur's offensive, the ship's magazine was stocked with more bombs than it had been designed to carry, and those that could not be secured in the munitions racks were lashed in place. Also securely tied down throughout the ship were all manner of smaller equipment and fixtures; everything from bomb-handling dollies to tool boxes and wardroom furniture. At the same time, Captain DeBaun hedged his bets in case the weather suddenly improved and Halsey ordered him to get his fighters into the air. Before securing the planes left on the flight deck with steel cables, the deckhands fueled them and spotted them for takeoff, meaning they could be made flyable in short order.

By dusk, the weather had grown even more ominous, with an eerie red glow on the horizon, and the white-capped sea darkening to charcoal. Captain Acuff's oilers kept trying to refuel the destroyers lowest on fuel, unsuccessfully attempting to rig lines over the stern, an effort that they abandoned as futile when night fell. The fleet undertook every possible measure to stretch out the destroyers' remaining fuel. They abandoned their usual practice of zigzagging to throw off submarines, and some ships secured all but one boiler and steamed at their most economical speed.

Aboard the *Cowpens*, all hands faced the prospect of a restless night aboard the pitching ship with grim determination. "And so to bed, not to sleep," the ship's history of the storm recorded, "but to devise ways and means of staying in our bunks since the tossing of ship continued and grew worse as the night advanced. No one was quite sure what was going to happen next, since there had been no evidence of a typhoon on the weather maps, yet it was all too obvious that this was no mean storm."[10] For his part, Captain DeBaun worried about the worsening conditions and that evening's turn back to the north, thinking it was a bad idea to head "back up in the general direction of something I didn't in my own mind believe was just a local storm."[11]

By midnight, Typhoon Cobra's western edge had met the cold front, but rather than bouncing off it as anticipated, the storm plowed directly through it. With the storm growing steadily closer, the weather worsened from dismal to vicious. Halsey, after briefly consulting Admirals McCain and Bogan before dawn, at 5 a.m. on the eighteenth, turned Third Fleet south again. He set no new refueling rendezvous, merely ordering all task groups to do so as soon as practicable after sunrise.

Typhoon Cobra Strikes

It must be understood that every man did his duty, steadily and carefully throughout the day. There was no panic although every man realized that he was closer to his maker than he had ever been before.
                    —USS *Cowpens* account of Typhoon Cobra,
                                  December 18, 1944[12]

The moment of *Cowpens'* greatest danger had arrived. Years after the war, when asked to consider their wartime experiences, the ship's veterans were virtually unanimous on what had scared them most. It was not the enemy—the countless close calls with Japanese bombs or torpedoes. It was this day, December 18, when Typhoon Cobra caught the Moo and the rest of Third Fleet in its full fury, and the howling winds and towering waves rocked the ship so wildly that it seemed she would capsize and sink. "The waves were like mountains and the ship pitched and rolled and shuddered like a wild horse," said ship's officer Francis MacBarron. "Of all the experiences I have had in my fifteen months at sea, nothing lives so vividly in my memory as that typhoon."[13] Weatherman Eugene Corde, too, explained the sense of terror and helplessness that all aboard felt that day. "I don't think any experience in my life has been so awesome and nerve wracking. The ship under enemy attack offered a better chance of survival."[14] The ship's war diary, normally written in a dispassionate style, on this day made clear all aboard knew they were standing at the edge of the abyss:

> Any resemblance between this report and an eulogy is not... coincidental; it is written with the full and complete realization that but for the grace of God it might have been a dirge written by our next of kin...New York Shipbuilding Company did build us a sturdy ship...but never for a moment did anyone forget that our creator was giving us the chance to fight for our lives and that a second's negligence and we were all gone.[15]

At dawn, Captain DeBaun passed the word to his men to secure for a typhoon, and he called all repair parties and damage control teams to their battle stations. DeBaun took position on the semi-enclosed bridge, where he remained until the storm passed. He pulled the gun crews and lookouts from their stations, directed all securing lines be checked and rechecked, and instructed all hands to stay clear of the flight deck, where the motion of the ship was the most dangerous. Despite these preparations, one look at the sea was enough to make the stomach of the most seasoned sailor plummet. Over the course of the morning, the waves grew into towering pyramidal monsters that threw the ships of the Third Fleet around like toys. The troughs were so deep or the crests were so high that from the bridge—more than one hundred feet to the waterline in normal seas—"one looked up to the tops of the waves when we were in the bottom of a swell."[16]

There was a rhythm to the pounding, and every fifteen minutes a rogue wave larger than all the rest slammed into the ship. The wind, too, worked up to a vicious crescendo, beginning the day at forty knots and steadily building up to more than one hundred over the course of the morning. It flung a combination of driving rain and spray from the towering waves against men and ship alike. It came in horizontally, working its way under the visors of the crew's weather gear, blinding them with spray that felt like needles against their skin. Visibility was only a few yards; from the bridge of the *Cowpens* the aft end of the flight deck was concealed under a blanket of flying seas, rain, and fog. Sometimes the veil of the storm drew back for an instant, just long enough for sailors aboard the Moo to spot the other Third Fleet ships a short distance away. They, too, were rolling drunkenly in the raging seas, clawing their way up each mammoth wave only to crash down into the trough in a massive spray of sea.

The oilers made a last, fruitless effort to fuel the neediest destroyers, but the wind and sea prevented the linkup and threatened to sweep overboard the men working the lines. After that failed, Task Group's 38.1's Admiral Montgomery tried fueling the destroyers from the fleet carriers, using the flattops' bulk to shield the destroyers from the wind, but this too was unsuccessful. After a final consultation with his aerologist, Halsey bowed to the inevitable and informed General MacArthur at 8 a.m. that he would not be able to return to the Philippines to resume air strikes the following day.

The fleet's southbound turn at 5 a.m. made the Moo's condition especially difficult. With her fuel tanks nearly full, *Cowpens* had a natural list to starboard, and the howling wind and pounding waves on her port side only worsened it. "In all its many months of operations," recorded the ship's narrative, "the Moo had performed some mad gyrations, but they were tame in comparison to what happened now."[17] Soon, the gun buckets on the starboard side, located just below the flight deck, were scooping up a generous helping of green water with each roll as the Moo wallowed in the pounding waves. The ship's inclinometer—a device for measuring the degree of roll—routinely indicated forty degrees and several times throughout the morning the needle bounced against the stop at forty-five degrees, indicating the ship had rolled beyond that point.

At 9 a.m. the howling wind pried loose one of the ship's heavy radar dishes, and a few on the bridge heard a quick whistle and looked up in time to see it hurtle off into the rain and fog. At about the same time, the number one whaleboat on the starboard side started to break loose from its mount, and the ship's navigator directed the officer of the deck to take a work party to try and save it. The whaleboat was swinging wildly in its cradle, and sailors attempted to lasso it as a first step toward tying it down. On their third attempt the whole party was nearly swept overboard. A chief boatswain's mate saw a huge wave approaching just as the ship rolled deeply toward the sea, and he yelled a warning. The entire work party scrambled up anything they could find—lines, girders, or ladders—to escape the wall of green water that crashed down on them. It was obvious that any further attempts to save the whaleboat would result in loss of life, and so the work party abandoned it to the sea.

Captain DeBaun knew the ship could not sustain the fleet's southern course for long, and decided to tack back and forth across that path and try to keep the wind on her starboard bow to contradict the ship's natural list to that side. At 9:10 a.m., he turned the ship to port, steering with the ship's engines. The change in course could help only so much in the towering seas, and *Cowpens* continued to violently pitch and roll. Every time the ship summited one of the towering waves and started down into the trough, her screws broke free of the water, and their vibrations, recalled Art Daly, "would almost shake the ship apart."[18] The old salts aboard had in the past joked that the sea is not considered rough until seawater comes down a vessel's smokestacks, but during several deep rolls as the morning went on the Moo's side-mounted stacks dipped into the ocean and spilled water down into the engineering spaces. Of this, the ship's narrative of the storm observed that "when an aircraft carrier ships green water down a stack God is near everyone on that vessel."[19]

All the ship's potentially movable objects had long since been tied to brackets in the walls, but to the horror of the crew, large pieces of previously secure furniture and equipment broke free and began hurtling around, posing risks to life and limb. VT-22 Avenger tail gunner Herbert Todd described how he helped secure several replacement Avenger engines to the bulkhead in the hangar bay, but with the ship's drunken rolls, the 2,045-pound engines tore the brackets out of the bulkhead and began sliding across the deck with the motion of the ship. Between the movements of the ship and the risk from flying equipment, Todd recalled, the storm was "quite an experience."[20]

Gangs of sailors were soon hard at work lashing down whatever had broken free and reinforcing the lines on whatever had not. Practically every heavy piece of furniture had disappeared behind a web of lines. But injuries were impossible to avoid, and the ship's medical department had their hands full. The docs organized what they called "St. Bernard groups" to retrieve the injured. One man fell into the aft elevator pit face-first, and a corpsman leapt in after him, cleaned the blood and broken teeth out of his mouth, and then recruited several sailors to carry him back to sick bay. Elsewhere, in one of the ship's enlisted messes, a man crashed the full width of the compartment when the ship lurched to one side, ending in a head-on collision with a bulkhead. So many injuries resulted from either flying furniture or men losing their footing that the captain finally ordered that all hands not on duty should tie themselves into their bunks.

Captain DeBaun was unsuccessfully trying to zigzag the ship in the general direction of the fleet's course, but every time he tried to bring it back to starboard the ship underwent a violent series of rolls. DeBaun's dilemma mirrored that of the infamous Captain Queeg in Herman Wouk's 1951 novel *The Caine Mutiny*. Wouk had served in the Pacific during the war, and many suspect he used Typhoon Cobra as the inspiration for a pivotal scene in his Pulitzer Prize–winning book, later adapted into an Academy Award–nominated movie starring Humphrey Bogart. In the novel's climax, when facing a violent storm very similar to the one in which DeBaun was now locked, Captain Queeg refuses to turn his ship, the USS *Caine*, out of formation to save it. DeBaun, in contrast, made the opposite decision. Knowing that continuing to the south was too dangerous for the Moo, and with the barometer continuing to drop, at 9:30 a.m. the captain informed Admiral Montgomery that he could no longer keep fleet formation and turned the Moo into the wind. This was a courageous move on DeBaun's part; Halsey did not release his vessels from maintaining fleet formation for another two and a half hours. But Admiral Montgomery supported DeBaun's decision and assigned two destroyers to escort the Moo as she broke away.

DeBaun noticed that using the rudder to steer only worsened the ship's rolls, so from this point on he ordered the ship to maneuver entirely by its engines. This, noted the ship's history, was "a fearful task, as the course of the wind shifted and the ship's head continually had to be brought to new courses."[21] But the engineering department, despite being partially flooded by seawater, was up to the challenge—and using the throttles they continually adjusted the Moo's course as directed by DeBaun on the bridge.

With the typhoon's winds steadily building up in intensity, by 10 a.m. the situation on the flight deck was looking more precarious by the minute. The hours of pitching and rolling had strained the lines and planes, and equipment began to work loose. The first thing to go was one of the small wheeled cranes used to clear wrecks on the flight deck. It tore loose from its lashings, then rolled crazily back and forth across the deck with the motion of the ship, repeatedly smashing into the ship's smokestacks. The ship's narrative likened it to the pied piper, for once it was loose, "all the tractors and jeeps immediately followed suit and the flight deck became a confused spectacle with the vehicles careening around."[22] The crane finally found a gap between the stacks and hurtled through it, into a gun tub and then the sea. One by one, the tractors and jeeps followed it over the side. The first plane to go was an Avenger that worked loose from its restraints and slipped back and forth on the wet deck, finally lodging against the ship's third smokestack. On the next roll, the fifteen-thousand-pound torpedo bomber backflipped into a gun bucket and then slid off the side into the waves. A few minutes later, three Hellcats with wings folded slipped off the deck into the storm. "No one heard a sound as they left," noted the ship's narrative, "but everyone again had the feeling of impotence as they helplessly watched them go."[23]

By 10:30, the Moo's rolls were worsening as the ship closed on the storm center, with conditions growing worse by the minute. One sailor recalled how "facing the wind head on, *Cowpens* pitched so violently that the bow would alternatively rise out of the water, then pitch so deeply that seawater crashed down across the forward flight deck, accompanied by the bellowing wind and the pounding and shuddering of the ship's hull."[24] Barometers plummeted off the bottom of the scale, dipping under twenty-seven inches, at the time the lowest reading ever recorded by the US Navy. Over the course of the morning the wind steadily increased in intensity; Captain DeBaun recalled how at the peak of the storm the needle on his anemometer (wind gauge) "was hard against the stop at 120 knots several times and always above 100 knots."[25] Eventually the wind tore one of the three cups off the device, and even then it still registered 105 knots. A 110-knot wind exerts seventy-eight pounds per square foot of force with an accompanying suction effect; every time a hatch opened from the outside, the wind sucked the air out of the adjacent compartments, popping ears and forcing the men to yawn to equalize the pressure. The towering waves, too, pounded against the ship's hull with unbelievable force. A cubic yard of water weighs more than 1,600 pounds and each wave was thousands of yards strong, slamming into the hull at speeds sometimes more than fifty miles per hour.[26]

The needle on the ship's inclinometer was repeatedly bouncing off the stop at forty-five degrees—and Captain DeBaun estimated the worst rolls were at least fifty degrees. From his perch on the bridge, DeBaun watched with a mix of fascination and terror as each starboard roll put the edge of the flight deck into the sea. The rolls to port were always about five degrees less due to the ship's built-in starboard list, DeBaun explained, but on the big rolls to starboard "one could reach down from the starboard wing of the bridge and touch green water."[27] The bridge crew called out over the ship's loudspeaker how many degrees the ship rolled, and each time she rolled all hands held their breath until she righted herself. The ship's war diary captured the collective terror and helplessness of those on board:

The suspense, the terrible moment came each time the ship hung at the end of a starboard roll waiting, waiting, waiting to see if she would come back again. Never again do any of us want to look that closely into the face of God. In the countless times that members of this ship have faced Nipponese dive bombers and torpedo bombers there has never been the fear, the dread that prevailed that day as all hands realized that we were in the grip of something bigger and greater and more omnipotent than any human agency.[28]

Fifteen minutes later, at 10:45, while the ship was tacking to the southeast in hopes of finding an easier-riding course, one of the Hellcats lashed down on the starboard side of the flight deck broke free of its moorings and skidded across the flight deck. A lurch of the ship threw it into the catwalk, where the impact and friction punctured the plane's fully fueled belly tank and set it alight. As DeBaun later described it, "The wind was on the starboard quarter at that time so I had no choice but to turn the ship as to keep the flames away from the other planes that were parked around it on the flight deck. Otherwise, I would soon have had the whole deck covered with burning planes."[29] Sounding fire quarters, he stopped the port engine and went ahead full on the starboard to heave to.

As the Moo turned to the north to shift the direction of the wind across the flight deck, Bob Price gathered the deckhands together and asked for volunteers to go with him topside to fight the fire; about a dozen men stepped forward. By then, the fumes from the spilled gasoline were starting to seep into the hangar deck, and there was the very real potential that a spark could set them alight there as well. The first group of volunteers stepped out onto the flight deck and were immediately battered down by the storm. It was impossible to stand upright against the howling wind, so the volunteers made their way across the deck toward the burning plane on their stomachs or hands and knees. It was 150 feet from the closest port side hatch to the fire, and they inched their way across the deck, lashing themselves to each aircraft tie-down like mountain climbers to prevent being swept off into the sea. No single hose was long enough to reach, and so the firefighters dragged several heavy coils of hose behind them, assembling it into a single length as they went. As the firefighters approached the plane, the ammunition on the fully loaded fighter had caught fire, and the .50-caliber rounds cooked off right over their heads. As the ship finally got into the wind, Bob Price arrived on the scene and ordered the men to cut the remaining lines tying down the plane in hopes that the next roll would send it over the side.

As one group worked its way across the flight deck, another approached from the hangar deck on the other side. Led by Chief Petty Officer Alphonse DeBoo, this group carried their water hose up the outside ladder on the starboard quarter. It was a slow, difficult process working their way toward the fire; waves broke over them countless times, and it was a seeming eternity until they could get the hose assembled and get enough water pressure to go to work. Finally, both firefighting parties were in position and had just turned their hoses on the blaze when the ship took a heavy plunge to the starboard and the burning Hellcat toppled overboard, taking with it a portion of the catwalk railing and life raft. The rolls were so severe, according to Captain DeBaun, "they could have been our last but the Good Lord was on our side."[30] Two men thought they saw someone go overboard with the plane but he was gone so quickly that no one could help him.

With the plane out of the way, the firefighters turned their hoses to the flaming deck. DeBoo directed his men to lash themselves to the tie-downs on the flight deck to better hold themselves in place, and by 11:10 the last flames were out. DeBoo wanted to linger a few minutes on the deck in case the fire started up again, but on reconsideration he thought the risk of more planes careening about was too high and so he ordered his men back inside. They had almost reached the safety of the ship's island when the last Avenger "snapped its lines with a sound like a rifle shot," hopped thirty feet into the air, flipped over, and dropped back on the deck right into the firefighters' midst.[31] Miraculously, no one was hurt. The firefighters attributed their narrow escape to the grace of God, and they scrambled back inside to avoid the plane, which was still careening back and forth across the flight deck. The Avenger finally slid between the stacks and into the sea, accompanied by several spare drop tanks, the last plane to be lost that day.

At about the same time that the firefighters were working their way across the deck to fight the fire, down in the belly of the ship Chief Gunnery Officer Edward Hinchey discovered that the bombs in the forward magazine had broken free of their lashings and were all over the deck, sliding back and forth with every lurch of the ship. Cowpens was carrying more bombs than she had racks to store, and the largest 2,000-pounders had been lashed in place because the ship's magazine had not been designed to hold bombs that large. As a result, the 500-pound bombs were bouncing around like tennis balls and the 2,000-pounders were slamming into the bulkheads with such force that Captain DeBaun could feel the impacts on the bridge seven decks above.

Knowing that if just one bomb went off nothing could save the ship, Hinchey and several other sailors charged into the magazine to get them under control. With *Cowpens* buttoned up against the battering of the storm, the heat in the magazine was overpowering, 120 degrees or more. The volunteers worked in shifts, staying inside as long as they could before coming out and collapsing from heat exhaustion. One junior ordnance-man by the name of John Hartpence went into the magazine with as much line as he could carry and refused to come out until the task was done. He scrambled to tie down each bomb in the few seconds when the ship was on an even keel. Then when the ship lurched away to either side, Hartpence leapt up and clung onto the overhead girders to avoid being crushed by the tons of bombs rolling on the deck beneath him—only to drop down and resume lashing as soon as the ship stabilized. Hartpence's overhead routine, cheered the ship's narrative of the storm, was "shades of Tarzan!"[32] Through tremendous effort, and almost three miles of line, Hinchey, Hartpence, and their colleagues lashed the bombs down and made them secure over the course of three hours.

DeBaun knew that his current northern course would not clear the storm as quickly, but the ship was rolling just too badly on a southward course. He hoped to swing slowly to the southwest as the wind hauled, gradually opening the distance to the storm center. At 10:50, he turned the Moo to the west, putting the wind on his starboard bow to get farther from the eye of the storm, and over the next hour DeBaun steered the Moo back and forth between the west and northwest trying to find the easiest-riding course.

Down in the galley, Baker First Class Charles Culp was off duty. The bake shop was partially flooded with water from the drains, which was running back and forth with every roll of the ship. The rolls were so bad, Culp recalled, that he could almost walk on the bulkheads. Despite the order to tie himself into his bunk, he went up topside to the catwalk under the aft end of the flight deck because he did not want to be trapped below if the ship rolled over and sank. Conditions topside took his breath away. "It was a sight to behold; no sky, just water and wind . . . [when] the ship rolled and laid on her side I had to grab the catwalk and hope she would come back . . . every time she would take one over the bow, the fantail would come out of the water showing her screws and shuddering like she wanted to break in two."[33] After hanging on for dear life for a few moments, Culp reluctantly went back below, where he discovered his chief petty officer on the phone with the bridge. Culp had to grab the chief and hold him in place so he could talk to the officer of the deck, who wanted to know why no one was serving chow. Culp recalled how the chief shot back, "I cannot even stand up and talk to you without help, how am I supposed to serve chow?"[34] Amazingly, some men's stomachs were solid enough to be hungry, and the mess made food available. The ship was rocking too badly to prepare a hot meal—even coffee or tea—and no one could have kept a tray steady to receive it anyway. So the cooks put out cold cuts and the men ate their sandwiches standing up, clinging to overhead safety lines with one hand.

Of the two destroyers that Admiral Montgomery had assigned to *Cowpens* when she broke away, only one managed to find her. Destroyer *Halsey Powell* somehow managed to identify the Moo on radar and joined up alongside, just out of visible range in the raging storm. Her assistance became essential after 10:30 a.m., when the relentless sea battered its way into the Moo's radio transmitter room, shorting out most of her communications and, half an hour later, her radar as well. This left the ship blind and nearly deaf and mute with the exception of one VHF radio channel. *Halsey Powell* became the Moo's eyes, transmitting her radar reports to the *Cowpens'* CIC, who relayed them to the bridge. It was a harrowing situation, as the raging storm cloaked countless ships all around the Moo, all on varying speeds and courses, trying to find an easier go of it. *Halsey Powell* tracked and reported each contact to the Moo; and at noon, with her faithful destroyer trailing 2,500 yards behind, *Cowpens* passed nearest to the eye of the typhoon, twenty-five miles away to the northeast. It passed so close to several Third Fleet carriers that it was clearly visible on their radar screens. Indeed, the photographs of the vortex on *Wasp*'s radar screen were probably the first ever taken of the eye of a storm and, in the words of Samuel Eliot Morison, had the ominous "appearance of an Edgar Allen Poe thriller."[35]

DeBaun turned the Moo on a westerly course for about an hour when at 12:19 p.m. *Halsey Powell* called out, "Go hard right, some ships have appeared on our screen and you are on a collision course."[36] DeBaun ordered all stop on the starboard engine to nose her bow to the northwest, then it was emergency full on all engines to pull away from the object in her path. A disabled fleet tug came out of the mist and the two ships missed each other by only fifty yards. But the turn toward the storm center took its toll, inducing a violent series of rolls, the worst of the day. The ship's narrative described how "the ship heeled way over from port to starboard, back and forth like a giant pendulum, building up momentum with each sway."[37] It was twelve long minutes of fighting the wind and waves until DeBaun could get the ship back heading westerly, whereupon she settled down.

The Moo soon had her chance to return the favor. At 1:25 p.m., *Halsey Powell*'s surface radar suddenly went out of action, and not ten minutes later the Moo's radar operator, Lt. James Noland, miraculously managed to get theirs working again. "We were on our way again," recorded the ship's narrative, "lame and halting but with eyes."[38] Now it was *Cowpens* threading *Halsey Powell* through the obstacle field of ships; minutes later the Moo's radar operators guided the destroyer away from an incoming contact, and *Halsey Powell* "barely had time to comply when a ship loomed out of the mists and shot past them."[39] For the rest of the afternoon, the Moo used this system of remote control to thread *Halsey Powell* through the maze of obstacles in her path.

With the ship finally opening the distance from the eye of the storm, all hands could appreciate the moments of levity that punctuated the hours of sheer terror. Captain DeBaun relayed how after one serious roll he was "sure that there were smiles...when [he] lost [his] footing and skated clear across the bridge from port to starboard on the seat of [his] pants."[40] Moreover, the captain savored reminding his weatherman that he had predicted the weather would improve on the eighteenth, and after the ship's wind gauge lost one of its cups in 120-knot winds, DeBaun invited the young lieutenant up to the bridge "to look the weather over." The man did not make an appearance until late that afternoon; DeBaun gleefully noted that "rumor has it that he was slightly under the weather and had so many life preservers on that he just couldn't make the long climb to the bridge."[41] DeBaun never publicly commented on the matter, but he transferred the lieutenant off the ship at the next port of call.

DeBaun also marveled at the cheerfulness and resilience of his crew even when *Cowpens* was in its greatest peril. At noon, when the ship was closest to the eye, and the weather, according to Samuel Eliot Morison, "was worse than the foulest epithet can describe," the Moo conducted her usual scheduled shift change.[42] The captain recalled the "youngsters in their teens who came up...to relieve the lookouts, and I heard one of them say to the lookout he was relieving: 'It's a stinker, ain't it?'" DeBaun was amazed that the young man was just enjoying the experience and was not the least bit fearful.[43]

The ship's first feeling of relief came at 12:20 p.m., when the barometer started to rise. The men in the aerology department "let out a war whoop combining joy and hope for salvation." Word spread like wildfire around the ship, and "all hands hardly dared to believe that maybe the worst was over."[44] As the afternoon wore on, DeBaun brought the ship around first to the southwest and then the southeast, braving the last few lashes from the departing storm. By midafternoon the winds had calmed to sixty-four knots, and when the ship passed seventy-five miles from the center of the storm the Moo broke out of the fog and rain and saw the sun for the first time. They had survived.

Aftermath

Fine men such as these do not leave this old world for no reason at all. We like to think of them as still carrying on for us wherever they are.

—Lt. Cmdr. Bob Price's letter to the
mother of a lost pilot[45]

As soon as *Cowpens* cleared the storm, all departments began taking stock and cataloging the damage. Seven planes had gone over the side: four Hellcats and three Avengers. In addition to the loss of the ship's radar, the storm battered several of the ship's antiaircraft guns out of action, while the twisting and bucking of the ship opened two twenty-four-inch cracks in the hangar deck bulkheads. All four of the ship's side-mounted smokestacks were smashed in on their undersides from waves, and water taken in through the stacks had to be drained out of the engine rooms. There was only superficial fire damage to the wooden flight deck, just a ten-foot-diameter charred area. The radio generator room was flooded; it was just off the flight deck between the stacks and wasn't fitted with a watertight door, as the designers never foresaw the possibility that the sea would enter the ship that far up. But all told, the damage was far less than it could have been. Captain DeBaun noted with some pride in the ship's damage report to Third Fleet that "the USS *Cowpens* was materially ready and able to fight at the end of the storm."[46]

While the *Cowpens* escaped major damage, other ships in the Third Fleet were not as lucky. In a two-hour period at the height of the storm, the typhoon sank three destroyers, damaged twenty-seven other ships, and swept 146 airplanes from carrier decks. Two other destroyers had very close calls with disaster, rolling as much as seventy degrees in the raging seas, and aircraft that broke loose aboard *Cowpens'* sister ship, *Monterey*, sparked a hangar bay fire that gutted that deck, killed three, and wounded forty. The total death toll was 790, more than twice the number of American casualties in the Battle of Midway in 1942, while the loss of planes was five times greater than US combat losses at the Great Marianas Turkey Shoot in June.

Unfortunately, the Moo did suffer one terrible loss. Once the seas subsided, DeBaun ordered a roll call taken, and one man was missing: Lt. Commander Bob Price. The man seen blown overboard must have been Price, and the witnesses' general description of the man's clothing matched what Price was wearing when he led the firefighting teams out on the flight deck. The Moo's log recorded that Price "was last seen in the vicinity of the burning plane on the flight deck as the ship hove to, and is believed to have been blown overboard at that time."[47] DeBaun recalled that Price "was an excellent officer and well-loved by his men," and his order of the day on December 19 commemorated Price's loss and offered thanks for the ship's survival.[48]

The Captain highly commends all hands in the execution of their duties during all emergencies yesterday. The heroic efforts of officers and men saved their ship at a time when she was in gravest danger. The response over and above the call of duty marks this ship and her personnel, among those who uphold the highest standards and traditions of the United States Naval Service. The loss of one of our heroic officers while fighting to save this ship and her personnel leaves us in that state of numbness brought on only by the courage exemplified by seafaring men. It is with devout reverence to the Almighty that we bow our heads in silent prayer. May God Have mercy on his soul.[49]

Price's widow, Josephine Virginia Price, first learned of her husband's death the same way that hundreds of thousands of other families did during the Second World War: via Western Union telegram. On December 23 she received the following notice:

THE NAVY DEPARTMENT DEEPLY REGRETS TO INFORM YOU THAT YOUR HUSBAND ROBERT HOYT PRICE IS MISSING AT SEA WHILE IN THE SERVICE OF HIS COUNTRY. THE DEPARTMENT APPRECIATES YOUR GREAT ANXIETY BUT DETAILS NOT NOW AVAILABLE AND DELAY IN RECEIPT MUST NECESSARILY BE EXPECTED. [signed] VICE ADMIRAL RANDALL JACOBS CHIEF OF NAVAL PERSONNEL.[50]

In contrast to the Navy's impersonal message, Bob's friends and colleagues wrote to offer heartfelt condolences to his widow. Hugh Nieman was the first to do so; he and Price had been aboard since the beginning and the two were close. While Price had beaten the odds at sea once before, Nieman did not want to give his wife any false hope.

I refrain from building you up to any chance of his survival as I fear there is no hope. No one could have survived but a short while in such a violent area. Ships or planes were unable to search the area before a lapse of 24 hours. However at that time it was thoroughly and completely covered by both ships and planes...would that in some way I might help you bear your heart-rending loss. Bobby was my friend and I cherished him as one of the cleanest cut and most devoted naval officers I shall ever know.[51]

One of Price's friends aboard, Francis MacBarron, described his feeling of powerlessness and wrote to Virginia, describing his own survivor's guilt:

I hope that you do not think us callous in terms of other men's lives because we are not. On that day it was impossible to throw a life ring, to send a destroyer to search the area or any of the things that are customarily done when a man goes over the side...what I am trying to tell you is that all of us that day were beyond the help of any human agency. I will never understand why Bob Price had to be the one to go on that day after the punishment he took last June. Some men are called upon to make a greater sacrifice than others, and your Bob...was one of these. Deep inside of me I feel both a personal loss for him and a complete humbleness before him. I hope you will accept these words as tribute to him and an awareness of your greater sorrow.[52]

CHAPTER 25

Luzon and the South China Sea: A Deplorable Situation

Cowpens and Third Fleet returned to Ulithi to patch up their storm damage and close out the year. All hands enjoyed recurring liberty ashore, regular mail deliveries, and nightly movies. Riding out the holiday at the fleet's supply depot in the Western Pacific offered a better Christmas Day than they could have hoped for at sea. The ship's menu for the meal—featuring a truculent *Cowpens* bull pulling Santa's sleigh—listed the available fare. There was roast turkey, baked spiced ham, two types of potatoes, fresh fruit and vegetables, freshly baked bread and pies, and hard candies, cigars, and cigarettes. It was a nice diversion, but Clem was less pleased with the relaxation of discipline aboard ship for the holiday. The stern officer wrote on Christmas Eve that there were a "surprising number of parties aboard tonight. Should be knocked off."[1]

Despite the holiday festivities, the months of combat had taken their toll and the squadron's cohesion was beginning to fray. Clem's journal detailed how fellow fighter pilot John Behr forced the removal of the squadron's commander, Lee Johnson. On Christmas Day, after noting he attended Christmas Mass, Clem wrote that "Behr on rampage to get Johnson by dirty methods if possible. Deplorable situation."[2] The following day, he added: "Situation is getting out of hand. Lee Johnson looks definitely on his way out. Behr carrying vicious whispering campaign."[3] Clem was vague on Behr's motive, noting only that it was "all apparently because of a personal desire for glory," perhaps meaning that Behr blamed Johnson's weak leadership for his lack of opportunities in combat.[4]

Clem had mixed feelings about Johnson. While the two got along, Clem was unhappy that the skipper had not done more to address the squadron's problems after the infamous September 9 mission where they remained on high cover without ever attacking ground targets. While Clem at the time rejected Captain Taylor's accusations that Johnson had not been sufficiently aggressive, since then he'd had a change of heart, writing that Behr's "only valid argument is on non-aggressiveness."[5]

Air group commander Tom Jenkins stepped in to try and smooth troubled waters, but Behr only escalated the dispute, appealing directly to the captain. On the twenty-seventh, Clem wrote: "Discovered today that Behr turned in written report direct to the captain of the ship, going over Jenkins completely just when he seemed to have everything under control."[6] DeBaun didn't tarry after receiving Behr's memo, and called an inquiry the following day. No copy of either Behr's memo or DeBaun's findings survive, and all we know is that DeBaun relieved Johnson on December 29. It might be that the captain found Behr's accusations credible, or perhaps just concluded that his departure was advisable given that Johnson had lost the confidence of some of his pilots. But whatever DeBaun's reasoning, Johnson's abrupt exit elevated Clem to VF-22 squadron commander. VF-22's personnel officer brushed off the drama, describing the change of leadership primarily in positive terms. "Craig became skipper of our squadron toward the end of a long tour which had seen morale drop badly. With him in command, high morale was restored, and the squadron's efficiency became tops."[7]

Jesus Christ Rings in the New Year—Back into Action

Cowpens' extended break at Ulithi finally came to an end on December 30, when Task Force 38 sortied for Luzon, beginning a cruise of more than eleven thousand miles that kept them at sea for almost a month. Task Force 38 put to sea with fewer flattops than usual, given the fleet's recent losses to kamikazes. Yet it still fielded a powerful punch, with seven fleet carriers and four light carriers in three task groups, plus two more operating as night carriers. *Cowpens* was again part of Task Group 38.1, along with fleet carriers *Yorktown* and *Wasp*, and fellow light carrier *Cabot*. The group's previous commander, Admiral Montgomery, was injured in a freak boat accident at Ulithi, and so Rear Admiral Radford assumed command.

The ship's history noted that as they set sail, "we had no knowledge of what the future would find, but, as usual, we were loaded for bear."[8] Word that Eric Rellis and Si Johnson had been rescued after their five weeks on the run behind enemy lines in the Philippines reached *Cowpens* over the holidays, and the squadron history described how "it was good news indeed and we all felt a lift."[9] Moreover, on New Year's Eve, the blue-jackets standing watch across the fleet shared a moment of spontaneous joy with the passing of the year. On the stroke of midnight, the TBS circuit came alive with what one sailor called a "release from ennui, from homesickness, and strain."[10] For a few brief moments, the channel was filled with merriment; holiday greetings, jokes, singing, and observations on the passage of time, the year to come, and on life in general. Finally, someone with authority broke in and tried to reimpose discipline. "Jesus Christ," the anonymous officer cursed. "This is a tactical circuit. Knock it off, will you?" Only a small, respectful voice responded. "This is Jesus Christ. Wilco. Out."[11]

Halsey, too, was upbeat, with his New Year's message stating: A MIGHTY WELL DONE IN 1944 AND A VERY HAPPY AND PROSPEROUS NEW YEAR IN 1945 X KEEP THE BASTARDS DYING.[12] One reason for Halsey's enthusiasm was that Nimitz approved his raid into the South China Sea, so long as the fleet provided air cover for the upcoming landings on Luzon at Lingayen Gulf. Halsey's plan was to arrive at the beachhead on the west coast of Luzon by looping around the north side of the island, allowing him to clear out Japanese airfields on Formosa before moving down to support the landings, scheduled for January 9.

The news was alarming to Clem Craig, who was worried about *Cowpens'* battle-worn state. Recalling their close calls in previous trips to Formosa, Clem worried that "this ship is not [in] too good shape and a heavy blow might open her up."[13] Clem was also concerned about his squadron's junior pilots. Steady casualties had thinned its roster of veterans, with only seven remaining from VF-22's first cruise aboard *Independence*. Backfilling the losses were an equal number of green replacements who had less than ninety days with the squadron. The disparity between the old hands and the newcomers was apparent in exercises. Of the ship's first day at sea, Craig wrote, "When our pilots are landing they are either good or terrible."[14]

The primary adversary at Formosa was the weather—a trend that plagued the task force throughout January 1945. Third Fleet nosed into a cold front, bringing with it a heavy overcast and soaking mists and rain. On the third and fourth the Moo's pilots struggled to find their targets under the sullen clouds, which at times were only one hundred feet off the deck. Coming in at practically treetop level to get under the overcast, Clem and his fliers found Formosan airfields thick with parked planes. The Japanese tried to conceal them under camouflage netting or piles of hay—or hid them among wooden dummies. Clem and his pilots were low enough to find them anyway, and worked them over with rockets and gunfire. Clem was pleased with the results, writing: "We got two divisions in over targets and again shared in the major damage of the day."[15]

The pilots also found new and interesting targets to shoot at. For example, in one instance at Giran on January 3, Lt. Jim Bryce and his division were wrapping up their strafing runs when, much to their surprise, a passenger train came chugging into view on the tracks along the edge of the airfield. For months *Cowpens'* pilots had been reading about Army pilots in Europe who were hunting German trains, and they were eager to follow suit. A steam locomotive is a large pressure vessel, and when you put enough .50-caliber holes into it, it detonates in spectacular fashion. Bryce and the three other Hellcats pounced on the engine, pouring long bursts into it before it blew up in a great cloud of steam and debris. They followed the tracks down the coast to a railroad yard with six parked locomotives. In the pilots' estimation this was less sporting, as the locomotives weren't moving, but they still destroyed one and damaged three more. After hearing Bryce's tales—and seeing the outline of a locomotive painted on the ship's island to celebrate the kill—the pilots recorded that "first locomotive blood" had gone to Jim Bryce and his division, and all the others vowed that they were going to go out and do likewise.[16]

As the Moo and Task Force 38 worked over airfields on Formosa, Admiral Kinkaid's Seventh Fleet approached the Luzon beachhead at Lingayen Gulf. They arrived offshore with more than eight hundred ships, and the Japanese responded with waves of planes and kamikazes. They struck or near-missed thirty Allied vessels, sank three, and damaged twenty-seven, while suicide boats sunk one transport ship and damaged several others. The savagery of these attacks dispelled any impression that the Japanese were beaten; the losses were so high that General MacArthur requested the carrier task force return to northern Luzon to help counter the threat.

Disappointing Strikes on Luzon

Third Fleet arrived off the northeast coast of Luzon early on the morning of January 6. In advance of the day's strikes, Halsey gave his pilots a stern talking-to. Describing Luzon as a "bloody battleground," he reminded his fliers of Seventh Fleet's casualties and warned that "every undestroyed enemy plane is potential death to many of our comrades. This is the time for great effort and great determination. Give it your best and God bless you."[17] Unfortunately, conditions were hardly conducive to the great efforts that Halsey hoped to achieve. Instead, the pilots described the situation as "weather very poor, targets almost nil."[18] Working against a thick overcast and high winds, the Moo's fighter sweep checked airfield after airfield and found more burned-out wrecks than they did operational planes.

Additionally, *Cowpens'* deck was bucking like a bull in the rough seas, making landings treacherous. There were a half dozen crashes over two consecutive days, resulting in two deaths. On the sixth, Staten Island's Gordon Cumming, who had been with the squadron about nine months, lost control of his Hellcat on approach and crashed into the sea. Although a destroyer recovered him, Cumming suffered major injuries in the crash and died three hours later without regaining consciousness. Ens. Charles Norton followed the next day; he barreled out of control and went over the side. He never emerged from the cockpit, and his Hellcat quickly sank out of sight. The mood aboard ship that afternoon as Task Force 38 pulled out to refuel was somber, tinged by disappointment for two days of fruitless missions, Ensign Norton's loss, and the burial services for Ensign Cumming, for which Captain DeBaun half-masted *Cowpens'* colors. Moreover, news of the heavy kamikaze attacks on MacArthur's landing forces was circulating through the ship's grapevine. "Suicide boys got to Seventh Fleet," Clem wrote grimly that evening.[19]

After drinking deep from the oilers, the task force turned back toward Formosa in hopes of cleaning out any reinforcements that had arrived in the previous few days. The dawn fighter sweep on Giran and Karenko airfields launched on time, but the weather had worsened from difficult to dogshit. The pilots made their way to the target mostly on instruments, and rocketed the revetments and dispersal areas even though the visibility was so poor they couldn't tell if anything was inside. In a later strike at Karenko, they headed back to the coast along some railroad tracks and by chance happened on a freight train. "One run was all that was needed to fix that train up," the pilots cheerfully reported, and they wrecked it with rocket and machine-gun fire before moving on.[20]

Formosa claimed one more of the Moo's fliers at Suo Harbor on the ninth. Fenced in by mountains on three sides, the small bay was difficult to get into, but Air Group 22 managed to set fire to four luggers. The antiaircraft fire was furious, with a crossfire from both sides of the harbor. Lt. Ormond Higgins had his engine shot out; he flew about five miles out to sea before he ditched. Higgins's wingmen, circling overhead, saw him escape the plane and get into his life raft, apparently uninjured. They relayed his position to the rescue submarine, but due to dwindling fuel they had to head back to the carrier while the sub was still twenty-five miles away. "He's still missing but Hig is a resourceful guy and we have high hopes," noted the squadron history.[21] Unfortunately, the sub did not arrive on scene until after dark, and by then the young Ohioan had drifted away. He was never seen again.

CHAPTER 26

Operation GRATITUDE: Into the South China Sea

Nimitz released Task Force 38 from its support duties for the Luzon landings on January 9, and Halsey set off for the South China Sea. The Navy's primary problem in the Philippines in January 1945 was protecting its three-hundred-mile supply chain from Mindoro to the beachhead at Lingayen Gulf. To the west across the South China Sea were numerous Japanese-held harbors and airfields on the east coast of Asia. Halsey planned to hit as many of these as possible, starting at Cam Ranh Bay in Indochina (now Vietnam), then working his way up the Chinese coast as far as Hong Kong. The orders were "received with some emotion" aboard the Moo, according to the ship's history.[1] No US ships had been in the South China Sea since the beginning of the war, it was stormy that time of year, and the area was within reach of countless enemy airfields stocked with kamikazes. The ship's history expanded on this nervousness: "Not that we haven't stuck our necks out at various and sundry times before—the Mighty Moo has led the parade on more than one occasion— but going into this area was reasonable justification [for] a gulp or two. But in we went, and as per usual, we were right out front as the number one carrier of the entire Task Force to go through the Bashi Channel."[2]

The sea itself put on quite a show that evening, as the currents in the channel boiled and foamed like rapids and churned up clouds of bioluminescence in the dim light of early evening. "We ran down wind continually overtaking great swells," described the ship's narrative history. "As we knifed through them clouds of spray would fly out on either side and the phosphorescence was so much in evidence that the spray looked like sheets of snow."[3] When the sun rose the next morning, some of the crew trooped topside to take a look at the water to gauge whether it looked any different from any of the other seas the Moo had been in. The consensus opinion was that it was not as blue as the Central Pacific and "had a decided green tinge."[4]

Indochina was a bust for the Moo—as were follow-on missions along the Chinese coast. Cowpens' pilots flew routine patrols and long-range searches while the rest of the task force hit docks, air installations, and fuel dumps all up and down the coast, sending more than 132,000 tons of shipping to the bottom. The pilots had high hopes for good hunting in China, but they searched multiple airfields in Canton and on the Luichow Peninsula and found little in the way of enemy planes. The raids caught the attention of Tokyo Rose, however, who claimed to have the American fleet right where she wanted it. She gloated, "Now you're in there at last. Let's see you get out." Halsey was quick to retort, stating, "When we get through with them, they will be glad to let us out!"[5] Captain DeBaun relayed this taunt over the ship's loudspeakers to the crew, who responded with raucous cheers.

Flak over Hong Kong: "From Intense to Unbelievable"

Cowpens and Task Force 38 spent the next two days waiting for a break in the weather—and in the interim her routine patrols were marred by a tragic accident. One of her Avengers was on final approach when the pilot, Lt. Robert "Red" Preston, lost control of his plane and spun into the ocean on the ship's port quarter. Almost immediately there was a large explosion as one of the plane's depth charges detonated, and after a moment or two a second followed suit. Destroyer Twining sprinted to the scene and found only the tail gunner, D. C. Menge, but not Preston or his radioman, Joseph Fockler.

Finally, by the sixteenth the weather eased, allowing the scheduled strike against Hong Kong—which proved to be one of the toughest of Air Group 22's career. Tom Jenkins and his pilots found the harbor filled with ships just off the Kowloon Wharves, on the north side of the narrow strait that divides the island from the mainland. Three freighters in particular were surrounded by a flock of escorts, suggesting they were something worth protecting. The Hellcats made a strafing run with rockets and machine guns in a vain attempt to silence the antiaircraft fire in advance of the bombers. It worked for a moment, but when the Avengers started on their dive, the Japanese ships and batteries below let them have it. The flak, in the words of one of the Moo's pilots, ranged from "intense to unbelievable."[6] The air was filled with projectiles of all sizes, from streams of tracers to heavy bursts from large-caliber guns. "Never before had our pilots seen AA that could compare with this," noted the account of the mission.[7] The enemy gunners knew their business, using different-colored bursts so they could identify which flak bursts were theirs and adjust their fire. The barrage of Technicolor explosions battered the Moo's planes while painting the sky in bursts of purple, red, yellow, and green, in addition to the usual sooty black.

Pressing through the hail of fire, the Avengers released their bombs on the freighters, scoring several hits and setting all three afire. Unfortunately, the murderous flak found its mark; Ens. George Clark had just pushed over into his bombing run when he took a hit in his engine. He pulled away, radioing his wingmen that he was about to ditch. His wingmen escorted Clark's wounded Avenger until he made a successful water landing eight miles out to sea and then circled overhead while a Chinese junk picked up Clark and his two crewmen, Donald Mize and Charles Meyers. Group commander Tom Jenkins was optimistic about their odds, noting in the after-action report that their rescue by Chinese locals meant that "the pilot and crew have an excellent chance to survive."[8]

Cowpens returned to Hong Kong later in the day, with VT-22's executive officer, Harold McMillan, leading five of the ship's Avengers. The mission was no less difficult; intelligence had decided that the Kowloon warehouse and port complex was a high-value target given it was smack in the center of the Japanese antiaircraft defenses. If one could get past the scores of gun batteries, there were numerous piers, office buildings, warehouses, and cranes clustered closely together. The formation made its approach at 12,500 feet, pushing over into a dive over Hong Kong's southeast coast. Preceding the Moo's planes in their attack run was a squadron from another carrier. Enemy gunners exacted a terrible price from this other squadron, shooting down two of its planes on their attack dive, two more as they pulled away after dropping their bombs, and damaging two others so badly that they crashed as they tried to head back out to sea. Following close behind, Air Group 22 escaped the bulk of the enemy fire and put all of its bombs in the target area before turning for home.

Although the other air group took the brunt of the flak, VT-22 did not escape unharmed. Lt. Billy Laughren went into his dive, dropped his bombs, and pulled out over the bay. He was a cheerful and gregarious young man from Monrovia, California, known to his fellow pilots as "Laughing Laughren." A bank teller in his civilian life, he grew a spectacular goatee while aboard that earned him the second moniker "Billy Goat." His wingman did not see Laughren take a hit but momentarily lost sight of him when his own plane was battered by flak. When he regained control, he saw what he thought was Laughren's plane plummet into the bay and explode when it hit the water. The wingman could not definitely identify the downed plane, but Laughren and his two crewmen, Albert Krska and William Styverson, never returned to the ship.

Clem's Red-Letter Day

After the last strikes on Hong Kong, *Cowpens* and the rest of the task force withdrew to refuel. The weather steadily worsened overnight, and when dawn broke on the seventeenth, the barometer was plummeting, with sustained winds of almost thirty knots. As if the storm was not enough, a destroyer darted across *Cowpens'* bow, and DeBaun threw her rudder hard to starboard to avoid a collision. The Moo heeled over thirty-two degrees;

two officers who were unlucky enough to be casually chatting on the flight deck when the ship suddenly lurched underneath them experienced what they described as the "thrill of the month" when they started sliding down the width of the ship toward the churning seas below. The pair dropped to the deck, managed to grab some aircraft tie-downs, and then held on for dear life until the ship's roll settled down. One of the officers quipped afterward that when he left the States he thought he had "given up skiing for the duration."[9]

By dawn on January 21, the Moo and the rest of the task force had cleared the Luzon Strait and arrived off the southeast coast of Formosa. The weather had finally improved, and both sides geared up for a day of intensive air operations. *Cowpens'* first targets for the day were the now-familiar airfields at Giran and Karenko, which the Moo's pilots had hit a half dozen times before. At Giran, the pilots spotted six real aircraft hidden among the dummies and burned-out wrecks, and enthusiastically strafed them as well as rocketed and bombed some nearby hangars and support buildings. With their work on the airfield completed, the pilots investigated the nearby railroad tracks, which had been the site of the first score in the pilots' train-killing game. Sure enough, to their delight they discovered a full train sitting there on the siding. "But not for long," the men cheerfully recounted. "A few well-placed tracers and POP! Went the engine."[10]

The Japanese, too, were out looking for targets. The Moo launched her eight-plane CAP about 7 a.m., and for ninety minutes they circled overhead, with the pilots "getting nothing but uncomfortable tails."[11] But about 8:30 a.m., bogeys began to light up the task group's radar screens, and *Cabot* sent the Moo's planes off to investigate. The FDO put them right on a Japanese Dinah, a twin-engine reconnaissance aircraft. The four Hellcats tore into the intruder, setting one engine afire and riddling the other with bullets. The Dinah fell off into a steep dive, and the pursuing pilots recalled the plane impacted the water "with a great splash and floated for a few minutes while flames consumed it."[12]

Not fifteen minutes later, *Cabot* had more business for the Moo's pilots.

It turned out to be a Jill torpedo bomber. "Dinah is bad enough to have around taking pictures," the pilots later observed, "but Jill is even worse because her mission whenever we have met her seems to be try to put a fish into us."[13] It made an attempt to run for the clouds, but Ensigns Francis Kelly and Kasameir Neverdauskey were hot on its tail. Both planes opened fire, but Neverdauskey did the most damage, wrecking its engine and riddling its wing tank with .50-caliber fire, sending the plane tumbling into the sea.

Later that afternoon, Clem and his two divisions of Hellcats were on their third hour of CAP. The Moo's FDO, Lt. Dan Arnold, spotted another group of bogeys on radar fifty miles out to the southwest. Two divisions of Hellcats went to investigate, with Clem leading the first and Jim Bryce the second. The Hellcats rushed to the scene at twenty thousand feet until Arnold was able to confirm the bogeys' altitude—only six thousand feet. He directed the Moo's pilots to come down to that altitude in a long, fast descent to build up speed. As the Hellcats came charging "down the hill," Arnold continuously updated them with the latest bearing to the bogeys until he finally called out: "You should have them in sight; Craig, go get 'em, don't let 'em through, Bryce is coming in right behind to back you up!"[14]

The Moo's planes broke out of the clouds above the bogeys, and what looked on radar to be four bogeys turned out to be eighteen: thirteen Tojos, two Oscars, and three Zekes stacked in four groups, the pilots recalled, "like a flight of stairs."[15] In the US pilots' estimation, eight Hellcats versus eighteen Japanese was about even odds. Clem and his three wingmen came down on the enemy formation in a high-speed dive, with Bryce a few moments behind. Clem plowed right into the enemy formation with a high side run at its forward edge, while Bryce started at the top. As soon as the Japanese pilots saw the Hellcats screaming down on them, they jettisoned their belly tanks and bombs and dove for the water. Clem and Bryce abandoned all thought of keeping their planes together and freed their pilots to go after the enemy—sparking a general melee.

As Clem dove into the formation, four Japanese aircraft attempted a defensive weave, but they swung too wide, and Clem "scooped up" one of the Tojos at the outside of the weave—putting a short burst into its cockpit and sending it plummeting into the sea. Clem methodically worked his way through a total of five kills that day; his second was a deflection shot on a Tojo, the third in a head-on pass, the fourth from behind with a burst to the cockpit, and the fifth from the port side into the engine.

The Moo's pilots were not impressed with the skill of the Japanese pilots or their flying tactics. They seemed to be little inclined to press their advantage and mostly seemed to be trying to get away. In the words of one pilot, they "relied too heavily on acrobatics to escape harm, which our boys countered by merely sitting out the performance, and when completed closed again for the kill."[16] The Moo's Hellcats used their speed advantage to take repeated runs at the enemy from all angles, while the Japanese attempted to counter by turning head-on into the attack, with sharp "flipper turns," and, in one inexplicable instance, through "a slow roll started at 75 feet over the water."[17] Several times the Japanese pilots were able to work their way onto the tail of a Hellcat, but their gunnery was inaccurate, and in each case a friendly plane swooped in to drive them off.

The fight was brief and explosive, lasting less than five minutes. When it was over, there were fourteen Japanese confirmed splashed plus three more probables—with the eighteenth and final enemy plane probably escaping. "Clem came out the winner," the squadron's history recorded, with his five kills—making him one of an elite few Navy pilots during the war to achieve the vaunted ace-in-a-day status.[18] He returned to the Moo with guns dry (no ammunition remaining) and the gun camera footage to corroborate all five of his kills. Bryce was close behind with four, one of them a probable.

But all eight *Cowpens* pilots in the air that day had a hand in the result. Roop and Roche had one and a half each; Ben Amsden, Francis Anchors, and Francis Myers each one; and Streetman two probables. Only one *Cowpens* plane was hit: Myers, who shook enemy fighters from his tail twice during the engagement, told the ship's mechanics that he thought his engine "ran a little rough."[19] That was a pretty significant underestimation of the problem; two of his engine's cylinders had been shot out.

The air group had an impromptu party to celebrate the victories in the ready room that evening, while congratulations from the entire chain of command came pouring in. Adding to the excitement of the day's events was the news that they were returning to Ulithi, with Air Group 22 looking forward to its relief and return to the US. Clem, in particular, was getting a lot of attention for his five aerial kills. "We are retiring and really drawing comments on yesterday's action," he wrote on the evening of the twenty-second. "Seems to be a lot of publicity in the offing. And an excellent chance for the CMH [Congressional Medal of Honor]. Another Navy Cross is a cinch."[20] Captain DeBaun lobbied up his chain of command in support of Clem's CMH nomination; after months of Captain Taylor's pointed skepticism toward his pilots, DeBaun's unwavering support must have been a welcome change for Clem. But despite the captain's best efforts, Clem received a second Navy Cross rather than the CMH. The citation described his "extraordinary heroism" in the face of overwhelming odds. "Lt. Commander Craig led his division against a numerically superior flight of enemy planes... [and] succeeded in personally shooting down five hostile aircraft while his splendidly directed division accounted for nine and possibly twelve more. His airmanship, courage, and devotion to duty reflect the highest credit upon Lt. Commander Craig and the United States Naval Service."[21]

Air Group 22 had a great deal to celebrate, for they had completed the most difficult tour of *Cowpens'* career. VF-22 recorded that they "headed for home with a feeling that it had carved out its share of the Jap carcass which already was beginning to rot in the Pacific sun."[22] Air Group 22 flew 3,066 sorties in the months they were aboard. They claimed 241 enemy aircraft damaged or destroyed, including 50 in the air—of which Clem accounted for 12.5, making him a double ace. They also damaged 5 Japanese warships, sunk 29 cargo ships, and damaged another 38.

Air Group 22 saw the most action of *Cowpens'* air groups, and it also took the most losses—twenty-three in all. Fifteen died during operations in the Philippines and five more in Hong Kong. Ten more were shot down but rescued; George Clark, downed in Hong Kong Harbor with his two aircrewmen, Charles Meyers and Donald Mize, successfully escaped through China. Moreover, Eric Rellis, Si Johnson, Robert Jones, and Alan Pray, shot down over Manila Bay in November, awaited the squadron's arrival at Pearl Harbor. In contrast, Doc Frellsen and Donald Stanley survived being shot down over Formosa, but were sent to a POW camp in Tokyo until war's end.

CHAPTER 27

Air Group 46 and the Iwo Jima Campaign

Luzon's capture in February 1945 put a stranglehold on the supply of vital raw materials reaching the Japanese home islands. US planners talked about "the Luzon bottleneck"—the relatively narrow stretch of water between the northern Philippines, Formosa, and the Chinese mainland. With both the US Army and Navy setting up shop on Luzon, this bottleneck was effectively corked. Any enemy ships trying to run the gap faced a fearsome array of Philippine-based aircraft and submarines.

But there was still the question as to how to advance toward Japan itself. Due to the geography, there were only two practicable routes: the Bonin and Ryukyu island chains. The Bonins, also known as the Volcano Islands, begin south of Tokyo and stretch some seven hundred miles to Marcus Island (Minami Shima), which is 615 miles north of Saipan. Most of the islands in this chain are too small for an airfield, consisting of only tiny volcanic cones sticking out of the Pacific. The Japanese set up shop on the two largest, Iwo Jima and Chichi Jima. The first US offensive would be "up the ladder of the Bonins" to Iwo Jima, starting on January 20, 1945. To the United States, the island's value was its location halfway between the home islands and the Marianas—625 miles north of Saipan and 660 miles south of Tokyo. The Japanese had built two airfields on the tablelands in the center of the island and were working on a third.

The New Guys in Town: Air Group 46

Air Group 46 replaced Air Group 22 aboard *Cowpens* on February 6, 1945. This air group's tour aboard the Moo was the shortest of the four groups who served aboard—only a month—and they barely had time to find their sea legs before being reassigned. In contrast to their predecessors, who arrived aboard the Moo already having tasted combat aboard another carrier, Air Group 46 was undertrained and very green. Only a handful had ever seen combat; one of the few was their commander, Lt. Cmdr. Carl Rooney, a graduate of the Naval Academy class of 1934, who flew fighters from *Wasp* and later from Guadalcanal. The air group's inexperience was not an isolated problem; the Navy had cut back its pilot training programs the previous year based on declining casualty numbers, only to face higher demand for pilots in late 1944 due to mounting attrition and burnout. Accordingly, by early 1945 the Navy was rushing fliers through training and out to the fleet. This left many new air groups like Air Group 46 less prepared for combat than their predecessors.

To make matters worse, while waiting in Hawaii for transportation to the *Cowpens*, the fighter squadron was cannibalized for talent by another air group. VF-46 lost under protest five pilots with more than three hundred hours in the Hellcat in return for five others who had only had sixty, far below the squadron average. In the weeks to come, one of these green pilots went missing in action and several of the others were involved in accidents, all of which the air group commander attributed to their inexperience. In retrospect, the only veteran hand that joined the squadron in Hawaii was its mascot, Frigate, a stray dog the Marines picked up on Saipan. Frigate made his way to Oahu by means unknown, where he gained some notoriety for successfully completing two parachute jumps from the 225-foot tower at Ford Island.

Arriving in Ulithi lagoon to join *Cowpens* on February 6, Air Group 46 was gobsmacked by the size of the fleet already there. Of the 1,108 total warships then in the US Navy, approximately four hundred were anchored in the lagoon—not counting the sizable number of oilers, tankers, and merchant ships waiting to deliver supplies. Air Group 46 was quickly thrown into the mix. Task Force 58 was bound for Tokyo, where they would attack airfields and aircraft factories in advance of the landings on Iwo Jima, scheduled to begin on February 19. Tokyo was a lucrative target; with a population of eight million people, the city was the political and industrial heart of Japan. It sits in the largest lowland region in the home islands, the Kanto Plain, roughly the size of Connecticut. Spruance hoped that three days of carrier strikes against airfields and aircraft factories there would paralyze the Japanese and prevent them from sending a flow of kamikazes south to interfere with the landings.

The pilots of Air Group 46 were stunned to learn of their objective. As their first combat mission, the squadron history noted with excitement, Tokyo was a "Homeric task for a curtain raiser to say the least."[1] While the newly arrived air group was eager for action, by now the Moo had been in the combat zone eighteen months. Her weary crew—many of whom had been aboard since August 1943—were hoping the ship would be sent home for its much-needed overhaul. Captain DeBaun's announcement that Tokyo was the next target had an electrifying reaction and helped the crew forget its fatigue. The enemy capital was a target they had been dreaming of since they left Philadelphia in 1943, something to reckon with. It would be wrong for the Moo to head home, the crew thought, just when the march across the Pacific reached its culmination and Fifth Fleet would need her the most.[2]

Cowpens and Task Force 58 put to sea on February 9, bound for Tokyo. Writing the previous day, Art Daly seemed to think it was about time: "Well, we have had a good rest. A few beers. A few swims. We are all supplied. Tomorrow we go out again..."[3] With the recent kamikaze attacks in mind, Captain DeBaun used every possible moment to prepare the ship for battle over the five-day northward steam to Japan. The pilots conducted practice intercepts, the Moo's gunners conducted endless exercises, and the crew simulated all manner of disasters and emergencies—running collision and abandon-ship drills until everyone could perform them blindfolded. "Not that we were scared," the ship's narrative said with a seeming wink and nod. "Just checking up."[4]

Air Group 46 endured the gauntlet of pre-mission briefings for the first time, committing the details of the mission to memory. Tokyo was heavily defended, with at least ninety airfields and five hundred or so anti-aircraft guns, and the pilots were told to expect the biggest air battle of the war. Given the air group's lack of combat experience, the tone of the briefings walked the line between bolstering their confidence and discouraging recklessness. One point repeated again and again in these briefings was that the emperor's palace was not, repeat *not*, to be bombed. This order was justified as for the pilots' own protection, but there was likely some input from the Navy's political masters in Washington, as the directive came with a lecture on the emperor's role in stabilizing postwar Japan. The firm guidance was almost certainly necessary, as by their own admission there were many pilots aboard the Moo who were eager to "drop a 500-pound message on the Mikado's palace."[5] Air Group 46 sheepishly acknowledged the order, noting that "we would have welcomed the opportunity to contribute toward the destruction of their Emperor-God. But ours was to do as we were told."[6]

Tokyo Protected by the Weather Gods

Air Group 46 would get not one but two trips to Tokyo. The weather was so bad on the first attempt on February 16 and 17 that few pilots could find their targets, and after supporting the landings on Iwo Jima from February 19 to 21, Admiral Spruance turned the fleet around for a second try on the twenty-fifth. The weather didn't cooperate for either attempt; on the morning of their first mission on the sixteenth, the pilots described how "it was black as the inside of a cow at dawn with forty knots of wind and sleet blowing across the deck."[7] The solid overcast, howling winds, and intermittent precipitation made for a cold, damp morning that turned into a gloomy, sunless day. Mere weather would not stop what Admiral Mitscher predicted would be "the greatest air victory of the war for carrier aviation," and so the task force's pilots readied to fly.[8] But one chief petty officer aboard the Moo with twenty years of sea duty was unconvinced as he watched the pilots warm up their engines on the flight deck. He noted that "this is the toughest flying weather I've ever seen. I wish to God I was back on the farm in Missouri!"[9]

The day's strikes included a series of attacks against airfields and aircraft manufacturing plants in and around the Tokyo region. Only by some miracle was there a gap in the weather over the Nakajima Tama plant—one of the four major aircraft engine factories in the Tokyo region. The Moo's Avenger pilots spotted the enormous facility through the clouds and poured rockets and bombs into it, sparking multiple fires. Airfields were another target; when the Moo's pilots found them under the blanket of clouds, they were often filled with parked planes—but they were not fueled for flight and the Japanese typically did not try to get them into the air. Enemy fighters only rarely made an appearance, and when they did they showed little enthusiasm for a fight. For example, four Oscars tentatively approached a flock of the Moo's Hellcats, and after Lt. Herbert Badger knocked one down, the rest turned tail and ran.

Given the weather, the Moo's fliers had to settle for hitting whatever targets of opportunity they could find beneath the overcast. In one instance, Lieutenant Commander Rooney and his two divisions spotted a cluster of ships and went to work with their rockets and machine guns. Two Hellcats, the first piloted by Lt. Richard McNees and the other by Ensign Omar Clark, peppered one with .50-caliber fire and then pulled away. Unfortunately, it exploded in a tremendous fireball just as Clark's plane passed over it. His wingmen saw his plane take the full force of the blast and then cartwheel into the water at high speed. The VF-46 squadron history eulogized him by saying "he was a fine pilot and officer whose loss was sharply felt."[10]

In another instance, pilot inexperience was the killer. Shortly after a fighter sweep northeast of Tokyo, Lt. (jg) Damon Bright, of Belvidere, Illinois, turned for home. He was one of the five inexperienced pilots traded to VF-46; his wingmen saw him pull out of formation, presumably to accompany another Hellcat with mechanical issues who needed to return to the carrier. Bright did not link up with the other pilot and was never seen again.

The Moo's second try for Tokyo on the twenty-fifth wasn't any better than the first. The weather was uncooperative the whole way there—heavy seas, low-lying clouds, and howling thirty-five-knot winds. Refueling was treacherous, and *Cowpens'* deckhands wrestled with the lines and hoses connecting her to the oiler steaming alongside. One sailor, John Primiano, was trying to secure the fuel connections when a rogue wave swept him off the deck into the raging sea. Sailors threw a dye marker into the water to mark the spot where he went in, but destroyer *Haynsworth* was unable to find him.

Cowpens' primary target in the second round of raids on the twenty-fifth—the Nakajima aircraft factory in Musashino—was socked in by weather, but the formation diverted to the Koizumi engine plant to the north.[11] This time, the clouds briefly parted, and the factory's defensive battery of guns punctuated the skies around the attacking planes with black bursts of flak. The multi-acre facility was an easy target, and Hellcats and Avengers alike scattered their bombs across a wide area. The accompanying photo Hellcat recorded the results—large fires burning in several target buildings.

Overall, enemy resistance during both trips to Tokyo was strangely muted, with the Moo's pilots describing the enemy air cover as "conspicuous by its absence."[12] Out at sea the task force was braced for a wave of kamikazes akin to what the Seventh Fleet encountered off Luzon, but the majority of radar contacts were friendly planes returning to their carriers. The lack of enemy air activity was both puzzling and a relief; and all hands speculated why Japanese resistance was far less than expected. "Lack of experienced pilots, a dearth of high octane gasoline, or both, may have contributed to their unwillingness to oppose us in the air," mused the squadron historian. "We didn't know."[13]

Cowpens underway, somewhere in the Pacific. From this angle you can see her narrow flight deck and small island. *(US Navy)*

Robert P. McConnell was the first captain of *Cowpens*. Respected by the crew, he narrowly survived the sinking of the USS *Langley* and *Pecos* in 1942 before assuming command of the Moo in January 1943. The inscription is dedicated to Bob Price, "with sincere personal regard and best wishes for continued success and good luck." *(Courtesy of Richard Price and the Price family)*

Robert "Bob" Price was an experienced fighter pilot and natural leader who escaped the fall of Singapore in early 1942. He served aboard *Cowpens* first as commander of one of its fighter squadrons, then as Air Group 25 commander, and finally as the ship's air officer. *(Courtesy of Richard Price and the Price family)*

Bob Price (left) and his division of fighter pilots from VF-25. Bill Stanton and Archibald "Big Mac" McIlwane (middle) disappeared after takeoff on their first combat mission to Wake in October 1943. Benny Farber (right) died in a landing accident off the Marianas Islands in February 1944. *(Courtesy of Richard Price and the Price family)*

On November 24, 1943, Lt. Alfred McGee was on approach for landing when a spray of gasoline from a leaking belly tank ignited a fireball. McGee was able to touch down successfully and then scampered across the wing as the ship's firemen extinguished the blaze. *(US Navy)*

Burial at sea for four Marines killed on December 4, 1943, when a damaged Hellcat fighter plowed through a gun bucket during an emergency landing. Ten other crewmen were injured in the accident. *(US Navy)*

King Neptune and his Royal Court initiate the *Cowpens* pollywogs into the Ancient Order of the Deep as the Moo crosses the equator for the first time, on January 22, 1944. *(US Navy)*

Ensign Ed Haley joined *Cowpens* as a replacement pilot in the winter of 1943. A thoughtful diarist during his time aboard, Ed earned the nickname Stump for his diminutive height. *(Courtesy of Glenn Haley)*

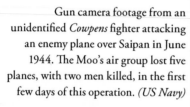

Gun camera footage from an unidentified *Cowpens* fighter attacking an enemy plane over Saipan in June 1944. The Moo's air group lost five planes, with two men killed, in the first few days of this operation. *(US Navy)*

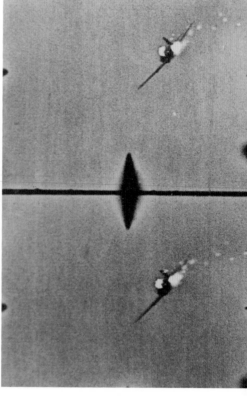

Herbert Watson Taylor was the Moo's second captain. Quiet and introspective, Taylor had a "still waters run deep" style of command that put him at odds with his pilots throughout the fall of 1944. *(US Navy/US National Archives)*

Lt. Commander Clement "Clem" Craig helped lead the *Cowpens* second fighter squadron, VF-22, and was the ship's greatest fighter ace. He finished the cruise with 12.5 aerial kills—including five shot down in a single mission, making him one of an elite few Navy pilots who could claim "ace-in-a-day" status. Clem and his fliers had a strained relationship with Captain Taylor for much of their time aboard. *(Courtesy of Jerry Craig)*

Captain George DeBaun was the third commanding officer of *Cowpens*. DeBaun's cheerfully profane personality and sense of humor quickly won over the crew. He was also a skilled sailor, a trait that helped pull the ship through its most difficult hours. *(Courtesy of Duncan Koler)*

The Moo faces the wrath of Typhoon Cobra, December 18, 1944. The top-heavy ship came close to capsizing, and most aboard described the experience as more terrifying than combat. "The waves were like mountains and the ship pitched and rolled like a wild horse," said one sailor. *(US Navy)*

The Moo arrives in San Francisco, March 24, 1945, for a much-needed overhaul after steaming more than 143,000 miles. Workmen on the Golden Gate Bridge (visible in background) cheered the ship as she passed underneath. *(US Navy)*

On February 25, 1945, one of VF-46's inexperienced pilots bounced his plane over the crash barrier and plowed into the aircraft spotted forward. Two crewmen were knocked overboard and lost. *(US Navy)*

A close-up of the Moo's combat tally painted on her island sometime in the spring of 1945, including her bovine logo. By war's end, *Cowpens* had destroyed 93 planes in the air and another 512 on the ground—and sank 16 ships. The scoreboard also records five kills for the pilots' "train game." *(US Navy)*

The scene in a squadron ready room aboard *Cowpens* after the announcement of the Japanese surrender, August 15, 1945. Frank Martinich is in the lower right corner, with his cigar. *(US Navy)*

The cover of the *Cowpens* newspaper after V-J Day, showing a triumphant Moo celebrating with the Allies. *(Author's collection)*

The Moo's last wartime captain, Herbert Duckworth. He served as air officer aboard *Lexington* during the Battle of the Coral Sea in May 1942, then helped pioneer some of the multi-carrier tactics and formations that helped the Navy on its march to Tokyo. Although he arrived aboard *Cowpens* in late July 1945, an assignment in occupied Japan delayed his assumption of command until after the surrender. *(US Navy)*

CHAPTER 28

Operation DETACHMENT: Iwo Jima

While the Japanese defense of Tokyo was inexplicably subdued, Iwo Jima was another matter. The battle was one of the most savage and costly in the Pacific War. US Marines waged a bloody, yard-by-yard campaign to wrest control of the island from nearly thirty thousand Japanese defenders determined to fight almost to the last man. In the more than monthlong campaign, the Marines lost 6,821 men, with more than seventeen thousand wounded. The Japanese defenders had fortified the island with layers upon layers of gun emplacements and bunkers capable of weathering an extended bombardment and exacting a terrible cost on the landing forces. Both the US Navy and the Army Air Corps threw every implement of destruction at their disposal at Iwo Jima in an attempt to soften it up in advance of the landings—including months of bomber raids and a three-day preparatory naval bombardment of more than 181,600 rounds. But it was largely for naught; so resilient were the Japanese defenses that in some cases the American heavy shells only succeeded in blasting away their camouflage.

Given the volume of firepower the Navy had already thrown at Iwo, the Moo's token contribution of two days of close air support on February 19 and 21 probably contributed little to the overall result. The area had been so thoroughly bombarded that most identifiable landmarks had been wiped out—even the outlines of the airfields were practically obliterated.

As a result, Air Group 46 struggled to find their targets amid the devastation. The VF-46 squadron history likened the terrain to a lunar landscape and noted that "it was extremely difficult to locate pinpoint targets in the ash heap."[1] Moreover, even when they did drop their bombs in the target area, the smoke and haze from the vicious fighting below made it difficult to determine how effective they were.

The Moo and Task Group 58.3 had more success screening the island from Japanese planes. For example, on February 21, the fleet intercepted enemy radio transmissions indicating enemy aircraft were bound for Iwo Jima. Sure enough, shortly before dark, groups of perhaps twenty bogeys showed up on radar, and they made their move after 7 p.m. In groups of one to two, they dropped to low altitude and tried to get in close—but in every case broke off about six thousand yards away, where the task force's flak grew intense and accurate. Deckhands aboard the Moo saw two Japanese planes flare up and go into the water after meeting antiaircraft rounds, and US night fighters chased off many of the rest. The survivors returned to circling at a distance before the attack came to an end. "They circled around for some time," the ship's narrative said, "and finally wandered off and we went to bed."[2]

The task force made one final swipe at Okinawa before turning their bows toward Ulithi. Although intelligence expected the island to be a hornet's nest of enemy fighters, the Japanese made no effort to contest the attack in the air. Moreover, the clear weather allowed the task force's photoreconnaissance planes to get nearly complete coverage of the island, vital to prepare for the amphibious landings scheduled for April. *Cowpens* and Air Group 46 hit two islands near Okinawa, Minami Daito and Ie Shima; with a little enthusiastic rocketing and strafing they demolished the handful of planes they found on airfields, and wrecked barracks, an ammunition depot, and two medium freighters.

While the enemy did not make an appearance, the day was not without its casualties. Ens. Alfred Adair—one of VF-46's five undertrained replacement pilots—was returning from his reconnaissance mission over Okinawa. He came in hot on landing, bounced once on the deck without catching a wire, cleared the barriers in full flight, and with a horrible crash plowed into the planes parked forward. Five aircraft were wrecked; but worse yet, two deckhands were flung over the side and lost. Sailors on the fantail threw a life preserver and dye marker to Seaman First Class Walter Clendaniel, who was not wearing a life jacket but was spotted swimming. His colleague, Aviation Machinist's Mate First Class Clarence Watt, was facedown in the water, probably knocked unconscious by the crash or the fall to the sea. By the time the plane guard destroyer arrived a few minutes later, both men had disappeared.

CHAPTER 29

A Gallant Lady,
Homebound at Last

After retiring the last of its planes from the strikes on Okinawa, the task force swung around and made its way toward Ulithi. Having accomplished their mission of supporting the Iwo Jima landings, the months-old question again sprang into the crew's mind: Is it our turn to go home? The answer came with a shrill piping over the loudspeaker system followed by: "This is the Executive Officer. I have a message which will please you all. We are ordered to report to the Port Director after our arrival at Ulithi for onward routing for Pearl."[1] The ship's narrative records what happened next:

> That's all he said, that's all he needed to say. Pandemonium broke loose throughout the ship. All the emotions that had been bottled up for so many months burst out: cheers, screaming, whistling. All the sounds and noises that men can make when they are lost in joy. The variations were endless: some did clog dances, some jumped up and down, some sat quietly in the corners weeping at the thought that home was soon to be over the horizon... sleep was impossible that night; far into the wee hours of the morning men lay in their bunks making plans, dreaming of their beloved.[2]

The ship's plank owners, the men who had been aboard since the ship first put to sea in August 1943, were both weary from continual operations and proud of the ship's service record. *Cowpens* carried her officers and men through every operation from Wake Island to Tokyo, and despite her rocky start and numerous close calls had never been hit by the enemy. The ship's narrative history waxed poetic when describing the pride they had for their humble and now battle-worn ship:

> She is a gallant lady who has served her country well; right now she is tired after 22 months of continuous operations. It is with considerable pride that all of us are bringing back to the states no longer an inert mass of steel but a living body whose name today is a tocsin for all who have or are still serving aboard her.[3]

Air Group 46, having spent only a month aboard, was not lucky enough to join the *Cowpens* on its trip home. They transferred ashore at Ulithi to await the arrival of the Moo's sister ship *Independence*, where they served out the rest of their tour. The squadron history records that the air group, "having made [their] adieus to good friends and wished them Godspeed on their well-earned journey back to Uncle Sugar, forlornly and unceremoniously went over the side on a rope ladder into an LST (landing ship)."[4]

It was with great jubilation that *Cowpens* weighed anchor from Ulithi on March 7, setting an easterly course for Pearl and home. Many sailors trooped up to the flight deck to see the atoll fade over the horizon—not for good, the ship's historian recorded, but "just long enough to patch up our scars and then we will be back to pick up the ball again."[5] As they steamed out of the lagoon, Admiral Mitscher and the Moo's comrades-in-arms signaled their congratulations for her well-earned overhaul and home leave.

As the ship pulled out into the open ocean, the Moo unfurled her homebound pennant, which by naval tradition can be flown by any warship bound for the United States that had been in foreign waters for more than nine months. The pennant is one foot long for each officer and man who had been aboard that whole time, not to exceed the length of the ship—and so the Moo's pennant fluttered out her whole 622-foot length, supported by balloons at its far end to keep it aloft. Upon arrival in the

US, the pennant's blue field and star is presented to the commanding officer, while its long red-and-white stripe is divided equally among all those who had been aboard since the ship last left the country.

While all hands were ready to go home, the Moo herself needed some convincing. The ship had just set course to the east when the gyro compass on the bridge swung around to due west. Perhaps *Cowpens* was not ready to be homebound, the men standing watch thought, or maybe she had steamed so long toward the enemy that she only knew that direction. The needle pointed west for a few minutes before finally getting the hint and slowly, almost reluctantly, turning to point back to the east. But the Moo was stubborn, and did not give up. About an hour later, the ship "apparently decided that it had enough of this going east stuff," and that it was time to get back into the fight. The compass swung back around to due west, but with the crew showing no indication of giving in, the ship accepted her course for home. The needle rotated back to the east and reported accurately for the remainder of the trip.[6]

It was a leisurely ten-day cruise to Pearl, and another five to San Francisco. Workmen on the Golden Gate Bridge waved to the Moo as she passed underneath, and a Navy band was playing a welcome as she tied up at the pier. In advance of their arrival, Chaplain Handran offered in the ship's newspaper some reflections on how her sailors had matured since the ship had left Philadelphia, twenty months before.

> You young fellows have changed since you came aboard. A lot of mothers are going to cry a little because their babies are gone forever. There aren't any kids aboard the *Cowpens*. You're men. Some of you will have years to go before you vote, but you're men...a national crisis separated the men from the boys, and you found yourself men before you knew it.[7]

Handran concluded his sermon by urging his readers to be the kind of men that their families hoped they would be: strong, courageous, and morally upstanding. While this was a noble sentiment, the chaplain's guidance did not survive liberty in San Francisco. DeBaun released the bulk of the crew upon arrival, and the bluejackets hit the town, determined to make up for more than a year and a half of lost time. Art Daly was unlucky enough to have to stand watch the first night, and while he did not see the carnage firsthand, he recorded his shipmates' (probably) exaggerated battle stories in his journal. "I did not get liberty for the first day but the bunch that did tore up all the bar rooms. One nut was arrested for biting a girl on her behind! A lot of the crew is in jail or in the brig."[8]

A Mostly Mightier Moo

On May 21, 1945, the Moo was again ready for sea. Her two-month overhaul, necessary after the wear and tear of more than 160,000 miles of steaming in wartime conditions, was now complete. Repair crews completely rebuilt her troublesome boilers, replaced all four of her six-ton screws, and located the source of the terrible vibration in the aft end of the ship at high speeds—missing teeth on the reduction gears between her power plant and propeller shafts. The Navy upgraded the Moo's radar and antiaircraft guns, added an additional catapult, and replaced more than 60 percent of the ship's wooden flight deck planking, fixing the leaks into the ship's hangar bay.

Much had happened while *Cowpens* was in drydock. On April 14, President Franklin Roosevelt died of a cerebral hemorrhage at the age of sixty-three at his vacation home in Warm Springs, Georgia. His death shocked the nation; news of the president's declining health had been kept secret from the public. FDR had been in office since 1933, and most of the seventeen- and eighteen-year-old servicemen fighting the war could barely remember a time when someone else was president. In contrast, Americans knew little about his successor, Harry Truman. He was FDR's third vice president, had occupied the office only since January, and many Americans didn't even know his name.

Almost three weeks later, the nation savored the defeat of Nazi Germany on May 8, 1945. Close to a million people took to the streets in New York City, and Broadway and Times Square turned on their illuminations for the first time since the war began. In San Francisco, just across the bay from where the Moo was in drydock, the response was muted. The city, as one of the major West Coast ports of embarkation for the Pacific War, did not have the emotional connection to the fight against Nazi Germany that New York City did—and upon learning the news the city government swiftly prohibited the selling of alcohol for twenty-four hours. "I remember all the yelling on V-E Day, but it didn't mean much to me," Art Daly noted in his journal. "The war was still on in the Pacific."[9]

And indeed it was—the latest example of the Japanese willingness to fight until the bitter end was Okinawa, where US forces landed on April 1. Operation ICEBERG, as it was known, was the last major US amphibious landing of the war, and resulted in the highest US casualties of any fight in the Pacific: 12,250 killed or missing and more than 36,000 wounded. These casualties included the bitter fighting out at sea, where the kamikaze campaign reached its terrible climax, with 1,465 suicide attacks over the course of three months. They sank 36 US ships—including 15 amphibious ships and 12 destroyers—and damaged 368 others.

Despite news of vicious fighting in the Pacific, only three of the Moo's crew failed to report in time for her sailing to rejoin the war. Captain DeBaun noted in the log that from a morale perspective, "the unusually low percentage of three stragglers out of thirteen hundred speaks for itself."[10] But the captain had a new problem; the ship that he received out of drydock was nowhere near as experienced as the one he put in. While the Moo was undergoing its repairs there had been a major turnover in its personnel. While some plank owners remained, their experience was diluted by an influx of new recruits who had never been to sea. DeBaun would have to rebuild his ship's fighting team nearly from scratch; he noted in the log that the ship had lost considerable experience and was in need of a training shakedown "almost as badly as when she was commissioned."[11]

Air Group 50: The Moo's Last Squadrons

Air Group 50 joined the *Cowpens* from the naval air station in Klamath Falls, Oregon, where both its fighter and torpedo squadrons formed. Each of the air groups that served aboard the Moo had its own personality, and this one was cheerful, with a lucky streak. While its pilots were eager to see action before the war ended, as it grew ever closer to its conclusion—and particularly after the atomic bombings—the pilots grew increasingly resentful of the risks they were being asked to take for diminishing returns. Cmdr. Raleigh Kirkpatrick led both the overall air group and its fighter squadron, VF-50. He was an experienced prewar naval aviator and member of the US Naval Academy class of 1935 who survived the sinking of the *Wasp* off Guadalcanal in 1942.

Klamath Falls was a good duty station, and the squadron and their families bonded over card games, hunting and fishing, and unit dinners. The torpedo squadron's (VT-50) history noted that "of course there were other forms of amusement, chiefly of a liquid nature, about which the less said the better."[12] But their time in Klamath Falls was not without incident, as Air Group 50 suffered its first casualties in training exercises there. They lost six men in crashes and midair collisions, including VT-50's commanding officer, Robert Pinz. The squadron's XO, Charlie Melhorn, assumed command. He was "old Navy"—the son of Adm. Kent Melhorn, formerly the fleet surgeon for the commander in chief of the US Fleet. Accordingly, Charlie was a stickler for procedure and rank, and frowned on foolishness during working hours. But his men respected him for it, and when the skipper stood up or started speaking all conversation around him came to a halt. Only after the day's business was concluded did Melhorn reveal his lighter side; his pilots recalled the many happy hours they spent in sing-alongs with the skipper, who played the accordion.

Melhorn took a circuitous path to naval aviation, one marked by several turns of bad luck that nearly killed him. He'd graduated from UCLA in 1940 and went to the Chilean Andes to become a professional snow skier, but this did not last long. That summer, Admiral Melhorn telegraphed his son—and the message was something to the effect of "there was going to be a war, and come home and get in it."[13] Melhorn volunteered for the Navy and transferred to PT boats operating out of Guadalcanal. An encounter with a Japanese destroyer in December 1942 put an end to that; the enemy ship blasted his tiny boat to pieces, flinging

Melhorn into the sea and killing nine of his eleven-man crew. Battered and bleeding from the ears, he swam four miles to the nearest island in his life jacket, terrified that his blood would attract sharks.

Melhorn's close call at sea crystalized his thoughts about a new career in the Navy. He had already been considering aviation, "if for no other reason than it was one way to get out of Guadalcanal."[14] But in flight school his luck was not much improved. One of his instructors flew Melhorn's training aircraft through some power lines; the subsequent crash totaled the aircraft but both men walked away unharmed. In another instance, one of Melhorn's wingmen collided with his Avenger during a formation flying exercise off Miami. He stayed in the plane as long as he could, bailing out only when the fire from his burning engine ate through the firewall and charred his flight suit. Unfortunately his gunner never made it out of his turret, and his radioman—who hurriedly bailed out without fully securing his chute—fell to his death after he tumbled out of his parachute harness. It was no wonder then that Melhorn did not find much joy in aviation. "Flying was never a great job for me," he said years after the war. "If you fly properly you've got to work at it, and I used to work at it pretty hard."[15]

Our best account of life in Air Group 50's fighter squadron, VF-50, comes from one of its junior pilots, Lee Nordgren. He was a Minnesotan, born in Mankato in 1924. From a young age, Nordgren had always been interested in aviation. His father was an aerial photographer in the First World War, and Lee enrolled in pilot training in his teens and first soloed in a Piper Cub at the age of fifteen. This flying experience put him well ahead of his peers when he enlisted as a naval cadet in 1942 at the age of eighteen. Nordgren didn't set out to be a fighter pilot. Because of combat attrition and the kamikaze threat, he noted that "it was just what the Navy needed at the time."[16] The Navy sent him to Daytona Beach to learn to fly the Hellcat, and he soon discovered he had a knack for it. As part of his training he had the opportunity for a mock dogfight with an Army Air Corps P-38; Nordgren handily beat the Army pilot twice and sent him home with his tail between his legs. But the training pipeline seemed endless to him, and by the time he joined VF-50 in Klamath Falls, he was getting frustrated and was "beginning to wonder if [he would] ever go to war."[17]

Air Group 50 joined *Cowpens* in Hawaii on June 10, and the ship weighed anchor for the war three days later. The ship's remaining plank owners were plenty salty, and they had seen it all before. But for the new air group, there was a feeling of anticipation as the Moo got underway. They gathered together on the flight deck as the ship cast off and the white-clad Navy band on the pier played the customary farewell songs— "Aloha" and "Anchors Aweigh." As the Hawaiian Islands faded astern, many of the pilots were preoccupied with their thoughts about heading into combat. All of them knew about the heavy losses off Okinawa and that carriers like *Cowpens* were the primary target for kamikazes. "It was a peculiar feeling," the torpedo squadron's narrative observed, "not knowing what was ahead and being possessed with the knowledge that whatever it was, it wouldn't be a joking matter as some were trying to make it out to be."[18]

CHAPTER 30

The Fleet That Came to Stay

Cowpens and Air Group 50 joined the last phase of the naval operations against Japan, intended to set the stage for the invasion of the home islands, Operation OLYMPIC. They were what historians have dubbed "the fleet that came to stay." Halsey's orders were to range up and down the Japanese coast, hitting anything that could bring the cost of the war home to the enemy. This included cities, factories, ports, and shipping, plus the last vestiges of the Japanese fleet.[1]

As the task force steamed north to the Japanese home islands, the Moo's intelligence officer called the squadrons together and announced that Tokyo was the first target. Now knowing what they faced, a case of nerves set in for the Moo's fliers. "We began sweating it out in earnest," the VT-50 squadron historian recalled. "The coming strike and home were all that we talked about those nine days."[2] Although comforted by the task force's tremendous naval power, they had no illusions about the dangers: "the ever-worrying thought of Japanese suicide planes again—of enemy submarines—of being forced down over the target, of living in a prison camp."[3]

Captain DeBaun did not allow any idle time to worry. He had a little less than a week before his gun crews and pilots faced combat for the first time, and he used every bit of it training—filling the days with drills and exercises. DeBaun noted with evident pride in the ship's log that his demanding regimen had "produced a crew fully ready for sleep at taps."[4] Though exhausting, DeBaun's rigorous training produced results. His men grew more practiced and well coordinated, his gunners accurate, and his pilots more capable.

Mission to Tokyo—Navigators, Not Heroes at Hokkaido

The attack on Tokyo on July 10 was the first mission the new air group had flown with the full task force. The weather was clear, and once the coast came into view, the Moo's pilots were struck by how much it looked like some parts of Northern California. Before long, however, the idyllic landscape began to emit flak, and the squadron history recorded that it "ceased to be either scenic or pretty."[5] The density of enemy defenses only increased as they approached the target; the Tokyo plain was so concentrated with airfields that from the air the pilots could count as many as a dozen at any given time—although there were few enemy planes to be found.

The air group hit several airfields around Tokyo that day, bombing revetments, hangars, and the operational planes they spotted among the wrecks and dummies. The flak was brisk, and in some cases uncomfortably close. But on their return to the ship the Moo's pilots were surprised to find all planes present and untouched by Japanese ground fire. Intelligence attributed the lack of Japanese fighters in the air to depletion of enemy stocks of planes and pilots; while they were correct that Japan had given up trying to destroy the fast carriers, they were mistaken on the reason why. What the US interpreted as impotence was a deliberate decision. The Japanese were stockpiling thousands of aircraft to oppose the US invasion of the home islands, and had issued orders not to employ them until US troops were about to land.

The pilots described how there was "much laughter and gaiety" aboard *Cowpens* that night. With all the Moo's planes safely back aboard, the stress of combat had passed, and there were congratulations to swap and war stories to be told. Down in the squadron ready room, flight surgeon Doc Simmons produced a bottle of whiskey and some beer and gave everyone who wanted it a drink, and everyone wanted it.[6] Captain DeBaun, too, was satisfied with the day's results, recording in the ship's log: "This was the first big job assigned to *Cowpens* air group, and they came through like veterans."[7] Hearing Radio Tokyo's mostly fictional version of events the following day only added to the pilots' morale. They had made the headlines and were proud of it.[8]

After Tokyo, Task Force 38 steamed north for two days of strikes in northern Japan. Hokkaido was a major supplier of the Japanese war economy, providing much of its iron and steel, and its industry was too far north for B-29 raids. It was also shielded by persistently lousy weather—heavy, low-hanging clouds, rain, and fog—making it difficult for the Moo's pilots to find their targets. Instead, they scoured the coast, bombing whatever they could find, including a destroyer and a variety of other cargo ships.

The greatest challenge in this series of missions was finding one's way from the ship to the target and back, with one flier from another carrier sardonically concluding that conditions were so bad—with visibility almost nothing at times—that the strikes "produced navigators, not heroes."[9] Avenger tail gunner Frank Martinich described how his pilot struggled to find their way back to the ship one particularly misty afternoon. Just as they began to really sweat their low fuel state, the onboard radar set started picking up a formation of ships. Martinich's pilot turned into the landing circle, and the Moo appeared out of the clouds in the final seconds of their approach. He wrote that evening that his plane "Got one wave off, came around a second time, and made a hard landing blowing out both tires...boy, what a hop. God was with us again today."[10]

Yokosuka and Kure: "We Might Not Hit the Target but We'll Always Be in the Uniform of the Day"

After Hokkaido, Halsey aimed to eliminate the last remnants of the Japanese fleet, which were anchored in two of Japan's most heavily defended ports—Yokosuka and Kure. There was not much left of the once-mighty Imperial Japanese Navy. Of Japan's twelve wartime battleships, only *Nagato* and *Haruna* remained—plus hybrid battlewagons *Ise* and *Hyuga*, partially converted to flattops—and five of twenty-five Japanese carriers, all of them damaged. These ships were bereft of fuel and no match for Third Fleet and US submarines if they put to sea. But Halsey had his orders from Admiral Nimitz to eliminate them, and he was characteristically boisterous about the task. "What's left of the Japanese Navy is helpless, but just for good luck we will hunt them out of their holes," he told a journalist. "My only regret is that the ships do not have wheels—so we could chase them inland after we drive them from the coast."[11]

The ship's first try for Yokosuka on the seventeenth was marred by one of her ugliest operational accidents of the war. The mission was scrubbed for poor weather once the Moo's planes were in the air, and so they returned to base. Lt. (jg) Albert Bradley was flying one of *Cowpens'* Hellcats; he tried to ditch his full 150-gallon drop tank, but despite his best efforts, it remained stubbornly attached to his plane. The impact of his hard landing jarred the belly tank loose, and it shot forward through his propeller, which slashed it open and sparked a fire. The tank rolled across the flight deck and splashed a wave of flaming gasoline over the starboard side of the ship, where it doused two men on the catwalk, aviation radioman Third Class Joe Cornwell and Seaman First Class Leonard "Bud" Wood, both of whom suffered serious burns. While the firemen had the blaze out in seconds, and there was no material damage to the ship, Cornwell and Wood lingered for two days before succumbing to their wounds.

Once the weather cleared on July 18, the Moo got the go-ahead for a strike on battleship *Nagato*. News of the attack left the air group "as excited as a hunter receiving news of big game ahead," as delivering a hit on an enemy warship offered good odds for commendation. The battleship was moored in Yokosuka Harbor, and the pilots hoped it would be a "sitting-duck pushover."[12] The intelligence briefing set them straight. *Nagato* was moored close to shore, hemmed in by steep mountains on three sides—meaning attacking aircraft could approach from only one direction, down a chute under the barrels of more than 150 heavy anti-aircraft guns and two hundred smaller automatic weapons. The pilots could expect to take fire from three separate directions and sometimes from above, as the Japanese had lugged some of *Nagato*'s guns to the tops of nearby hills. The briefing was sobering; the pilots grumbled, "It's bad enough to attack a gun-studded battleship in open sea, but to attack one anchored in harbor, amongst protecting harbor batteries, is another factor again." The layered defenses, they concluded, made "a very unpleasant picture."[13]

Cowpens' planes joined more than three hundred other planes flying to Yokosuka, where the antiaircraft fire was even denser than predicted. VT-50's Frank Martinich recalled how it had the US planes' range even before they started on their attack runs, and all of the air group later agreed the Japanese gunners "were in rare form."[14] The stream of tracers and exploding flak was heavier than anything the squadron had seen. With so many planes in the air, and with such a narrow approach path, the carrier planes couldn't do much to evade the ground fire, and in trying three of the Moo's planes narrowly avoided colliding in midair. The squadron claimed one bomb hit on the ship and several near misses— although amid the smoke and confusion of the attack they couldn't be sure. Miraculously, all of *Cowpens'* planes returned home safely.

After dinner that evening, the pilots of VT-50 retired to their ready room to discuss the day's events. Nerves were still raw, and most pilots were too wired to sleep even after one of the ship's flight surgeons, Doc Silva, handed out shot bottles of brandy. They were amazed that the squadron escaped unscathed from that hornet's nest of flak, particularly after learning that fourteen aircraft from other squadrons were lost on the day's mission. The more superstitious among them began to wonder if the squadron had some special blessing of providence—were they "Lucky Fifty"?[15]

After topping off its fuel and supplies, Task Force 38 turned north again, bound for Kure Harbor, outside Osaka. Kure was the cradle of the Imperial Japanese Navy; many of its warships were built in the city's yards, and its officers trained in the nearby Naval Academy. A few surviving warships were moored in coves around the harbor, guarded by clusters of antiaircraft guns. While the flak at Yokosuka was tough, intelligence thought Kure was likely better guarded. The Navy's plan was to overwhelm these defenses with nearly 1,400 sorties on the harbor and surrounding airfields over the course of the day. The number of planes involved meant midair collisions were a real risk, so the task force's planners choreographed the strikes in five-minute waves to bring formations in and out of the target zone safely.

The task force hit Kure three times, on July 24, 25, and 28—delivering the coup de grace to battleships *Haruna* and hybrid battleships *Ise* and *Hyuga*. Two other previously damaged or partially completed aircraft carriers also took hits from bombs, and one capsized. The combination of the murderous flak and the repeated hits on Japanese warships produced record commendations; more than 170 US pilots earned the Navy Cross during the three days of strikes—five posthumously—more than were awarded at the 1942 Battle of Midway.[16]

After their close call at Yokosuka, the men of Air Group 50 weren't thrilled to attack yet another heavily defended harbor, and the pilots debated among themselves how long their luck would hold:

> We were still expecting trouble somewhere along the line. Lady Luck would not play that much of a favorite with us. Would her favor desert us on the next strike? Or would she toy with us...play us along for several more days... [or] weeks to build up a false feeling of security, only to be brought back to the reality of war when least expected? Though none knew the answer to this...some harbored guesses.[17]

It was cloudy over Kure that morning, and Air Group 50 did not find its primary target, the battleship *Haruna*. A merchant ship was occupying the berth that intelligence had reported the battlewagon in; tail gunner Frank Martinich grumbled to his diary the enemy "must have moved her."[18] The antiaircraft fire was every bit as heavy as at Yokosuka, however, and the Japanese gunners added some color and special effects so gunners could tell which burst of flak was theirs. The pilots described how "there were bursts of every color of the rainbow, some with balls of fire shooting out of them like roman candles, some with a pinwheel effect and many with streamers...it was very much like a 4th of July celebration until they had [our] range."[19]

Between the cloud cover and the flak, the Moo's pilots had a hard time putting bombs on the targets. After failing to find the *Haruna*, they made a run on heavy cruiser *Tone*, anchored nearby. She had seen action in almost every major battle of the Pacific, including Pearl Harbor, Midway, Guadalcanal, the Philippine Sea, and Leyte Gulf. She was heavily camouflaged with netting to look like an island, but she betrayed her position by opening fire. Frank Martinich noted that "when those 5-inch guns started shooting at us we knew something big was down there."[20] Bombing through intense flak and the cloud cover, the best the Moo's Avengers could do was to unload their bombs somewhere in the vicinity of the ship, scoring no hits. A second raid on *Tone* later that afternoon went slightly better; the air group put four 500-pound bombs close enough to her that they hoped they might have split a few of her seams beneath the waterline.

While Commander Melhorn was disappointed in the results, his fliers were relieved it was behind them and there were no casualties. Lucky 50 had again come through mostly unscathed except for a few minor holes from the flak, while the casualties ran high in other squadrons, with more than thirty planes lost.[21] The pilots focused on the positive, saying that their lack of results reminded them of the squadron's unofficial motto: "We might not hit the target, but we'll always be in the uniform of the day."[22]

Dodson and Nordgren Go It Alone at Kure

Much to the frustration of the Moo's pilots, the task force planned to repeat its strikes against Kure the following day, and *Cowpens* was assigned the hybrid battleship-carrier *Ise* and the harbor facilities as targets. The strike lifted off into a heavy weather front, with clouds down to the wave tops and visibility of less than a quarter mile. The pilots tried to get above the overcast but they were never able to break out, and so the strike commander scrubbed the whole mission for weather.

Several of the Moo's fliers tried to reach the target anyway. Frank Martinich described how his pilot and a handful of other Avengers with perhaps six fighters for escort headed ashore at low altitude. With visibility of only a few hundred feet, they made landfall and nearly collided with a hill, which suddenly emerged out of the thick clouds right in front of them. As all the planes frantically pulled up to avoid a collision, they scattered and were unable to find one another afterward. Finally, Martinich's pilot thought better of the whole scheme, jettisoned his bombs, and turned for home. Martinich wrote of the wasted munitions in his diary that evening, noting: "poor taxpayers."[23]

Lt. Charles Dodson had similar ambitions and told his wingman, Lee Nordgren, of his intention to go "over the top" and asked if he wanted to come along. Lee was eager for action and knew that Dodson would need his help to get to Kure, as he was a poor navigator. He told Dodson, "My job as your wingman is to go where you go."[24] The two headed toward the target, staying close so they wouldn't lose each other in the clouds. Nordgren described the combination of instrument and formation flying as "a hairy experience...there's an ugly feeling when you're in the clouds, and nothing seems right. You just have to trust the instruments."[25]

Dodson and Nordgren broke out of the clouds at seventeen thousand feet and after a brief search found the city of Kure. At first, the pair were going to attack two bridges in town, but then Dodson spotted the *Ise* tied up along a wharf. Nordgren called to Dodson: "We'll spread out and attack. Two planes instead of 200!"[26] The pair turned toward the battleship and dropped into a steep dive, Dodson in the lead and Nordgren close behind. The *Ise* and the harbor gun batteries opened up with everything they had, while the two Hellcats dropped their bombs at three thousand feet and pulled away at high speed. In the final dive, Nordgren kept his machine guns firing, primarily to document the attack with his gun camera. Both bombs were close misses; Dodson's bomb splashed alongside the port side close aboard next to the ship's number two turret, and Nordgren on the opposite side amidships.

With every gun in the harbor firing at them, the duo beat a hasty retreat, making a single strafing pass on a few small boats in the harbor along the way. They returned aboard the Moo hours after everyone else had returned and with less than twenty gallons of fuel per plane. Nordgren described the collective reaction as "Where the hell have you been?"[27] No one believed they bombed the *Ise* until they saw the gun camera footage. Years after the war, Nordgren mused they had been both incredibly stupid and lucky. "We were fortunate to have gotten out of there—we should have gotten shot down and no one would have ever known what happened to us."[28] Admiral McCain, however, was impressed. In his dispatch that day, he offered his thanks: FOR THE PILOTS WHO PUNCHED THROUGH THE WEATHER TO HIT THE ISE, AND ALL THOSE WHO SMACKED THE TARGET UNDER TOUGH CONDITIONS, CONGRATULATIONS AND WELL DONE, MCCAIN.[29] Both men received the Navy Cross for the mission, and Nordgren's colleagues joked that it was the only time that commendation was ever given for disobeying orders.

"Lucky 50" No More

Captain DeBaun's replacement arrived aboard the Moo as the ship prepared for another round of strikes on Kure in late July. Herbert Duckworth was forty-five years old, a seasoned aviator and carrier officer with an Errol Flynn mustache. He had the best professional pedigree of all the Moo's wartime captains, but he had taken an unconventional path to command. He graduated in the Naval Academy class of 1922, where he earned the inevitable nickname of "Ducky," and went on to earn his aviator's wings at Pensacola in 1925. He was a bold and aggressive officer, but not naturally inclined toward aviation—what his son called "a warrior first, a sailor second, and an aviator last."[30] Duckworth had a knack for teaching, and over the following fifteen years he alternated between assignments in the fleet and multiyear stints as a flight instructor at Pensacola.

In the early days of the war, Duckworth served as the air officer aboard *Lexington* under Ted Sherman before her sinking at the Battle of the Coral Sea. Afterward, Sherman adopted Duckworth as his chief of staff, and together the two men helped pioneer some of the multicarrier formations and tactics that served the Navy well in its Pacific campaign. He was also the primary planner and tactician for the October 1943 raid on Wake, which was the "dress rehearsal" for the much larger multicarrier raids that followed. Staff work was not typically a path to command in the Navy, and rather than returning to sea, he was sent home to help run the Naval Air Operational Training Command in Jacksonville. Duckworth wrangled his return to the fleet only in the last days of the war, and was all set to take command of the Moo in August—although intervening events would soon force a delay.

Halsey wasn't done with the Japanese fleet, and he planned to throw the bulk of his strength against Kure Harbor again on July 28. *Cowpens* received orders for two strikes on battleship *Haruna*, with instructions to use general purpose (GP) bombs rather than armor-piercing ones. With the battlewagon anchored in shallow water, close misses alongside might split her seams below the waterline. Charlie Melhorn was unconvinced about the tactics, but the decision had been made above him in the chain of command, so he could do little about it. Moreover, he gave his squadron a stern talking-to in advance of the mission. Remembering the lackluster results the previous time they hit Kure, Melhorn told them, "If we're going in here, and we're going to be against all this flak again, let's make damn sure we get this ship. If not, they're going to send us back in this afternoon."[31] But the old saying "The third time is the charm" didn't hold true on this day, for the squadron suffered its first combat casualties.[32]

Battleship *Haruna* was anchored near the beach right where fleet intelligence said it would be. The Moo's pilots nosed over into their dives at fourteen thousand feet as the multicolored flak opened up all around them. This time the Japanese gunners found their mark. Ens. William Maguire's plane took a direct hit soon after he released his bombs, and his stricken Avenger caught fire, plummeted into a small village, and exploded on impact. Maguire got free of the cockpit at low altitude, but he struck the ground before his chute opened—and his crewmen went down with the plane. Flak also found Ens. Dana Overman's Avenger; a shell exploded in its equipment bay, and the shrapnel shattered radioman Clarence Mortensen's arm and mangled his hand. After Overman dropped his bombs and pulled away, tail gunner James Helms scrambled to Mortensen's aid, applying a tourniquet and giving him morphine for the pain.

The air group was distraught to have suffered their first casualties of the deployment. "The false feeling of security had been broken," the squadron history said. "We lost the favor of lady luck. War's reality struck home."[33] Frank Martinich's wounded friend Mortensen was transferred to the hospital ship *Rescue*; Doc Simmons didn't think he would ever regain the full use of his hand, but thought that Mort could have lost it entirely if Helms hadn't been so quick to apply the tourniquet. [34] Martinich was sad to see his friend go and commented in his diary that night, "[It] looks as though that's all Mort will see of this war."[35]

Despite the casualties, Charlie Melhorn was satisfied with the six bomb hits they claimed on the *Haruna* over the course of two missions, later saying, "We really did a job on the ship." While their bombs exploded on the battleship's armored hide, Melhorn later thought it was sufficient to at least "clean off the topside." He added, "You don't sink battleships with GP bombs, but we certainly put her out of action at least as an anti-aircraft platform."[36] Melhorn received the Navy Cross for the attack, but denied he deserved it, saying that half the Third Fleet received medals that day. "They were giving them out like popcorn," he said somewhat dismissively years later. "We were getting decorated in 1945 for things that they wouldn't even have gotten a pat on the back for in 1942."[37]

More stormy weather closed out the month, with an approaching typhoon forcing Halsey to withdraw the task force out of striking range. The pilots recalled how Admiral Halsey "led us hastily hither and yon" to avoid the storm's path up the coast.[38] As *Cowpens* bucked and pitched in the unsettled sea, the old hands aboard told the new air group of the Moo's close call during Typhoon Cobra—of the terrible rolling of the ship, the great waves breaking high over the flight deck, and the loss of three destroyers and several hundred men, among them Bob Price. Like any sea story, the tale became more dramatic with each telling, and by this point the Moo's sailors had exaggerated her rolls to an incredible sixty degrees.

The lengthy break at sea was longer than the usual diversion to refuel and replenish—rather than a few days, Halsey kept the fleet out to sea for a week. The long period of inactivity was so uncharacteristic of Halsey that some of his subordinate commanders began to wonder what was going on. Halsey's staff insisted the admiral wanted to avoid a typhoon forming to the northwest, which was a plausible excuse considering the Bull's bad luck with storms. But others were suspicious, such as the Moo's task group commander, Admiral Radford. He noted that "something more than a typhoon seemed to be delaying our operations, but on *Yorktown* we did not know what it could be."[39] Radford's suspicions were correct: Admiral Nimitz had ordered Halsey to stay clear of the Japanese coast. He knew that the Army Air Corps intended to employ the atomic bomb as soon as weather allowed, and he wanted Third Fleet to be well away from any fallout.

CHAPTER 31

The Final Act

Word of the atomic bombing of Hiroshima reached the Moo on August 7, coming as a complete surprise to everyone aboard. Captain DeBaun shared the news over the ship's loudspeaker, and the reaction ranged from excitement to confusion to disbelief. The VT-50 squadron history described the bomb in excited tones, noting that they didn't know what it was for sure, "but must be terrific."[1] Some thought it sounded more like science fiction than reality. One of these was sailor John Ingraham, whose friends turned to him for explanation of what an atomic bomb was. Ingraham had a couple of classes in chemistry at the University of California at Berkeley before the war, and he joked that made him the scholar in residence to his friends. Ingraham was initially dismissive of the prospect of an atomic weapon, saying, "That's a bunch of nonsense. Everything's made out of atoms. There couldn't be a bomb that wasn't made out of atoms." The men resolved the question by taking up a collection and buying a bottle of medical alcohol. "And that solved that," Ingraham concluded.[2]

As more information reached the Moo, realization of the bomb's potential set in. It was the talk of the ship, and all hands debated its effectiveness and whether it would help end the war. Most favored anything that would accelerate the enemy's defeat. "Atomic bomb the greatest thing in war," the VT-50 squadron history proclaimed. "We have the Japs against the wall now."[3] Ship's officer Henry Ortland was probably representative of many aboard who supported the bomb because he dreaded the prospect of invading the home islands. He had a recurring nightmare where he died while commanding a landing craft in the first wave of amphibious landings—which he regarded as an ill omen for his overall odds of survival if the war continued. As a result, Ortland's support for the bombing was unequivocal; as far as he was concerned it was "the right thing to do."[4] But that view was not universal aboard the Moo, with Frank Martinich left wondering why the bomb was necessary if continued conventional attacks had already pushed the Japanese to the brink of surrendering.

A second atomic bomb followed on August 9, and news of the bombing and the subsequent Soviet declaration of war on Japan stirred up the anticipation aboard ship to a fever pitch. "What a day!" the VT-50 squadron history cheered. "It looks like it's about over now. Everyone expects the Japs to toss in the sponge...excitement everywhere on the ship."[5] The two atomic bombings had the unintended side effect of prompting many of the Moo's carrier pilots to question why they were being asked to risk their lives flying combat missions. Why waste additional American lives, they reasoned, if the bomb could win the war all by itself? One such man was VT-50 commander Charlie Melhorn, who described the growing sense of futility that he experienced in the closing days of the war. After Hiroshima, he felt, "as did many other pilots, obsolete from that moment on."[6] The torpedo squadron history echoed that sentiment, noting, "There seems to be little sense in our dropping these little bombs we have."[7]

"My Boy, They're Pau, as the Hawaiians Say..."

The final few days were an emotional roller coaster for the men aboard the Moo as the war moved in fits and starts toward surrender. At times it seemed like an end to hostilities was imminent, and at others like the Japanese would fight on. On the ninth, the enemy sued for peace, although it tried to haggle over terms. Over Radio Tokyo, the Japanese government announced it was ready to accept the terms of the Allies' final ultimatum, known as the Potsdam Declaration, "with the understanding that the said declaration does not comprise any demand which prejudices the prerogatives of his Majesty as sovereign ruler."[8] As Washington considered the offer, sailors aboard the Moo and across the task force were abuzz with excitement. "The ship is going crazy," the VT-50 squadron history stated. "Everybody around radios waiting for our answer. I hope the stateside strategists accept... if they were out here they sure as hell would."[9] Naturally, betting pools quickly sprung up throughout the ship, with officers and men alike putting down money for or against the surrender, as well as when it might happen.

Initial elation about the Japanese peace feelers turned into frustration and skepticism as the days passed. All hands aboard the Moo and among US military and civilian leadership waited nervously throughout the weekend of August 11–12, while the Moo refueled at sea. The wait grew even more interminable with the arrival of more stormy weather. "We ate sandwiches for a couple of days, that's all the cook could prepare because the ship was like a cork on the water," Frank Martinich described. "We didn't do much but fight the ocean and the typhoon."[10]

Halsey was characteristically adamant about keeping the pressure on, and Air Group 50 briefed up for another strike on the thirteenth, this time against the Tokyo Shibaura electric plant, a major manufacturer of radio tubes. With surrender seemingly imminent, the Moo's pilots, along with many others across the fleet, were unhappy about flying additional missions—and Shibura was the worst of the lot. The plant was reputed to have the toughest antiaircraft defenses in Japan, and other air groups who had bombed it earlier in the year dubbed it "old bloody."[11] The plant was in downtown Tokyo, and when the intelligence officers drew the range of all the antiaircraft guns protecting Shibura on the map, Charlie Melhorn recalled, "you could scarcely see the target area for all the flak circles."[12] The fact that the plan called for a low-level attack did not improve the pilots' view of the odds.

The mood in the Cowpens' pilot ready rooms grew increasingly resentful as the mission drew ever closer. The VT-50 squadron history stated bluntly: "Dammit, why do we have to fly again? It's the worst target of all."[13] Commander Melhorn managed to reimpose discipline among his pilots, but even he believed the risk outweighed the gain. "We thought, what are we doing going in here, when they could really wipe this thing out with one of these new weapons with no expenditure of life?"[14] As the Japanese surrender was potentially so close at hand, Melhorn regarded any additional US deaths as senseless. "I'm sure they felt that way in the First World War," he noted. "Those soldiers in the Argonne on November 10 who were ordered into action knowing the armistice was coming any minute. If anyone got killed it was futile."[15]

For once, the poor weather worked in *Cowpens'* favor. Conditions were lousy for flying, with persistent rain and wind, a ceiling of less than five hundred feet, and visibility of less than a half mile. The Moo made two good faith efforts to get to the target, but in both cases—and likely much to the relief of the pilots—thick overcast concealed the plant under a blanket of clouds. Martinich spoke for many in the air group when he wrote that evening: "Bad weather—thank God. Didn't have to go over electric plant."[16] Instead, the Moo's planes found Tateyama airfield in the gloom and gave it another dose of bombs, rockets, and strafing, leaving hangars and barracks afire. Martinich described how several of the Moo's Avengers got hits with two-thousand-pound bombs on a hangar full of planes and "blew it all to hell."[17] In the afternoon they bombed and rocketed three secondary airfields, destroying ten planes on the tarmac.

Task Force 38 retired off the coast of Honshu to refuel on the fourteenth; there was no flying besides routine patrols, and the air group briefed up for the electric plant again the following day. And again, no one was happy about it. "We'll all get knocked off yet if they keep this up," grumbled the VT-50 squadron history.[18] But the belief that the surrender was close at hand raised hopes that the mission would be preempted by the end of the war, and the pilots described how "nobody can eat or sleep we are so excited."[19] Chief among the optimists aboard was the ship's genial senior medical officer, Dr. C. C. Tronsegaard. The doc's bet in the surrender pool had passed some seventy hours before, but he was as confident as ever in the ultimate result. Throughout this tense period, he reassured everyone: "My boy, they're *pau* [finished], as the Hawaiians say. They'll give up."[20]

A Last-Minute Reprieve—The Final Bloodletting

On the evening of the fourteenth, Radio Tokyo claimed that the Japanese had accepted the surrender terms, but Admiral McCain warned his pilots that strikes for the fifteenth had not yet been canceled by Admiral Nimitz and so they could not let their guard down. He signaled his carriers: OUR ORDERS TO STRIKE [on August 15] INDICATE THAT THE ENEMY MAY HAVE DROPPED AN UNACCEPTABLE JOKER INTO THE SURRENDER TERMS. THIS WAR COULD LAST MANY MONTHS LONGER. WE CANNOT AFFORD TO RELAX. NOW IS THE TIME TO POUR IT ON. The surrender offer was indeed genuine; President Truman announced it from the White House at 7 p.m. on the fifteenth, Washington time, and declared a two-day holiday. Orders to cease fire were transmitted to the Pacific Fleet almost at once after President Truman's announcement.

It took some time before the official notification reached Task Force 38's fliers, who were beginning their dawn missions. Aboard the *Cowpens*, the last day of the war, August 15, 1945, started as just another strike day, with the target the infamous Shibaura electric plant. The mission began as scheduled at 5:30 a.m., and the Moo's fliers despaired that the surrender had not come in time to save them from the fearsome rings of guns surrounding their target.[21]

At 6:33 a.m. Admiral Halsey relayed to his ships Nimitz's order to cease offensive operations against Japan. The reaction in the Moo's ready room was nothing short of explosive. "All hands jumped up with startled looks and as the meaning of the news sunk in, shouts and loud yells broke out everywhere. Hands were shaken, backs pounded, chairs jumped on ... hell was raised. The joy and happiness caused by the announcement gave vent to the stored-up feelings of hope, tension, and nervousness of the previous days."[22] Frank Martinich was not scheduled to fly until that afternoon; he was asleep in his rack when his friends woke him with the word that the war was over. "I rushed into the ready room and everyone was jumping up and down and hollering," Martinich wrote that evening.

"Pictures were taken in the ready room of our reactions, and I just had to smoke a cigar."[23]

The first wave of carrier strikes had already dropped their bombs; but the cease-fire message reached the second wave—including all of the Moo's aircraft—en route to their targets, just before they crossed the Japanese coast. General chaos reigned as soon as the formation learned they had been recalled to the carriers. In an expression of spontaneous relief and happiness, the pilots gleefully jettisoned their bombs and rockets and broke out of formation, doing spins, rolls, and some stunts that weren't even in the books. While the squadron history called it a "great show by happy and relieved pilots," not everyone was thrilled to be in the middle of it.[24] One of the Moo's aviators, Merlie Jordahl, described it as the most dangerous flight he'd ever been on, saying "it was really quite a melee on the way back to the *Cowpens*."[25] Lee Nordgren recalled how a plane above and ahead of him in the formation, upon hearing the war was over, jettisoned his bombs, which only narrowly missed crashing through Nordren's wing. Dying at the last minute in a friendly fire incident, Nordgren concluded, "would have been a bad way to end the war."[26]

The jubilation aboard the Moo reached its peak as her returning planes entered the landing circle and one by one touched down on deck. A crowd gathered topside, and the sailors cheered the returning pilots with chants of "Victory! Victory!" V-J Day had come at last, and officers and men alike shared a moment of jubilation that the United States had won the war and they would live to see home again. Admiral Halsey made a brief speech, telling Task Force 38: "Our fame and immortality on land, sea, and air shall go down in history and will always be remembered—God bless you all, well done."[27] But Halsey's most appreciated gesture among the bluejackets that morning was his order to "splice the mainbrace," the traditional naval order to distribute alcohol to the crew. Across the fleet, ships' pharmacies opened their liquor cabinets, and soon every drop of it was gone.

The war had come to an end quite suddenly, and American forces in Japanese waters were taking no chances that the surrender was a ruse. CAP and other routine patrols continued just as they had before, and every ship remained on alert. Halsey ordered his pilots to shoot down any Japanese snoopers that approached the fleet, "not vindictively, but in a friendly sort of way."[28] Sure enough, that morning Japanese fighters ambushed several patrols over Tokyo, while the task force shot down eight aspiring kamikazes. Captain Duckworth was in *Cowpens'* CIC listening to Halsey make his victory speech and watching on radar as the CAP splashed each one in turn. "We shot down a Jap as [Halsey] commenced, one during his speech, and two within 15 minutes after. There is still some bloodletting to be done," he wrote in a letter home.[29] Duckworth, like many others across the fleet, was pessimistic about the chances of long-term peace. He believed that only a total defeat would convince the Japanese to abandon their militaristic ways, while the surrender allowed them a face-saving escape. In a letter home, Duckworth mused that a little humiliation might make the Japanese "possible residents in this world."[30]

CHAPTER 32

A Postwar Moo

The Moo's Moment of Glory

Planning for the end of the war had been underway since mid-June, so when the Japanese surrender came, the machinery of the occupation, known as Operation BLACKLIST, swung into action. As General MacArthur—now supreme commander for the Allied powers—and the Japanese worked out the logistics of the surrender, out at sea *Cowpens* prepared for her own starring role. Admiral Halsey selected a group of ships to split off from the task force and anchor in Tokyo Bay to support the occupation, and much to the surprise of everyone, he selected only one US carrier to do so—*Cowpens*.[1] Adm. Ted Sherman, recently promoted to command of the fast carriers, protested to Halsey that his flattops had earned a greater right to participate. Halsey responded by curtly telling Sherman to mind his own business.[2] It seemed somewhat inexplicable that *Cowpens* had been selected over all others, and Commander Melhorn speculated that Halsey always had a soft spot for the humble Moo since his daughter Margaret christened her back in 1943. That might have contributed to the admiral's decision, but other, more practical reasons probably played a larger role. Halsey feared the Japanese might commit some act of treachery and wanted his fleet carriers safely out at sea. The irony was not lost on the Moo's complement; she had probably earned the proudest moment in her wartime career not in recognition of her sterling battle record, the skill of her crew, or the bravery of her pilots. She was going to be the first US aircraft carrier in Tokyo Bay because she was expendable.

Many aboard the Moo shared Halsey's concerns that the Japanese would not live up to their end of the bargain. "We were still worrying," noted the VT-50 squadron history. "Being the first fleet units to enter Tokyo Bay might be an honor or it might be a trap. We still didn't trust the two-faced Japs. These thoughts kept our nerves on edge."[3] Also preoccupied was Captain Duckworth, who received orders to take a contingent of bluejackets ashore to occupy the Japanese airfield at Yokosuka. While he was initially intrigued with the assignment because of the potential for publicity, as time progressed he became more despondent that it might prevent him from assuming command of *Cowpens*. "As originally planned it would have been all right I guess but the way the thing has turned out it is just a mess. I should have taken over [the ship] a week ago...my one opportunity for a command if even for only one day—shot to hell."[4]

Cowpens spent nearly two weeks in limbo, waiting for orders to head into Japanese waters. As a result, the Moo's old adversary of boredom became a serious issue. The pilots kept up a busy flying schedule searching for POW camps and confirming the demobilization of Japanese forces, but the bluejackets had little to occupy their time. The officers did their best to keep the men engaged with mundane tasks and with as much sports as they could manage. Martinich wrote of the period that the men were scrubbing a different airplane every day, noting: "Peacetime Navy is really clean."[5] But no matter how much the officers tried, they couldn't distract from the one thing that everyone was wondering: "How soon can I go home?" The Navy Department did not keep them waiting long; on August 16 it announced its demobilization plan with requirements of forty-nine points for officers and forty-four points for enlisted men necessary to muster out. Each man accumulated a half point for every year of age and month of service, as well as additional credits for being married, having dependent children, and the numbers and types of medals and commendations earned.

Anchoring in Japanese Home Waters: "There Aren't Enough Lights!"

Cowpens split from Third Fleet to form the naval component of the occupation forces, known as Task Group 35.1, bound for their first stop of Sagami Wan, the waters just outside Tokyo Bay. While she was the only US carrier in this force, in case of Japanese betrayal she was accompanied by a considerable collection of firepower, including a host of battleships, cruisers, and destroyers. The morning of August 27 was a beautiful one, with ribbons of clouds framing a picturesque Pacific sunrise. The Moo was at general quarters in case of trouble, but many men not on duty trooped to the flight deck to watch the ship sail into the heart of the former empire. There was an air of excitement; the crowd topside could see Mount Fuji, and VT-50's squadron history recalled that "when the sun set behind this pride of Japan that night, it was a sight that we'll never forget. It reminded some of us of Mount Rainier, at Seattle, and others of Mount Shasta, south of Klamath Falls."[6]

The Moo kept her guard up in Sagami Wan. Across the task group, ships remained at general quarters, manning their guns in case hostilities resumed. *Cowpens'* planes stood ready to fly, armed guards patrolled her deck, and although she was anchored, her engineers kept her ready to get underway at a moment's notice. DeBaun had been warned about a threat from frogmen, so a whaleboat circled the ship checking for divers. As time passed and the feared Japanese attack failed to materialize, the fleet gradually relaxed its guard. The boat patrols were soon discontinued. On the second day in Sagami Wan, August 28, Admiral Halsey instructed all ships there to show standard anchor and gangway lights, and directed that movies be shown topside. Halsey intended the order to demonstrate to the Japanese the American naval strength in what was once their harbor. This simple order was shocking to many commanding officers—for the last four years at war, all US warships ran completely darkened as a defense against attack. It was a hard habit to break, and the US warships in Sagami Wan were slow to comply. Soon, a second order arrived to emphasize the first: "There are not enough lights showing!"[7]

As *Cowpens* stood at anchor, she began her transformation from a man-o'-war to a peacetime naval ship. Much of this came at the direction of the Moo's executive officer, Cmdr. Frederick Brush. He believed that more discipline and structure were needed to sustain morale and ordered all hands except those on duty to attend early morning muster on the flight deck for calisthenics. Sports leagues and field days helped pass the time in the afternoon. And finally, the men were put to work repairing the ship from her long, hard months of combat duty. Her paint was faded and flaking, her equipment battered and corroded. "Men never knew there was so much brass work, so many hose nozzles, so many rust stops on the deck to be buffed and polished, scraped, sanded and painted," wrote one observer of the transformation.[8]

Captain Duckworth, who was still waiting to go ashore, was upbeat in a letter to his wife about the sailors aboard. "None of the kids have let down so far and they take this all very quietly and in their stride. Everyone has been cleaning up the ship and seeming to enjoy it. Lots of athletics. Still shoot the guns though just to keep their hands in. These kids are really great."[9] Perhaps the officers were fooling themselves that the work would improve morale, especially for those men like Art Daly, who hoped to get out of the Navy as soon as he could. "Our asshole executive officer has us crazy working our ass off all over the ship," Daly grumbled to his journal. "We thought we could relax a bit now that the war is over, but this jerk has working parties going all the time. This was supposed to improve our morale...bullshit!"[10]

Fifty Was First: "Any Claims to the Contrary Are Damn Lies"

Recovery of Allied POWs swung into action soon after the occupation forces anchored in Tokyo Bay. Commodore Rodger Simpson was in overall command but heading up the Navy side of the effort was Cmdr. Harold Stassen, a former governor of Minnesota and later a prominent figure in the Republican Party. Stassen's political star was bright at the time, and many Americans thought he would be Truman's challenger in the next presidential election. On the morning of the twenty-eighth, two of the Moo's Avengers transported Commander Stassen and his staff ashore to Atsugi airfield, thirty miles southwest of the capital. They were the first naval squadron to touch down on Japan; they did not receive a warm welcome, but this time the hostility was from the US Army, not the Japanese. The Eleventh Airborne Division had arrived on the airfield two days earlier, taking up residence in barracks that only days before had been occupied by kamikaze pilots. As far as the Army was concerned the Navy was not welcome.

Commander Melhorn's Avenger—with Stassen in the back—blew out a tire when he landed, and he limped his plane down the runway, looking for a place to deliver his passenger. As the damaged plane came crawling in, Melhorn described how an Army colonel "[came] charging out on the taxiway, waving this .45 [pistol] and motioning for me to take off, to get out. Obviously I had no business there that this was an Army show."[11] Melhorn was disappointed and annoyed that the war was barely over and interservice rivalries had reemerged, a turn of events he described as like the bad old days of 1940 all over again. But the arrogant colonel got his comeuppance when Commander Stassen stepped out of the back of the plane. Melhorn described him as doing the "double take of all double takes" and suddenly becoming very deferential to Stassen's direction.[12]

The Japanese were waiting to meet the arriving US officials in a little striped tent just off the runway. They made some attempt at pleasantries, offering lemonade and snacks for the arriving Americans. Stassen had no time for such things and walked right up to the senior Japanese general present and started making demands how he wanted the prisoner of war returns accomplished. The general blanched, responding, "I have no authority to do this." Stassen got right up into his face, poked him in the chest, and said, "Buster, you have no authority, period." Melhorn was impressed; Stassen "didn't hesitate to throw his weight around...he was absolutely fearless."[13]

That evening, Melhorn and company returned to *Cowpens*. As this was the first interaction anyone aboard had with the Japanese, a curious crowd gathered in the ready room to hear all about it. Frank Martinich

wrote in his journal that evening that the pilots brought back some souvenirs and "mostly unbelievable stories about how good the Japs treated
them."[14] Even though only a fraction of the air group had gone, all of
them were immensely proud of having been the first squadron to touch
down on occupied Japan. To recognize their accomplishment, Air Group
Cmdr. Raleigh Kirkpatrick printed up brag cards to distribute to his men.
Decades after the war, some of these veterans still proudly kept the cards
in their wallet:

> In the interest of public safety and the future well-being of all bars,
> clubs, beer-joints, pubs, juke-joints, cocktail lounges, night spots,
> dives, shower rooms, bowling alleys, football stadiums, and other
> places of amusement where liquor and argument lead to bloodshed
> and mayhem; this is to certify that [name] is of the stalwart company
> of Air Group Fifty, which led Naval Aviation into Japan by making
> the first group landing on Japanese home soil, at Atsugi Airfield on
> the Tokyo plain, at 0951 on the morning of August 28th, 1945, AD.
> Any claims to the contrary are damn lies. [signed] R.C. Kirkpatrick,
> Commander US Navy, Commanding Air Group 50.[15]

Duckworth Goes Ashore

Captain Duckworth took off from *Cowpens* on the morning of August
30, bound for Yokosuka airfield with seventeen planes, eight officers, and
eighteen enlisted men. Duckworth's flight was timed to coincide with the
arrival of Admiral Halsey and the Fourth Marine Regiment, but Duckworth's plane touched down ten minutes ahead of Halsey landing at his
new headquarters at the Yokosuka Naval Yard, and a full thirty minutes
ahead of the Marines. There were still some lingering doubts about Japanese intentions, and every warship in Sagami Wan was standing by to
open fire in case of trouble. Duckworth was just as cautious, and once the
plane came to a halt, he ordered his bodyguard, USMC Private First Class
Bernard "Mac" McCarty, to get out and check out the situation.

McCarty was prepared for a firefight, with a loaded Thompson submachine gun in one hand and his pistol ready for action in its holster. But he was so nervous about getting out of the Avenger that he accidentally pulled the lever to jettison the hatch rather than open it. McCarty described how it "came off in my hand as I climbed out, and there I stood with my Tommy gun in one hand, and the damn hatch in the other, looking like a goddamn Roman gladiator holding a shield."[16] Fortunately, there was no one on the airfield around to witness his mistake—although there was a brief moment of excitement when a car full of American war correspondents sped toward the plane. It was unmarked, and McCarty later said that if the journalists hadn't started swearing in English when they saw his rifle leveled at them then he would have opened fire. But despite their initial introduction over the barrel of a gun, the journalists warmed to McCarty, and several articles identifying him as the first US Marine in Japan appeared in papers stateside.

After a brief search, the *Cowpens* contingent found their Japanese counterparts, and Duckworth received their formal surrender in a small seaplane hangar nearby. Halsey hoisted his four-star flag at 10:45 a.m., and so as not to beat his superior officer to the punch, Duckworth delayed hoisting his own flag until about twenty-five minutes later. A US war correspondent watching the ceremony described how there was an honor guard, a call to attention, and then the Stars and Stripes went up the flagpole. He said that "as the flag was raised, we had that same old thrill that makes one feel like yelling at a football game."[17]

Lee Nordgren was one of the lucky few who accompanied Duckworth ashore, and he was in a state of disbelief as the Japanese peaceably moved aside. That first evening, he drew the assignment as the post duty officer. Still expecting a Japanese attack, Nordgren had a restless night sleeping in the Japanese admiral's quarters. "I could look out the window and there was a big cave right there," he said after the war. "I had this vision of a Japanese soldier coming out of that cave in a banzai attack." Nordgren slept with his pistol on the bedstand, but he had so little training with it that he quipped, "It's a good thing I didn't have to use it or I probably would have shot my foot off."[18]

The day also brought the ship's final operational casualty: Ens. Robert Atchinson, of Birmingham, Alabama, was waved off from landing, but his Hellcat couldn't summon the power to fight its way back into the air. It struck the flight deck ramp, skidded the full width of the ship, and then careened over the side into the bay. It swiftly sank with no sign that Atchinson had extracted himself from the cockpit. The LSO, Lt. Walter Lumpkin, who had nearly been mowed down in the crash, regained his feet and dove over the side in an attempt to save the pilot. He was unharmed by the nearly seventy-foot fall to the water but could not reach the sinking plane in time.

With the Japanese minefields and submarine nets finally cleared, Cowpens steamed into Tokyo Bay late on the afternoon of August 31, the first American carrier to do so. Much of her task group was already there, and the Moo was nearly the last to arrive. While passing the already-anchored battleship King George V, men topside were treated to the sight of their British colleagues-in-arms standing at the rails, offering a salute to the Moo while their band played "The Star-Spangled Banner."

CHAPTER 33

The Moo Wraps Up Her Affairs

The Second World War officially ended on September 2, 1945, aboard the battleship *Missouri* in Tokyo Bay—a venue chosen by President Truman, in honor of his home state. All hands aboard the *Cowpens* were in dress whites for the occasion, and Captain DeBaun assembled the men at morning quarters. But then attention turned to the *Missouri*, anchored some six hundred yards away. She was too far away for anyone aboard the Moo to get a clear view of the ceremony without binoculars, but the event was broadcast over the ship's loudspeaker system, and all hands listened with rapt interest.

The war was over, but *Cowpens* wasn't homebound just yet. While her presence in the occupation force was a singular honor, it also meant she was required to linger another month. Captain Duckworth remained in command at Yokosuka airfield until General MacArthur's interim government began on September 8, when his flag went up at the US Embassy in Tokyo. By that point, Allied troops were pouring into Japan, filling out fourteen separate designated military zones. By the end of that month, there were more than 230,000 soldiers in Japan, beginning an occupation that lasted until 1952.

Captain Duckworth finally got his long-sought-after carrier command—plus a bronze star for his time ashore—beginning on September 10. In one of his last acts as departing commander, Captain DeBaun did an interview with the Armed Forces Radio network for a spot entitled "Meet Your Navy," which was played over *Cowpens'* loudspeaker for the benefit of the ship. The announcer detailed the Moo's enviable combat record and described how she was the only US carrier in Tokyo Bay before turning to DeBaun. The captain started off his remarks by stating how proud he was "to speak for the carrier men of our great fleet"—a comment that must have grated on Adm. Ted Sherman and all the other fleet carrier officers out at sea. After discussing the Moo's participation in every combat operation from Wake to Tokyo with the exception of Okinawa, the announcer asked DeBaun if it was true that "today was the first time [he had] left [his] ship in 65 days?" DeBaun confirmed this, saying that he was "still waiting to get on some good dry land." The announcer inquired if he meant ashore in Japan, and DeBaun wistfully responded: "No, give me land, lots of land, in the good old USA."[1] DeBaun's wish was soon granted; he departed for home and a position on Admiral King's staff in Washington soon after turning over command to Duckworth.

Aboard the Moo, another one of the lucky few sent home early was Chaplain Ralph Handran. He received orders to transfer stateside midsummer, but in time of war the captain makes the final decision on when personnel leave the ship, and DeBaun held on to his ship's religious authority until it was all over. DeBaun was upfront about his reasons for doing so, telling Handran: "Chaplain, while you were aboard, we didn't get hit once. I didn't want you leaving while there was shooting going on."[2] Although undoubtedly grateful for the compliment, Handran was relieved to depart. He wrote to the head of his religious order, saying that: "I've had enough battle experience to last a lifetime. If I never see another Jap dive-bomber I shall not be the least bit unhappy."[3]

As the ship's crew painted the Moo, her air group stayed on the move, expanding their search for POWs beyond Tokyo. On September 3, Hellcat pilots Lee Nordgren and Bill Sutherland scouted out a prison camp on the north shore of Honshu as an advance team for Commander Stassen. The pair landed on a grass airstrip near Niigata to let the POWs know that help was on the way. Nordgren was a little anxious about the assignment, as he suspected the Navy thought two ensigns were more expendable than Commander Stassen. But the two pilots received a friendly welcome from a crowd of curious locals. Nordgren had little four-packs of cigarettes that came in US ration packs and started handing them out. The Japanese gratefully accepted the Chesterfields, a brand they hadn't seen in years. With a little fast talking, Nordgren convinced one of the crowd to give them a lift to the camp on the back of a water truck. But on arrival, he recalled that "what I saw there turned my stomach."

> The men were so emaciated. We stood up on a table and talked to them. I asked if they had any questions. The first thing they wanted to know about was baseball. Imagine all that time in Japanese camps—some of those guys had been prisoners for four years—and the first thing you want to know about is baseball. I didn't know about baseball, and so I turned to Bill and said, "Bill, you're going to have to help out here." So Bill got up and told them everything about that baseball season and they ate it up.[4]

With the task force's guard gradually lessening, sailors were now authorized to go ashore for sightseeing, liberty, and recreation parties. Almost everyone wanted to go, so passes were issued via lottery. Some aboard the Moo complained that the drawings were rigged to select men who were all six feet of height or more, presumably in an effort to discourage Japanese attacks against isolated Americans. But this was unnecessary, as the visits were uneventful and most sailors had a pleasant time. Groups went to Yokosuka, Yokohama, and Tokyo, and each sailor was issued a small quantity of yen to purchase souvenirs—although bartering for liquor and cigarettes was prohibited.

Frank Martinich headed into Yokosuka, which he described as deserted. "Everybody was gone except one or two people that we ran into."[5] Ship's officer Henry Ortland, too, had a similar experience, seeing mostly elderly people on the streets. He speculated that the men were in the military and the women were in hiding, as the wartime Japanese authorities had informed the public that American servicemen would rape Japanese women. Those people that Ortland did encounter were always friendly; an elderly couple invited him in for tea, and he was struck by their honest welcome. "They seemed glad we were there and that the war was over."[6]

The Moo's sailors were astounded by the damage done in the B-29 fire-bomb raids on Tokyo, memories that remained vivid years after the war. They toured the city's central business district, which had been gutted by the raids. All that remained of the wood-framed buildings was their concrete foundations and their steel business safes, encircled by the ashes and rubble of the building that had burned down around them. For Carswell Wynne it wasn't the look of the place that stuck in his memory. "There were still bodies in the wreckage," he recalled. "You could smell them."[7] But despite the damage, even in Tokyo the people were friendly. Wynne described how everyone he encountered "did not give us even one dirty look...they didn't want the war. They were real nice." Plus the local police, Carswell recalled with a smile, "saluted us like we were admirals."[8]

Captain Duckworth staged his first captain's inspection and presentation of awards on September 20, with both Air Group Commander Raleigh Kirkpatrick and Charlie Melhorn receiving the Navy Cross. At the conclusion of the morning's presentations, the executive officer notified the cheering crew that the ship was scheduled to depart for home in just a few days. Others left sooner, including Lee Nordgren. His Navy Cross gave him enough points to get out early, and so the Navy booked him a berth on a transport ship. Nordgren was happy to be homebound, but the seas were rough and filled with sharks, mostly of the card-playing variety. "I was the only guy on the ship who didn't get seasick," Nordgren explained. "But on the way home I got in a bridge game with three army guys and they took me for $200. I realized later they were in cahoots."[9]

Cowpens departed Japanese waters for good on October 1 as part of a large convoy, bound for Okinawa and then San Diego. The long transit home was a quiet one, although not entirely without incident. Commander Brush made sure the days were filled with routine maintenance on the ship, sports leagues, and every other distraction the officers could devise. Working parties painted and cleaned every compartment—and when they were done with that they painted the decks (floors) and the undersides of the chairs, too. The trip also brought the Moo's final death—late on October 13, Seaman Adron Stimson went overboard into the frigid North Pacific. Martinich recorded of the event that "all the ships had their search lights on and were covering the area but it was so cold out that he probably went under before they started looking for him."[10] The ship's official records offer no clues as to what happened, but Carswell Wynne later said he had heard the man was "trying to goof off in a lifeboat."[11]

The Moo's homebound convoy split up as it drew closer to the West Coast. *Cowpens* continued to San Diego with only two destroyers and two troop transports for company, arriving on the afternoon of October 21 to a tumultuous welcome. It was a beautiful day, and a cheering crowd and a Navy band were at the pier to meet them. *Cowpens* and her compatriots disembarked more than three thousand veterans that day, and the city rolled out the red carpet, declaring a four-day holiday, with a packed schedule of parades and pageants celebrating their accomplishments.

True to form, however, the humble Moo was upstaged in her victorious homecoming by another ship. The climax of San Diego's Navy Day celebration was the arrival of the city's namesake cruiser on the twenty-sixth. Accompanied by a crowd of civilian yachts and speedboats, *San Diego* pulled up along the pier as tens of thousands cheered their welcome and sirens and whistles across the city announced her arrival. The Navy threw open the doors to the public, and tens of thousands lined up to tour the Moo, *San Diego*, and the other Third Fleet ships in port. Commander Brush's work details paid off, and the Moo was gleaming from bow to stern, with one wall of her elevator well painted with a map of her travels during her months in combat. It was a fine closing note for an illustrious combat career.

The Moo's days were numbered. She made two more trips to Pearl Harbor, Guam, and Okinawa before February 1946 as part of Operation MAGIC CARPET. Between October 1945 and May 1946, more than one million men returned to the United States from Europe and the Pacific. Aircraft carriers were pressed into service as makeshift troop transports. Flattops like the Moo operated with a skeleton crew and with bunks stacked five high in their hangar deck so they could carry the maximum number of passengers. By late fall 1945, virtually everyone who had the points to be discharged was gone, and those left aboard the Moo were men who had arrived in the final weeks of the war. One such man was Bill Kuntz. On one of the MAGIC CARPET trips back from the Pacific, he was passing through the hangar deck to attend to some task when he encountered a large group of Marines who were trading war stories. Most had fought on Iwo Jima, Okinawa, or both, and Kuntz paused for a minute to listen to their tales. Noticing his youth and low rank, one of the Marines turned to him and condescendingly asked, "Sailor, what did you do for the war effort?" Kuntz didn't hesitate at all. He looked the Marine right in the eye and told him he had an important job—"I'm taking you home." The Marines looked at him, smiled, and patted him on the back before Kuntz walked away with his head held high.[12]

CHAPTER 34

Cowpens Is Put Out to Pasture

The Moo spent twenty-six months in wartime service—from June 1943 to August 1945. Although short by modern standards—US Navy ships now routinely serve thirty or more years—her service was as eventful as it was brief. She participated in all the major offensive carrier operations of the war from Wake Island to Tokyo Bay, with only the exception of a ninety-day period for her much-needed overhaul from March to May 1945. The ship's history records that over the course of the war, she steamed more than 200,000 miles, launched 11,275 sorties from her flight deck, and dropped 620 tons of bombs. She sank 16 ships, damaged many others, and destroyed 93 planes in the air and another 512 on the ground. She accomplished all of this without ever being hit by the enemy. For her service, *Cowpens* earned twelve battle stars, the most of all her light carrier sisters. Although characteristically overlooked for the more prestigious Presidential Unit Citation, the Moo earned a Navy Unit Commendation, which reads:

> For outstanding heroism in action against the enemy Japanese forces in the air, ashore, and afloat in the Pacific War Area, from October 5, 1943 to August 15, 1945. Operating continuously in the most forward areas, USS *Cowpens* and her air groups struck crushing blows towards annihilating Japanese fighting power; they provided air cover for our amphibious forces; they fiercely countered the enemy's aerial attacks and destroyed his planes; and they

inflicted terrific losses on the Japanese in fleet and merchant marine units sunk or damaged. Daring and dependable in combat, the Cowpens and her gallant officers and men rendered loyal service in achieving the ultimate defeat of the Japanese Empire.[1]

The Navy needed the Moo and her *Independence*-class sisters early in the war when losses had thinned the number of available carriers. But now the war was over, and the situation was far different; American industry had caught up with wartime losses. By the end of 1945, the US Navy had nineteen of the larger, more capable *Essex*-class, as well as two of the even larger, armored *Midway*-class battle carriers. Accordingly, it had no need for the humble "stopgap sisters."

Cowpens' service had come to an end. She was inactivated in February 1946. By then, Captain Duckworth had moved on to his next assignment and so the ship's executive officer, Frederick Brush, oversaw her decommissioning. The remaining crew, most of whom had arrived too late to witness her in her wartime prime, celebrated her inactivation in grand style with a party in San Francisco, which the program for the evening dubbed the Mighty Moo's "Last Rendezvous."[2]

The Navy was not ready to dispose of *Cowpens* just yet, and she was mothballed at anchor outside San Francisco in a way that she could be restored to service quickly if needed. It took more than a year to make her ready, but by January 1947, all her hatches, portholes, and windows were sealed and her interior spaces were dehumidified. All her exposed surfaces were covered in protective insulation and corrodible parts coated with plastic paint. Every piece of machinery was coated with preservative, her electrical system disconnected and tagged with instructions for reassembly. Her gear topside was cocooned under weatherproof hoods, and her gun mounts covered with metal igloos that were sealed at the base.

A survey of her condition in September 1959 found that she was in good shape and capable of being restored to service. But the Navy saw little utility in retaining her, and concluded that "there is no existing requirement for this ship in either its present configuration or any planned conversion to permit is utilization . . . it would be most uneconomical to maintain her in the reserve fleet without justifiable reason for her maintenance."[3] The government estimated her worth in raw materials as $422,560, but was unable to get even that. The valiant little *Cowpens* was sold for $273,389 in May 1960 to a scrapping company, and by October 1961 she was gone.

CHAPTER 35

Lives and Careers After the War

The postwar lives of the men who served aboard *Cowpens* were as varied as they were. Many of her officers remained in the Navy, especially those who had started their career before the war. Of her four captains, only **Herbert Duckworth** had the connections and professional pedigree to continue to advance into first-line assignments in the Navy. In December 1946 he assumed command of *Midway*, then the largest aircraft carrier in the world. After eight months aboard, Duckworth switched to the role of a student at the National War College in preparation for a subsequent assignment as the senior naval officer on the faculty at the Air Force University. Duckworth described his role there as keeping the Air Force from "telling lies about the Navy."[1] In 1950, he became director of aviation plans for the chief of naval operations, where he managed the Navy's worldwide inventory of aircraft. Duckworth hoped to return to command at sea, but a 1952 heart attack ended his career. He retired in 1956 as a vice admiral. In his civilian life, Duckworth became a skilled photographer and learned to paint. He was elected president of the Jacksonville Art Museum in 1957. He died in 1990 at the age of ninety.

Despite his rocky start, **Robert P. McConnell** had a successful Navy career. He served in the Pacific again after the war, commanding Carrier Division 15 and then Fleet Air Guam. He returned to Washington, DC, to oversee the Navy's Discharges and Dismissals Committee until 1953. Upon retirement that year he was promoted to vice admiral on the basis of the combat award he earned aboard *Cowpens*. He died in 1973.

Herbert Taylor never served at sea again, spending the rest of his career in staff positions or commanding shore installations. He was promoted to rear admiral shortly before his retirement in 1951, and died nine years later. Like Taylor, **George DeBaun** spent the rest of his career ashore. He served for two years on the communications staff of the office of chief of naval operations, and then was the first director for a naval research lab in Pennsylvania. He retired as a rear admiral in 1950 and died in 1979.

Cowpens' greatest ace, **Clem Craig,** had a distinguished career in the Navy. He flew another thirty combat missions in the Korean War as commander of fighter squadron VF-193. Clem accumulated over the course of his twenty-three-year career a Navy Cross—with gold star in lieu of a second—a Distinguished Flying Cross, a Silver Star, and an Air Medal with twenty-two service stars. But Clem's unwillingness to play politics left him passed over for captain, and he retired in July 1962. Clem worked several years as a recruiter for Lockheed and flew cargo planes for Air Zambia for nine months before hanging it up for good. Clem indulged his passion for horses and fishing in retirement, and died in 2002 at the age of eighty-seven.

Air Group 25 commander **Bob Price** has two memorials, the first a marker in his family cemetery in Shelbyville, Illinois. His name is also one of 36,286 inscribed on the tablets of the missing at the American Military Cemetery in Manila, in the Philippines. Price left behind his widow, Virginia, and two small children, Richard and Julie. His son said that his last memory of his father was seeing him when he returned to Shelbyville after his rescue from his raft in the Pacific in June 1944. Virginia remarried, to a local school principal in 1956; she died in 1995 at the age of seventy-eight. But she kept all of Price's wartime letters to her and his scrapbooks.

Mark Grant never returned to combat after he was relieved of command of Air Group 25 for exhaustion in late 1943. He spent the rest of the war in stateside training billets, and in late 1945 briefly commanded the escort carrier *Barnes* as she prepared for inactivation. He commanded the Naval Air Station on Tinian Island in the Marianas in 1947, and then a Fleet Air Wing in 1948. In 1950, Grant helped bring a transport ship, the *Marine Phoenix*, out of mothballs for use in the Korean War. Starting in 1952 he got a job as the executive officer of the US Naval Mines Countermeasures Station in Pensacola. Late one night in July of that year, a paper shade on a nightlight in the living room of his home caught fire and quickly spread into a blaze. Grant managed to flee the building, and his wife and daughter escaped out a bathroom window. Thinking his daughter was still inside, he charged back in to rescue her, but was overcome by the smoke and fire. He was forty-one.

While his Navy Cross sent him home early, VF-50 pilot **Lee Nordgren** stayed in the Navy reserves for twenty-seven years, retiring as commander. He went back to his hometown of Mankato, Minnesota, to run the family photo and camera business, married his high school sweetheart, Donna, and had five children. Nordgren was a hard charger until the end. He played tennis until he was eighty, and as of 2017 was the longest standing member of the Mankato Kiwanis Club, which he'd joined in 1950. Prior to his death in 2018 at the age of ninety-four, his daughter Lynn asked him about the happiest times of his life. He responded: "Marrying your mom. And oh boy, I loved flying that Hellcat."[2]

Father Ralph Handran returned to Villanova after the war. Despite his insistence that he had seen enough conflict, in 1951 he volunteered for active duty again for the Korean War. He picked up where he'd left off, serving as the chaplain for another aircraft carrier, the *Bennington*. Handran remained in the Navy until 1968, retiring as a commander. Afterward, the self-described "crotchety old buzzard" who ministered to the Moo's complement through its most difficult times became the director of the Augustinian House in Ocean City, New Jersey, where he remained until his death in 1972. When asked in 1971 what his greatest ambition was, Father Handran responded that he had accomplished two of his three goals, becoming a priest and a commander in the Navy—but he was still working on saving his own soul.[3]

VT-50's commander, **Charlie Melhorn**, continued the family tradition and made a career of the Navy. While flying was always work for him, he stayed close to aviation, serving aboard several different carriers. He retired in 1961 and reinvented himself as an academic, teaching history at San Diego State College starting in 1967. He earned a PhD from the University of California at San Diego in 1973, and converted his thesis about the early development of naval aviation into a book, entitled *Two-Block Fox: The Rise of the Aircraft Carrier, 1911–1929*. In his final years, Melhorn devoted himself to community service. He moved to Los Angeles and served as the president of a residents' association representing more than one hundred thousand homes. He also advised the Los Angeles city government on its low-cost housing and landfill policies. He died of a heart attack in 1983, at the age of sixty-five.

VF-25's **Anderson Bowers** made a career of the Navy. He overcame his initial troubles with navigation and night flying, and volunteered for an assignment with plenty of both—a night fighter squadron aboard the carrier *Antietam*. In 1955, Bowers was grounded due to tunnel vision but served in a variety of staff jobs until retiring in 1962. After the Navy, Bowers worked as a stockbroker for Merrill Lynch until his death in 1969 at the age of forty-seven. Bowers's death at such an early age meant that his children were too young to ask him about his wartime service, but his daughter Emily concluded that Bowers "really enjoyed his time flying a Hellcat, even when he was being shot at."[4]

VF-25 pilot **Ed Haley** completed a second deployment in the Pacific with the squadron aboard escort carrier *Chenango*, racking up another eighty-five combat missions. Ed believed the peacetime Navy was not for him, saying, "I felt that I had used up a lot of my luck during my two combat tours and that maybe I should look for a new career."[5] He was discharged in December 1945 with thirteen Air Medals and the Distinguished Flying Cross. He had a successful postwar career as a manager for AT&T. In 2017, at the ripe old age of ninety-five, Ed and his family visited the *Lexington* at Patriots Point Museum in Charleston, South Carolina, where he had the opportunity to climb into a Hellcat for the first time in more than seventy years. Once in the cockpit he seemed instantly at home, and his hands flew to the instrument panel to check the settings—leading one member of his family to cheer, "He's gonna take off!"[6] When asked what it was like to be in a Hellcat again after all these years, Haley smiled wistfully. "It's heaven . . . it just feels very nice."[7] He passed away in March 2021.

Art Daly returned to his native Massachusetts, where he joined the Boston Police Department in 1949. Art loved the job and made a career of it, retiring in 1981. He died in February 2022, at the age of ninety-nine—after more than forty years of retirement.

Frank Martinich returned to Detroit and became a draftsman and tool and die designer, eventually transferring to a forge outside his hometown of Milwaukee, where he worked for more than thirty-two years. He retired as a supervisor in their engineering department and was proud of the work he did on the solid rocket boosters for the Space Shuttle. He died in June 2021 at the age of ninety-six.

After his tour of duty in VT-22 aboard *Cowpens*, **Herbert Todd**, my grandfather, was discharged from the Navy in October 1945 and returned to his hometown of Cortland, New York. He married and had five children, and worked as a carpenter until his retirement. My grandfather never talked about his service, although he enjoyed watching reruns of *Victory at Sea*, NBC's documentary series of naval warfare during World War II. He caught a glimpse of himself in one episode, suntanned and stripped to the waist working on the Moo's flight deck, but his family has never been able to identify the footage. My grandfather died in 2010 at the age of eighty-nine.

Epilogue

March 9, 1991, was a crisp southern spring day in Charleston, South Carolina. The brand-new guided missile cruiser USS *Cowpens* (CG-63) sat tied up to the pier, smartly dressed for her commissioning in pennants, signal flags, and red, white, and blue bunting from bow to stern. The ship had little resemblance to her illustrious forebear. At 9,800 tons and 567 feet long, she was 2,000 tons lighter and 50 feet shorter than her carrier predecessor, with a boxy superstructure on a sleek, greyhound hull. Her complement of 330 was a quarter of the size of the original Moo, and while the carrier could reach thirty-two knots on four screws, the cruiser could match that speed on only two. The new *Cowpens* was equipped with a battery of electronics and weapons that would have made a World War II task group green with envy; her computer-controlled radar and AEGIS combat system could track hundreds of targets simultaneously, feeding guidance data to the missiles sitting in her 122 vertical launch tubes. Two five-inch guns, two triple torpedo mounts, two 25mm chain guns, and two Phalanx close-in defense guns rounded out her armament, while the small flight deck on her stern hosted two helicopters.

As a Navy band played Sousa marches, a crowd of several thousand people gathered pierside for the ship's commissioning, with a special section for the now elderly CVL-25 carrier veterans. The two-hour ceremony was filled with all the pageantry that the pressures of war had curtailed when the original *Cowpens* was commissioned in May 1943. The ship's new commanding officer, Capt. Edward Moore Jr., read his orders from the chief of naval personnel instructing him to take command of the ship and report to duty with the US Pacific Fleet. Moore turned to his executive officer and directed: "Set the first watch."[1] Aboard ship, Harold Dahl, representing the original *Cowpens* veterans group, rose to his feet to be symbolically relieved by a much younger naval officer dressed in a Revolutionary War–era uniform. The veterans had symbolically "maintained the watch" for forty-four years, preserving the history and legacy of their now-departed carrier. With the construction of a new ship, they were ready to pass this responsibility to a new generation. The young lieutenant advised the older veteran: "I relieve you, sir." Dahl responded: "The CVL veterans stand relieved. We wish you fair winds and following seas."[2] With that, Captain Moore called his crew to quarters. With a collective yell of "Aye, sir!" they charged up the gangways to take their stations aboard as the band struck up "Anchors Aweigh."

The path to a second *Cowpens* had begun as before in its tiny namesake town, but it took nearly three decades to come to fruition. In the immediate aftermath of the war, few men wanted to reminisce about their service, and most just wanted to resume the civilian lives they left behind when they joined up "for the duration." Even men like Capt. Herbert Duckworth, who made a career of the Navy, explained why so many veterans found virtue in forgetting. "One must remember that a lot of us...have tried to dismiss the war and all its details from our minds in an honest effort to keep abreast of our times, of new developments, and to live for the future, not the past."[3]

The passage of years dulls past hardships and trauma, and as the nineteen- to twenty-year-old sailors of 1945 grew into their fifties, more and more found their thoughts returning to their wartime service. By 1976, some of the Moo's veterans began talking to one another about setting up regular reunions, while the town of Cowpens came to the same conclusion on its own. In 1977, it advertised an invitation for a reunion in newspapers across the Southeast. Only one veteran turned up, but he brought two more in 1978. There was a two-year lapse in 1979 and 1980, and the town feared the idea might die out. But they tried again, and the gatherings gained momentum thereafter. Fifteen veterans came to Cowpens in 1981, 96 in 1982, 150 in 1983, and more than 250 in 1984.

The annual reunions offered an opportunity to reconnect for men who shared a common coming-of-age experience aboard *Cowpens*. Some men reconnected with old friends or met shipmates who served aboard at different times. For other men, the reunions helped them share with wives and families a part of their lives that they had never talked much about before. The gathering also provided opportunities to resolve lingering regrets about the war. One Cowpens resident, Bobby Dowis, recalled a conversation he had with one of the ship's fighter pilots. The man confessed to him that he always regretted he'd never had the opportunity to thank a shipmate who had helped pull him from his burning plane when he'd crashed on the Moo's flight deck. Dowis responded by pointing to another veteran on the other side of the room, saying, "Well, why don't you? He's right over there." The two men shared a tearful reunion.

The reunion gradually blossomed into a multiday celebration of the ship's service, dubbed the "Mighty Moo Festival." Added to the social events were all the hallmarks of a small-town fair, including a potluck dinner, a high school beauty pageant ("Ms. Cowpens"), a golf tournament, a crew-versus-town baseball game, and a parade where the veterans rode on a float as the guests of honor. As the reunions grew, so did the bond between the town and the veterans. Local residents started an adopt-a-crewman program where they took a veteran as one of their own and kept in touch with him throughout the year. This program made the vets feel like part of the community and resulted in at least one marriage. The veterans, in turn, helped fund the creation of a small museum dedicated to the Moo in the town's historic train depot and set up a Cowpens memorial student scholarship fund. One veteran, Jack Kittrell, explained how the relationship between the town and its veterans was unique. "I have many friends who are veterans, and they go to their reunions, and they're never in the same place... and it's hard for them to understand the feeling we have for this particular place. It's simply because of the people in the little town of Cowpens that we've become involved with. We've gotten to know them and feel like they're personal friends, and we're just as close to them as we are to a lot of our own people here."[4]

With the Navy's dramatic expansion in the 1980s, the Cowpens town council lobbied the Navy for a second ship bearing the *Cowpens* name. With guided missile cruisers having taken over from carriers as carrying the name of historic battles, the Navy agreed to name the seventeenth *Ticonderoga*-class cruiser *Cowpens*, with Bath Iron Works laying her keel in December 1987. News of a second ship gave the reunions additional momentum. "All of the guys from the original ship are real excited," said Don Moss, the 1990 festival chairman. "The idea of the new ship seems to have given them new life, and there's excitement about the fact that there'll be a new set of young guys to help the namesake live on."[5] While the original carrier had passed into history almost three decades before, the town made clear that they considered the new ship, CG-63 (for cruiser, guided missile, number 63), an extension of the town and its legacy. During his commissioning speech dockside in 1991, the town's then mayor, C. Tyrone Courtney, pointed out the connection between his citizens and *Cowpens*' naval tradition. "We consider this ship to be ours," he told Captain Moore. "But we gladly entrust it to your safekeeping."[6] U.S. Rep. Elizabeth Patterson offered a similar benediction, describing the ship as an embodiment of the community and its values. "May you and your crew continue the tradition of our town, our battlefield, our citizens, and the valor of the carrier *Cowpens*."[7]

The Mighty Moo Festival has now been held every Father's Day weekend for more than forty years, with the exception of the initial two-year lapse in 1979–80 and an unfortunate cancellation in 2020 due to the COVID-19 pandemic. Every year, the remaining World War II veterans gather in Cowpens with the CG-63 plank owners, and the Navy sends a delegation of sailors, often including its captain or other senior officer. The close relationship between the town, the crew, and the Navy is unique— no other ship or veteran's organization in the US Navy does anything like it. "We say, and very proudly... that we are the only community in the United States that has this type of event," said Jan Humphries, a member of the town's reunion committee. "I've had military career sailors, veterans tell me, 'I've served on six or seven ships and I've never seen anything like what Cowpens has done with the Mighty Moo.' Never, it's not done."[8] Carswell Wynne, who had reported aboard the original *Cowpens* in March 1945 as a nineteen-year old with "salt in his blood," could not speak more highly of the small town he grew to know over the course of four decades' worth of reunions. "These people are the absolute finest people you will find anywhere in America," Wynne said. "They wear their patriotism on their sleeve and really open more than their town to us, they open their hearts...people just have to experience it first hand to really know how much this town loves their country and those who serve in the military."[9]

In his semi-autobiographical account of the Pacific War, *Tales from the South Pacific*, famed author and veteran James Michener discussed the inevitability of time and his generation's passing to the next. "They will live a long time, these men...they, like their victories will be remembered as long as our generation lives...After that...longer and longer shadows will obscure them, until their Guadalcanal sounds distant on the ear like Shiloh and Valley Forge."[10] In recent years, the shadows that Michener predicted have become all too apparent in Cowpens. Where more than 250 veterans attended the reunion in 1984, in 2022 there were only two, both of them in their nineties. Their departure leaves a painful void for the community; many of these men attended year after year, often bringing their wives and families—and forging close ties with the town that welcomed them home every June. Their declining numbers has at times given the reunions a somber tinge. "It's very hard and sad," said Jan Humphries. "It breaks your heart because we are family."[11]

The "new" *Cowpens* at the time of this writing is now thirty years old and has just completed a midlife modernization. While the Navy has threatened to retire her despite the $148 million spent on her rebuild, she has many more years of life in her, and may continue to serve into the 2030s if the service allows. With luck, there will be many more sailors in the years to come who can carry on the Moo's legacy, who like their forebears can claim with a mix of pride and cheerful self-derision, "I am a *Cowpens* man." The mixing of the generations between the old and new Moo crews at the annual reunions gave the World War II veterans confidence that their modern successors would carry on in their stead. Carswell Wynne died just days before the 2019 reunion, but the previous year he told a reporter that he thought the legacy was in good hands. "The new ship is picking up where us old guys left off."[12]

In Memoriam for the Sixty

There be of them, that have left a name behind them, that their praises might be reported. And some there be, which have no memorial; who are perished, as though they had never been... their bodies are buried in peace; but their name liveth forevermore.

—Ecclesiasticus 44:8–9, 14

Archibald Graham McIlwaine IV	Pilot, VF-25	Wake Island	5 October 1943	Missing in action
William O. Stanton	Pilot, VF-25	Wake Island	5 October 1943	Missing in action
Orson Thomas	Pilot, VF-25	Wake Island	6 October 1943	Shot down / lost at sea
Eldin "Whitey" Arms	Pilot, VF-25	Wake Island	6 October 1943	Landing accident
Charles Grange	USMC	Kwajalein	4 December 1943	Landing accident
Ted McKay	USMC	Kwajalein	4 December 1943	Landing accident
Curtis Miller	USMC	Kwajalein	4 December 1943	Landing accident
Herman Pusey	USMC	Kwajalein	4 December 1943	Landing accident
Wilbur Steven	Pilot, VF-25	Hawaii	1 January 1944	Disappeared on training flight
Benjamin Farber	Pilot, VF-25	En Route— Marianas	21 February 1944	Landing accident

Kenneth Dye	Pilot, VF-25	Saipan	29 March 1944	Lost overboard
Donald Sealey	Crew	Eniwetok	7 April 1944	Drowned during beach party
James Martin	Crew	Eniwetok	7 April 1944	Drowned trying to rescue Sealey
Donald Rouch	Pilot, VF-25	Truk	29 April 1944	Shot down by AA
Albert Sanchez	Pilot, VF-25	Truk	29 April 1944	Shot down by AA
John Chmura	Aircrew, VT-25	Truk	30 April 1944	Wounded by AA, later died
Anthony Limpinsel	Aircrew, VT-25	Truk	9 May 1944	Wounded by AA, later died
Paul "Papo" Parker	Pilot, VF-25	Saipan, Marianas	11 June 1944	Shot down / missing in action
James Maddox	Aircrew, VT-25	Saipan, Marianas	12 June 1944	AA fire
Robert Wright	Pilot, VF-25	Pagan, Marianas	12 June 1944	Missing in action
George Massenburg	Pilot, VF-25	Philippine Turkey Shoot, Marianas	19 June 1944	Engine failure / lost at sea
Frederick Stieglitz	Pilot, VF-25	Philippine Turkey Shoot, Marianas	19 June 1944	Missing in action
John Maxey	Pilot, VF-22	Hawaii	1 August 1944	Catapult accident
Robert K. Ashford	Pilot, VF-22	Philippines	13 September 1944	Enemy action / missing in action
Paul Reeder	Pilot, VT-22	Philippines	13 September 1944	Shot down and executed by Japanese
Joseph A. Brunson Jr.	Aircrew, VT-22	Philippines	13 September 1944	Shot down by AA
William G. Stevens Jr.	Aircrew, VT-22	Philippines	13 September 1944	Shot down by AA

Earl Snell	Pilot, VT-22	Philippines	22 September 1944	Lost at sea after ditching
John Shoemaker	Crew	Philippines	26 October 1944	Lost overboard in deck accident
Joel Bacon	Pilot, VF-22	Philippines	5 November 1944	Shot down / lost at sea
Thomas Gunter	Pilot, VF-22	Philippines	5 November 1944	Enemy action
Charles Stewart	Aircrew, VT-22	Manila, Philippines	13 November 1944	Shot down / drowned after water landing
Ralph Bridges	Aircrew, VT-22	Philippines	13 November 1944	Shot down / drowned after water landing
Steve Korus	Pilot, VT-22	Manila Bay, Philippines	14 November 1944	Enemy action
Richard Eschbach	Aircrew, VT-22	Manila Bay, Philippines	14 November 1944	Enemy action
Joseph Budak	Aircrew, VT-22	Manila Bay, Philippines	14 November 1944	Enemy action
Kenneth Strandt	Pilot, VF-22	Philippines	22 November 1944	Landing accident / mechanical failure
George Whitehouse	Pilot, VF-22	Luzon, Philippines	14 December 1944	Shot down by AA
Robert H. Price	Air Officer	At Sea	17 December 1944	Typhoon
Charles Norton	Pilot, VF-22	Okinawa	6 January 1945	Flight deck accident
Gordon Cumming	Pilot, VF-22	Okinawa	7 January 1945	Enemy action
Ormond Higgins	Pilot, VF-22	Formosa	9 January 1945	Shot down / lost at sea
Robert "Red" Preston	Pilot, VT-22	Hong Kong	14 January 1945	Landing accident

Joseph Fockler	Aircrew, VT-22	Hong Kong	14 January 1945	Landing accident
Billy Laughren	Pilot, VT-22	Hong Kong	15 January 1945	Enemy action
Albert Krska	Aircrew, VT-22	Hong Kong	15 January 1945	Enemy action
William Styverson	Aircrew, VT-22	Hong Kong	15 January 1945	Enemy action
Omar Clark	Pilot, VF-46	Honshu	16 February 1945	Enemy action
Damon Bright	Pilot, VF-46	Konoike, Honshu	17 February 1945	Missing in action
John Primiano	Crew	At Sea	23 February 1945	Lost overboard
Walter Clendaniel	Crew	Iwo Jima	25 February 1945	Landing accident
Clarence Watt	Crew	Iwo Jima	25 February 1945	Landing accident
Joseph Petipas	Pilot, VF-50	Wake Island	20 June 1945	Enemy action
Joe Novis Cornwell	Crew	Off Honshu	17 July 1945	Landing accident / drop tank fire
Leonard "Bud" Wood	Crew	Off Honshu	17 July 1945	Landing accident / drop tank fire
Gerald George Coon	Aircrew, VT-50	Kure Harbor, Japan	28 July 1945	Shot down by AA
James Kenneth Daniel	Aircrew, VT-50	Kure Harbor, Japan	28 July 1945	Shot down by AA
William Charles Maguire	Pilot, VT-50	Kure Harbor, Japan	28 July 1945	Shot down by AA
Robert Atchinson	Pilot, VF-50	Sagami Wan, Tokyo	29 September 1945	Landing accident
Adron Stimson	Crew	South of Aleutians	13 October 1945	Lost overboard

Acknowledgments

This book has been a long and at times difficult journey. Winston Churchill said that "writing a book is an adventure. To begin with it is a toy and an amusement. Then it becomes a mistress, then...a master, then it becomes a tyrant. The last phase is that just as you are about to be reconciled to your servitude, you kill the monster and fling him to the public." I could not have vanquished the monster without the loving support of my wife, Sarah, and two sons, Henry and Zachary, who even through the tough times of the pandemic year of 2020 were forgiving when my focus was seventy-five years distant. I hope that in my writing this book my sons will learn something about a great-grandfather they never knew, as well as a little about their old man.

The journey from draft to publication is a military campaign of its own, and I am thankful for the assistance of a variety of family, friends, professionals, and subject matter experts who all helped along the way. First and foremost is my intrepid agent, Jane Dystel, who took a chance on a first-time author with a lengthy draft, and to fellow writer Charlie Goodyear, who introduced me to Jane. I am also grateful to Sean Desmond, Zoe Karimy, and everyone at Grand Central Publishing, whose unflagging enthusiasm for the *Cowpens* story and hard work on the manuscript helped make it a reality.

Famed spy novelist John le Carré once said that he always had five trusted readers review his draft before sending it to his publisher, and I added one to that. My wife, Sarah, was the first of these—I could always count on her to provide clear-eyed advice on the draft's content and direction. Michael Panchyshyn served as expert technical reader, providing invaluable corrections on topics as diverse as the US and Japanese naval order of battle to the ballistic characteristics of a .50-caliber round. Dave Fichtner sharpened my generalizations of naval operations and could always recommend additional sources to substantiate important details. Rich Hegmann went above and beyond on edits, helping me find the elusive convergence of militarily accurate and readable prose. Mike Wussow lent his journalist's eye to the draft, improving the overall flow and catching many stylistic inconsistencies. He also played a vital role in helping me strategize my pitch to agents and publishers. Fidel Damian provided a final sanity check, leveraging his encyclopedic knowledge of military history.

This book is a selective rather than comprehensive account of the Moo's service—regrettably, I could not share every story of courage, sacrifice, and humanity that I found in my research. But I am grateful for the assistance of a long list of remarkable people who helped provide the material to write this book. With only one exception, the veterans and their families were always eager to help someone who wanted to tell the *Cowpens* story—volunteering not only their time to answer my questions but in many cases providing copies of diaries, photos, and other materials. I am grateful to Robert Price's children for donating their father's letters and scrapbooks to the National Naval Aviation Museum in Pensacola, and to Jared Galloway and the rest of the museum's archivists for helping me access them. I'm also grateful to the McConnell and Johnson family for information on Adm. Robert McConnell. Ed Johnson was particularly helpful in allowing me to speak with his mother—the admiral's daughter, Doreen, who has a remarkable life story of her own.

Several of the people I met had already published extensive accounts of their relatives' service. Although these were done primarily to preserve their story for the benefit of their family, they were essential in helping me put a human face on the ship's often sterile official records. I'm proud to now share their story with a broader audience. Jerry Craig's biography of his father, Clem Craig, entitled *Ace Pilot: The Biography of Clement M. Craig*, is the best account of the turbulent times of Air Group 22 aboard the Moo. Maureen Daly allowed me to quote her father Art's war diary, entitled *USS* Cowpens: *The Raging Bull*. Art recorded not only his personal experiences but also collected press articles and the notable radio traffic that passed through his hands. Similarly, Glenn Haley's story of his father's service, *From Yellow Perils to the Big Blue Umbrella: The Memoirs of Edgar W. Haley*, was a remarkable account of life in Air Group 25. I would never have found Ed without the Patriots Point Museum of Charleston, South Carolina, who allowed "Stump" into the cockpit of one of their Hellcats in 2017, and then posted the video on Facebook. Glenn was kind enough to allow me to interview his father, who was still a lively guy in his midnineties. Kent Soule was also very helpful in providing me copies of the video interviews of his father, Robert, documenting his life and times as an Avenger pilot in Air Group 22. Emily Bowers humored my endless questions about her dad, Anderson, and provided me copies of his letters, which she has been transcribing.

Idaho attorney Duncan Koler went through a trunk in his attic filled with the papers of his grandfather, Adm. Herbert DeBaun, and sent me scans. Paulette "PK" Johnson, the daughter-in-law of VT-22 pilot Silas "Si" Johnson, also graciously shared Si's papers and helped me learn more about my grandfather's flights during the war. Brother Richard from the Augustinian Order, Province of St. Thomas of Villanova, went through Father Ralph Handran's papers in their archives on my behalf when their facility (which is also a retirement home for the Augustinians) was closed to visitors due to COVID. James Cottingham, the son of VT-22 commander Richard Cottingham, scanned his collection of his father's documents, maps, and photos. I'm also grateful to the family of fallen *Cowpens* pilot Paul Parker, who allowed me access to his papers, and East Carolina University History professor Gerry Prokopowicz and his students, who created an online tribute to Papo's life and service aboard the Moo. Special thanks also to Anne Cox of the State Historical Society of Missouri, who sent me a scan of the only surviving copy of Robert M. Wright's *Naval Biography: A Chronicle of Service*.

Like the CVL-25 veterans, I can't say enough about the people of Cowpens, South Carolina, for their hospitality and for preserving the *Cowpens* legacy. Their patriotism and small-town values are, as Carswell Wynne suggested, the best of America and even won over a cynical Washingtonian like me. Many thanks to the late Brenda Adair, the guardian of the

Cowpens Depot Museum, for the countless ways she helped my research, including allowing me to scan and inventory the museum's holdings. I'm also grateful to the late Bobby Dowis, who told me his stories of the reunions of years past.

I had the opportunity to interview a number of *Cowpens* veterans either personally or on the phone. It's sometimes easy to forget that these senior citizens were once eighteen- and nineteen-year-old hell-raisers. But once they start telling their stories, it is easy to see that mischievous gleam in their eye is still there. Frank Martinich welcomed me into his retirement home in Florida and proudly showed me the "First in Japan" brag card that he had been carrying in his wallet for seventy years. He also allowed me to copy his shipboard diary, which proved to be a great account of the Moo's final weeks in combat. Kris Nordgren allowed me to talk to her father, Lee, who told me how he and his wingman, Charles Dodson, earned their Navy Crosses by attacking Kure Harbor on their own. Other *Cowpens* veterans who told me their stories and helped me understand what life was like aboard the Moo were Don Saylor, Don Brady, Carswell Wynne, Bill Kuntz, Merlie Jordahl, and Ray Williams. *Cowpens* veteran John Ingraham, who has written several books on microbiology for Harvard Press, cheerfully advised me, "Don't get hooked on writing. You might never recover." But as this manuscript demonstrates, by then I was too far gone to be saved.

Bibliography

"7 Battle Craft Land 3000 Vets at Local Docks: San Diegans Welcome Pacific Fighters as Ships Berth at Piers." *San Diego Union* (San Diego, CA), October 22, 1945, 1–2.

"24 Pilots, Aircrewmen from Famous VT-25 Arrive at NAS after 10 Months at Sea." *The Avenger* (Naval Air Station, Ft. Lauderdale, FL), September 23, 1944.

Adamson, Hans Christian, and George Francis Kosco. *Halsey's Typhoons: A Firsthand Account of How Two Typhoons, More Powerful Than the Japanese, Dealt Death and Destruction to Admiral Halsey's Third Fleet.* New York: Crown Publishers, 1967.

Air Group 22. *Aircraft Action Reports for the Period of 2 October 1944 to 1400 on 15 October 1944.* 1944.

———— *Aircraft Action Reports for the Period of 7 September to 24 September 1944.* 1944.

———— *Aircraft Action Reports for the Period of 21 October 1944 to 27 October 1944.* 1944.

———— *Aircraft Action Reports for the Period of 1400 on 15 October 1944 to 2230 on 17 October 1944.* 1944.

Air Group 25. *Aircraft Action Reports for the Period 11 June–3 July 1944.* 1944.

———— *Aircraft Action Reports: Period 16 February Through 22 February.* 1944.

Air Group 46. *Aircraft Action Reports for the Period of 16 February 1945 Through 1 March 1945.* 1945.

Applebaum, Yoni. "Publishers Gave Away 122,951,031 Books During World War II." *Atlantic*, September 10, 2014. https://www.theatlantic.com/business/archive/2014/09/publishers-gave-away-122951031-books-during-world-war-ii/379893/.

"Aroma." *Mighty Moo*, September 28, 1944.

Associated Press. "Herbert S. Duckworth, Retired Admiral, 90." *New York Times* (New York, NY), June 1, 1990. https://www.nytimes.com/1990/06/01/obituaries/herbert-s-duckworth-retired-admiral-90.html.

Ayers, George. "Interview with VF-50 Pilot George Ayers." By Scott Ayers. Library of Congress, American Folklife Center, Veterans History Project. 2017.

Babits, Lawrence Edward. *A Devil of a Whipping: The Battle of Cowpens.* Chapel Hill: University of North Carolina Press, 1998.

Bailey, Beth L., and David R. Farber. *The First Strange Place: The Alchemy of Race and Sex in World War II Hawaii.* New York: Free Press, 1992.

Barber, Noel. *Sinister Twilight: The Fall of Singapore.* Cassell Military Paperbacks. London: Cassell, 2002.

Bergerud, Eric M. *Fire in the Sky: The Air War in the South Pacific.* Boulder, CO: Westview Press, 2000.

Bernstein, Marc. "Hail Storm at Truk." *Naval History,* February 1994.

Blanchard, Robert. "Sobering Stats: 15,000 U.S. Airmen Killed in Training in WW II." Real Clear History, February 12, 2019. https://www.realclearhistory.com /articles/2019/02/12/staggering_statistics_15000_us_airmen_killed_in_train ing_in_ww_ii_412.html.

Boomhower, Ray E. *Fighter Pilot: The World War II Career of Alex Vraciu.* Indianapolis: Indiana Historical Society Press, 2010.

Borneman, Walter R. *The Admirals: Nimitz, Halsey, Leahy, and King—The Five-Star Admirals Who Won the War at Sea.* New York: Little, Brown, 2012.

Bowers, Anderson Jr. The Wartime Letters of Anderson Bowers. 1943–1944.

Bowers, Emily. Interviewed by author. 2020.

Brady, Don. Interviewed by author. 2018.

Buell, Thomas B. *Master of Sea Power: A Biography of Fleet Admiral Ernest J. King.* Annapolis, MD: Naval Institute Press, 2012.

Byerly, John. "USS *Cowpens* CG-63 Commissioning." YouTube, May 19, 2013. https://www.youtube.com/watch?app=desktop&v=tGTMdN2t_Qk&fb clid=IwAR1WlNcDo8aCvJiPof37EHZohkF91xTffzsjlGXWUl-w4Ryw _4v0ZST5who.

Cannon, M. Hamlin, and Center of Military History. *Leyte—The Return to the Philippines.* Washington, DC: Center of Military History, United States Army; U.S. Government Printing Office, 1993.

Carr, Harry L. *The Goose on the Loose: USS* Goss, *DE-444, 1944-1945.* Coronado, CA: Self-published, 1988.

"Charles Melhorn, Naval Hero." Obituary. *Los Angeles Times* (Los Angeles, CA), October 25, 1983. https://www.newspapers.com/clip/51275136/charles-melhorn -obituary/.

Clark, J. J., and Clark G. Reynolds. *Carrier Admiral.* New York: D. McKay, 1967.

"Commander Handran on Duty." *Augustinian Order Provincial Newsletter,* January–February, 1973.

Commander in Chief, Pacific Fleet. *Court of Inquiry to Inquire into All the Circumstances Connected with the Loss of the USS* Hull *(DD-350), USS* Monaghan *(DD-354). And the USS* Spence *(DD-512), and Damage Sustained by the USS* Monterey *(CVL-26) and USS* Cowpens *(CVL-25) and Other Damage Sustained by Ships of the Third Fleet as the Result of Adverse Weather on or About December 18, 1944*. 1945.

Commander, US Naval Forces Southwest Pacific. "Operations, Action, and Sinking of USS *Langley*, Period from February 22 to March 5, 1942." 1942.

Composite Squadron 25. *Aircraft Action Report, Wake Island Action, October 5th and 6th 1943*. 1943.

Connell, Royal W., and William P. Mack. *Naval Ceremonies, Customs, and Traditions*, 6th ed. Annapolis, MD: Naval Institute Press, 2004.

Costello, John. *The Pacific War*. New York: Quill, 1982.

Cowpens Bicentennial Committee. *History of Cowpens, South Carolina*. Edited by Linda Dearybury Taylor. Cowpens, SC: Intercollegiate Press, 1982.

Cowpens Reunion Association. USS Cowpens' Veterans Memories of Typhoon Cobra. Letters collected by the Cowpens Reunion Association, Cowpens Depot Museum, Cowpens, South Carolina. 1994.

Craig, Jerry. *Ace Pilot: The Biography of Clement M. Craig*. Blurb, 2018.

Daly, Arthur. *The World War 2 Diary of Arthur Daly*. Unpublished memoir, 1945.

Davidson, Joel R. *The Unsinkable Fleet: The Politics of U.S. Navy Expansion in World War II*. Annapolis, MD: Naval Institute Press, 1996.

DeBaun, George. *Biography of Rear Admiral George H. Debaun*. 1979.

Drury, Bob, and Thomas Clavin. *Halsey's Typhoon: The True Story of a Fighting Admiral, an Epic Storm, and an Untold Rescue*. New York: Atlantic Monthly Press, 2007.

Duckworth, Herbert. The Papers of Herbert Duckworth. National Aviation Museum, Pensacola, FL. 1945.

Dull, Paul S. *A Battle History of the Imperial Japanese Navy, 1941–1945*. Annapolis, MD: Naval Institute Press, 1978.

Ewing, Steve. *Thach Weave: The Life of Jimmie Thach*. Annapolis, MD: Naval Institute Press, 2004.

Ewing, Steve, and John B. Lundstrom. *Fateful Rendezvous: The Life of Butch O'Hare*. Annapolis, MD: Naval Institute Press, 1997.

Fahey, James J. *Pacific War Diary, 1942–1945*. Boston: Houghton Mifflin, 1992.

Faltum, Andrew. *The Independence Light Aircraft Carriers*. Charleston, SC: Nautical & Aviation Pub. Co. of America, 2002.

Fighting Squadron 22. *History of Fighting Squadron Twenty Two from 30 September 1942, Date of Commissioning, Through 31 December 1944*. 1945.

Fighting Squadron 25. *A History of Fighting Squadron 25*. 1944.

———— "Narrative of Events Surrounding Eleven Days' Survival in a One-Man Life Raft." 1944.

Fighting Squadron 50. *History of Fighting Squadron 50*. War diary for VF-50. 1945.

Fighting Squadron Six. *Fighting Squadron Six: History*. 1944.

Ford, Douglas. *The Elusive Enemy: U.S. Naval Intelligence and the Imperial Japanese Fleet*. Annapolis, MD: Naval Institute Press, 2011.

Freuer, A. B. "Saving the Torpedoed Cruiser Houston." *World War II*, November 1996.

Frick, L. M. "Occupation Carrier: To the USS Cowpens Fell the Honor of Being the First Fast Carrier into Tokyo Bay." *Our Navy*, 1946.

Friedman, Norman. "CVLs: The Independence Class." In *Warship*, edited by Robert Gardiner. Annapolis, MD: Naval Institute Press, 1980.

———— *U.S. Aircraft Carriers: An Illustrated Design History*. Annapolis, MD: Naval Institute Press, 1983.

Gadbois, Robert O. *Hellcat Tales: A U.S. Navy Fighter Pilot in World War II*. Bennington, VT: Merriam Press, 2011.

Gannon, Robert. *Hellions of the Deep: The Development of American Torpedoes in World War II*. University Park, PA: Pennsylvania State University Press, 1996.

Gilbert, Alton Keith. *A Leader Born: The Life of Admiral John Sidney Mccain, Pacific Carrier Commander*. Philadelphia, PA: Casemate, 2006.

Goodman, Sherwin. "Memories of 50 Years." Library of Congress, American Folklife Center, Veterans History Project. Unpublished memoir, 2001.

———— "Oral History of Sherwin Goodman." Library of Congress. Sherwin H. Goodwin Collection. Legacies: Stories from the Second World War. 2001.

"Grant Funeral Held Monday, Flags at Half-Staff at Naval Station." *Panama City News-Herald* (Panama City, FL), July 29, 1952.

Guttridge, Peter. "Kathleen Winsor, Author of the Racy Bestseller *Forever Amber*." Obituary. *Independent*, May 29, 2003. https://www.independent.co.uk/news/obituaries/kathleen-winsor-36575.html.

Haley, Ed. Interviewed by author. 2018.

Haley, Edgar W., and Glenn Haley. *From Yellow Perils to Big Blue Umbrella: The Memoirs of Edgar W. Haley*. Self-published, 2011.

Hall of Valor Project. "Clement Melvin Craig." Navy Cross commendation. Accessed 2020. https://valor.militarytimes.com/hero/21089.

———— "Herbert Watson Taylor." Navy Cross commendation. Accessed 2020. https://valor.militarytimes.com/hero/21123.

———— "Thomas H. Jenkins." Navy Cross commendation. Accessed 2020. https://valor.militarytimes.com/hero/5969.

——— "George C. Bullard." Prisoner of War Medal commendation. Accessed 2020. https://valor.militarytimes.com/hero/300319.

Halsey, Ashley Jr. "The CVLs' Success Story." In *The History of the USS* Cabot *(CVL-28)*. Annapolis, MD: US Naval Institute, 1946.

Hammel, Eric M. *Aces Against Japan: The American Aces Speak*. Pacifica, CA: Pacifica Military History, 1995.

Hammond, James W. Jr. *The Treaty Navy: The Story of the US Naval Service Between the World Wars*. Victoria, British Columbia: Wesley Press, 2001.

Handran, Ralph. The Papers of USS *Cowpens'* Chaplain Ralph Handran. The Archives of The Augustinian Order, Province of St. Thomas of Villanova. 2020.

Hargis, Robert. *US Naval Aviator: 1941–45*. Oxford, UK: Osprey Publishing, 2002.

Hastings, Max. *Retribution: The Battle for Japan, 1944–45*. New York: Vintage Books, 2009.

Hay, Gerald. "Veteran Recalls Heyday of Olathe Naval Air Station." *Gardner News*, November 10, 2010. https://web.archive.org/web/20201031193551/gard nernews.com/2010/11/10/veteran-recalls-heyday-of-olathe-naval-air-station/.

Heinrich, Thomas R. *Warship Builders: An Industrial History of U.S. Naval Shipbuilding, 1922–1945*. Studies in Naval History and Sea Power. Annapolis, MD: Naval Institute Press, 2020.

Hembree, Mike. "Mighty Moo Ballyhoo." *Greenville News* (Greenville, SC), June 23, 1990. https://www.newspapers.com/clip/64800532/the-greenville-news/.

Herder, Brian Lane. *The Naval Siege of Japan 1945: War Plan Orange Triumphant*. Oxford, UK: Osprey Books, 2020.

——— *World War II US Fast Carrier Task Force Tactics 1943–45*. Edited by Martin Windrow. Oxford, UK: Osprey Books, 2020.

"History and Development of New York Shipbuilding Corporation." *Bulletin of American International Corporation* 3, no. 1 (June 1920).

History of the Chaplain Corps, United States Navy, The. Vol. 6. Washington, DC: Government Printing Office, 1960. https://books.google.com/books?id=ZexHAQ AAIAAJ.

Holmes, John H. "Art Challenges an Admiral." *Palm Beach Post* (West Palm Beach, FL), January 20, 1957.

Hone, Thomas. "Replacing Battleships with Aircraft Carriers in the Pacific in World War II." *Naval War College Review* 66, no. 1 (2013): 56–76.

Hone, Thomas, and Trent Hone. *Battle Line: The United States Navy, 1919–1939*. Annapolis, MD: Naval Institute Press, 2006.

Hone, Trent. *Learning War: The Evolution of Fighting Doctrine in the U.S. Navy, 1898–1945*. Studies in Naval History and Sea Power. Annapolis, MD: Naval Institute Press, 2018.

"Hope Keeps You Alive Says Flyer Who Spent 11 Days on Raft at Sea." *Seattle Daily Times* (Seattle, WA), August 19, 1944.

Hornfischer, James D. *The Fleet at Flood Tide: America at Total War in the Pacific, 1944–1945*. New York: Bantam Books, 2016.

———— *The Last Stand of the Tin Can Sailors*. New York: Bantam Books, 2004.

Hudson, J. Ed. *The History of the USS* Cabot *(CVL-28): A Fast Carrier in World War II*. Self-published, 1986.

"IJN *Naka*: Tabular Record of Movement." Combined Fleet (website). Accessed 2020. http://www.combinedfleet.com/naka_t.htm.

"IJN *Noshiro*: Tabular Record of Movement." Combined Fleet (website). Accessed 2020. http://www.combinedfleet.com/noshiro_t.htm.

"I'll Be Home for Christmas." Song Collection, Library of Congress, 2002. https://www.loc.gov/item/ihas.200000010/.

Ingraham, John L. Interviewed by author. 2018.

———— *March of the Microbes: Sighting the Unseen*. Cambridge, MA: Belknap Press of Harvard University Press, 2010.

Irons, Martin. *Phalanx Against the Divine Wind: Protecting the Fast Carrier Task Force During World War 2*. Hoosick Falls, NY: Merriam Press, 2017.

James, Michael. *The Adventures of M. James: A Sailor's Diary Aboard the U.S.S.* Monterey, *CVL-26*. Dublin, NH: Turn of the Screw Press, 2005.

James, Savanna. "Cowpens Festival Honors Veterans." *Carolina News and Reporter*, July 2, 2018. https://carolinanewsandreporter.cic.sc.edu/cowpens-festival-honors-veterans/.

Jarman, E. B. *Draft War Diary: The Notes of USS* Cowpens *Assistant Navigator E. B. Jarman*. 1944–1945.

J.C.H., *Nine out of Fifty: A Narrative History of Torpedo Squadron 50*. 1945.

Johnson, Doreen McConnell. Interviewed by author. 2018.

Johnson, Jess. "*Cowpens*' Namesake Hosts 33rd Mighty Moo Festival." US Navy Public Relations, 2010.

Jordahl, Merlie. Interview with author. 2018.

Kehn, Donald M. Jr. *In the Highest Degree Tragic: The Sacrifice of the U.S. Asiatic Fleet in the East Indies During World War II*. Lincoln: Potomac Books, 2017.

"Kerr's Comments." *Mighty Moo*, July 22, 1945.

Kilduff, Peter. *US Carriers at War*. Annapolis, MD: Naval Institute Press, 1997.

Klieger, P. Christiaan. *The Fleischmann Yeast Family*. Images of America. Charleston, SC: Aradia, 2004.

Krohn, Tim. "Life Remembered: Navy War Hero, Artcraft Camera Owner a 'Hard Charger.'" *Free Press* (Mankato, MN), September 21, 2018. https://www.mankatofreepress.com/news/local_news/life-remembered-navy-war

-hero-artcraft-camera-owner-a-hard-charger/article_076e5f1a-bce2-11e8-bf45
-2780aa6e4778.html.

Kuntz, Bill. Interviewed by author. 2018.

Kuntz, Bill, and Don Saylor. Interviewed by author. 2017.

Lambert, John G., and Donald E. Labudde. *USS Independence CVL-22: A War Diary of the Nation's First Dedicated Night Carrier.* J. G. Lambert, 2009.

Langan, Michael D. "Commentary: 'I'll Be Home for Christmas, If Only in My Dreams.'" NBC2, December 9, 2020. https://nbc-2.com/features/com mentary/2020/12/09/commentary-ill-be-home-for-christmas-if-only-in-my -dreams/.

Lavender, Chris. "*Cowpens* Celebrates the Mighty Moo." *GoUpstate*, June 16, 2018. https://www.goupstate.com/news/20180616/cowpens-celebrates-mighty-moo.

Lee, Robert M. *A Record of the USS* Cowpens *as Compiled by Robert M. Lee, 1943– 1944.* Cowpens Depot Museum, Cowpens, SC.

Lindemann, Klaus P. *Hailstorm over Truk Lagoon.* Singapore: Maruzen Asia, 1982.

Lingeman, Richard R. *Don't You Know There's a War On?: The American Home Front, 1941–1945.* New York: Thunder's Mouth Press / Nation Books, 2003.

"Little Tug That Could, The." *World War II*, July–August 2005, 58–64.

Lockwood, Charles A. *Sink 'Em All; Submarine Warfare in the Pacific.* New York: Dutton, 1951.

Lockwood, Charles A., and Hans Christian Adamson. *Zoomies, Subs, and Zeros.* New York: Greenberg, 1956.

Loughlin, John. "Allied POWs Flogged by Brutal Japs." *Argus* (Melbourne, Austra-lia), September 3, 1945. https://trove.nla.gov.au/newspaper/article/973695.

Lundstrom, John B. *Black Shoe Carrier Admiral: Frank Jack Fletcher at Coral Sea, Midway, and Guadalcanal.* Annapolis, MD: Naval Institute Press, 2006.

———. *The First Team and the Guadalcanal Campaign: Naval Fighter Combat from August to November 1942.* Annapolis, MD: Naval Institute Press, 1994.

———. *The First Team: Pacific Naval Air Combat from Pearl Harbor to Midway.* Annapolis, MD: Naval Institute Press, 1984.

Mahoney, Kevin A. *Setting the Rising Sun: Halsey's Aviators Strike Japan, Summer 1945.* Guildford, CT: Stackpole Books, 2019.

Martinich, Frank. Interviewed by author. 2018.

———. *The Wartime Diary of Frank Martinich.* Unpublished, 1945.

Mason, Theodore C. *Battleship Sailor.* Annapolis, MD: Naval Institute Press, 1982.

McIntyre, George. *The Wartime Journal of* Cowpens *Crewman George McIntyre.* Unpublished, 1943–1944.

"*Meet Your Navy* Interview with Captain George H. Debaun." *Meet Your Navy.* Radio program. Armed Forces Radio Network, 1945.

Melhorn, Charles M. *Two-Block Fox: The Rise of the Aircraft Carrier, 1911–1929*. Annapolis, MD: Naval Institute Press, 1974.

Melton, Buckner F. *Sea Cobra: Admiral Halsey's Task Force and the Great Pacific Typhoon*. Guilford, CT: Lyons Press, 2007.

Messimer, Dwight R. *Pawns of War: The Loss of the USS* Langley *and the USS* Pecos. Annapolis, MD: Naval Institute Press, 1983.

Michener, James A. *Tales of the South Pacific*. New York: Dial Press Trade Paperbacks, 2014.

"Mighty Moo Head Big Entertainment." *Mighty Moo*, May 28, 1944.

Miller, John Grider. *The Battle to Save the* Houston, *October 1944 to March 1945*. Bluejacket Books. Annapolis, MD: Naval Institute Press, 2000.

Miller, Richard E. *The Messman Chronicles: African Americans in the U.S. Navy, 1932–1943*. Annapolis, MD: Naval Institute Press, 2004.

Mooney, James L., United States. Naval History Division. *Dictionary of American Naval Fighting Ships*. 8 vols. Washington: Navy Dept., Office of the Chief of Naval Operations, 1959.

Morin, Howard. "Navy Day, 1945, Finds US Fleet World's Greatest." *San Diego Union* (San Diego, CA), October 27, 1945.

Morison, Samuel Eliot. *History of United States Naval Operations in World War II*. 1st ed. 15 vols. Individual volumes are cited below.

———. Vol. 3, *Rising Sun in the Pacific: 1931–April 1942*. Boston: Castle Books, 1948.

———. Vol. 7, *Aleutians, Gilberts, and Marshalls: June 1942–April 1944*. Boston: Castle Books, 1951.

———. Vol. 8, *New Guinea and the Marianas: March 1944–August 1944*. Boston: Castle Books, 1953.

———. Vol. 12, *Leyte: June 1944–January 1945*. Boston: Castle Books, 1958.

———. Vol. 13, *The Liberation of the Philippines, 1944–1945*. Boston: Castle Books, 1959.

———. Vol. 14, *Victory in the Pacific: 1945*. Boston: Castle Books, 1960.

Naval History and Heritage Command, "Captured Zero Fighters Yielded Intelligence for Allies." History Up Close, 2014. https://www.history.navy.mil/content/history/museums/nnam/education/articles/history-up-close/captured-zero-fighters-yielded-intelligence-for-allies.html.

———. "US Navy Personnel Strength, 1775 to Present." https://www.history.navy.mil/research/library/online-reading-room/title-list-alphabetically/u/usn-personnel-strength.html.

Naval History and Heritage Command. Bureau of Naval Personnel. *Aviation Personnel Fatalities in World War II*. Washington DC: Navy Department, 1947.

Naval History and Heritage Command. Bureau of Naval Personnel, Historical Section. *The Negro in the Navy: United States Naval Administrative History of World War II, #84.* 1947. https://www.history.navy.mil/research/library/online-reading-room/title-list-alphabetically/n/negro-navy-1947-adminhist84.html.

Navy Biographies Section. *Biography of Rear Admiral Herbert Watson Taylor.* Washington DC, 1951.

———. *Biography of Vice Admiral Herbert S. Duckworth, US Navy Retired.* Washington, DC, 1952.

———. *Biography of Vice Admiral Robert P. McConnell.* Washington, DC, 1953.

"Navy Pilot Tells of Evading Japs for Five Weeks." *Fort Worth Star-Telegram* (Fort Worth, TX), March 16, 1945.

Navy Recruiting Bureau. *Men Make the Navy...The Navy Makes Men.* US Navy, 1942.

New York Shipbuilding Company. *50 Years: New York Shipbuilding Corporation.* Camden, NJ, 1949.

New York Shipbuilding Corporation (website). Accessed 2020. https://newyorkship.org/.

"*New York Times* from June 20, 1943, The." The Times Machine, *New York Times.* Accessed 2020. https://timesmachine.nytimes.com/timesmachine/1943/06/20/issue.html (log-in required).

Nordgren, Lee. Interviewed by author. 2018.

Office of Naval Records and History, Ships' Histories Branch. *History of USS Cowpens (CVL-25).* Washington, DC, 1945.

Office of the Chief of Naval Operations. *Report of Surrender and Occupation of Japan.* 1946.

Ortland, Henry III. "Interview with Henry Ortland." By Morgen Koelker and Jonathan Mathews. Library of Congress. Illinois WW2 Memorial Board Classroom Project. 2001.

"Our Executive Officer." *Mighty Moo,* February 18, 1945.

"Overdose of Pills Kills C. R. Holmes." *New York Times* (New York, NY), February 6, 1944. https://timesmachine.nytimes.com/timesmachine/1944/02/06/96567799.html?pageNumber=28 (log-in required).

Pahl, Herschel. "Interview with Herschel Pahl, VF-6 Pilot." By Jodi Lindsay and Beverly Simmons. Library of Congress, American Folklife Center, Veterans History Project. Washington, DC, 2001.

———. *Point Option: Carrier Warfare in the Pacific Through the Eyes of a Junior Fighter Pilot.* 2nd ed. Ava, MO: Self-published, 2002.

Parshall, Jonathan B., and Anthony P. Tully. *Shattered Sword: The Untold Story of the Battle of Midway.* Washington, DC: Potomac Books, 2005.

Patriots Point Naval & Maritime Museum. "YKTV: WWII Pilot Climbs into Hell-cat Cockpit at 95." Facebook, December 13, 2017. https://www.facebook.com /PatriotsPoint.org/videos/10156526569522788/.

Patterson, D. Larry. *First Marine on Japan*. Self-published, 2013.

Pawlowski, Gareth L. *Flat-Tops and Fledglings: A History of American Aircraft Carriers*. South Brunswick, NJ: A. S. Barnes, 1971.

Prados, John. *Storm over Leyte: The Philippine Invasion and the Destruction of the Japanese Navy*. New York: NAL Caliber, 2016.

Price, Robert H. The Papers of Robert H. Price. Collected letters, paperwork, flight logs, and memorabilia of Robert H. Price. National Naval Aviation Museum, Pensacola, FL. 1944.

"Ralph E. Handran, O.S.A." Obituary. The Augustinians, Province of St. Thomas of Villanova, 2020. https://www.augustinian.org/necrology-page/ralph-e-hand ran-osa.

Rellis, Eric. *50th Anniversary of 'My Philippine Odyssey': The Diary and Memoirs of Eric Rellis*. Library of Congress, American Folklife Center, Veterans History Project. Unpublished memoir, 2001.

Remember When Videos. *World War II: Legacy of Valor—Starring Robert M. Soule*. Salt Lake City, UT. DVD interview, undated.

Reynolds, Clark G. *Admiral John H. Towers: The Struggle for Naval Air Supremacy*. Annapolis, MD: Naval Institute Press, 1991.

———. *The Fast Carriers: The Forging of an Air Navy*. Huntington, NY: R. E. Krieger, 1978.

———. *On the Warpath in the Pacific: Admiral Jocko Clark and the Fast Carriers*. Annapolis, MD: Naval Institute Press, 2005.

Riley, Robert Boyd. "Interview with Robert Boyd Riley, USS *Cowpens* Shipfitter." By Neil Kaiser. Library of Congress, American Folklife Center, Veterans History Project. 2016.

"Robert McConnell, a Retired Admiral." *New York Times*, February 12, 1973. https://www.nytimes.com/1973/02/12/archives/robert-mconnell-a-retired -admiral.html.

Rowland, Buford, and William Lloyd. *US Navy Bureau of Ordnance in World War II*. Washington, DC: Government Printing Office, 1953.

Scheiber, Harry N., and Jane L. Scheiber. *Bayonets in Paradise: Martial Law in Hawai'i During World War II*. Honolulu: University of Hawai'i Press, 2016.

Scott, James. *Target Tokyo: Jimmy Doolittle and the Raid That Avenged Pearl Harbor*. New York: W. W. Norton, 2015.

Sears, David. *Pacific Air: How Fearless Flyboys, Peerless Aircraft, and Fast Flattops Conquered a Vast Ocean's Wartime Skies*. Cambridge, MA: Da Capo Press, 2011.

Sherman, Frederick C. *Combat Command: The American Aircraft Carriers in the Pacific War*. New York: Dutton, 1950.

Smith, Bruce. "'Rawhide' and 'the Herd': USS *Cowpens* Becomes Newest Ship in US Navy." *Times and Democrat* (Orangeburg, SC), March 10, 1991. https://www.newspapers.com/clip/62259026/the-times-and-democrat/.

Smith, Colin. *Singapore Burning: Heroism and Surrender in World War II*. London: Viking, 2005.

Smith, D. Scott. "USS *Cowpens*." South Carolina Educational Television, 1983. (DVD interview).

Sommers, Sam. *Combat Carriers, and My Brushes with History: World War II, 1939–1946*. Montgomery, AL: Black Belt Press, 1997.

"S.S. Victory Feat Awaits Jap Defeat." *San Francisco Examiner* (San Francisco, CA), May 8, 1945.

Stafford, Edward Peary. *The Big E: The Story of the USS* Enterprise. Classics of Naval Literature. Annapolis, MD: Naval Institute Press, 1988.

"Swish—Bang!!!!" *Mighty Moo*, September 10, 1944.

Taylor, Theodore. *The Magnificent Mitscher*. Annapolis, MD: Naval Institute Press, 1991.

Terrell, George. *Semper Fi: An Account of My Experiences in the Marine Corps in World War 2*. Library of Congress, Veterans History Project. Unpublished memoir, 1984.

Thomas, Evan. *Sea of Thunder: Four Commanders and the Last Great Naval Campaign, 1941–1945*. New York: Simon & Schuster, 2006.

Thomas, Willie. "Interview with USS *Independence* Stewards Mate Willie Thomas." Interviewer: J. Bryant. Library of Congress, American Folklife Center, Veterans History Project. 2019.

Thomason, Tommy H. "Waving Them Aboard—The LSO." *US Navy Aircraft History* (blog), November 7, 2012. http://thanlont.blogspot.com/2012/11/waving-them-aboard-lso.html.

Tillman, Barrett. *Avenger at War*. Annapolis, MD: Naval Institute Press, 1990.

——— *Clash of the Carriers: The True Story of the Marianas Turkey Shoot of World War II*. New York: New American Library, 2005.

——— *Hellcat: The F6F in World War II*. Annapolis, MD: Naval Institute Press, 1979.

——— "Hellcats over Truk." *Proceedings*, March 1977.

——— *Whirlwind: The Air War Against Japan, 1942–1945*. New York: Simon & Schuster, 2010.

Todd, Herbert. Interviewed by author. 2010.

Toland, John. *But Not in Shame: The Six Months After Pearl Harbor*. New York: Random House, 1961.

Toll, Ian W. *The Conquering Tide: War in the Pacific Islands, 1942–1944*. New York: W. W. Norton, 2015.

———— *Pacific Crucible: War at Sea in the Pacific, 1941–1942*. New York: W. W. Norton, 2012.

———— *Twilight of the Gods: War in the Western Pacific, 1944–1945*. New York: W. W. Norton, 2020.

"Torpedo Juice." Tom Pynchon's Liquor Cabinet, January 4, 2018. https://drunk pynchon.com/2018/01/04/torpedo-juice/.

Torpedo Squadron 22. *History of Torpedo Squadron 22 from Commissioning Through 31 December 1944*. San Francisco, CA, 1944.

Torpedo Squadron 50. *History of Torpedo Squadron 50 (VT-50), 1943–1945*. 1945.

Tuohy, William. *America's Fighting Admirals*. St. Paul, MN: Zenith Press, 2007.

United States National Archives, National Military Personnel Records Center. Personnel Records of Mark Grant. St. Louis, Missouri. Accessed 2020.

————. Personnel Records of Robert McConnell. Accessed 2020.

————. Personnel Records of Herbert Watson Taylor. Accessed 2020.

United States Naval Academy. *The Lucky Bag: The Annual of the Regiment of Midshipman*. Annapolis, MD: United States Naval Academy, 1921.

United States Strategic Bombing Survey. *The Campaigns of the Pacific War*. Washington, DC: Government Printing Office, 1946.

US Naval Institute. "A Hundred Years Dry: The US Navy's End of Alcohol at Sea." *USNI News*, July 1, 2014. https://news.usni.org/2014/07/01/hundred-years-dry-u-s-navys-end-alcohol-sea.

————. *The Reminscences of Rear Admiral Kent Melhorn, Medical Corps, USN (Ret.) and Cdr. Charles M. Melhorn, USN (Ret.)*. Edited by USN (Ret.) Cdr. Etta-Belle Kitchen. Annapolis, MD: Naval Institute Press, 1983.

US Navy Board of Inspection and Survey. *Report of Material Inspection of Cowpens (CVL-25)*, 1959.

USS *Belleau Wood*. *Flight Quarters: The War Story of the USS* Belleau Wood. Edited by Lt. John W. Alexander. Los Angeles, CA: Cole-Homquist Press, 1946.

USS *Cowpens*. *Aircraft Action Reports for the Period of 1 January 1945 Through 22 January 1945*. 1944.

————. *Anti-Aircraft Action—Covers Action on 14 October 1944 During Air Strikes Against Formosa in Support of Leyte Operation in Task Group 38.1*. 1944.

————. *Award Nominations for the USS* Cowpens, *1943–1944*. 1943–1944.

————. *Daily War Diary, USS* Cowpens. 1943–1945.

————. "History of the USS *Cowpens* (CVL-25)." 1945.

————. Invitation to the Mighty Moo's Last Rendezvous: The Inactivation of the USS *Cowpens*. February 22, 1946.

———. *The Mighty Moo Reviews the Month of January 1945*. 1945.

———. *The Mighty Moo Rides Again*. 1945.

———. *The Mighty Moo: The Story of the USS* Cowpens *(CVL-25)*. Army & Navy Pictorial Publications, 1946.

———. *Narrative Account of the Activities of the USS* Cowpens *Covering Period from 2 November 1944 to 24 November 1944*. 1944.

———. *Narrative Account of the Activities of USS* Cowpens *Covering Period from 10 December 1944 to 20 December 1944*. 1944.

———. *Report of Action 5 and 6 October 1943 (Wake Island)*. 1943.

———. *Report of Action for the Period 21 April 1944 to 28 April 1944 (Operation Desecrate II)*. 1944.

———. *Report of Action for the Period 29 April 1944 to 1 May 1944 (Operation Post-Desecrate II)*. 1944.

———. *Report of Actions During Period 19 November to 5 December 1943 (Galvanic and Post-Galvanic Operations)*. 1943.

———. *Report of Actions During the Period 1 July to 15 August 1945*. 1945.

———. *Report of Actions During the Period 2 November 1944 to 7 November 1944*. 1944.

———. *Report of Actions During the Period 2 October 1944 to 1400, 15 October 1944, and 0705 21 October 1944 to 28 October 1944*. 1944.

———. *Report of Actions During the Period 5 January to 2400, 7 January 1945*. 1945.

———. *Report of Actions During the Period 6 June 1944 to 6 July 1944*. 1944.

———. *Report of Actions During the Period 10 December 1944 to 16 December 1944*. 1944.

———. *Report of Actions During the Period 10 January to 2400 20 January 1945*. 1945.

———. *Report of Actions During the Period 12 February 1944 to 23 February 1944*. 1944.

———. *Report of Actions During the Period 21 January to 1400, 26 January 1945*. 1945.

———. *Report of Actions During the Period 29 August 1944 to 25 September 1944*. 1944.

———. *Report of Actions During the Period 29 January 1944 to 4 February 1944*. 1944.

———. *Report of Actions During the Period 1400, 15 October 1944 to 2230, 17 October 1944*. 1944.

———. *USS* Cowpens *Action Report, 13 June to 20 June 1945: Wake Island*. 1945.

———. *USS* Cowpens *(CVL-25) Action Report 10 Feb. to 4 March 1945*. 1945.

———. *USS* Cowpens *(CVL-25): Action Report, 16 August–2 September 1945*. 1945.

————. USS Cowpens *(CVL-25)—Ramming of by USS Abbot.* 1943.

————. USS Cowpens *(CVL-25)—Report of Storm Damage.* 1944.

————. USS Cowpens *Selected Message Traffic.* 1943–1945.

USS *Skate* (SS-305). USS Skate, *Report of War Patrol Number One.* 1943.

Walton, Bill. "Vought's Kingfisher Sure Was Slow but It Saved Plenty of Aviators." Avgeekery, October 18, 2017. https://www.avgeekery.com/voughts-king fisher-sure-was-slow-but-it-saved-plenty-of-aviators/.

"Watch Out Artie Shaw—Mighty Moo Forms Swing Band." *Mighty Moo*, March 19, 1944.

Williams, Ray. Interviewed by author. 2017.

Willman, Chris. "How 'Have Yourself a Merry Little Christmas' Became One of the Season's Most Beloved Songs." *Entertainment Weekly*, updated December 23, 2020. https://ew.com/article/2007/01/08/history-popular-holiday-song/.

Winston, Robert A. *Fighting Squadron: A Sequel to Dive Bomber.* Annapolis, MD: Naval Institute Press, 1991.

Wooldridge, E. T. *Carrier Warfare in the Pacific: An Oral History Collection.* Smithsonian History of Aviation Series. Washington, DC: Smithsonian Institution Press, 1993.

Wouk, Herman. *The Caine Mutiny: A Novel of World War II.* Garden City, NY: Doubleday, 1952.

Wright, Robert M. *The United States Navy: A Chronicle of Service—On Active Duty, in Ready Reserve, and to Retired Status (October 1940 to March 1977).* Kirksville, MO: Self-published, 1978.

Wukovits, John F. *Dogfight over Tokyo: The Final Air Battle of the Pacific and the Last Four Men to Die in World War II.* New York, NY: Da Capo Press, 2019.

Wynne, Carswell. Interviewed by author. 2018.

Y'Blood, William T. *The Little Giants: U.S. Escort Carriers Against Japan.* Annapolis, MD: Naval Institute Press, 1987.

———— *Red Sun Setting: The Battle of the Philippine Sea.* Annapolis, MD: Naval Institute Press, 1981.

Zdon, Al. "First to Set Foot in Japan." *Minnesota American Legion and Auxiliary* 96, no. 10 (2014).

Ziesing, Hibben. *History of Fighting Squadron Forty-Six: A Log in Narrative Form of Its Participation in World War 2.* New York: Plantin Press, 1946.

Notes

Introduction
1. USS *Cowpens, Mighty Moo Rides Again*, 1.
2. J.C.H., *Nine out of Fifty*, 1–2.

Chapter 1. Origins: The Stopgap Sisters
1. Lambert and Labudde, *USS* Independence *CVL-22*, 3.
2. Craig, *Ace Pilot*, 31.
3. Buell, *Master of Sea Power*, 244.
4. Cowpens Bicentennial Committee, *History of Cowpens*, ix.
5. Wukovits, *Dogfight over Tokyo*, 76.

Chapter 2. The Moo's Veteran Officers: McConnell and Price
1. D. M. Johnson, interview.
2. Messimer, *Pawns of War*, 132.
3. Commander, US Naval Forces Southwest Pacific, "Operations, Action, and Sinking of USS *Langley*."
4. Toll, *Conquering Tide*, 10.
5. Toll, *Pacific Crucible*, 167.
6. D. M. Johnson, interview.
7. Price, Papers.
8. Price, Papers.
9. Price, Papers.
10. Price, Papers.
11. Price, Papers.
12. C. Smith, *Singapore Burning*, 264.
13. Toll, *Pacific Crucible*, 248.

Chapter 3. The *Cowpens* Crew
1. Terrell, *Semper Fi*.
2. Sommers, *Combat Carriers*, 45.

3. USS *Belleau Wood, Flight Quarters*, 17.

4. *Cowpens* Reunion Association, "Memories of Typhoon Cobra."

5. Sommers, *Combat Carriers*, 12.

6. Kehn, *Highest Degree Tragic*, 10.

7. Kuntz, interview.

8. Daly, *World War 2 Diary.*

9. Daly, *World War 2 Diary.*

10. Terrell, *Semper Fi*, 6.

11. Terrell, *Semper Fi*, 6–7.

12. Zdon, "First to Set Foot in Japan," 9.

13. Terrell, *Semper Fi*, 9.

14. Terrell, *Semper Fi*, 10.

15. Connell and Mack, *Naval Ceremonies*, 181.

16. Miller, *Messman Chronicles*, 120.

17. Willie Thomas, interview.

18. Terrell, *Semper Fi*, 76.

19. Terrell, *Semper Fi*, 77.

Chapter 4. Air Group 25

1. Craig, *Ace Pilot*, 55.

2. Wright, *United States Navy*, 13.

3. Remember When Videos, *World War II.*

4. Ayers, interview.

5. Ingraham, interview.

6. Haley, *From Yellow Perils*, iii.

7. Haley, *From Yellow Perils*, 2.

8. Haley, *From Yellow Perils*, 2.

9. Gadbois, *Hellcat Tales*, 17.

10. Haley, *From Yellow Perils*, 4.

11. Haley, *From Yellow Perils*, 6.

12. Remember When Videos, *World War II.*

13. Remember When Videos, *World War II.*

14. Remember When Videos, *World War II.*

15. Kilduff, *US Carriers at War*, 64.

16. Kilduff, *US Carriers at War*, 64.

17. Haley, interview.

18. Haley, interview.

19. Tillman, *Hellcat*, 58.

20. Bergerud, *Fire in the Sky*, 296.

21. Remember When Videos, *World War II.*

22. Wright, *United States Navy*, 21.
23. A. Bowers, Wartime Letters.
24. A. Bowers, Wartime Letters.
25. A. Bowers, Wartime Letters.
26. A. Bowers, Wartime Letters.
27. A. Bowers, Wartime Letters.
28. A. Bowers, Wartime Letters.

Chapter 5. *Cowpens* Takes Her First Steps Toward the War

1. Ships' Histories Branch Office of Naval Records and History, *History of USS Cowpens*, 1.
2. Sommers, *Combat Carriers*, 56.
3. Sommers, *Combat Carriers*, 50.
4. Ingraham, interview.
5. Todd, interview.
6. M. James, *Adventures of M. James*.
7. Martinich, interview.
8. Daly, *World War 2 Diary*.
9. Daly, *World War 2 Diary*.
10. M. James, *Adventures of M. James*, 4.
11. Daly, *World War 2 Diary*.
12. Ingraham, *March of the Microbes*, 105.
13. Wynne, interview.
14. "Our Executive Officer."
15. Price, Papers.
16. Haley, interview.
17. A. Bowers, Wartime Letters.
18. Pahl, *Point Option*, 97.
19. Price, Papers.
20. Price, Papers.
21. A. Bowers, Wartime Letters.
22. Hone and Hone, *Battle Line*, 94.
23. Halsey, "CVLs' Success Story," 138.
24. Wright, *United States Navy*, 17.
25. Wooldridge, *Carrier Warfare in the Pacific*, 189.
26. Price, Papers.
27. Price, Papers.
28. Sommers, *Combat Carriers*, 54–55.
29. Office of Naval Records and History, *History of USS Cowpens*, 1.
30. Terrell, *Semper Fi*, 51.

31. National Military Personnel Records Center, Personnel Records of Robert McConnell.

32. Price, Papers.

Chapter 6. Hawaii

1. Terrell, *Semper Fi*, 59.
2. Bailey and Farber, *First Strange Place*, 40.
3. Toll, *Conquering Tide*, 293.
4. Sommers, *Combat Carriers*, 65.
5. Toll, *Conquering Tide*, 292.
6. Bailey and Farber, *First Strange Place*, 43–44.
7. Bailey and Farber, *First Strange Place*, 24.
8. Lee, *Record of the USS* Cowpens.
9. Toll, *Conquering Tide*, 293.
10. Daly, *World War 2 Diary*.
11. Mason, *Battleship Sailor*, 23.
12. Borneman, *Admirals*, 146.

Chapter 7. A Dress Rehearsal at Wake Island

1. Price, Papers.
2. Price, Papers.
3. Ewing and Lundstrom, *Fateful Rendezvous*, 188.
4. Boomhower, *Fighter Pilot*, 54.
5. Pahl, *Point Option*, 79–80.

Chapter 8. *Cowpens'* Baptism by Fire at Wake

1. Fighting Squadron 25, *History of Fighting Squadron 25*, 5.
2. Pahl, *Point Option*, 80.
3. A. Bowers, Wartime Letters.
4. Bergerud, *Fire in the Sky*, 358.
5. Bergerud, *Fire in the Sky*, 358.
6. Bergerud, *Fire in the Sky*, 369.
7. Bergerud, *Fire in the Sky*, 369.
8. Daly, *World War 2 Diary*.
9. Pahl, *Point Option*, 85.
10. A. Bowers, Wartime Letters.
11. A. Bowers, Wartime Letters.
12. A. Bowers, Wartime Letters.
13. A. Bowers, Wartime Letters.
14. Lockwood and Adamson, *Zoomies, Subs, and Zeros*, 25.

15. Lockwood and Adamson, *Zoomies, Subs, and Zeros*, 29–30.
16. Lockwood, *Sink 'Em All*, 104.
17. Fighting Squadron 25, *History of Fighting Squadron 25*, 25.
18. Fighting Squadron 25, *History of Fighting Squadron 25*, 25.
19. Price, Papers.
20. Price, Papers.
21. Price, Papers.
22. National Military Personnel Records Center, Personnel Records of Robert McConnell.
23. National Military Personnel Records Center, Personnel Records of Robert McConnell.

Chapter 9. Back to Pearl: The *Cowpens* Jinx Strikes Again

1. Price, Papers.
2. Price, Papers.
3. Price, Papers.
4. Price, Papers.
5. Lee, *Record of the USS* Cowpens, 4.
6. Terrell, *Semper Fi*, 68.
7. USS *Cowpens*, USS Cowpens *(CVL-25)—Ramming of by USS* Abbot.
8. Terrell, *Semper Fi*, 68.
9. Lee, *Record of the USS* Cowpens, 4.
10. Sommers, *Combat Carriers*, 81.

Chapter 10. GALVANIC and FLINTLOCK: The Marshall and Gilbert Islands Campaigns

1. Price, Papers.
2. Price, Papers.
3. Pahl, *Point Option*, 97.
4. Daly, *World War 2 Diary*.
5. Fighting Squadron 25, *History of Fighting Squadron 25*, 6.
6. Sommers, *Combat Carriers*, 85.
7. Reynolds, *On the Warpath*, 289.
8. Daly, *World War 2 Diary*.
9. Terrell, *Semper Fi*, 73–74.
10. Terrell, *Semper Fi*, 73–74.
11. Lee, *Record of the USS* Cowpens, 5.
12. McIntyre, *Wartime Journal*.
13. Morison, *History of United States Naval Operations*, vol. 7, 195–96.
14. Sommers, *Combat Carriers*, 85.

15. Morison, *History of United States Naval Operations*, vol. 7, 196.
16. Lee, *Record of the USS* Cowpens, 5.
17. Connell and Mack, *Naval Ceremonies*, 72.
18. Sommers, *Combat Carriers*, 73.
19. National Military Personnel Records Center, Personnel Records of Robert McConnell.
20. Price, Papers.

Chapter 11. Passing the Hours
1. Haley, *From Yellow Perils*, 32.
2. J.C.H., *Nine out of Fifty*, 5.
3. Applebaum, "Publishers."
4. Price, Papers.
5. Price, Papers.
6. Price, Papers.
7. Handran, Papers.
8. *History of the Chaplain Corps*, vol. 6.
9. Handran, Papers.
10. Handran, Papers.
11. Daly, *World War 2 Diary*.
12. J.C.H., *Nine out of Fifty*, 15–16.
13. Sommers, *Combat Carriers*, 123.
14. "Hundred Years Dry."
15. Sommers, *Combat Carriers*, 110.
16. Haley, *From Yellow Perils*, 34.
17. Hammond, *Treaty Navy*, 119.
18. Ingraham, interview.
19. Hornfischer, *Last Stand*, 91.
20. Riley, interview.
21. Ziesing, *History of Fighting Squadron Forty-Six*, 2.
22. J.C.H., *Nine out of Fifty*, 15.
23. "Kerr's Comments."
24. Lee, *Record of the USS* Cowpens, 6.
25. Price, Papers.
26. Price, Papers.
27. Bergerud, *Fire in the Sky*, 403.
28. "Aroma."
29. Martinich, interview.
30. Haley, *From Yellow Perils*, 30.
31. Kilduff, *US Carriers at War*, 66.

32. Price, Papers.
33. McIntyre, *Wartime Journal*, 11–12.
34. Haley, *From Yellow Perils*, 33.
35. Haley, *From Yellow Perils*, 34.
36. Fighting Squadron 25, *History of Fighting Squadron 25*, 7.
37. Price, Papers.

Chapter 12. Strikes in the Marshall Islands

1. USS *Cowpens, Mighty Moo: The Story*, 8.
2. Tillman, *Clash of the Carriers*, 18.
3. Melton, *Sea Cobra*, 33.
4. Taylor, *Magnificent Mitscher*, 201.
5. Taylor, *Magnificent Mitscher*, 178.
6. Fighting Squadron 25, *History of Fighting Squadron 25*, 8.
7. Price, Papers.
8. Daly, *World War 2 Diary*.
9. Daly, *World War 2 Diary*.
10. Price, Papers.
11. Terrell, *Semper Fi*, 94.
12. Terrell, *Semper Fi*, 105.
13. Sommers, *Combat Carriers*, 103.
14. Terrell, *Semper Fi*, 95.
15. Lee, *Record of the USS* Cowpens, 7.
16. Price, Papers.
17. Daly, *World War 2 Diary*.
18. Fighting Squadron 25, *History of Fighting Squadron 25*, 8.
19. Haley, *From Yellow Perils*, 39.
20. Fighting Squadron 25, *History of Fighting Squadron 25*, 8.
21. Fighting Squadron 25, *History of Fighting Squadron 25*.
22. Haley, *From Yellow Perils*, 39.
23. Haley, *From Yellow Perils*, 40.
24. Fighting Squadron 25, *History of Fighting Squadron 25*, 8.
25. Haley, *From Yellow Perils*, 41.
26. McIntyre, *Wartime Journal*, 15.
27. Sherman, *Combat Command*, 226.
28. Price, Papers.
29. Tillman, *Clash of the Carriers*, 16.
30. Terrell, *Semper Fi*, 75.
31. McIntyre, *Wartime Journal*, 18.
32. Haley, *From Yellow Perils*, 44.

Chapter 13. Truk: Operation HAILSTONE

1. Taylor, *Magnificent Mitscher*, 181.
2. Morison, *History of United States Naval Operations*, vol. 7, 317.
3. USS *Cowpens, Mighty Moo: The Story*, 9.
4. Haley, *From Yellow Perils*, 44.
5. Pahl, "Interview with Herschel Pahl."
6. Fighting Squadron 25, *History of Fighting Squadron 25*, 10.
7. Fighting Squadron 25, *History of Fighting Squadron 25*, 10.
8. Fighting Squadron 25, *History of Fighting Squadron 25*, 10.
9. Daly, *World War 2 Diary*.
10. Lee, *Record of the USS* Cowpens, 8.
11. Williams, interview.
12. Williams, interview.
13. Williams, interview.

Chapter 14. "We'll Fight Our Way In!"

1. Fighting Squadron 25, *History of Fighting Squadron 25*, 11.
2. Fighting Squadron 25, *History of Fighting Squadron 25*, 11.
3. Taylor, *Magnificent Mitscher*, 186.
4. Fighting Squadron 25, A *History of Fighting Squadron 25*, 11.
5. Fighting Squadron 25, *History of Fighting Squadron 25*, 11.
6. Fighting Squadron 25, *History of Fighting Squadron 25*, 11.
7. Fighting Squadron 25, *History of Fighting Squadron 25*, 12.
8. McIntyre, *Wartime Journal*, 25.
9. Fighting Squadron 25, *History of Fighting Squadron 25*, 12–13.
10. Price, Papers.
11. Price, Papers.
12. Price, Papers.
13. Klieger, *Fleischmann Yeast Family*, 88.
14. Fighting Squadron 25, *History of Fighting Squadron 25*, 13.
15. Haley, *From Yellow Perils*, 46.
16. Price, Papers.

Chapter 15. Palau, Hollandia, and Truk

1. Price, Papers.
2. Fighting Squadron 25, *History of Fighting Squadron 25*, 13.
3. Tillman, *Whirlwind*, 191–92.
4. Fighting Squadron 25, *History of Fighting Squadron 25*, 13–14.
5. Price, Papers.

6. Lee, *Record of the USS* Cowpens, 11.

7. Terrell, *Semper Fi*, 79.

8. Price, Papers.

9. Winston, *Fighting Squadron*, 123.

10. USS *Cowpens, Report of Action for the Period 21 April 1944 to 28 April 1944*, 59.

11. Haley, *From Yellow Perils*, 51.

12. Haley, *From Yellow Perils*, 51.

13. Daly, *World War 2 Diary*.

14. Fighting Squadron 25, *History of Fighting Squadron 25*, 15.

15. Haley, *From Yellow Perils*, 46. Ed believed this incident occurred in February.

16. Price, Papers.

17. Fighting Squadron 25, *History of Fighting Squadron 25*, 16.

18. Fighting Squadron 25, *History of Fighting Squadron 25*, 16.

19. Wright, *United States Navy*, 43.

20. Haley, *From Yellow Perils*, 45. Haley misattributed his experiences on the second Truk raid to the first attack in February.

21. Haley, *From Yellow Perils*, 45.

22. Fighting Squadron 25, *History of Fighting Squadron 25*, 16.

23. USS *Cowpens, Report of Action for the Period 29 April 1944 to 1 May 1944*, 1.

24. Haley, *From Yellow Perils*, 53.

25. Haley, *From Yellow Perils*, 53.

26. Price, Papers.

27. Price, Papers.

28. Price, Papers.

29. United States Naval Academy, *Lucky Bag*.

30. Price, Papers.

31. McIntyre, *Wartime Journal*.

32. Daly, *World War 2 Diary*.

33. Price, Papers.

Chapter 16. Operation FORAGER: The Invasion of the Marianas

1. Fighting Squadron 25, *History of Fighting Squadron 25*, 17.

2. Haley, interview.

3. Fighting Squadron 25, *History of Fighting Squadron 25*, 17.

4. Price, Papers.

5. Sommers, *Combat Carriers*, 100.

6. Sommers, *Combat Carriers*, 100.

7. Haley, *From Yellow Perils*, 50.

8. Haley, *From Yellow Perils*, 55.

9. Haley, interview.

10. Price, Papers.
11. Price, Papers.
12. Price, Papers.
13. Price, Papers.
14. Reynolds, *On the Warpath*, 348.
15. Fighting Squadron 25, *History of Fighting Squadron 25*, 17.
16. Tillman, *Clash of the Carriers*, 78.
17. Fighting Squadron 25, *History of Fighting Squadron 25*, 18.
18. Daly, *World War 2 Diary*.
19. USS *Cowpens, Mighty Moo: The Story*, 12.
20. Tillman, *Clash of the Carriers*, 100.
21. Tillman, *Clash of the Carriers*, 77.
22. Air Group 22, *Aircraft Action Reports for the Period of 2 October 1944 to 1400 on 15 October 1944*, 11.
23. Toll, *Conquering Tide*, 477.
24. Hammel, *Aces Against Japan*, 197.
25. Hammel, *Aces Against Japan*, 197.
26. Y'Blood, *Red Sun Setting*, 104.
27. Haley, *From Yellow Perils*, 56.
28. Hammel, *Aces Against Japan*, 197.
29. Fighting Squadron 25, *History of Fighting Squadron 25*, 18.
30. Kilduff, *US Carriers at War*, 70.
31. Kilduff, *US Carriers at War*, 71.
32. Kilduff, *US Carriers at War*, 71.
33. Air Group 25, *Aircraft Action Reports for the Period 11 June–3 July 1944*, 42.
34. Hammel, *Aces Against Japan*, 198.
35. Haley, *From Yellow Perils*, 57.
36. Haley, *From Yellow Perils*, 57.
37. Haley, *From Yellow Perils*, 57.
38. Haley, *From Yellow Perils*, 57.
39. Haley, *From Yellow Perils*, 57.
40. Fighting Squadron 25, *History of Fighting Squadron 25*, 18.
41. Tillman, *Clash of the Carriers*, 196.
42. Fighting Squadron 25, *History of Fighting Squadron 25*, 18.
43. Air Group 25, *Aircraft Action Reports for the Period 11 June–3 July 1944*, 44.
44. Daly, *World War 2 Diary*.

Chapter 17. Left Behind

1. Fighting Squadron 25, *History of Fighting Squadron 25*, 18.
2. "Hope Keeps You Alive."

3. Price, Papers.

4. Fighting Squadron 25, "Narrative of Events," 4.

5. Fighting Squadron 25, "Narrative of Events," 5.

6. Fighting Squadron 25, "Narrative of Events."

7. Price, Papers.

8. Fighting Squadron 25, *History of Fighting Squadron 25*, 18.

9. USS *Cowpens, Report of Actions During the Period 6 June 1944 to 6 July 1944*, 56.

10. Fighting Squadron 25, *History of Fighting Squadron 25*, 18.

11. Fighting Squadron 25, *History of Fighting Squadron 25*, 19.

12. Fighting Squadron 25, *History of Fighting Squadron 25*, 19.

13. Price, Papers.

14. Price, Papers.

15. Fighting Squadron 25, *History of Fighting Squadron 25*, 19.

16. Price, Papers.

17. Price, Papers.

18. Haley, *From Yellow Perils*, 59.

Chapter 18. The Recapture of the Philippines

1. Remember When Videos, *World War II*.

2. Craig, *Ace Pilot*, 11.

3. Craig, *Ace Pilot*, 133.

4. Craig, *Ace Pilot*, 133.

5. Craig, *Ace Pilot*, 133.

6. Drury and Clavin, *Halsey's Typhoon*, 14.

7. Toll, *Pacific Crucible*, 201.

8. Thomas, *Sea of Thunder*, 1.

9. Toll, *Conquering Tide*, 159.

10. Borneman, *Admirals*, 473.

11. Craig, *Ace Pilot*, 136.

12. Craig, *Ace Pilot*, 136.

13. Craig, *Ace Pilot*, 136–37.

14. Craig, *Ace Pilot*, 138.

15. Craig, *Ace Pilot*, 139.

Chapter 19. Lackluster Strikes in Palau: Captain Taylor's Decision

1. Air Group 22, *Aircraft Action Reports for the Period of 7 September to 24 September 1944*, 104.

2. Air Group 22, *Aircraft Action Reports for the Period of 7 September to 24 September 1944*, 2.

3. Air Group 22, *Aircraft Action Reports for the Period of 7 September to 24 September 1944*, 2–3.

4. Air Group 22, *Aircraft Action Reports for the Period of 7 September to 24 September 1944*, 172.

5. Craig, *Ace Pilot*, 153.

6. Price, Papers.

7. Torpedo Squadron 22, *History of Torpedo Squadron 22 from Commissioning Through 31 December 1944*, 18.

8. Craig, *Ace Pilot*, 143.

9. Torpedo Squadron 22, *History of Torpedo Squadron 22 from Commissioning Through 31 December 1944*, 13.

10. Prados, *Storm over Leyte*, 83.

11. Craig, *Ace Pilot*, 148.

12. Goodman, "Memories of 50 Years," 8.

13. Goodman, "Memories of 50 Years," 8.

14. Goodman, "Memories of 50 Years," 8.

15. Daly, *World War 2 Diary*.

16. Craig, *Ace Pilot*, 151.

17. Torpedo Squadron 22, *History of Torpedo Squadron 22 from Commissioning Through 31 December 1944*, 20.

18. Craig, *Ace Pilot*, 152.

Chapter 20. Operation KING II: The Buildup for Leyte Gulf

1. Craig, *Ace Pilot*, 153.

2. Craig, *Ace Pilot*, 153.

3. Craig, *Ace Pilot*, 153.

4. Craig, *Ace Pilot*, 154.

5. Craig, *Ace Pilot*, 153.

6. Craig, *Ace Pilot*, 154.

7. Craig, *Ace Pilot*, 154.

8. Sommers, *Combat Carriers*, 117.

9. Goodman, "Memories of 50 Years," 8.

10. Goodman, "Memories of 50 Years," 8–9.

11. Daly, *World War 2 Diary*.

12. Sommers, *Combat Carriers*, 117.

13. Craig, *Ace Pilot*, 154.

14. Remember When Videos, *World War II*. Soule described this as the December typhoon, but the fact pattern fits the October storm.

15. Remember When Videos, *World War II*.

16. Remember When Videos, *World War II*. Soule thought the officer who had called was Admiral Halsey, but he was on the battleship *New Jersey*. Task Force commander Adm. Slew McCain had his flag on *Hornet*. So this was probably the ship's captain, O. A. Weller.
17. Craig, *Ace Pilot*, 154.
18. Craig, *Ace Pilot*, 154.
19. Craig, *Ace Pilot*, 154.
20. Craig, *Ace Pilot*, 155.

Chapter 21. Raid on Formosa: The Moo Rides Herd on *Houston* and *Canberra*

1. Morison, *History of United States Naval Operations*, vol. 12, 95.
2. Stafford, *Big E*, 437.
3. Goodman, "Memories of 50 Years," 9.
4. Hall of Valor Project, "Thomas H. Jenkins."
5. Goodman, "Memories of 50 Years," 10.
6. Craig, *Ace Pilot*, 159.
7. Prados, *Storm over Leyte*, 142.
8. Craig, *Ace Pilot*, 163.
9. Freuer, "Saving the Torpedoed Cruiser *Houston*."
10. USS *Cowpens, Anti-Aircraft Action*.
11. Goodman, "Memories of 50 Years," 10.
12. Toll, *Twilight of the Gods*, 171.
13. Morison, *History of United States Naval Operations*, vol. 12, 103.
14. USS *Cowpens, Mighty Moo: The Story*, 16.
15. Craig, *Ace Pilot*, 171–72.
16. USS *Cowpens, Mighty Moo: The Story*, 16.
17. USS *Cowpens, Report of Actions During the Period 1400, 15 October 1944 to 2230, 17 October 1944*, 14.
18. Air Group 22, *Aircraft Action Reports for the Period of 1400 on 15 October 1944 to 2230 on 17 October 1944*, 7.
19. Craig, *Ace Pilot*, 176.
20. Morison, *History of United States Naval Operations*, vol. 12, 103.
21. Craig, *Ace Pilot*, 176.
22. Craig, *Ace Pilot*, 176.
23. Craig, *Ace Pilot*, 175.
24. Craig, *Ace Pilot*, 175.
25. Daly, *World War 2 Diary*.

Chapter 22. The Battle of Leyte Gulf

1. Hastings, *Retribution*, 157.
2. Goodman, "Oral History."
3. Goodman, "Memories of 50 Years," 12.
4. Goodman, "Memories of 50 Years," 12.
5. Goodman, "Oral History."
6. Goodman, "Memories of 50 Years," 12.
7. Goodman, "Oral History."
8. Goodman, "Memories of 50 Years," 12–13.
9. USS *Cowpens*, "History," II-16.
10. Craig, *Ace Pilot*, 198.
11. Craig, *Ace Pilot*, 199.
12. Craig, *Ace Pilot*, 199–200.
13. Hall of Valor Project, "Thomas H. Jenkins."
14. Hall of Valor Project, "Herbert Watson Taylor."
15. Drury and Clavin, *Halsey's Typhoon*, 56.
16. Craig, *Ace Pilot*, 136.
17. Craig, *Ace Pilot*, 200.
18. Price, Papers.
19. Price, Papers.
20. Price, Papers.

Chapter 23. Black November

1. Toll, *Twilight of the Gods*, 364.
2. Craig, *Ace Pilot*, 201.
3. USS *Cowpens, Narrative Account of the Activities of the USS Cowpens Covering Period from 2 November 1944 to 24 November 1944*, 2.
4. Craig, *Ace Pilot*, 202.
5. Craig, *Ace Pilot*, 202.
6. USS *Cowpens, Narrative Account of the Activities of the USS Cowpens Covering Period from 2 November 1944 to 24 November 1944*, 2.
7. USS *Cowpens, Report of Actions During the Period 2 November 1944 to 7 November 1944*, 2.
8. Goodman, "Memories of 50 Years," 13.
9. Craig, *Ace Pilot*, 203.
10. USS *Cowpens, Narrative Account of the Activities of the USS Cowpens Covering Period from 2 November 1944 to 24 November 1944*, 2.
11. Rellis, *50th Anniversary*.
12. Rellis, *50th Anniversary*, 3.
13. "Navy Pilot Tells of Evading Japs."

14. Goodman, "Memories of 50 Years," 14.

15. USS *Cowpens, Narrative Account of the Activities of the USS Cowpens Covering Period from 2 November 1944 to 24 November 1944*, 3.

16. USS *Cowpens, Report of Actions During the Period 2 November 1944 to 7 November 1944*, 18.

17. Lockwood, *Sink 'Em All*, 251.

18. Price, Papers.

19. Price, Papers.

20. Craig, *Ace Pilot: The Biography of Clement M. Craig*, 204.

21. USS *Cowpens, Report of Actions During the Period 2 November 1944 to 7 November 1944*, 18.

22. National Military Personnel Records Center, Personnel Records of Herbert Watson Taylor (1945).

23. Craig, *Ace Pilot*, 206.

24. Morison, *History of United States Naval Operations*, vol. 12, 360.

25. Toll, *Twilight of the Gods*, 378.

26. Daly, *World War 2 Diary*.

27. Craig, *Ace Pilot*, 206.

28. Craig, *Ace Pilot*, 206.

29. Price, Papers.

30. Craig, *Ace Pilot*, 207.

31. Price, Papers.

32. Price, Papers.

Chapter 24. The Mighty Moo Faces Typhoon Cobra

1. USS *Cowpens, Mighty Moo: The Story*, 18.

2. Craig, *Ace Pilot*, 208.

3. USS *Cowpens, Report of Actions During the Period 10 December 1944 to 16 December 1944*, 20.

4. Adamson and Kosco, *Halsey's Typhoons*, 11.

5. Adamson and Kosco, *Halsey's Typhoons*, 31–32.

6. USS *Cowpens, Daily War Diary*.

7. *Cowpens* Reunion Association, USS Cowpens' Veterans Memories of Typhoon Cobra.

8. Adamson and Kosco, *Halsey's Typhoons*, 73; Commander in Chief, Pacific Fleet, *Court of Inquiry*.

9. USS *Cowpens, Narrative Account of the Activities of USS* Cowpens *Covering Period from 10 December 1944 to 20 December 1944*, 1.

10. USS *Cowpens, Narrative Account of the Activities of USS* Cowpens *Covering Period from 10 December 1944 to 20 December 1944*, 1–2.

11. Commander in Chief, Pacific Fleet, *Court of Inquiry*.

12. USS *Cowpens, Narrative Account of the Activities of USS* Cowpens *Covering Period from 10 December 1944 to 20 December 1944*, 10.

13. Price, Papers.

14. *Cowpens* Reunion Association, USS Cowpens' Veterans Memories of Typhoon Cobra.

15. USS *Cowpens, Narrative Account of the Activities of USS* Cowpens *Covering Period from 10 December 1944 to 20 December 1944*, 10.

16. USS *Cowpens, Narrative Account of the Activities of USS* Cowpens *Covering Period from 10 December 1944 to 20 December 1944*, 2.

17. USS *Cowpens, Narrative Account of the Activities of USS* Cowpens *Covering Period from 10 December 1944 to 20 December 1944*, 2.

18. Daly, *World War 2 Diary*.

19. USS *Cowpens, Narrative Account of the Activities of USS* Cowpens *Covering Period from 10 December 1944 to 20 December 1944*, 4.

20. Todd, interview.

21. USS *Cowpens, Mighty Moo: The Story*, II-19.

22. USS *Cowpens, Narrative Account of the Activities of USS* Cowpens *Covering Period from 10 December 1944 to 20 December 1944*, 5.

23. USS *Cowpens, Narrative Account of the Activities of USS* Cowpens *Covering Period from 10 December 1944 to 20 December 1944*, 5.

24. *Cowpens* Reunion Association, USS Cowpens' Veterans Memories of Typhoon Cobra.

25. Adamson and Kosco, *Halsey's Typhoons*, 72.

26. Adamson and Kosco, *Halsey's Typhoons*, 12; Melton, *Sea Cobra*, 53.

27. Adamson and Kosco, *Halsey's Typhoons*, 71.

28. USS *Cowpens, Narrative Account of the Activities of USS* Cowpens *Covering Period from 10 December 1944 to 20 December 1944*, 4.

29. Adamson and Kosco, *Halsey's Typhoons*, 72.

30. Adamson and Kosco, *Halsey's Typhoons*, 72.

31. USS *Cowpens, Narrative Account of the Activities of USS* Cowpens *Covering Period from 10 December 1944 to 20 December 1944*, 6–7.

32. USS *Cowpens, Narrative Account of the Activities of USS* Cowpens *Covering Period from 10 December 1944 to 20 December 1944*, 3.

33. *Cowpens* Reunion Association, USS Cowpens' Veterans Memories of Typhoon Cobra.

34. *Cowpens* Reunion Association, USS Cowpens' Veterans Memories of Typhoon Cobra.

35. Morison, *History of United States Naval Operations*, vol. 13, 68.

36. USS *Cowpens, Narrative Account of the Activities of USS* Cowpens *Covering Period from 10 December 1944 to 20 December 1944*, 10.

37. USS *Cowpens, Narrative Account of the Activities of USS* Cowpens *Covering Period from 10 December 1944 to 20 December 1944*, 9.

38. USS *Cowpens, Narrative Account of the Activities of USS* Cowpens *Covering Period from 10 December 1944 to 20 December 1944*, 10.

39. USS *Cowpens, Narrative Account of the Activities of USS* Cowpens *Covering Period from 10 December 1944 to 20 December 1944*, 10.

40. Adamson and Kosco, *Halsey's Typhoons*, 73.

41. Adamson and Kosco, *Halsey's Typhoons*, 73.

42. Morison, *History of United States Naval Operations*, vol. 13, 68.

43. Adamson and Kosco, *Halsey's Typhoons*, 73.

44. USS *Cowpens, Narrative Account of the Activities of USS* Cowpens *Covering Period from 10 December 1944 to 20 December 1944*, 9.

45. Price, Papers.

46. USS *Cowpens, Report of Storm Damage*, 4.

47. USS *Cowpens, Daily War Diary*.

48. Adamson and Kosco, *Halsey's Typhoons*, 10.

49. Price, Papers.

50. Price, Papers.

51. Price, Papers.

52. Price, Papers.

Chapter 25. Luzon and the South China Sea: A Deplorable Situation

1. Craig, *Ace Pilot*, 216.

2. Craig, *Ace Pilot*, 216.

3. Craig, *Ace Pilot*, 216.

4. Craig, *Ace Pilot*, 216–217.

5. Craig, *Ace Pilot*, 216–217.

6. Craig, *Ace Pilot*, 216.

7. Craig, *Ace Pilot*, 217.

8. USS *Cowpens, Mighty Moo Reviews the Month of January 1945*, 1.

9. USS *Cowpens, Mighty Moo Reviews the Month of January 1945*, 1.

10. Carr, *Goose on the Loose*, 28.

11. Carr, *Goose on the Loose*, 28.

12. Daly, *World War 2 Diary*.

13. Craig, *Ace Pilot*, 218.

14. Craig, *Ace Pilot*, 218.

15. Craig, *Ace Pilot*, 220.

16. USS *Cowpens, Mighty Moo Reviews the Month of January 1945*, 1

17. Sherman, *Combat Command*, 325.

18. USS *Cowpens, Mighty Moo Reviews the Month of January 1945*, 3.

19. Craig, *Ace Pilot*, 221.
20. USS *Cowpens*, *Mighty Moo Reviews the Month of January 1945*, 3.
21. Torpedo Squadron 22, *History of Torpedo Squadron 22 from Commissioning Through 31 December 1944*.

Chapter 26. Operation GRATITUDE: Into the South China Sea

1. USS *Cowpens*, *Mighty Moo Reviews the Month of January 1945*, 4.
2. USS *Cowpens*, *Mighty Moo Reviews the Month of January 1945*, 4.
3. USS *Cowpens*, *Mighty Moo Reviews the Month of January 1945*, 4.
4. USS *Cowpens*, *Mighty Moo Reviews the Month of January 1945*, 4.
5. Daly, *World War 2 Diary*.
6. USS *Cowpens*, *Aircraft Action Reports for the Period of 1 January 1945 Through 22 January 1945*, 115.
7. USS *Cowpens*, *Mighty Moo Reviews the Month of January 1945*, 6.
8. USS *Cowpens*, *Aircraft Action Reports for the Period of 1 January 1945 Through 22 January 1945*, 115.
9. USS *Cowpens*, *Mighty Moo Reviews the Month of January 1945*, 7.
10. USS *Cowpens*, *Mighty Moo Reviews the Month of January 1945*, 8.
11. USS *Cowpens*, *Mighty Moo Reviews the Month of January 1945*, 8.
12. USS *Cowpens*, *Mighty Moo Reviews the Month of January 1945*, 8.
13. USS Cowpens, The Mighty Moo Reviews the Month of January 1945, 8.
14. USS *Cowpens*, *Mighty Moo Reviews the Month of January 1945*, 8–9.
15. USS *Cowpens*, *Mighty Moo Reviews the Month of January 1945*, 9.
16. USS *Cowpens*, *Mighty Moo Reviews the Month of January 1945*, 9.
17. USS *Cowpens*, *Aircraft Action Reports for the Period of 1 January 1945 Through 22 January 1945*.
18. USS *Cowpens*, *Mighty Moo Reviews the Month of January 1945*, 9.
19. USS *Cowpens*, *Aircraft Action Reports for the Period of 1 January 1945 Through 22 January 1945*, 79.
20. Craig, *Ace Pilot*, 233.
21. Hall of Valor Project, "Clement Melvin Craig."
22. Torpedo Squadron 22, *History of Torpedo Squadron 22 from Commissioning Through 31 December 1944*, 21.

Chapter 27. Air Group 46 and the Iwo Jima Campaign

1. Ziesing, *History of Fighting Squadron Forty-Six*, 8.
2. USS *Cowpens*, *Mighty Moo Rides Again*, 1.
3. Daly, *World War 2 Diary*.
4. USS *Cowpens*, *Mighty Moo Rides Again*, 2.

5. Ziesing, *History of Fighting Squadron Forty-Six*, 10.

6. Ziesing, *History of Fighting Squadron Forty-Six*, 10.

7. Ziesing, *History of Fighting Squadron Forty-Six*, 10.

8. Morison, *History of United States Naval Operations*, vol. 14, 22.

9. Ziesing, *History of Fighting Squadron Forty-Six*, 10.

10. Ziesing, *History of Fighting Squadron Forty-Six*, 11.

11. USS *Cowpens*, *Mighty Moo Rides Again*, 6.

12. Ziesing, *History of Fighting Squadron Forty-Six*, 11.

13. Ziesing, *History of Fighting Squadron Forty-Six*, 11.

Chapter 28. Operation DETACHMENT: Iwo Jima

1. Ziesing, *History of Fighting Squadron Forty-Six*, 12.

2. USS *Cowpens*, *Mighty Moo Rides Again*, 5.

Chapter 29. A Gallant Lady, Homebound at Last

1. USS *Cowpens*, *Mighty Moo Rides Again*, 8.

2. USS *Cowpens*, *Mighty Moo Rides Again*, 8.

3. USS *Cowpens*, *Mighty Moo Rides Again*, 8.

4. Ziesing, *History of Fighting Squadron Forty-Six*, 14.

5. USS *Cowpens*, *Mighty Moo Rides Again*, 9.

6. USS *Cowpens*, *Mighty Moo Rides Again*, 9.

7. Handran, Papers.

8. Daly, *World War 2 Diary*.

9. Daly, *World War 2 Diary*.

10. USS *Cowpens*, *Daily War Diary*.

11. USS *Cowpens*, *Daily War Diary*.

12. J.C.H., *Nine out of Fifty*, 26.

13. US Naval Institute, *Reminscences of Rear Admiral Kent Melhorn*, 78.

14. US Naval Institute, *Reminscences of Rear Admiral Kent Melhorn*, 117.

15. US Naval Institute, *Reminscences of Rear Admiral Kent Melhorn*, 120.

16. Nordgren, interview.

17. Nordgren, interview.

18. J.C.H., *Nine out of Fifty*, 2.

Chapter 30. The Fleet That Came to Stay

1. Reynolds, *Fast Carriers*, 354.

2. J.C.H., *Nine out of Fifty*, 7.

3. J.C.H., *Nine out of Fifty*, 7.

4. USS *Cowpens*, *Daily War Diary*.

5. J.C.H., *Nine out of Fifty*, 2.

6. J.C.H., *Nine out of Fifty*, 10.

7. USS *Cowpens, Daily War Diary.*

8. J.C.H., *Nine out of Fifty*, 11.

9. Mahoney, *Setting the Rising Sun*, 40.

10. Martinich, *Wartime Diary.*

11. Hornfischer, *Fleet At Flood Tide*, 432.

12. J.C.H., *Nine out of Fifty*, 12.

13. J.C.H., *Nine out of Fifty*, 12.

14. J.C.H., *Nine out of Fifty*, 12.

15. J.C.H., *Nine out of Fifty*, 13.

16. Tillman, *Whirlwind*, 217.

17. J.C.H., *Nine out of Fifty*, 30.

18. Martinich, *Wartime Diary.*

19. J.C.H., *Nine out of Fifty*, 30.

20. Martinich, *Wartime Diary.*

21. US Naval Institute, *Reminscences of Rear Admiral Kent Melhorn*, 126.

22. J.C.H., *Nine out of Fifty*, 31.

23. Martinich, *Wartime Diary.*

24. Nordgren, interview.

25. Zdon, "First to Set Foot in Japan," 9.

26. Zdon, "First to Set Foot in Japan," 9.

27. Nordgren, interview.

28. Nordgren, interview.

29. Fighting Squadron 50, *History*, III-1.

30. Duckworth, Papers.

31. US Naval Institute, *Reminscences of Rear Admiral Kent Melhorn*, 127.

32. J.C.H., *Nine out of Fifty*, 33.

33. J.C.H., *Nine out of Fifty*, 34.

34. J.C.H., *Nine out of Fifty*, 33.

35. Martinich, *Wartime Diary.*

36. US Naval Institute, *Reminscences of Rear Admiral Kent Melhorn*, 127.

37. US Naval Institute, *Reminscences of Rear Admiral Kent Melhorn*, 134.

38. J.C.H., *Nine out of Fifty*, 35–36.

39. Wukovits, *Dogfight over Tokyo*, 193.

Chapter 31. The Final Act

1. J.C.H., *Nine out of Fifty*, 39.

2. Ingraham, interview.

3. J.C.H., *Nine out of Fifty*, 39.

4. Ortland, interview.
5. J.C.H., *Nine out of Fifty*, 40.
6. US Naval Institute, *Reminscences of Rear Admiral Kent Melhorn*, 127.
7. J.C.H., *Nine out of Fifty*.
8. Office of the Chief of Naval Operations, *Report of Surrender and Occupation of Japan*, 80.
9. J.C.H., *Nine out of Fifty*, 40–41.
10. Martinich, *Wartime Diary*.
11. Wukovits, *Dogfight over Tokyo*, 206.
12. US Naval Institute, *Reminscences of Rear Admiral Kent Melhorn*, 128.
13. J.C.H., *Nine out of Fifty*, 40.
14. US Naval Institute, *Reminscences of Rear Admiral Kent Melhorn*, 128.
15. US Naval Institute, *Reminscences of Rear Admiral Kent Melhorn*, 128.
16. Martinich, *Wartime Diary*.
17. Martinich, *Wartime Diary*.
18. J.C.H., *Nine out of Fifty*, 41.
19. J.C.H., *Nine out of Fifty*, 41.
20. Frick, "Occupation Carrier," 13.
21. J.C.H., *Nine out of Fifty*, 41.
22. J.C.H., *Nine out of Fifty*, 42.
23. Martinich, *Wartime Diary*.
24. J.C.H., *Nine out of Fifty*, 42.
25. Jordahl, interview.
26. Zdon, "First to Set Foot in Japan," 10.
27. Martinich, *Wartime Diary*.
28. Sherman, *Combat Command*, 373.
29. Duckworth, Papers.
30. Duckworth, Papers.

Chapter 32. A Postwar Moo

1. Some contemporary sources, including the Naval History and Heritage Command and Wikipedia, state that light carriers *Bataan*, *San Jacinto*, or escort carrier *Salamaua* were also in Tokyo Bay on September 2. This is incorrect; according to their war diaries *Bataan* and *San Jacinto* were out to sea, while *Salamaua* anchored in Sagami Wan, outside of Tokyo Bay.
2. Reynolds, *Fast Carriers*, 377.
3. J.C.H., *Nine out of Fifty*, 42.
4. Duckworth, Papers.
5. Martinich, *Wartime Diary*.
6. J.C.H., *Nine out of Fifty*, 43.

7. Frick, "Occupation Carrier," 60.

8. Frick, "Occupation Carrier," 14.

9. Duckworth, Papers.

10. Daly, *World War 2 Diary*.

11. US Naval Institute, *Reminscences of Rear Admiral Kent Melhorn*, 130.

12. US Naval Institute, *Reminscences of Rear Admiral Kent Melhorn*, 130.

13. US Naval Institute, *Reminscences of Rear Admiral Kent Melhorn*, 130–31.

14. Martinich, *Wartime Diary*.

15. Martinich, interview.

16. Patterson, *First Marine on Japan*, 14, 23.

17. Patterson, *First Marine on Japan*, 88.

18. Zdon, "First to Set Foot in Japan," 10.

Chapter 33. The Moo Wraps Up Her Affairs

1. "*Meet Your Navy* Interview with Captain George H. DeBaun."

2. Handran, Papers.

3. Handran, Papers.

4. Zdon, "First to Set Foot in Japan," 9.

5. Martinich, *Wartime Diary*.

6. Ortland, interview.

7. Wynne, interview.

8. Wynne, interview.

9. Zdon, "First to Set Foot in Japan," 10.

10. Martinich, *Wartime Diary*.

11. Wynne, interview.

12. Kuntz, interview.

Chapter 34. *Cowpens* Is Put Out to Pasture

1. Pawlowski, *Flat-Tops and Fledglings*, 207.

2. USS *Cowpens*, Invitation.

3. US Navy Board of Inspection and Survey, *Report of Material Inspection*.

Chapter 35. Lives and Careers After the War

1. Duckworth, Papers.

2. Krohn, "Life Remembered."

3. "Commander Handran on Duty."

4. E. Bowers, interview.

5. Haley, *From Yellow Perils*, 92.

6. Patriots Point Museum, "Ed Haley."

7. Patriots Point Museum, "Ed Haley."

Epilogue

1. Byerly, "USS *Cowpens* CG-63 Commissioning."
2. Byerly, "USS *Cowpens* CG-63 Commissioning."
3. Duckworth, Papers.
4. D. S. Smith, "USS *Cowpens*."
5. Hembree, "Mighty Moo Ballyhoo."
6. B. Smith, " 'Rawhide' and 'the Herd.' "
7. B. Smith, " 'Rawhide' and 'the Herd.' "
8. S. James, "Cowpens Festival Honors Veterans."
9. J. Johnson, "Cowpens' Namesake."
10. Michener, *Tales of the South Pacific*, 6.
11. S. James, "Cowpens Festival Honors Veterans."
12. Lavender, "Cowpens Celebrates the Mighty Moo."

Index